The Cambridge Companion to
Modern Italian Culture

This book provides a comprehensive account of the culture of
modern Italy. Specially commissioned essays by leading
specialists focus on a wide range of political, historical and
cultural questions. The volume provides information and
analysis on such topics as regionalism, the growth of a national
language, social and political cultures, the role of intellectuals,
the Church, the left, Feminism, the separatist movements,
organized crime, literature, art, design, fashion, the mass media
and music. While offering a thorough history of Italian cultural
movements, political trends and literary texts over the last
century and a half, the volume also examines the cultural and
political situation in Italy today and suggests possible future
directions in which the country might move. Each essay contains
suggestions for further reading on the topics covered. *The
Cambridge Companion to Modern Italian Culture* is an invaluable
source of materials for courses on all aspects of modern Italy.

ZYGMUNT GUIDO BARAŃSKI is Professor of Italian Studies at
the University of Reading. He has published extensively on
Dante, medieval poetics, modern Italian literature and culture,
post-war Italian cinema and literary theory. He is the editor of the
interdisciplinary journal *The Italianist* and co-editor, with
Professor Laura Lepschy, of the book series 'Italian Perspectives'
(Northern Universities Press).

REBECCA J. WEST is Professor of Italian and Cinema/Media
Studies in the Department of Romance Languages and
Literatures at the University of Chicago. She is the author of
Eugenio Montale: Poet on the Edge, which won the Howard Marraro
Prize in 1982, and of *Gianni Celati: The Craft of Everyday Storytelling*,
winner of the Scaglione Publication Prize in 1999. She is also co-
editor, with Dino S. Cervigni, of *Women's Voices in Italian Literature*
and editor of *Pagina, pellicola, pratica: studi sul cinema italiano*. She
has published extensively on modern and contemporary Italian
literature, culture, and film.

Cambridge Companions to Culture

The Cambridge Companion to Modern German Culture
Edited by EVA KOLINSKY *and* WILFRIED VAN DER WILL

The Cambridge Companion to Modern Russian Culture
Edited by NICHOLAS RZHEVSKY

The Cambridge Companion to Modern Spanish Culture
Edited by DAVID T. GIES

The Cambridge Companion to Modern Italian Culture
Edited by ZYGMUNT G. BARAŃSKI *and* REBECCA J. WEST

The Cambridge Companion to
Modern Italian Culture

edited by
ZYGMUNT G. BARAŃSKI *and* REBECCA J. WEST

CAMBRIDGE
UNIVERSITY PRESS

CAMBRIDGE UNIVERSITY PRESS
Cambridge, New York, Melbourne, Madrid, Cape Town, Singapore, São Paulo

Cambridge University Press
The Edinburgh Building, Cambridge CB2 8RU, UK

Published in the United States of America by Cambridge University Press, New York

www.cambridge.org
Information on this title: www.cambridge.org/9780521559829

First published 2001
Fourth printing 2007

Printed in the United Kingdom at the University Press, Cambridge

A catalogue record for this publication is available from the British Library

Library of Congress Cataloguing in Publication data
The Cambridge Companion to modern Italian culture / edited by Zygmunt G. Barański
and Rebecca J. West.
       p.   cm. – (Cambridge companions to culture)
    Includes bibliographical references and index.
    ISBN 0 521 55034 3 – ISBN 0 521 55982 0 (pb.)
    1. Italy–Civilization–20th century.   2. Italy–Civilization–19th century.   3. Italy–
    Intellectual life–20th century.   4. Italy–Intellectual life–19th century.
    5. Arts, Modern–20th century–Italy.   6. Arts, Modern–19th century–Italy.   I. Title: Modern
    Italian culture.   II. Barański, Zygmunt G.   III. West, Rebecca, J., 1946–   IV. Series.
DG451.c35   2001
945'.08–dc21   00-053014

ISBN-13 978-0-521-55034-5 hardback
ISBN-13 978-0-521-55982-9 paperback

In memory of our friends
Gian-Paolo Biasin, Tom O'Neill and John Waterhouse

Contents

Illustrations

Contributors

PERCY ALLUM is Professor of Political Science at the Istituto Universitario Orientale in Naples. He is the author of *Politics and Society in Postwar Naples* (1973), *Italy: Republic without Government?* (1973) and *State and Society in Western Europe* (1995).

ZYGMUNT BARAŃSKI is Professor of Italian Studies at the University of Reading. He has published extensively on Dante, Dante reception and modern Italian culture. He is editor of *The Italianist*.

GIAN-PAOLO BIASIN was, until his death in 1998, Professor of Italian Literature at the University of California, Berkeley. He was a leading authority on the literature and culture of nineteenth- and twentieth-century Italy. His books include *Montale, Debussy, and Modernism* (1989), *The Flavors of Modernity: Food and the Novel* (1993) and *Le periferie della letteratura. Da Verga a Tabucchi* (1997).

PETER BONDANELLA is Chairman of the Department of West European Studies and Distinguished Professor at Indiana University. He has written or edited numerous books on Italian cinema and literature, including *Dictionary of Italian Literature* (1979; revised edition 1996), *Italian Cinema: From Neorealism to the Present* (1983; revised edition 1990), *The Cinema of Federico Fellini* (1992) and *Umberto Eco and the Open Text* (1997).

ANNA CENTO BULL is Professor of Italian at the University of Bath. Her research interests focus on socio-political cultures and subcultures, as well as small-scale industrialization. She has recently published various studies on the Northern League. A book on social identities and political culture in Italy is forthcoming.

ALESSANDRO CARRERA teaches Italian literature at New York University. He has published books on music, philosophy and literature, as well as a collection of poetry, *La sposa perfetta/The*

Perfect Bride (1997), and a work of fiction, *A che punto è il Giudizio Universale?* (1999). In his youth, he was a singer–songwriter.

JOHN DICKIE is Lecturer in Italian at University College London and General Editor of *Modern Italy*. His *'Darkest Italy': The Nation and Stereotypes of the Mezzogiorno* was published in 1999.

ROBERT DOMBROSKI is Distinguished Professor and Director of Italian Graduate Studies at the City University of New York. His most recent books are *Properties of Writing: Ideological Discourse in Modern Italian Fiction* (1994) and *Creative Entanglements: Gadda and the Baroque* (1999).

JOSEPH FARRELL, Senior Lecturer in Italian at Strathclyde University, is the author of *Leonardo Sciascia* (1995) and editor of *Understanding the Mafia* (1997) and of *Carlo Goldoni and Eighteenth Century Theatre* (1997).

LAURA LEPSCHY is Emeritus Professor of Italian at University College London. Among her books is *Narrativa e testo fra due secoli. Verga, Invernizio, Svevo, Pirandello* (1984). She is one of the founder members of the Pirandello Society and has been the main editor of its journal, *Pirandello Studies*.

TOM O'NEILL was, until his death in 2001, Emeritus Professor of Italian in the University of Melbourne and a Professorial Fellow in the University's Department of French and Italian Studies. He has published extensively on nineteenth- and twentieth-century poetry and on modern Sicilian narrative.

EUGENIA PAULICELLI is Associate Professor in the Department of European Languages and Literatures at Queens College, City University of New York. She is the author of *Parola e immagine. Sentieri della scrittura in Leonardo, Marino, Foscolo, Calvino* (1996). She is currently completing a book on the aesthetic, social and political functions of fashion.

BRIAN RICHARDSON is Professor of Italian Language at the University of Leeds. He has edited Machiavelli's *Il principe* (1979) and *Trattati sull'ortografia del volgare* (1984), and is author of *Print Culture in Renaissance Italy* (1994) and *Printing, Writers and Readers in Renaissance Italy* (1999).

PENNY SPARKE is a Professor at the Royal College of Art and Course Director of the Joint Victoria and Albert Museum/Royal College of Art History of Design Programme. Her principal publications include *An Introduction to Design and Culture in the Twentieth Century* (1986), *Italian Design from 1860 to the Present* (1989), *As Long as It's Pink: The Sexual Politics of Taste* (1995) and *A Century of Design: Design Pioneers of the Twentieth Century* (1998).

SHIRLEY VINALL is Senior Lecturer in Italian Studies at the University of Reading and a co-editor of *The Italianist*. She has published especially on the modern novel, the early twentieth-century avant-garde and the influences of French literature on Italian culture.

CHRISTOPHER WAGSTAFF is Senior Lecturer in Italian Studies at the University of Reading, and has published articles on Italian literature, media and cinema.

DAVID WARD is Associate Professor in the Department of Italian, Wellesley College. He is the author of *A Poetics of Resistance: Narrative and the Writings of Pier Paolo Pasolini* (1995) and *Antifascisms: Cultural Politics in Italy, 1943–46. Benedetto Croce and the Liberals, Carlo Levi and the 'Actionists'* (1996).

JOHN WATERHOUSE, until his death in 1998, taught at the University of Birmingham. He published widely on modern Italian music, and was the author of *La musica di Gian Francesco Malipiero* (1990).

REBECCA J. WEST is Professor of Italian and Cinema/Media Studies at the University of Chicago. She has published widely on modern Italian narrative prose and verse, cultural studies, women's studies and cinema.

SHARON WOOD, Professor of Italian at Leicester University, is the author of *Italian Women's Writing 1860–1990* (1995) and *Woman as Object: Language and Gender in the Work of Alberto Moravia* (1990), and editor of *Italian Women Writing* (1993).

Acknowledgments

This has been a difficult project, and we owe debts of gratitude to many people. Sarah Stanton, Kate Brett and Linda Bree, all of Cambridge University Press, have given us sterling support and advice at different stages of the book's genesis. We have also received important assistance from the following colleagues: Bojan Bujić, Anna Cento Bull, John Dickie, Christopher Duggan, Sarah Hill, Giulio Lepschy, Laura Lepschy, David Robey, Shirley Vinall and John Waterhouse.

We should also like to express a special thanks to all the contributors not only for their excellent articles, but also, and more specifically, for their patience.

We should like to dedicate this book to the memory of Gian-Paolo Biasin, Tom O'Neill and John Waterhouse, friends and collaborators, who sadly died without seeing the *Companion* in print.

Note on translation

All quotations from Italian sources have been translated into English. Only in the chapter on poetry are texts given in both Italian and English. Unless otherwise stated, translations are by the author of the chapter or part of the chapter in which they appear.

The titles of books, paintings, films, etc., as well as the names of organizations, political parties, etc., are given in Italian and English. Since it is far from unusual for the English titles of Italian books translated into English, and of Italian films distributed in English-speaking countries, to be misleading and inaccurate, we have decided to translate all titles as literally as possible. We appreciate that this may create difficulties for anyone trying to find the English translation of many Italian books. To help our readers in this task, we have placed the symbol ‡ after our English version of titles of books which, as far as we are aware, have appeared in an English translation. For bibliographical information on English translations of modern Italian literature see Robin Healey, *Twentieth-Century Italian Literature in English Translation. An Annotated Bibliography 1929–1997*, Toronto, Buffalo and London: University of Toronto Press, 1998.

Chronology

1796–7	Napoleonic campaigns in Italy
1797	Treaty of Campoformio (Venice to Austria)
1798–9	Republic in Naples
1799	French defeats. Collapse of Naples Republic
1800	Second Napoleonic invasion of Italy
1800	Napoleon defeats Austrians at Marengo
1802	Proclamation of the Italian Republic
1805	Proclamation of Kingdom of Italy under Napoleon
1806	French occupy Naples
1808	French occupy Rome
1814	Austria regains Lombardy and Veneto
1815	Congress of Vienna. Restoration of pre-Napoleonic Italy
1820	'Carbonari' conspirators arrested in Milan
1820–1	Insurrections in Naples and Turin
1831–49	Carlo Alberto King of Savoy
1831–4	Insurrections in Modena, Parma, Papal States, Piedmont, Genoa
1839	First Italian railway opened: Naples–Portici
1844	Insurrection in Calabria
1846	Pius IX elected Pope
1848–9	Insurrections and first War of Independence. Roman Republic established. Austrian intervention and repression
1855	Piedmont joins France in Crimean War
1857	Pisacane's insurrectionary landing near Salerno fails
1859	Second War of Independence
1860	Garibaldi's expedition to Sicily ('the Thousand')
1861–78	Vittorio Emanuele II King of united Italy

1866	Third War of Independence: the Veneto joined to Italian Kingdom
1870	Italian troops enter Rome
1871	Rome proclaimed capital of Italy
1874	Pius IX's denunciation of Italian state
1882	The Triple Alliance (Italy, Germany, Austria)
1885	Italian troops occupy Massawa (Eritrea)
1890	Eritrea becomes Italian colony
1892	Italian Workers Party founded (banned 1894)
1895	Workers Party named Socialist Party (PSI)
1899	FIAT founded
1912	Italy occupies Libya, Rhodes and Dodecanese. Suffrage extended for literate male adults
1913	Engineering workers' right to organize recognized
1915	Italy declares war on Austro-Hungarian Empire
1917	October: Italians defeated at Caporetto
1918	October: Italian offensive. Armistice
1919	First 'fascio di combattimento' founded in Milan. D'Annunzio occupies Fiume (–1920)
1920	Strikes and occupation of factories
1921	Communist Party of Italy (PCI) formed as breakaway from PSI. Fascist National Party formed
1922	October: Fascist march on Rome. Mussolini head of government
1924	General elections. Social-Democrat Deputy Matteotti murdered
1925	*Manifesto of Fascist Intellectuals* issued
1926	Opposition parties and non-Fascist unions suppressed
1928	Gramsci sentenced to twenty years by Special Tribunal
1929	Concordat between Church and State
1935–6	Invasion of Ethiopia. Empire proclaimed. Rome–Berlin Axis
1937	Anti-Fascist Rosselli brothers assassinated in France
1938	Racial Laws promulgated
1939	Italy occupies Albania. Pact of Steel with Germany
1940	Italy enters Second World War
1943	25 July: Mussolini removed from power
	8 Sept.: Armistice declared. Committees of National Liberation (CLN) formed
	11–23 Sept.: Mussolini, freed by Germans, creates the Italian Social Republic
1944	4 June: Allied forces enter Rome

1945	28 April: Mussolini executed by partisans
	20 June: Parri government with Committee of National Liberation
	10 Dec.: First De Gasperi Christian Democrat (DC) government
1945	Women's suffrage granted
1946	2 June: Referendum. Italy becomes a republic
1947	De Gasperi evicts PCI and PSI from government
1948	Constitution of Italian Republic comes into effect
	Attempted assassination of Togliatti, leader of PCI
1949	Italy enters NATO. Church excommunicates Communists
1950	Cassa per il Mezzogiorno (Development Fund for the South) created
1951	Fiscal reform
1953	Electoral reform ('legge truffa') approved
	Ente Nazionale Idrocarburi (ENI) founded
1955	Italy enters UNO
1963	Moro heads centre–left government
	Compulsory schooling extended to fourteen-year-olds
1968	Students' occupation of universities
1969	Terrorist attack in Piazza Fontana, Milan
1974	Terrorist attacks in Brescia and on 'Italicus' train. Referendum confirms divorce law of 1970
1976	Lockheed bribery scandal
1978	Moro kidnapped and murdered by Red Brigades
1980	Terrorist bombing of Bologna railway station
1981	Masonic P2 Lodge uncovered. Abortion referendum. Abortion law passed
1990	The Gladio arms-cache exposure
1991	Communist Party dissolved and refounded as PDS (Democratic Party of the Left)
1992	Tangentopoli bribery scandal begins. Collapse of DC at general election
1993	Referendum leads to new electoral law
1994	Parliamentary election won by coalition of Forza Italia and allies
1996	Parliamentary election won, for the first time in the post-war period, by a centre–left coalition
1999	Italy became part of the Euro zone

SWITZERLAND   AUSTRIA — HUNGARY

SAVOY
to France
1860
                                    T Y R O L

Magenta× Milan   VENETIA
1859   LOMBARDY   1866
Turin   Novara   Solferino× ×Custoza
                        1859   1866
PIEDMONT   Venice•   Trieste

                                        ISTRIA   Fiume
Genoa•   PARMA
          1860   OTTOMAN
          MODENA   PAPAL LEGATIONS
            1860   ROMAGNA 1860   EMPIRE
NICE   •Bologna
to France
1860
                                        DALMATIA
MASSA
1829 to Modena
LUCCA   •Florence Rep. of SAN MARINO
1847 to Tuscany   from 1861 under
                            Italian protection
          TUSCANY
          1860   MARCHE
                    1860
Elba•   Adriatic Sea
          •Perugia
          PAPAL   Lissa×
          UMBRIA   1866
CORSICA   1860
to France STATES
1768   Mentana
            × 1867
          Rome×   N
          THE PATRIMONY•
            1870   A

SARDINIA   •Teano   P

            Naples   L
            Entered by Garibaldi
            7 Sept. 1860   E

Tyrrhenian   KINGDOM   S

    Sea   of the

                TWO SICILIES

Calatafimi× •Palermo
        1860
      •Marsala   ×Aspromonte
                      1862
            SICILY   Straits of   N
                    Messina

                                      S

0   100   200   300 km
0   100   200 miles

                Malta
                to Britain 1814

Map 1. The unification of Italy.

Map 2. Italy since 1919.

ZYGMUNT G. BARAŃSKI

Introducing modern Italian culture

A companion to modern Italian culture

Putting together a collective volume that intends to provide an overview on a complex issue such as the culture of a modern nation state is fraught with problems. Any overarching assessment cannot but be partial, since it is based on a process of selection and synthesis which offers the means to arrive at a series of generalizing descriptions and evaluations which can form the key moments of a broad analytical 'narrative'. This is true not just as regards the editorial choices determining the basic make-up of the book, but also as regards the critical efforts of individual contributors to whom the responsibility for granting substance to the editorial schema is delegated. In addition, the collaborative nature of the project does not always make it easy for the volume to present a unified front. However, this is no bad thing. I am persuaded that, beyond all that may unite its different parts, the success of a synthesis like the present 'companion' is also to a large degree dependent on the fragmentation of its vision. In order to prepare their 'narratives' of their respective corners of modern Italy, the contributors have had to undertake a job of drastic pruning. Yet the impetus behind this operation is different in each case, conditioned as it is by divergent methodological sympathies, as well as by contrasting perceptions both of what 'Italy' can signify and of the nature of its achievements. Hence, just as much as in the chapters' points of contact, it is in the robust tensions that arise from the competing claims of a panoply of different expert voices that a revelatory glimpse of the multifaceted complexity that is 'modern Italian culture' can be espied.

Our book thus attempts to strike a balance between congruence – the hope that, through collaboration, it is possible to suggest a broad, largely unified, impression of Italy – and difference – the recognition that such an impression is constantly put into crisis, first by the variety of events and experiences that have marked the recent history of the peninsula, and secondly by the differing reactions which these same events and experiences have elicited and continue to elicit. In order to avoid compartmentalizing Italy into a series of self-contained units, we would encourage readers to approach our volume in an open and flexible manner. In particular, they should consider the ways in which the chapters can usefully interact; and, in this regard, so as to ensure that rapprochements can be effected as freely as possible, we have not organized groups of chapters into separate sections. Bringing different chapters together cannot but expand understanding and break down barriers of perception. Such a way of reading, especially with the help of the index, also provides fuller information on matters which are not specifically discussed in a single chapter but which are examined in various areas of the book, such as the reverberations of the divisions between the North and South of the country.[1] Equally, it helps to foreground many of the key events, movements, institutions and figures of modern Italy: from the Risorgimento to Fascism and from the Resistance to Tangentopoli ('Kickback City'); from *verismo* to Futurism and from Neorealism to the Neo-avant-garde; from the Catholic Church to the Italian Communist Party; and from Alessandro Manzoni to Benedetto Croce and from Antonio Gramsci to Pier Paolo Pasolini. Finally, it offers a sense of how the relative weight of any set of circumstances, even of a crucial phase of Italian history such as Fascism which aimed to affect every sphere of life, changes depending on whether one considers this in terms of the development of architectural style, social policy or the film industry. Our survey has its limits; however, there are ways in which these can be not just countered, but also turned to the book's and the reader's advantage.

A fundamental consequence of recognizing the restrictions which constrain the present book is the need to justify as precisely as possible the criteria governing its make-up. To put it in a slightly different way, it is important to acknowledge not just what may be found in its pages, but also what is missing. The problem of what is omitted is a crucial one; and certainly our choices have in part been driven by what we deem to be vital about post-unification Italy, and, hence, are evaluative in nature. Although it is important for judgments of discrimination to be made, and all the contributors to this book reveal their studied preferences, I am aware of the relative character of our selections and appraisals. I am also cognizant that it is easier to make evaluative assessments within a single area of human enterprise than to do this between different types of activity; just as I appreciate that distorted judgments can result from applying the measures belonging to one sphere to define the significance and traits of another. Thus, on the one hand, it would not be difficult to make a case for the intellectual, ethical and artistic superiority of Rossellini's cinematic *œuvre* in relation to the productions of Berlusconi's three television channels, not least because Rossellini's ambitions are intellectual, ethical and artistic, while these attributes do not seem to be a priority as far as the television stations are concerned. On the other hand, there is no doubt that Berlusconi's brash programming strategies and even brasher programmes have had a much more profound impact on post-war Italian society than Rossellini's films with their restrained humanism. In a book which attempts to provide an introduction to 'modern Italian culture', both Rossellini the film-maker and Berlusconi the media entrepreneur have to be found a niche. The issue is not whether Berlusconi is 'better' than Rossellini, or whether the opposite is true, but of ensuring that their respective, and different, importance is adequately highlighted. There is thus no grand, all-seeing juncture from which modern Italy can be conveniently assessed; just as it is impossible for a 'companion' such as ours to provide more than the faintest of sketches of the country, its history and culture. At most, we can offer a kind of rudimentary map that will allow interested readers to set out on a journey of discovery – a journey during the course of which they can formulate their own preferences and increasingly recognize the limits of the image of Italy that we are presenting.

How were these limits fixed? What conditioned the choices that determined this drawing of boundaries?

Our ambitions for this book have always been primarily practical. To begin with, *The Cambridge Companion to Modern Italian Culture* fills a not insignificant gap in the literature on post-unification Italy. As far as we are aware, there is no single-volume study in English – and we suspect that the same is true as regards the Italian book market – that attempts to provide a general introduction to the cultural life of the peninsula since 1860. Precisely because of this, we feel that the main stress of the 'companion' has to be on providing information; and that for this information to be meaningful, it has to be both historically rooted and critically assessed. In addition, given the book's introductory character, we hope that it will appeal to a wide audience, ranging from students at every stage of their studies of Italy to the many people with an interest in the country. However, we would like to think that Italian specialists, too, will find the book useful, especially as a first point of reference, when seeking information on subjects outside their main areas of expertise. In the light of these aspirations, we decided that, in part, the book had to have a traditional remit (hence the strong emphasis on history, litera- ture, history of art, and what John Waterhouse, somewhat provocatively, terms 'serious music'), so that readers would find what many of them would conventionally expect from a 'companion' to a national culture. At the same time, we also believed that it was important that we call into question some of these conventional assumptions, thereby encouraging readers to begin to reassess their ideas both of Italy and of culture. John Dickie's deconstruction of 'The Notion of Italy' plays a vital role in this respect, as should be clear from the prominent position we accord his chapter at the book's opening. Equally, Anna Bull's historical survey, which follows Dickie's presentation, with its emphasis on 'Social and Political Cultures', intends to underline how historical events and changes in society are closely intertwined with people's attitudes and values; and 'attitudes and values' can usefully serve as one broad defini- tion of culture (others will be examined in due course). The discussions of the mass media, film, design, fashion, popular music, political, worker and religious mass organizations, and 'Other Voices' (this chapter focuses on groups and movements, such as the Catholic Church, organized crime, terrorism, the separatist regional Leagues, and Feminism, that, at one time or another, have questioned the legitimacy of the unified state) also intend to cast light on matters which are often ignored when a restricted view of culture is embraced.

'Cultural studies' and Italy

As with so much of our book, its basic structure was influenced by our desire to find a balance which would permit readers to grasp something of the complexity of the issues that cohere around the concept of Italy and to become aware of the variety of ways in which these issues can be approached. At the same time, however, our conviction that 'culture' cannot be reduced to what traditionally has been described as 'high culture' constitutes a clear expression of our own intellectual sympa- thies. This sense comes to us, as does our book's strong emphasis on relativism and on the need for interdisciplinarity, from the important work which for several decades has been done under the ever-broadening umbrella of 'cultural studies'.[2] Despite the wealth of academic work that is now included under this designation, what unites it is the belief that different forms of communication and of social practice should not be evaluated on the basis of critically untested value judgments. Instead, 'cultural studies' advocates that attempts be made to recognize the significance of as wide an array of these forms as possible, while placing special emphasis on those subordinate discourses and groups which, traditionally, have been marginalized in socio-political terms and in the academies. As a result of the eclecticism of 'cultural studies' and its intent to undertake a process of cultural revaluation, the relationship between it and longer-established academic disciplines has often been quite difficult. Our book tries to avoid such polemicizing. Admittedly, at their best, these academic disputes have succeeded in usefully redefining scholarly concerns; and the impact of 'cultural studies' on educational curricula in Britain and in North America has been profound.[3] At the same time, however, the reductionism of many other exchanges has usually been clear to all but the entrenched combatants. Thus, while acknowledging its debts to 'cultural studies',[4] *The Cambridge Companion to Modern Italian Culture* also vigorously asserts the worth of traditional humanistic disciplines, as well as the value of the achievements of artists who quite deliberately create their works for a narrow and intellectually sophisticated audience, and who see themselves as contributing to an élite tradition. Our book, therefore, is not concerned to conform to specific preferences of method. The emphasis is on breadth and 'openness', as regards both the information provided and the ways in which these facts can be interpreted. Where a particular approach can be of benefit to achieving these ends, I would hope that its influence is discernible. In this respect, it is reassuring to note that our position is strikingly similar to the principles adopted by Dombroski and Cervigni, the editors of the most recent collection on 'Italian Cultural Studies'.

Yet, for all our attempts at inclusiveness, there are significant areas of modern Italy for which we have failed to find room in the pages of our book. This is true as regards both topics which conventionally belong under the rubric of 'high culture', such as architecture and education, and subjects which might be comprised under the marker of 'low culture', such as sport and food. Equally, other important matters have only been included by being combined in a single generic category. This is the case as regards the press, radio and television, which have been subsumed under the catch-all heading 'the media'. Finally, a further group of topics is not treated systematically, though some understanding of them can be achieved by bringing together the relevant sections of different chapters. A noteworthy instance of this kind of 'fragmentary' presentation is the large amount of information about the development of Italian thought that can be gathered by amalgamating the chapters on left-wing ideology, Church doctrine, intellectuals and 'other voices'.

The decision regarding what to include and what to exclude was largely conditioned by what we think are the salient aspects of post-unification Italy. At the same time, we were helped in making our selections by the knowledge that three other collaborative books were due to appear (all three have now been published) which intended to cover some of the same ground and appeal to a not dissimilar audience as our 'companion'. While providing a balanced assessment of Italian culture, therefore, we felt it would be an advantage if our book, whether methodologically or as regards coverage, could, whenever possible, refrain from intruding too much on to the spaces marked out for themselves by these volumes. Ideally, we consider *The Cambridge Companion to Modern Italian Culture* to exist in a complementary relationship to these three works, and we would encourage readers to compare our treatment of particular issues with theirs.[5] Equally, we would hope that readers of these volumes would turn to our book to find information on areas, such as literature, music, art and political thought, where our coverage is generally fuller than theirs, and to get a broad sense of post-unification Italy – something which none of the three aims to offer, since their sights are overwhelmingly fixed on the twentieth century and on quite particular ways of looking at Italy. Similarly, Dombroski and Cervigni's collection, though it ranges from the Renaissance to the present, also has a relatively narrow, as well as an unsystematic, focus: it concentrates on analysing a disparate array of specific texts, figures and issues rather than on offering a series of broad interrelated overviews.

The three books are: *Italian Cultural Studies. An Introduction*, edited by David Forgacs and Robert Lumley (Oxford University Press, 1996); *La cultura italiana del Novecento*, edited by Corrado Stajano (Rome and Bari: Laterza, 1996) and *Revisioning Italy. National Identity and Global Culture*, edited by Beverly Allen and Mary Russo (Minneapolis and London: University of Minnesota Press, 1997). The basic differences between these volumes and our 'companion' should be evident from their titles.

Revisioning Italy is an overtly committed collection which 'cross[es] disciplinary boundaries and explodes the category "Italy" from within its traditional regional, peninsular, and European contexts and, from the outside, through its multitudinous occurrences and transmissions in Africa, Asia, and the Americas'. Drawing on 'contemporary trends in transnational cultural studies',[6] it explores issues – such as Italy's position in Europe and in the world, immigration, ethnicity and colonization – that our book addresses in a much less emphatic manner. *La cultura italiana del Novecento*, too, is a committed collection: 'the book wants to be a contribution to knowledge, a memory, a profile that can help [readers] face up to the year 2000'; and, like the Allen–Russo volume, it sets out to do this by assessing Italy against a global backcloth. However, unlike both *Revisioning Italy* and the present 'companion', the focus of Stajano's book is crucially restricted by an élite sense of what is important about a national culture:

> What is [. . .] the condition of Italian culture within the framework of
> a world undergoing a great transformation? What is the condition of
> the arts, of the sciences, of the legal and economic disciplines [. . .]
> culture as history and as national life? [. . .] [The] 26 essays recount the
> past and the present of the fundamental disciplines which constitute
> the framework of twentieth-century culture [. . .]. Each essay [. . .] aims
> to offer a kaleidoscope of the ideas, opinions and figures that have
> characterized the century in its various moments.[7]

And the twenty-six essays fulfil these aims rather well, offering excellent syntheses of academic disciplines as diverse as medicine, archaeology, demography and psychology. Thus, *La cultura italiana del Novecento* proffers a fuller view of Italian intellectual life than our book intends to provide. On the other hand, where our two volumes overlap, given Stajano's stress on 'ideas' and on intellectuals, his book is often less able to give an impression of the complexity of a problem than our less constrained surveys. Similarly, its sense of the variety of Italian culture is considerably narrower than ours.

The remit of *Italian Cultural Studies*, even though it concentrates exclusively on post-war Italy, is broad:

> Cultural studies is not so much a discipline as a cluster of disciplines.
> In Britain, where the term originated [. . .], these disciplines have
> come to include literature, social history, media studies, human
> geography, cultural anthropology, and the sociology of deviance [. . .].

Work in these diverse areas has been loosely unified by a common set of concerns: to deal with culture as a set of signifying practices and symbolic social forms; to look at a wide variety of cultural materials and avoid prior evaluative rankings of high and low; to bring new theoretical considerations to bear on the study of culture.

The aim of 'cultural studies' is to 'interrogate and deconstruct' the distinctions between 'high' or 'élite' culture and 'mass' or 'popular' culture, as well as their different forms.[8] Forgacs and Lumley's book is especially strong in dealing both with the sociological and anthropological dimension of culture and with 'low' forms: it ranges widely between youth cultures and corruption, and between gender relations and film stars. It is less concerned, however, to deal with 'high' culture and its implications. Of the three books under discussion, *Italian Cultural Studies* is the one which we see as having the closest complementary relationship with our 'companion'. Our broad historical perspective is countered by its more tightly focused chronological purview; our restricted treatment of popular and mass culture is balanced by its wide-ranging exposition of this topic; and our concern with 'high' culture corrects its limited and somewhat idiosyncratic treatment of this area.

'Culture', 'Italian', 'modern'

The title of our book, *The Cambridge Companion to Modern Italian Culture*, and especially the designation 'companion', indicate that its coverage intends to be wide. On account of the catholicity of our vision, each of the three key locutions constituting our title – 'modern', 'Italian' and 'culture', terms whose meaning is problematic whatever the context – raises special problems, and hence needs to be explained and defined with a modicum of care.

The most amorphous and fluid of the terms is 'culture'. This fact should already have been evident from the different values which so far have been attached to it in this Introduction. For instance, the quotation from *La cultura italiana del Novecento* reveals that, as is typical of Italian usage, Stajano uses *cultura* to refer specifically to 'high' culture, namely, to the intellectual and artistic achievements of a sophisticated élite. In addition, his view of this *cultura* is essentially optimistic: *cultura* is intrinsically valuable; it can help improve life; it can offer a safe haven during times of trouble. Stajano's faith in the benefits of 'high' culture is not unusual; it is deeply embedded in Italian society, even among non-intellectuals. Indeed, the idea has often been canvassed that many of Italy's problems could be alleviated if more of its citizens could be made to share in this *cultura*. Given the fairly restricted remit of what is deemed worthy to be described as culture, this means that, in general, Italian *cultura* is not as volatile a term as English 'culture'. Equally, this same élitist perception of culture can in part explain why 'cultural studies' as a distinct discipline has not managed to find acceptance in the Italian academic world – though this does not mean that popular culture and the mass media are not studied. They are, but independently of each other, and, of course, independently of 'high' culture.[9] Yet it is also clear on reading Stajano that there are meanings of *cultura* which are broader and less precise than 'high culture'. It is enough to think of his allusion to 'culture as history and as national life'. Furthermore, in Italian usage, *cultura* is coupled to the epithets *popolare* and *di massa* to refer, respectively, to activities developed by the people for their own use, and to mass-produced forms and their consumption.[10]

It is the more extended notion of 'culture' that, in recent years, has played an active role in British and North American thinking about culture. The concept is associated with 'experience', 'consciousness', 'ideological configuration', 'values and attitudes' (what the French have termed *mentalités*) and with the symbolic forms through which these states are expressed. It is also utilized to allude to 'ways of life', 'forms of organization' – the symbolic means and rituals to which different groups have recourse in order to establish their own identity, often through opposition to one another. This sense of culture, which potentially succeeds in embracing any type of intellectual, aesthetic or semiotic behaviour, is not just extremely wide, but also challenges the distinctions between 'high' and 'low', 'élite' and 'subordinate', 'mass' and 'popular', since it highlights the shifting nature of the particular area of cultural activity covered by each of the terms. It also foregrounds the relationship between cultural practices and power; and, by extension, the relationship between academic discourse, cultural value and power.[11]

The Cambridge Companion to Modern Italian Culture subscribes to this flexible view of culture. Indeed, at different points in the book, all the above-mentioned aspects of culture are given prominence. At the same time, however, by affording a notable amount of space to matters which commonly have been defined as belonging to 'high culture', it attempts to redress what has become something of an imbalance in many of the analyses that have been done in the field of 'cultural studies'. If the boundaries between different symbolic forms and practices are to be tested effectively, and the specificities of each of these are to be recognized, then key areas cannot be downgraded. To do this simply mimics the exclusive attitudes of the most haughty traditions of élite learning. Furthermore, as I clarify in the following paragraph, 'cultural studies', which not infrequently has relied rather too heavily on grand yet transient theorizing, can learn useful lessons from the procedures of established disciplines. Although such methodological problems obviously lie beyond the remit of our 'companion', it can nonetheless be useful to remind readers of their existence.

In contrasting Italian with British and American approaches to the study of culture, I should not like to create the impression that Italian scholarship is incapable of appreciating the implications of looking at culture from a mobile and interdisciplinary perspective. If anything, my impression is that the Italian emphasis on context, history and respect for the literal meaning of texts offers the best means to understanding the complexity of any cultural expression. In particular, given Italy's millennial regional, political and linguistic fragmentation, questions relating to culture, albeit with 'high culture' very much to the fore, have long been posed by Italian scholars in a manner receptive to geographical, historical, social and textual difference.[12] Indeed, such work has helped to establish that it is extremely difficult to make claims for a strong and overarching Italian national culture. This is true even as regards 'high' literature, given that Italy is alone in the Western world in having two major, yet distinct, élite literary traditions – one in Italian, the other in dialect. Although, since the Second World War, education and the mass media have diminished social, linguistic and regional differences, the continuing lack of a clearly identifiable national culture cannot but pose grave questions about the nature of national identity in Italy whether today or in the past. Equally, this absence can offer a first reason why, for centuries, Italy has found it far from difficult to assimilate foreign influences.

Naturally, this lack of an easily recognizable national cultural core raises doubts about the value of the epithet 'Italian' in the title of our book. At a very crude level, anything that occurs or is produced within the confines of the unitary Italian state can be termed 'Italian'. However, such a premise creates confusion regarding the status of cultural manifestations which appeared within those same confines before 1860, the year in which the country was largely unified. This is particularly so as regards pre-unification cultural forms which in some way make claims to being Italian. It is misleading, and not just when thinking about Italy, to imagine that well-defined geographical and political boundaries will determine and guarantee national identity and belonging, and so eliminate difference. It is vital, therefore, to remember both the fragility and deceptiveness of tags which are supposed to circumscribe a national area, and the shifting wealth of experiences which such tags are supposed to embrace – experiences that frequently are not even significantly shaped within the frontiers of the country. However, as long as its limitations are kept in mind, the epithet 'Italian' can, of course, serve a useful purpose. Bonds of geography, politics, history, religion and language do tie communities and cultures together (and all these elements do indeed underlie our book's use of 'Italian'). The problem is the strength of these ties and their significance, as well as their relationship to all those other forces, from regionalism to the artistic avant-gardes, whose thrust is towards separation rather than unity.

Italy may very well be marked by fragmentation; however, that is a general condition which it shares with every nation-state. This is an important fact. For too long, Italy's perceived lack of strong and tangible centralizing features has led people, including many Italians, to consider the country as 'anomalous', even backward, in respect to other advanced Western capitalist countries. The effect of this viewpoint has been to downplay Italy's achievements, which, especially in the post-war period, both economically and socially have been noteworthy. At the same time, it is undoubtedly the case that there are elements – such as the lack of linguistic unity, the inability of the state to gain legitimacy among its citizens, and the reluctance of those same citizens to think and feel in national terms except when celebrating the achievements of some great figure of the pre-unification past or when shouting support for an athlete or team donning the country's blue international shirt – which create the impression that Italy is little more than a name, and even that it is permanently on the verge of collapse. Ever since 1860, efforts have been made – without too much success – to counter such impressions by creating unifying national heroic myths such as that of the Risorgimento (the glorification of the unification process) or that of the anti-Fascist Resistance. More recently, as the idea of the country disintegrating under the combined pressure of the separatist movements, organized crime, corruption and the collapse of the First Republic has begun to seem to many a real possibility, various intellectuals have argued that, despite the country's recent unification and the failure of the state to bring its citizens together, a specific and definable *identità italiana* not only exists but has existed for centuries. Arguments in favour of this position have largely been based on highlighting the existence of a 'tendentious cleavage between national identity and Italian identity, namely the split separating the way in which the national state was born and its mode of being from the historical past of the country, which has become its nature'.[13] Unfortunately, the arguments put forward to support such views are largely unpersuasive: they are heavily laced with subjectivism and vagueness (what precisely does 'nature' mean in the passage cited in the preceding sentence?). As this Introduction has attempted to argue, matters of (national) identity are extremely difficult to define. Indeed, a genius of the stature of Dante Alighieri, when trying to establish certain common Italian characteristics in the *De vulgari eloquentia* ('On Vernacular Eloquence'), lapsed into unexpected banality: 'in so far as we act as Italians [*homines latini*], we have certain basic traits [*simplicissima signa*], of custom, clothing and speech, which allow the actions of Italians to be weighed and measured' (1, xvi, 3).

As a consequence of the claims relating to Italy's 'backwardness' and 'anomalousness', it is not unusual to hear the argument that the country's contacts with and contribution to modernity have been essentially negative. Some commentators have actually gone so far as to damn Italy's relationship to modernity, ascribing the country's faults to the 'difficulty Italian modernity has in creatively combining historical materials and deposits of our identity, of adapting that which is peculiarly Italian to its needs and vice versa'. 'As a result Italian modernity becomes with the greatest of ease corporativism, familism, tax evasion, mass illegality, and whatever else.'[14] Such assertions are plainly overwrought. It is certainly true that Italy's rapid transition from a primarily rural economy at the time of unification to a successful neo-capitalist economy since the 1950s has been anything but straightforward: both the successes and failures have been striking. It is equally true that Italy has found it difficult to develop bureaucratic and state structures to complement the social, political and economic changes through which the country has passed since 1860. At the same time, it should not be forgotten that, as our chapters on art, literature, music, the cinema, design and fashion illustrate, a far from negligible amount of what is perceived by people all over the world as characteristically 'modern' in these areas is Italian in origin. As regards the use of the term in the title of our book, it is not meant to suggest that thanks to unification Italy somehow became part of the modern world. The transition to modernity – the passage from a traditional oligarchic, agrarian and mercantile society to one dominated by capitalist economic, political, social and cultural forms – was irregular. In parts of Northern Italy, it had begun before 1860, while for the bulk of the peninsula the change did not occur until after the Second World War. On the one hand, the epithet is useful as a way of suggesting that, in general terms, the book covers the period when the shift to modernity painfully, unevenly and gradually took place. On the other hand, 'modern' is purely conventional: it is a cliché of much writing on Italy to consider the modern era as commencing with the country's unification.

Despite its position as one of the leading industrialized nations, modern Italy plays a secondary role in the world. Its greatness lies squarely in its past: during the centuries-long spread of Roman civilization; during the later Middle Ages, when, in comparison to the rest of Europe, it not only hosted the greatest thinkers (St Bonaventure and Thomas Aquinas), the greatest artists (Cimabue and Giotto) and the greatest writers (Dante, Petrarch and Boccaccio), but was also the seat of the most important banking and trading interests; and, finally, during the fifteenth and sixteenth centuries, when it spearheaded that revolution in Western culture which we now remember as the Renaissance. Modern Italy suffers under the yoke of this history. Indeed, many of those who bemoan the country's present condition do so by comparing it unfavourably to idealized versions of this illustrious past. Our book is not affected by such critical nostalgia. Its inspiration, as I suggest above, is not polemical but practical; and no one is more aware than Rebecca and I of our book's provisionality. As I write, late in 1998, things are changing. A new centre–left government, led 'scandalously' by an ex-Communist, the leader of the Democratici di Sinistra ('Democrats of the Left', formerly the Partito Democratico della Sinistra, 'Democratic Party of the Left'), Massimo D'Alema, has just come to power; major constitutional reform is being seriously discussed. For obvious reasons, such matters must perforce lie beyond the remit of our book. In any case, it is not our intention to give an up-to-the-minute account of modern Italy, but to offer a spyhole onto nearly 150 years of Italian culture. And if, by doing this, we can encourage some readers to recognize that, despite the burden of its past, modern Italy, to use Gian-Paolo Biasin's suggestive words, 'is a tiny but all-important place in the world',[15] then we will consider that our efforts have been more than worthwhile.

NOTES

1. See Robert Lumley and Jonathan Morris (eds.), *The New History of the Italian South* (Exeter: University of Exeter Press, 1997).

2. See Simon During (ed.), *The Cultural Studies Reader* (London: Routledge, 1993); Lawrence Grossberg *et al.* (eds.), *Cultural Studies* (London: Routledge, 1992); Fred Inglis, *Cultural Studies* (Oxford: Blackwell, 1993).

3. See Robert S. Dombroski, 'Forward', in Robert S. Dombroski and Dino S. Cervigni (eds.), *Italian Cultural Studies*. Special issue of *Annali di Italianistica* 16 (1998), pp. 11–14 (pp. 12–13); Ian Taylor *et al.* (eds.), *Relocating Cultural Studies* (London: Routledge, 1993); Graeme Turner, *British Cultural Studies* (London: Routledge, 1990).

4. For a succinct yet sympathetically incisive critique of the methods of 'cultural studies', see Paolo Barlera, 'Toward a Genealogy and Methodology of Italian Cultural Studies', in Dombroski and Cervigni (eds.), *Italian Cultural Studies*, pp. 15–29 (pp. 28–9).

5. For other studies dealing in general terms with modern Italy, see Further Reading.

6. Beverly Allen and Mary Russo, 'Preface', in Allen and Russo (eds.), *Revisioning Italy*, pp. ix–xi (pp. ix–x).

7. Corrado Stajano, 'Introduzione', in Stajano (ed.), *La cultura italiana del Novecento*, pp. vii–xviii (pp. xviii, xi–xii).

8. David Forgacs and Robert Lumley, 'Introduction: Approaches to Culture in Italy', in Forgacs and Lumley (eds.), *Italian Cultural Studies*, pp. 1–11 (pp. 1–2).

9. Ibid., pp. 3–8.

10. Zygmunt G. Barański and Robert Lumley, 'Turbulent Transitions: An Introduction', in Barański and Lumley (eds.), *Culture and Conflict in Postwar Italy* (Basingstoke and London: Macmillan, 1990), pp. 1–17 (pp. 10–12).

11. John Frow, *Cultural Studies and Cultural Value* (Oxford: Clarendon Press, 1995).

12. Barański and Lumley, 'Turbulent Transitions', pp. 11–15.

13. Ernesto Galli della Loggia, *L'identità italiana* (Bologna: Il Mulino, 1998), p. 65.

14. Ibid., pp. 154, 148. 'Familism' is the accentuation of exclusive family values and actions.

15. See below p. 168.

FURTHER READING

Clark, Martin, *Modern Italy 1871–1995*. London and New York: Longman, 1996.

De Grand, Alexander J., *Italian Fascism*. Lincoln and London: University of Nebraska Press, 1982.

Di Scala, Spencer M., *Italy from Revolution to Republic: 1700 to the Present*. Boulder and Oxford: Westview Press, 1998.

Duggan, Christopher, *A Concise History of Italy*. Cambridge University Press, 1994.

Ginsborg, Paul, *A History of Contemporary Italy: Society and Politics 1943–1988*. London: Penguin Books, 1990.

Levy, Carl (ed.), *Italian Regionalism*. Oxford and Washington: Berg, 1996.

Locke, Richard M., *Remaking the Italian Economy*. Ithaca and London: Cornell University Press, 1995.

Mack Smith, Denis, *The Making of Italy 1796–1866*. London: Macmillan, 1988.

Schneider, Jane (ed.), *Italy's 'Southern Question'*. Oxford and New York: Berg, 1998.

Schiavone, Aldo, *Italiani senza Italia. Storia e identità*. Turin: Einaudi, 1998.

Seton-Watson, Christopher, *Italy from Liberalism to Fascism 1870–1925*. London: Methuen, 1967.

Tannenbaum, E. R., *Fascism in Italy. Society and Culture 1922–1945*. London: Allen Lane, 1973.

1

The notion of Italy

Introduction

Of what is one writing when one writes a history of Italy? What, if any, is the thread of continuity that allows us to mean the same thing when we refer to Italy at the fall of the Roman Empire, the death of Dante, the French invasions of 1494 or 1796, the Congress of Vienna, unification, the end of the First World War, the fall of Fascism, or the 1994 election? The first aim of this essay is to argue that there is no single thread of continuity, no common plane of analysis of Italian history. When we examine two of the elements that might serve as that thread or plane, geographical space and culture, what we find is that the historiographical utility of the concept of Italy has to be demonstrated rather than assumed. Italy has to be constructed; it is not given to us directly by the historical sources. My second aim is to show that the notion of Italy is an important dimension of Italian history itself. Using examples from the post-unification era, I will suggest some of the ways in which varying notions of Italy have informed and been influenced by the key problem of nation- and state-formation.

My argument can be better defined through a brief comparison with a well-known earlier critique of the 'unity of Italian history' carried out in the 1930s by the idealist historian, philosopher and literary critic, Benedetto Croce. Croce's principal target is a nationalistic historiography that either treats 'race' as the factor of continuity in a nation's history or, in Croce's words, transforms the unity of Italian history into an issue of public order by branding as unpatriotic all who fail to see oneness in the peninsula's development. Against these positions, Croce baldly asserts that the unity of Italian history begins only in 1860 with the foundation of the unified state, but has a 'prologue' that stretches back to the Enlightenment. Croce adds that, since terms such as 'France', 'England' and 'Italy' are primarily political concepts, his point applies to political history. But this is certainly not, he argues, because there is a unitary history of Italian culture; rather it is because moral, religious, scientific and artistic histories have universal rather than national concerns. Croce regards as absurd and sterile the search for unity at a factual level in national histories: there can be no such thing as a fact which generates and gives unity to other facts.[1]

Croce's argument has many flaws. Perhaps the most telling is that he does not mention social history. If the subject of our analysis were, say, kinship or religion, the date 1860, although important, would obviously not be a neat dividing line. Moreover, in seeking to liberate the 'universal' concerns of philosophy and the arts from jingoism, Croce cuts them off from the social contexts in which they were produced. We might also be reluctant to share the confidence with which Croce circumscribes 'Italy' as a political concept. As Croce was well aware, that idea has had an important place in the literary sphere, whence its influence has travelled into politics and back at many different moments in Italian history. Another problem relates to the status Croce attributes to historiography: the historian seems to work on the plane of the universal, unconstrained, at least potentially, by the concerns of the contemporary era.

Nevertheless, it seems to me that Croce's insistence on the lack of unity in Italian history before 1860 remains basically valid. Indeed, I would go further than Croce in arguing that the 'disunity' of Italian history, or better, its open-endedness and internal diversity, continue to this day. Going further still, I would argue that, on the theoretical level at which Croce is working in most of his article, the same lack of a 'factually generated' unity can be seen in any history whose subject matter and/or premise is the nation or one of the entities often hyphenated to it (-people, -state). The way we view histories and societies in national terms has tended to involve us in making the mistaken assumption that they are or should be unities, that underlying them there is some profound and exclusive connection. Thus, in stressing the artificiality of 'Italy', I wish neither to imply that other national spaces are more objective and genuine, nor to rain undifferentiated scepticism over the possibility of identifying long-term continuities within some important dimensions of Italian history before and after 1860. What I am arguing is that not only the 'Italian nation', but also 'Italy' itself, are not givens, and can bring with them costs as well as benefits when they are used in historical analysis: Italy is an artificial, internally differentiated space which is, and has always been, traversed by a variety of historical forces. In this respect, as in many others, it is not anomalous.

The geographical space

The notion of Italy as a natural geographical entity, a distinct part of the Mediterranean area, dates back some twenty-two or twenty-three centuries. For almost as long, much has been made of the boundaries provided for Italy by Nature: to the North, the *chiostra alpina*; to the West the Mediterranean; to the East the Adriatic. However, in this section, I want to identify three ways in which Italian geography is an unreliable criterion of historical analysis: first, because geographical features do not provide a natural reason for the existence of a homogeneous social, cultural or economic field in Italy; secondly, because the space of Italy has always been both open-ended and internally varied and divided; and thirdly, because human interaction with geographical space is always mediated by conceptions of geography. Ultimately, we cannot write a history of Italy without taking into account the historical force of the various 'imaginary Italies', of which the land providentially guarded by the Alps and the sea is just one example.

Many of Italy's geographical characteristics have actually hindered the creation of a unified peninsula. To take just one example: much of Italy lacks easily navigable rivers. The Apennines, the country's mountainous 'backbone', impede the formation of large rivers. As one goes further south, sharper contrasts in relief, allied to problems of aridity and evaporation in summer, produce short rivers, with an irregular flow, some of which are torrents in winter and trickles in summer. The Po, at 652 kilometres one of Europe's major rivers, clearly gives a different character to the northern alluvial plain through which it meanders. Unstable soils, shifting bottoms and distributaries have meant that five or six centuries of human labour have been necessary to adapt the Po valley for agriculture, industry and transport. Indeed, across large parts of Italy, the instability of land forms and the uneven topography have also made road and railway construction difficult. Italy's physical geography has also helped to make it an open-ended space. The Alps, crisscrossed by trade routes since before Roman times, did not prevent invasion by Alaric's Visigoths in 408 or Attila's Huns in 452. Before 1860, when it became the first capital of Italy, Turin was the capital of the Kingdom of Sardinia which straddled the Alps and included Genoa, Piedmont, Nice and Savoy. At the other end of the peninsula, for many centuries after its invasion by the Vandals in 440, Sicily was conquered by a long and varied succession of Mediterranean sea powers.

Italy was the crossroads of European, African and Asian trade in the later Middle Ages, when a period of relative political autonomy permitted the precarious emergence of many independent city republics in the North and Centre, and great economic growth and integration in some areas. As a result, the 'commercial revolution' that began in the eleventh century has been used by some scholars as a starting-point for the history of Italy. It has even been argued that in the twelfth century, for the first time since the end of the *pax romana*, Italy began to function as an economic unit inasmuch as cities such as Florence and Genoa became more dependent for their basic foodstuffs on the Kingdom of Sicily and on Sardinia, whose trade they managed.[2]

Nonetheless, 'the concept of "Italy" remains one of questionable value in this period'.[3] The northern communes also went as far afield as the Crimea and Morocco in search of basic foodstuffs. Catalans as well as Genoese and Pisans were heavily involved in exports from Sicily and Sardinia. Corsica too was colonized, as were Dalmatian towns by the Venetians. The limited utility of the notion of Italy in this context becomes all the more apparent if we move beyond the specific question of the relations between the northern cities and the South. The political and social environment in which the merchants operated was certainly not 'Italian' in any very concrete sense. Rather it was based on the newly expanded towns and cities of the North and Centre. There was no comparable growth of *comuni* in the South where the more centralized political situation placed a ceiling on the development of mercantile interests. Each city republic was set in patterns of alliance and enmity with its neighbours; and the external influence of the Empire was often a factor in these conflicts. There were strong, even deadly rivalries among Italy's maritime powers such as Amalfi, Pisa, Florence, Genoa and Venice. Moreover, it is clear that at no point during the later Middle Ages were the economic spheres within which Italy's cities operated coterminous with the peninsula. In many cases their primary economic relations were with the subject territory (*contado*) immediately around them. The peninsula's thalassocracies conducted trade with, between and beyond Dalmatia, Crete, Constantinople, the Black Sea, Central Europe, Cyprus, the Levant, Egypt, Tripoli, Tunis, Corsica, Southern France, the Balearic islands, Spain, and Northern European cities such as Rheims, Troyes and later London and Antwerp.

Clearly, it is misleading to think of the economic geography in the period of the autonomous city-states as being 'Italian'. Thereafter, Italy's place, and the place of various parts of Italy, in Mediterranean, European or global configurations of economic power has changed radically over time. In the sixteenth century, for example, Europe's economic centre of gravity shifted to the North, leaving Italy marginalized.

Even after unification, the nation-state must be treated with great caution as a frame of reference for economic analysis. Given any modern state's need to quantify, understand and promote economic activities within its jurisdiction, it should not surprise us that such a national frame of reference became dominant in Italy: after 1860, there was, for example, a rapid and massive accumulation of statistical information premised on the notion of Italy. For most of Italy's history as an industrialized country, the most powerful sectors of its economy have been closely linked to the state: this can only have fostered the tendency to think economic problems in national terms. Yet, of course, after the establishment of the united state, the peninsula continued to be marked by economic dislocation, diversity and imbalance, and to be intersected by non-national economic forces.

The Giolittian era, named after Giovanni Giolitti, the dominant politician of the period from the turn of the century to the start of the First World War, saw the first wave of substantial industrial growth. But that period also serves to illustrate my points about the non-national nature of many historical transformations. The gradual integration of the internal market after unification, together with protectionist government policies and the role of the state itself as a customer for industry, certainly contributed to this phase of rapid growth. But industrial development was heavily concentrated in the north-western 'industrial triangle' of Milan, Turin and Genoa; the monopolization of investment by this area actually worsened the imbalance between North and South. Luciano Cafagna has argued that, in some respects, 'the process of industrialization of the three north-western regions of Italy was akin to that of an autonomous "small country"'.[4] There was little complementarity between the economies of North and South: there was only limited production, by the latter for the former, of raw materials and foodstuffs. Cafagna also maintains that a purely 'national' point of view has tended to neglect the functional integration of north-western Italy into the industrial economies of Europe. And of course, Italy's dramatic growth would have been unthinkable without the great worldwide acceleration in industrial production, and in the movement of goods, capital and labour in the same period. Some aspects of protectionism were socially divisive: the costs were passed on to consumers, mostly the less well off; public intervention in the economy often meant private collusion between competing cliques of politicians, bankers and industrialists; in the South, socially conservative grain interests were shielded, while the more dynamic sectors, such as the citrus-fruit growers and wine-makers, were denied full access to international markets. Italy's first spurt of industrial growth was also greatly aided by the reorganization of the banking system in the mid 1890s which was carried out with German capital and on the German model. The Giolittian era also saw a great increase in the mobility of labour across national boundaries. Emigration from Italy, overwhelmingly by peasants, peaked at 872,598 in 1913: about half this number headed across the Atlantic. Approximately half of all emigrants in the period 1896–1914 came from the South, notably Calabria and Sicily. Paradoxically, the savings sent back by emigrants began to constitute one of the most important sources of the 'domestic' capital invested in Italian industry.

Even when frontiers are natural barriers or are given regulated, concrete existence by modern nation-states, they are predominantly places of exchange rather than of closure; the spatial promiscuity of commerce, capital, disease, warfare, people and ideas reveals them to be porous, artificial and contingent. Nations as categories of historical study have exactly the same qualities.

Geography as a historical force is not only mediated by the ways humans interact with each other and the environment; it is also mediated by thought and perception. The idea of space is greatly impoverished as a historical instrument unless we take account of how people have thought of and lived out their relations to geography. The notion of Italy as a geographical given neglects the diverse perceptions of space and territory which have informed the lives of different social groups at different times.

Until well into the twentieth century, most Italians were peasants. One study of the Sicilian village of 'Milocca' in the late 1920s showed that its inhabitants had a complex set of spatial perceptions. The Milocchese tended to feel a semi-serious rivalry with the towns in the immediate vicinity and a pride in being Sicilian as opposed to Italian. Attitudes to Italy were vague and ambivalent. America, a place in which almost any oddity seemed possible, embraced much of the rest of the world, and continental divisions were not recognized. Loyalties revolved around the family and the neighbourhood. Saints were the focus for local patriotism. The individual's familiarity with localities even within the village territory was strictly bounded by his or her economic and social relationships. Women were restricted in their knowledge of the village: only the midwife had been to every one of its scattered neighbourhoods. Water supplies were felt to belong to God, whereas land belonging to the commune or the church was thought of as private. Some places in Milocca were said to be haunted by spirits, while others were deemed to conceal hidden treasure. Various biblical episodes were thought to have taken place in the village.[5]

For much of the country's history, the Italians have had world-pictures in which Italy was not the primary point of reference. Nor are the peasantry the only group of which this is true. The Catholic Church is the most obvious case: its geographical conception of its role has always had a strong global dimension. Many of Italy's problems of political integration after the Second World War have been attributed to the political subcultures of Catholicism and Communism, both regionally rooted, and both to some extent internationally minded.

The culture

In a recent debate on national identity in the journal *Passato e Presente*, Jens Petersen argued that Italy had a national culture for a long time before it had a national state:

> Italy is only a 'young nation' in terms of its construction as a state. As a people, as a culture, as a form of self-awareness, it begins in the fourteenth century at the latest. Dante's works remain the foundation of the collective consciousness. As the father of the Italian language he is also the father of the nation and the symbol of national greatness through the centuries. Metternich's notorious expression about Italy being merely a geographical concept was already wrong at the very moment he pronounced it.[6]

Petersen's identification of *italianità* with a cultural, predominantly literary tradition dating back to Dante has a certain superficial force to it.

Dante certainly had a conception of Italy as a linguistic and geographical area, a conception galvanized by opposition to cultural and political influences from France. In the *De vulgari eloquentia*, he theorized the use of an Italian 'illustrious vernacular' which, in opposition to the different regional languages spoken in the Italian peninsula, could serve as the transregional vehicle for the loftiest amorous, martial and ethical themes. Subsequently, in the *Divine Comedy*, Dante abandoned his idea of an 'illustrious vernacular' and demonstrated instead the effectiveness of Florentine as a literary medium capable of dealing with any subject and of reaching out beyond the intellectual élite. The influence of the *Divine Comedy* on the development of Italian language and letters is undoubtedly immense. However, those who hail Dante as the progenitor of Italian national culture are courting anachronism. Dante's politics, based on a division of temporal and religious power between the Holy Roman Empire and the Church respectively, held no place for Italy as any kind of 'power container'. His political and cultural concerns, moreover, were subordinate to his religious views: if Dante's Florentine medium can be seen, in retrospect, as 'Italian', his message is incompatible with any 'national culture' that it might be claimed he founded.

Nor does Italian literary culture become linear and unitary in Dante's wake. For example, for approximately three hundred years after his death, it was by no means obvious to intellectuals that the (Florentine) vernacular would or should win out over Latin as the tool of their trade. Some saw the vernacular as a threat to the national and international unity of scholars which was guaranteed by the language of ancient Rome. Indeed, the *questione della lingua*, the question of what form Italian should take, has exercised Italy's intellectuals to this day. The notion of Italy, and of Italian culture and language, has changed radically over time. For Petrarch, who lived only a generation after Dante, the notion of Italy was not even primarily a linguistic one, but involved an élite, scholarly identification with classical antiquity. In literary history, as in other contexts, 'one should not therefore think of one Italy, but rather of various Italies that are often contrasted, as powerful ideas are needed to oppose other powerful ideas, dominant myths set against oppositional myths'.[7] The Italian literary tradition, like any other national cultural tradition, is not an unbroken line through time. The myth of sequence is constructed retrospectively through the creative misreading of a set of heterogeneous moments. The past is constantly revised on terms conditioned by each new intellectual and social conjuncture. Petersen's own idea of the Italian literary tradition is not new. It has its roots in the Romantic assumption that literary culture is or should be rooted in a spoken language, the spontaneous voice of a 'people' through the ages. Its most famous formulations, including Francesco De Sanctis's *Storia della letteratura italiana* ('History of Italian Literature', 1870), belong to the period immediately after unification when literary history was being rewritten as the history of an idea of Italy which began with Dante and was destined to find its realization in the Savoyard state. Dante's own pre-eminent place in the canon was only (re-)established in the eighteenth century, and it is to the period following the French Revolution that we owe the growth of the cult of Dante as a living symbol of *italianità*. Since Croce, Italian critics have expressed dissatisfaction with the Dante cult and with De Sanctis's model of literary history. The unity and linearity of Italian literary culture has been revealed as a teleological patriotic myth.

The near-identification of literature and culture in Petersen's remarks is itself, of course, very problematic. It only holds together on the basis of the implicit and very selective idea that Italy is best embodied in the high literary culture of a social stratum which was, at the very least until this century, an exiguous élite of people able to read and write Italian. Few scholars have been bold enough to make claims for the long-term historical existence of cultural *italianità* at any other level: games and forms of social life, eating and drinking, particular religious practices, for example. In the pre-industrial era, it is anachronistic to treat these anthropological features as 'national'. They are more appropriately understood on other planes, such as the locality or the Mediterranean area. To identify Italy with culture at this level is also to presume that such features as diet and forms of social life do not change, and it risks undervaluing other long-term continuities which do not coincide with the national framework, such as Catholicism.

However, it is also difficult to point to a moment in the *modern* era when Italy might be thought of as having a popular national culture. The peasants of 'Milocca' show us that parts of Italy continued to have a localized, 'pre-national' culture well into the twentieth century; while industrialization brings with it a globalization of the market for cultural artefacts and trends. Indeed, David Forgacs has argued that, in the twentieth century, the strong influence of imported books, films, television programmes, popular music and comics has been a striking characteristic of a country which has displayed 'an unusually high degree of openness to non-national cultural goods, such as to throw into doubt the existence of a cohesive "national" culture from the consumer's point of view'.[8]

As James Clifford has reminded us, we tend to see cultures, and particularly national cultures, as isolated worlds. This is a conception which harks back to an organicist nineteenth-century anthropology.[9] Against this, he argues that we must learn to see cultures in relational terms: as Claude Lévi-Strauss has written, the idea of a culture existing on its own makes no sense.[10] All cultures are ways of relating to other cultures: it is misguided to analyse or judge them in the light of the expectation of unity that nationalism generates. Italian culture, like Italian geography, is not exceptional in its openness and diversity. What Italian history shows us is a great array of historically specific forms of openness and diversity.

Nation-building: the Italian state and the notion of Italy

The existence of a national state is Croce's basis for the unity of Italian history after 1860. Nonetheless, it is by now something of a historiographical commonplace that the central problem of Italian history since that date has been nation-building. There was no historical precedent for the unified Italy which was established in 1860: the dominion of ancient Rome grew from city-state to empire without passing through an intermediate stage that could be considered analogous to the modern nation-state. After the decline of the Western Empire, the peninsula was for centuries carved up between a host of powers, both internal and external. The establishment of a state and, within the space of a few years, of a national ruling cadre did not resolve the nationality question. The often-cited but still eloquent statistics on Italy's very low proportion of literate, Italophone citizens at and after unification clearly demonstrate that the population over which the state held sway was not geographically, socially or linguistically integrated.

The nation-building problem is often seen as having two aspects. The first is the cultural and social diversity within the peninsula, which can make identification with an Italian nation problematic. Broadly speaking, following great internal migration, and the spread of the mass media after the Second World War, this problem has largely been overcome. The second and more tenacious aspect of the problem of nation-building is that of political and institutional culture and of the relationship between citizen and state. For a long time the Italian state struggled to gain automatic acceptance of its legitimacy, not least because the Catholic Church, deprived of its temporal power by the unification of Italy, remained alienated from the state until 1929. With its frequently authoritarian and exclusionary response to the challenges of a modern society, most notably during the two decades of Fascism, the state itself has not helped the nation-building cause. Despite this, excluded groups such as Radicals, Catholics, Republicans, Socialists, Communists and post-Fascists have slowly, and often painfully, been brought within the boundaries of the political sphere. Yet the Italian state has failed, and continues to fail, consistently to base its own workings and its relationship with society on the kind of criteria associated with the Enlightenment. Italy still lacks such things as an efficient, transparent, honest and impartial bureaucracy, or a political arena where there is a contest between parties who accept each other's legitimacy and base their appeal to the voter on clearly enunciated legislative programmes. The problem of Italian political culture has many other facets which I can only allude to here: the way family ties and private patron–client networks often override the public interest within the institutions (familism and clientelism); the particularly close-knit ranks of the economic élite; collusion between organized crime and representatives of the state. In this section, I want to use two specific instances to illustrate some of the ways in which the concept of Italy, and specifically of Italy as nation, has been involved in the history of the Italian state seen in terms of nation-building: first, the problem of political corruption; second, the 'neo-absolutist' political thought of Alfredo Rocco.

In 1992 a web of corruption was revealed amongst the élites of Italy's economic capital, Milan. The arrest, on 17 February, of Mario Chiesa, the Socialist president of a retirement home, led directly to the arrest of thirty-six politicians, thirty-one business people and six civil servants. Over a longer period, what the newspapers dubbed the Tangentopoli ('Kickback City') investigations proved fatal for the whole system of clientelistic power based on the Christian Democrat and Socialist Parties. The Milan cases in particular reveal how the system was centred on 'business politicians' who operated in a strategic location between three spheres: the administration of public resources and services over which the politicians had a *de facto* control; those parts of the private sector seeking to do business with the state on privileged terms; and politics, both local and national. These men (the role was a very masculine one) would create rings of connivance between individuals in all three spheres, involving payments that ranged from huge international bank transfers to gifts of cash and watches. Building companies that wanted to secure work in the extension of the Milan underground, or even funeral parlours wanting to collect corpses, would pay a bribe to an administrator, who in turn would channel a percentage of the funds on to the politicians of his own party who controlled his appointment, as well as to politicians from other parties, in a formalized system of dividing up and sharing out of the spoils. By increasing the demand for favours from him, and by increasing the state resources at his disposal, the business politician could increase his own influence at a national level within the party structure.

Practices like these are only the most recent, and most visible, example of problems that have beset the state and society since 1860, albeit with varying degrees of intensity in different periods and places. The selective distribution of privileges, rather than the generalized administration of rights, is an unstable basis for the construction of political consensus. For example, any reduction in the resources available for distribution, or any injudicious monopolization of privileges, may upset the power balance between those who oppose the system of privileges, those excluded from it, those with access to it, and those who hang on in the hope of getting access to it. But even when they are working 'well', the occult practices of corruption and clientelism inevitably undermine the credibility of what politicians say in public: corruption fosters a closed value system amongst those involved, a realm outside the ethical sphere created by identification with the national state and the national interest; corrupt elements within parties have a positive interest in reducing moral and political discourse to empty formulae. Far from building a nation, people within the state and the great bodies of collective representation (parties, unions) have often acted to discredit the collective interest that the term 'nation' encodes in political discourse, by acting through channels that, even when not actually corrupt or clientelistic, have often been familial or private. The value of the notion of Italy in political culture can only have been debased further by the patriotic rhetoric of many politicians involved in corrupt practices: one thinks of the 'tricolour Socialism' promoted by Bettino Craxi's Socialist Party in the early 1980s.

Corruption, familism, clientelism and patronage are recurrent features of modern Italian history. Yet we should be very careful not to treat them as if they were invariable – anthropological prime movers of Italy's problems of state-formation. One of the reasons why this warning needs to be given is that ahistorical or otherwise superficial understandings of patronage, familism and corruption have played a central part in what can be called a culture of denunciation. Italy is unusual in Europe in the degree to which aggressive nationalism has been marginalized since the fall of Fascism. Yet a kind of inverted patriotism, a patriotism of pathos marked by worry about the state of the nation and pessimism about the 'national character', remains a striking feature of Italian culture. A recent example, that almost reaches the point of self-parody, is a newspaper article by Eugenio Scalfari published on 15 January 1995. At the time Scalfari was the editor of Italy's best-selling daily, *La Repubblica*. The article was written soon after the start of the Lamberto Dini government that followed the end of media magnate Silvio Berlusconi's brief period as Prime Minister. Scalfari gives a profile of the Italian national character: his countrymen are hard-working, individualistic, wily and deceitful; they are very attached to their mothers, and lack morality and a 'spirit of service'. Like Mussolini before him, Berlusconi is a typical Italian, 'the materialization of the nation's characteristic elements', which is what makes him a dangerous person to govern the country. By contrast, all of Italy's best leaders, from Cavour to De Gasperi, 'had almost nothing Italian about them'.

It would be tempting, in the absence of further proof, to attribute homespun theories of this kind to a chronic shortage of copy, were it not for the fact that they chime with ideas present at many levels of Italian public and academic life in different historical periods. For example, liberals have long lamented that Italy is the corruption, distortion or parody of an idealized form of the modern national state, an Enlightenment or 'Anglo-Saxon' polity. The tradition of denunciation, and the concomitant dream of making Italy into a 'normal' or 'modern' country, has been a powerful and often positive force. The magistrates who, since the early 1990s, have challenged organized crime and political corruption across Italy – with some success – could be seen as the latest manifestation of this tradition. However, many less admirable figures also have their place in it (including Alfredo Rocco, about whom I have more to say below). The tradition of denunciation has also frequently taken the form of a disgust with politics in general. For many people across the political spectrum, Italy is deemed to be unique because of its endlessly repeated failure to achieve putative standards of nationhood and institutional maturity or modernity. A great deal of historical work remains to be done on the specific nature of the notions of Italy and of political normality which inform such laments.

Given Italy's perceived status as a 'failed' nation in which the public sphere is enervated by clientelism, the collective interest is an elusive ideal, and political homogeneity is undermined by cultural diversity, it is perhaps ironic that Italian history should offer so many instances of political projects and actions legitimated and motivated by reified notions of Italy. Even some of those who, like Vincenzo Gioberti in his *Del primato morale e civile degli Italiani* ('On the Moral and Civil Primacy of the Italians', 1844), have argued that the Italians as a unified people do not exist, have still managed to regard an abstract notion of Italy as a reality. There is no limit to the range of political positions that can draw on reified concepts of Italy. The thought of Alfredo Rocco provides one of the clearest instances of the way the notion of Italy has actually informed Italy's history, in his case through a project to construct an authoritarian state. From 1914, Rocco, a law professor and leading ideologue of the Associazione Nazionalista Italiana, set forth a body of ideas which he himself, as Mussolini's Minister of Justice between January 1925 and July 1932, was later to turn into laws that were the basis of Fascism's transformation from government into régime.

Rocco saw the modern era in dualistic terms, as a long war between the forces of social cohesion and anomie. Only the state could prevent society's dissolving under the pressure of competing individual interests. Democracy, Socialism and Feminism were all secret allies of this individualistic threat to society. The state, for Rocco, was an organic entity with rights which transcended those of individuals singly and, at any one point in time, of the people collectively. Because Italy was caught up in a struggle for survival between societies, the state had to be in the hands of an élite able to intuit society's overriding aims. Any such élite in Italy faced a difficult task: the country had had only a few decades of fitful state-building to counteract centuries of individualism; its territory did not provide the raw materials it needed; mass emigration was draining away its life-blood. But the Italian race was fertile. If the state could orchestrate the economic efforts of the masses and encourage the monopolistic trend in capitalism, Italy would be able to expand by increasing production and wresting colonies from nations in decline.

It is striking and instructive to note how vague and ambivalent Rocco's notion of the Italian nation reveals itself to be when examined closely, especially in the light of his reputation for intellectual rigour. Emilio Gentile points to an oscillation between different meanings in Rocco's thought on the nation:[11] at some moments he thinks of the nation as an organic group or race; at others he maintains that 'nationality is a spiritual fact, not a physical phenomenon'. While Gentile's critique is certainly valid, it does not exhaust Rocco's contradictoriness, nor does it show how the contradictions within Rocco's thought are not so much flaws as rhetorical tactics. For example, reifying the nation as race or stock allows Rocco to transform it into the subject of Social Darwinist narratives of evolutionary struggle. Alternatively, treating the nation as something spiritual makes it into a way of identifying and stigmatizing the un-Italian: 'the office workers holding the state to ransom, the politicking Socialists, and the fanatical advocates of full bellies are not part of the nation. Nationality is a spiritual fact, not a physical phenomenon.'[12] Consciously or not, Rocco's nation changes radically according to the needs of his argument.

But I would argue that it is not just Rocco and the other Nationalists who use the term nation in a systematically vague way. The notion of Italy as a nation is frequently the product of a shifting mosaic of miniature textual strategies whose common assumption is the construction of the nation as a concrete fact, or group of people, or a single idea, existing independently of the concepts people have of it. Paradoxically, the vagueness of the language of the nation, and the logical sleight of hand with which it is often used, both contribute to the production of the mirage of a single, simple idea or thing. The very ambiguity of the terminology of nationhood allows 'Italy' to be constructed in a variety of fantasy scenarios, narratives, imperatives and arguments that help to give this notion its intellectual and emotional hold over us.

Conclusion

The name 'Italy' has no single clear etymology, but its origins seem to be Greek. From the fifth to the third century BC, the Samnites of the South of the peninsula adopted the Greek name for their own territory. Once the term was taken over by the Romans, the area it embraced spread northwards as Roman hegemony spread. During the rapid expansion of the late fourth and early third centuries BC, 'Italy' reached the Arno. However, only with Diocletian's administrative reforms at the end of the third century AD were the islands included. Gradually, over the same arc of time, the name came to have an ethnic as well as a geopolitical sense.

Of course etymology tells us only a limited amount about meaning. In its search for origins, moreover, it can nourish the illusion that, at some point between the Middle Ages and 1870, the word 'Italy' settled into a single, stable modern meaning. The implication of what I have argued above is that this is not the case. The advent of the nation-state, with what Croce called its 'preface' in nineteenth-century Nationalism, has given 'Italy' a concrete political referent. It has also become a necessary point of identification for the citizens of a state that presides over what is now one of the world's most powerful economies. But by being tied in with discourses of political and cultural nationhood in this way, the notion of Italy has become the stake and instrument in a great many forms of antagonism and division: all Italians have a notion of Italy, but they do not all agree on what that notion means, particularly in the political context. Italy is, as it has always been, a geographical expression (as Metternich famously remarked). It is an expression, as I have suggested, with a profusion of different meanings across time and space. Yet, for all its slipperiness, the word 'Italy' can have real effects, as Metternich himself was well aware, and as the case of Alfredo Rocco demonstrates.

For Benedetto Croce, facts are to history as individual words are to poetry: between them lies the synthesizing work of the mind. It is in the domain of ideas, rather than in the material realm, that the unity of a history is to be found; it resides in the historian's morally driven 'mental process'. I would agree with Croce that, as a historiographical category, 'Italy' is not authorized by any form of intrinsic unity in all that it denotes. However, there is more than the intellect of the historian holding it in place. However selective, mythical, muddled or contested notions of Italy can be, some of them have come to form the discursive premises of a whole range of national institutions – institutions which, in their turn, authorize the currency of the term. In their own small way, university departments of Italian Studies are part of this process. As we have seen, notions of Italy also shape the way citizens relate to those institutions, even when they are very critical of them. 'Italy' does not objectively define a self-contained field of study. Yet it is still an immensely important plane of analysis for many reasons, not least because it legitimates and delimits the administrative influence of a state.

NOTES

1. Benedetto Croce, 'Recenti controversie intorno all'unità della storia d'Italia', in *La storia come pensiero e come azione*, 2nd edn (Bari: Laterza, 1938), pp. 307–20.

2. David Abulafia, *The Two Italies. Economic Relations between the Norman Kingdom of Sicily and the Northern Communes* (Cambridge University Press, 1977), p. 5.

3. David Abulafia, 'Southern Italy, Sicily and Sardinia in the Medieval Mediterranean Economy', in *Commerce and Conquest in the Mediterranean, 1100–1500* (Aldershot: Variorum, 1993), pp. 1–32 (p. 8).

4. Luciano Cafagna, *Dualismo e sviluppo nella storia d'Italia* (Venice: Marsilio, 1989), p. 321.

5. Charlotte Gower Chapman, *Milocca. A Sicilian Village* (London: Allen & Unwin, 1973).

6. Simonetta Soldani (ed.), 'Nazione e Stato nazionale in Italia: crisi di una endiadi imperfetta', *Passato e Presente* 33 (1994), pp. 13–30 (p. 12).

7. Maria Serena Sapegno, ' "Italia", "Italiani" ', in A. Asor Rosa (ed.), *Letteratura italiana*. v: *Le Questioni* (Turin: Einaudi, 1986), pp. 169–221 (p. 170).

8. David Forgacs, *Italian Culture in the Industrial Era 1880–1980* (Manchester University Press, 1990), p. 28.

9. James Clifford, 'On *Orientalism*', in *The Predicament of Culture* (Cambridge, Mass. and London: Harvard University Press, 1988), pp. 255–76 (p. 273).

10. Claude Lévi-Strauss, *Race et histoire* (Paris: Gonthier, 1961), pp. 16–17.

11. Emilio Gentile, 'L'architetto dello stato nuovo: Alfredo Rocco', in *Il mito dello stato nuovo dall'antigiolittismo al fascismo* (Rome and Bari: Laterza, 1982), pp. 167–204 (p. 177).

12. Alfredo Rocco, 'L'amnistia, il disgregamento dello Stato e gli stranieri d'Italia' (1915), in *Scritti e discorsi politici* (Milan: Giuffrè, 1938), vol. I, pp. 235–38 (p. 238).

FURTHER READING

Antonelli, Roberto, 'Storia e geografia, tempo e spazio nell'indagine letteraria', in *Letteratura italiana. Storia e geografia*. i: *L'età medievale*. Turin: Einaudi, 1987, pp. 5–26.

Bethemont, Jacques and Pelletier, Jean, *Italy. A Geographical Introduction*. London: Longman, 1983.

Bollati, Giulio, 'L'italiano', in R. Romano and C. Vivanti (eds.), *Storia d'Italia*. i: *I caratteri originali*, vol. ii. Turin: Einaudi, 1972, pp. 949–1022.

della Porta, Donatella, 'Milan: Immoral Capital', in S. Hellman and G. Pasquino (eds.), *Italian Politics: A Review*, vol. viii. London: Pinter, 1993, pp. 98–115

Dionisotti, Carlo, 'Varia fortuna di Dante', in *Geografia e storia della letteratura italiana*. Turin: Einaudi, 1967, pp. 205–42.

'Regioni e letteratura', in R. Romano and C. Vivanti (eds.), *Storia d'Italia*. v: *I documenti*, vol. ii. Turin: Einaudi, 1973, pp. 1373–95.

Galasso, Giuseppe, *Introduzione. L'Italia come problema storiografico*. Turin: UTET, 1979.

Gambi, Lucio, 'I valori storici dei quadri ambientali', in R. Romano and C. Vivanti (eds.), *Storia d'Italia*. i: *I caratteri originali*, vol. i. Turin: Einaudi, 1972, pp. 3–60.

Pizzorno, Alessandro, 'Introduzione: La corruzione nel sistema politico', in Donatella della Porta, *Lo scambio occulto. Casi di corruzione politica in Italia*. Bologna: Il Mulino, 1992, pp. 13–73.

Tucci, Ugo, 'Credenze geografiche e cartografia', in R. Romano and C. Vivanti (eds.), *Storia d'Italia*. v: *I documenti*, vol. i. Turin: Einaudi, 1973, pp. 47–85.

Waley, Daniel, *The Italian City-Republics*, 2nd edn. London: Longman, 1978.

Zamagni, Vera, *The Economic History of Italy 1860–1990*. Oxford: Clarendon Press, 1993.

2

Social and political cultures in Italy from 1860 to the present day

Introduction

It is almost inevitable for historians to look back upon the past with an eye on the present, partly because they are influenced by later developments, and partly because contemporary debates relating to culture, politics and society actively lead them to reconsider past events in a new light, bringing out analogies with and meanings for the present. The collapse of Communism and the end of the Cold War have accentuated this tendency. This is not surprising, since the most pressing issues facing Italy today, namely, regional disparities, the need for electoral and institutional change (the creation of a 'Second Republic'), clientelism and corruption, and national unity itself, can be considered as the resurfacing of unresolved problems. Now that the period dominated by the Cold War can be encapsulated within a precise time span, and the transition to a Second Republic is proving less smooth than might have been expected in the early 1990s, it is as if Italy's political agenda is being directly linked to concerns which predate that period and go back to the process of unification. One of these debates focuses on questions of nationhood and identity, questions which Italy is asking together with the rest of Europe, since, almost inevitably, such matters become prominent at moments of great political change. Nevertheless, in Italy these questions seem to revolve specifically around the country's failure to create a collective national identity. According to the sociologist Roberto Cartocci, Italy's present-day task is still the one d'Azeglio succinctly summarized after unification in his famous saying: 'Italy is made; now the Italians must be made.'[1] Closely related to this is the issue of clientelism and corruption, which also appears as a constant of Italian history since unification, and which is judged to stem from the poor degree of legitimacy of the Italian state.

Current debates on nationhood, clientelism and familism are once again privileging a long-term view of historical change. As Putnam wrote, with reference to the uneven performance of the Italian regional system: 'Institutional history moves very slowly. Time is measured in decades.'[2] This view of history has been successfully applied to other fields, including political parties and party systems, social and political cultures and economic structures. The tendency of scholars of contemporary Italy to look backwards has now met with a comparable tendency on the part of historians of nineteenth-century Italy to look forward:

> The new research has begun to sketch out elements of continuity that link Liberal Italy not to Mussolini's Fascist state but to the Italian republic that took shape after 1947 [...] the new Italian historiography has established new perspectives that will widen the debate on the course of contemporary Italian history both synchronically and diachronically, opening the ways to broader comparative exploration and bringing into new focus the elements of continuity in the longer-term formation of the state and society in Italy.[3]

Alongside this long-term view of history, recent studies of Italy also seem dominated by a pre-eminence of culture over structure. In particular, the nature and functioning of the country's economic and political set-up are judged to depend on the prevailing collective orientations of its citizens. Interpersonal trust and co-operation underpin successful socio-political institutions; conversely, distrust and particularism largely explain institutional malfunctioning. In a way this approach is not surprising, precisely because cultural values and beliefs change only gradually. 'Once established, these orientations have a momentum of their own, and may act as autonomous influences on politics and economics long after the events that gave rise to them.'[4] Culture, however, at least in the form of a group's aspirations and collective will, is also seen as capable of imposing a rapid pace on political change in the face of socio-economic continuity. What the two viewpoints have in common is the idea that socio-economic, political and cultural change need not be synchronized. On the contrary, there can be serious dislocations between them. This can be seen clearly in the case of Italy. The starting-point of a history of modern Italy is generally the country's unification, achieved in 1860 and completed in 1870 with the conquest of Rome. These dates, which used to indicate the end of one historical period and the beginning of another, are now considered arbitrary. The drive towards unification, once interpreted as a cumulative and converging process involving economic, social and cultural change, has now been redimensioned and largely reduced to the powerful attraction the myth of Nationalism and national identity exercised over a relatively small intellectual minority.[5] Economically and socially, but also culturally if we exclude the modernizing élites, there was much continuity after 1860 with the pre-unification period. This meant continuity with the regional states which had previously made up the peninsula, leading to the existence of significant divisions within the newly formed nation-state.

Subnational divisions can have different origins and natures: they can be class- or religion-based, or they may reflect the urban/rural dichotomy. Such cleavages may play a significant role within a nation (one only has to think of an urban/liberal versus a rural/conservative society); however, typically, they tend to be fairly uniformly distributed across the national territory. There can, however, be cases where religious allegiances or the rural/urban dichotomy split a country into two or more geographical divisions. There are also territorial/cultural cleavages, which are often related to internally cohesive local and regional communities, bent on defending their shared culture and identity in opposition to the nation-building efforts of a new unitary state. Class, religious and territorial cleavages are not neatly compartmentalized but interact with and even reinforce each other in various ways. A nation will be the more successful at fostering a common sense of identity among its people, the more it 'defuses' the danger posed by the existence of its internal cleavages, in particular, by preventing them from developing into rigid politico-ideological divisions.

The point I want to make is that, after unification, Italy can be characterized as a country where dramatic political change clashed with the relative inertia of pre-existing regional processes of development, and where, therefore, territorial/cultural cleavages were especially strong. My analysis of the period 1860 to the present takes this view as its starting-point and looks at the complex interaction between culture and structure against a background of both continuity and change.

Socio-economic structures and political cultures after unification

Italian unification was achieved late compared to other European countries. Once the process started, however, it developed fairly rapidly. Favourable international circumstances, especially in the decade 1850–60, contributed to its successful outcome. It has even been claimed that 'Italian Unification had little to do with Liberal or Nationalist plans [. . .] Unification was a product of French and Piedmontese territorial ambition.'[6] This judgment is too harsh; however, the patriots were undoubtedly a small minority, divided between the socially and politically moderate Liberal current, headed by the Piedmontese Count of Cavour, and the democratic and Republican wing, led by Mazzini. The predominance of the northern-based moderate Liberals gave the movement a degree of cultural and ideological homogeneity, even though Liberalism itself had been put into practice only in Piedmont, in the years preceding unification. The result was that a fairly homogeneous subgroup found itself presiding over a non-homogeneous country.

The primary task of Italy's new Liberal rulers consisted in the construction of a sense of nationhood, a task made very difficult by the fact that only a small percentage of the population spoke Italian (as opposed to regional dialect), and could read or write. The élites were able to communicate with each other and the process of Italian unification had largely been the result of their efforts, with some participation on the part of the lower-middle class and the urban-based artisans, but only sporadic – and by no means welcome to the élites – participation of the rural masses, who formed the vast majority of the population. The cultural distance between the élites and the masses was one factor militating against nationhood. However, socio-economic structures also differed widely within Italy and cut across both the élites and the masses, accounting for strong regional and subregional cultures. These regional differences can be briefly described.

In the hilly areas below the Alps and in central Italy share-cropping was the dominant land-tenure system. Share-cropping families were generally extended ones, usually under the authority of a male head. Seasonal emigration abroad and employment in the textile sector for women and children complemented work done on the land. The main cultural trait associated with the peasantry in this type of structure is family-centred social stability. Relations between share-croppers and landowners were largely characterized by a culture of paternalism, which often involved a third party: the Church and the parish priest. In the eyes of the landowners this was a highly desirable system, guaranteeing both industrial (mainly textile) and rural production and, above all, social peace.

In the Po Valley, share-cropping was also fairly widespread; however, a process of proletarianization of the share-croppers had already begun. This was the most fertile area of Italy, where the development of a system of capitalist intensive farming with large tenant farmers employing landless labourers was accompanied by innovative irrigation and drainage schemes. Specific cultural traits developed among the region's peasantry: collective strategies alongside family strategies, a potential for the creation of stable workers' organizations, but also greater social instability. As for the tenant farmers, they favoured change to a larger extent than the landowners in the other regions. There was little trade-off in this area between productivity and social peace. As a result, relations between labourers and tenant farmers were characterized by direct confrontation. Up to the 1880s it was Anarchism, based on the idea of spontaneous rebellion against authority and the state, which dominated the political culture of the local labourers and impoverished share-croppers. Later it was Socialism, with its emphasis on trade-union organization and municipal government, which prevailed.

In the South, the latifundia system, consisting of very large estates extensively cultivated and absentee landowners, was the dominant socio-economic model. The peasants were land hungry, rather than landless, since they often possessed a tiny plot of land, which was insufficient to meet their needs. They were therefore employed on the latifundia on an irregular basis. This involved long-distance travel, the use of rudimentary tools, and working in isolation. Associated with the latifundia system was a peasant culture of instability, fear and mutual distrust, where interpersonal contacts were often limited to the village, a large agglomeration of houses lacking the most elementary forms of hygiene and where humans mixed with animals. This culture is often referred to as 'semi-feudal', a rather inappropriate term given the transition of the latifundia system to a market-oriented economy. Nevertheless, the term does convey a sense of the social distance between landowners and peasants, as well as an idea of the often destructive, short-lived, 'pre-modern' violence of the peasants. Brigandage, a mixture of social revolt and widespread banditry affecting the southern regions between 1861 and 1866, is the most famous example of this type of violence. Far from expressing any specific social or political demands, the unrest showed a destructiveness which increased in brutality the more the peasants' hopes for land redistribution following unification were thwarted.

Clearly, regional differences in 1860 were considerable. We cannot speak of *one* landowning class or of *one* peasant class. To the subnational inter-class divisions, therefore, we need to add regionally and even locally based intra-class cultural differences. The Italian governments after unification had to strive for the formation of a national identity by trying to reconcile the masses to the élites (the *paese reale*, i.e., the vast mass of the population excluded from citizenship, to the *paese legale*, the legal and institutional system devised for a small minority), but also the élites to themselves. That the masses too were composed of vastly different social groups mattered less in the early decades, since these cleavages had not yet fed into political groups and/or demands. Potentially more dangerous was the split between Church and state, symbolized by the Italian troops entering Rome by force on 20 September 1870 and by the Pope, Pius IX, declaring himself a prisoner of the Italian state. The Catholic Church commanded support among all social groups and could have organized a political force in open conflict with the governing Liberals. Instead, the Pope forbade all Catholics to participate in the political life of the new state, thus opting for a policy of isolationism. On the other hand, the Church–state divide and the supranational nature of the Catholic Church deprived the ruling élites of a powerful unifying *national* culture, in contrast to those Protestant countries, such as Britain and Scandinavia, where the Church had been successfully integrated into the nation-state.

In this context, Italian Liberalism enjoyed a fragile but politically unchallenged existence in the first decades after unification. The suffrage was extremely restricted, since only 2% of the population, or 600,000 adult males, had the right to vote. Despite this, two political parties managed to emerge, the Right and the Left, which had their roots in the pre-unification division between those who favoured a monarchical and Liberal Italy, and those who supported Mazzini's ideals of a Republican and democratic state. As was to be expected, given the restricted suffrage, the two parties did not differ substantially in terms of the social origins of their supporters. Rather, they reproduced the territorial divisions between the country's élites.

The governments of the Historic Right (1861–76), led by Prime Ministers of Piedmontese origins (such as Urbano Rattazzi and Giovanni Lanza), or from Tuscany and Emilia (such as Bettino Ricasoli and Marco Minghetti), represented primarily the landowning classes of the North and Centre. They believed in the rule of law, long-term education of the lower classes and, somewhat reluctantly, administrative centralization. The last policy was largely embraced as a result of southern brigandage and the grave danger of national disintegration that this appeared to pose for the new state. The government was worried about brigandage turning into an organized political revolt in favour of the deposed southern monarchy, and decided to intervene with drastic measures, including the imposition of martial law. In other words, the abrupt awareness of deep territorial and social divisions and the fear that these could translate into centrifugal political forces convinced the ruling élites that if 'harmonization' was not to come as a spontaneous process of social and cultural bonding, then it had to be imposed from above. It is ironic, therefore, that when the governments of the Historic Right fell, this was largely as a result of the continuing strength of subnational boundaries, particularly of regional divisions within the élites. It was a split between the Piedmontese and the Tuscan members of Parliament that precipitated the fall in 1874, while the pressure exercised by the southern deputies to end their exclusion from government also played a part.

In 1876 the New Left (so-called to distinguish it from Mazzini's old Democrats) was securely in government, under the leadership of Agostino Depretis, a Piedmontese who had taken part in the 1860 Garibaldi expedition to Sicily. The Left had now moved a long way from Mazzini's ideas, and was mainly in favour of a loose, pragmatic, down-to-earth political programme, as opposed to Mazzini's idealistic and Romantic vision of a nation where 'the people' were united and indivisible. The governments of the New Left (1876–87) took on board the interests of the southern landowners and of the professional classes. The latter were numerous throughout Italy but were especially influential in the South. Depretis was able to devise a specific solution to Italy's social and cultural divisions, namely, the parliamentary practice known as *trasformismo*, which consisted of gaining a majority in Parliament on the basis of private agreements with individual deputies or groups of deputies. Thus political Liberalism in Italy assumed a peculiarly 'distorted' character. There was no alternation of parties in power, only reshuffles within the established majority, with groups of deputies alternately joining and leaving the majority. *Trasformismo* was heavily criticized at the time as a source of corruption and political stagnation, but it was obviously a direct consequence of the fragmented character of Italy's ruling and middle classes which required of its political leaders skills of mediation and power-broking, rather than the ability of purposeful leadership stemming from a unitary vision of the state. This was reflected in the social composition of Parliament and governments after 1876, when landowners and members of the military élite were gradually replaced by professional politicians, mainly lawyers and journalists, who were especially adept at persuading and mediating. *Trasformismo* was in this context a recognition that the new Italian state lacked legitimacy in the eyes of the middle classes as well as in the eyes of the peasant majority. The extension of the suffrage in 1882, enfranchising almost 7 per cent of the population (slightly more than 2 million adult males), had, if anything, aggravated the situation. An increased electorate meant increased demands on the state.

From Crispi to Giolitti: old and new cleavages, 1887–1914

With Francesco Crispi, Prime Minister from 1887 to 1891 and again from 1893 to 1896, we enter a new period of Italian history, characterized by a determined effort to forge a national culture based on patriotism and colonialism. Political compromise and *trasformismo* faded into the background, replaced by authoritarianism and militarism.

Compared to his predecessors' unifying projects, Crispi's was less problematic in relation to the élites. The introduction of protectionist tariffs in 1887 was due largely to the perceived need to accelerate Italy's economic development and promote industrialization. Nevertheless the tariffs also united the élites by favouring northern industrialists, the landowners and tenant farmers of the Po Valley, and wheat producers (including the southern landowners, who were also given fiscal incentives to compensate for export losses). They all now had a financial stake in the Italian nation.

In relation to the lower classes, however, Crispi's political and cultural vision was complicated both by economic crises and by the formation of two subnational political cultures, Socialism and political Catholicism. The Socialist subculture was strongest among the impoverished share-croppers and landless labourers of the Po Valley, where it started to absorb the Anarchist tradition, whereas the Catholic subculture developed among the share-croppers of Lombardy and the Veneto. Each subculture put up a defence of the local/regional society against the processes of modernization, urbanization and proletarianization, seen as endorsed by the Liberal state. The Socialists offered their supporters the protection of increasingly effective workers' leagues and later developed farming co-operatives. The Catholics guaranteed the continuation of paternalistic practices, promoting self-help measures, rural banks and charity schemes among the northern share-croppers. The development of these two subcultures reinforced subnational boundaries in two ways. On the one hand, it led to the creation of two mutually exclusive ideologies. Socialism was strongly anti-clerical, partly because it inherited the anti-clerical tradition of the regions which had historically been part of the Papal States, and partly because it developed almost as a religious movement. Catholicism was both anti-Socialist and anti-Liberal; indeed, Pope Pius IX had condemned both doctrines with the publication, in 1864, of the *Syllabus of Errors*. On the other hand, while seemingly blurring the territorial conflict, the ideological conflict actually provided it with clear-cut collective identities and symbols based upon an idea of community. Admittedly, the type of community constructed by universalistic ideologies such as Socialism and Catholicism is supposedly devoid of a territorial context, but, in concrete historical terms, it has often coincided with a territorial community. Thus, for industrial workers in urban areas, the 'Socialist community' tended to equate with both a class and a territorial unit (a factory, a neighbourhood, a suburb), while for agricultural workers in the Po Valley it became increasingly equated with a region. It is not a coincidence that the Italian Socialist Party itself, founded in 1892, was born out of a fusion of distinctly regional Socialist movements.

Crispi's attempted solution to these growing class (and regional) divisions was to appeal directly to the lower classes over the heads of their political representatives. Had the economy been on an upward trend, and had his expansionist and colonialist foreign policy been successful, his strategy might very well have proved workable. As it was, the defeat of the Italian army at Adua on 1 March 1896, during a military expedition against Ethiopia intended to turn that country into an Italian protectorate, brought humiliation and embarrassment to the government, and forced Crispi to resign, thereby signalling the end of his vision of a strong unitary state.

After Adua, there followed four years of uncertainty and instability, with direct class conflicts and disagreement within the élites as to which political strategy to implement. The state repeatedly resorted to ruling by force, as when the army opened fire upon demonstrators in Milan in May 1898. However, it was unable to stop the opposition – Socialists, Republicans and Radicals – from increasing its votes at the general elections of 1897 and 1900. Internal divisions became even more prominent when, on 28 July 1900, the king, Humbert I, was assassinated by an Anarchist. With the left-wing Liberal Giovanni Giolitti (Prime Minister, with only brief interruptions, between 1901 and 1914) the country returned to a renewed and refined system of *trasformismo*. The system was extended to political parties as well as to deputies and groups of deputies. Unlike Crispi, Giolitti accepted that political relations with the lower classes had to take place through the medium of their representatives: Socialist and Catholic trade-union and political organizations. As for the Socialist Party, Crispi's iron rule and the state's repeated use of force at the turn of the century convinced many of its leaders, as well as its founder, Filippo Turati, of the need to collaborate with left-wing Liberals and settle for a 'minimalist' programme of social and political reforms, including universal male suffrage, proportional representation, civil liberties, nationalization of public utilities, and social and protective measures for workers.

What allowed *trasformismo* to resurface was economic growth. Between 1896 and 1913 Italy experienced her first industrial take-off. The economy grew at an annual rate of around 6 per cent between 1896 and 1907, while new sectors, such as the engineering, chemical, metalworking and hydro-electric industries and the banking sector, rapidly expanded, leading to the development of the so-called industrial triangle of Turin, Genoa and Milan. Economic growth allowed Giolitti to mediate on a much larger scale than in the days of Depretis. His aim was to modernize Italian society and narrow the wide gap between the various social groups within the general framework provided by protectionism. Giolitti was genuinely convinced that the state had to maintain an impartial role in labour disputes, but also that it had to adopt a much more proactive attitude towards the workers. To this end he established a Ministry for Labour in 1902, and encouraged prefects to think of their function less in terms of law and order and more in terms of devising ways to alleviate and improve social and economic conditions. The Socialists were granted many of the economic and social reforms they advocated. They were also rewarded with, and largely settled for, concessions for their followers (such as farming co-operatives subsidized by the state and centrally funded public works), as well as local and regional political power. The Socialist Party's political constituency, in fact, was somewhat limited. The Party was caught between its aspiration to represent the interests of all workers and its fear that the southern peasant masses and women represented deeply conservative groups, which were not 'ready' for emancipation. Despite a growing Feminist movement at the turn of the century, the Socialist Party refused to demand the vote for women or press for the introduction of divorce. The Socialist Party's influence was limited largely to male skilled workers, landless labourers and proletarianized share-croppers. Women textile workers, numbering more than one million in the 1890s, were generally unorganized or had started to join Catholic organizations. As for the Catholics, they were also offered, and accepted, concrete rewards for their followers, together with an understanding that the government would not introduce anti-clerical legislation. In their northern strongholds the Liberal deputies began to be replaced by Catholic-approved ones.

In the South, however, the government's alliance with the absentee landowners meant that the state remained a guarantor of the existing social structure, with only minimal concessions to the lower classes. Here the disorganized character of the peasantry allowed Giolitti to rely upon the use of force. Mass emigration abroad also came to the rescue, representing an individualistic response embedded in the culture of isolation and insecurity of the southern peasantry (and to a lesser extent in the family-centred culture of the share-cropping regions). Giolitti made full use of the southern deputies, just as his predecessors had done, exploiting to his advantage the mutually exclusive nature of Italy's socio-political cultures. Thanks to his pivotal role and to the regional entrenchment of his opponents, Liberalism continued to dominate national politics.

Towards the end of the Giolittian period, however, all three political cultures, namely, Liberalism, Catholicism and Socialism, had become regionalized, with a fourth, Nationalism, aspiring to become the new, truly national culture. Italian Nationalism started as a cultural and literary movement, particularly around the Tuscan-based review *Il Regno* ('The Kingdom', 1903–5), developing into a political association in 1910. Its ideology and aspirations, at first varied and confused, became increasingly well defined, with the aim of detaching the idea of the nation from its Liberal-democratic cradle. In particular, individual and political liberty became subordinated to the need to turn the nation into a powerful and cohesive body. Indeed the close link between Liberalism and Nationalism which had characterized the Risorgimento was turned by the new movement into one of cynical expediency, no more than a clever tactic to achieve unification.

Nationalism's aim was to overcome both territorial and class cleavages. To the subnational and supranational 'communities' constructed by the Socialist and Catholic ideologies, it opposed an imagined community which explicitly coincided with the nation. It strove to overcome the class divide born out of the industrialization process by developing a national 'industrial' culture and appealing directly to both employers and employees with the vision of a corporatist and productivist state, as well as with the allure of colonial expansion. The desire on the part of the Nationalists to overcome class divisions should not make us overlook the fact that their idea of the nation was deeply class-based and undemocratic, being conceived not as a community of citizens, but as providing the middle classes with a powerful political instrument and cultural identity in an age increasingly dominated by class conflicts.[7] Around this core project the Nationalists wanted to create a new, conservative and openly anti-Socialist political alliance, to which 'pro-national' Liberals and Catholics would eventually turn. Within the envisaged nation of unequal citizens, the lower classes, particularly industrial workers, were offered a politically subordinate, though materially advantageous, position. Industrial workers, however, did not appear very receptive to Nationalism's advances, remaining loyal to the Socialist and Catholic subcultures. In addition, Nationalism failed to take account of rural Italy. Nonetheless, the new movement succeeded to a large extent in modifying the political climate of the country.

Changes in Italian society during the Giolittian period help us to understand the new cultural and political climate. At the turn of the century, Italy was predominantly a rural country. Manufacturing industry was relatively well developed in the North; however, it was predominantly made up of textile production and only partially built around modern mechanized plants. Protectionism encouraged the growth of heavy industry, linked to the state and to the new German-style 'mixed banks', which carried out the dual role of commercial and merchant banks. A new, more aggressive and determined generation of industrialists emerged, who came to consider Giolitti's mediating skills and non-interfering attitude in labour disputes as a hindrance to Italy's economic development, particularly following the slowing down of industrial growth after the general depression of 1907–8. The hardening of the employers' attitude was paralleled in the Socialist camp by the dominance of the intransigent wing of the Socialist Party at the 1912 National Congress. Changes in the internal composition of the labour force, with a shift away from well-paid, highly trained skilled workers towards a more standardized, lower-paid unskilled workforce, contributed to a weakening of the reformist wing of the Socialist Party and Trade-Union Confederation and the concomitant emergence of a revolutionary Syndicalist wing.

The confrontational and increasingly anti-government stance of both employers and workers' organizations marked the end of Giolitti's version of *trasformismo*. Giolitti turned to all his opponents for support. In 1911 he went to war with Turkey to conquer Libya, in an attempt to placate the Nationalists. The war was both popular and successful, but it had the effect of strengthening the resolve of the Nationalists and alienating the Socialists. In 1912 a new electoral law was introduced, based on almost universal male suffrage, as a concession to the Socialists. The following year general elections took place and Giolitti resorted to an electoral pact with the Catholics. Thanks to this alliance, the Liberals remained in command of a comfortable majority. However, they had to rely increasingly on the South and its corrupt clientelistic cliques of deputies. They also lacked a wide network of supporters across the country, something which the Nationalists, on the other hand, were openly striving for, with some degree of success, particularly in the North. The Liberal 'Party' was a rather loose amalgam of different tendencies and currents as well as individual personalities, and it also included a group of young Liberals who had strong sympathy for the Nationalists.

At the start of the new century, therefore, Italy was no nearer the formation of a national culture than it had been in 1860. Indeed, at the political level there had been something of a setback. Whereas Italy's secularized middle classes had previously been represented by only one party, they were now split between the Liberal Party and the Nationalist Association. Nor had class-based cleavages superseded territorial ones. This was to a certain extent inevitable, since industrialization only affected some areas of the country and regional rural structures persisted in others.

The First World War provided Nationalism with an important platform. The Nationalists believed that participation in the conflict would impose a sense of identity and a strong discipline upon all Italians, thereby justifying a return to an authoritarian style of government. To this end the Nationalists rallied around the 'interventionist' cause against those who advocated neutrality. They managed to become the fulcrum of an alliance which included ex-Socialists like Mussolini, revolutionary Syndicalists, right-wing Liberals and Catholics and representatives of big business, as well as some democrats like Salvemini and reformist Socialists like Bissolati, who believed that the war represented a fight between democratic and authoritarian nations. An *alternative* political alliance to Giolitti's coalition system was therefore in place in 1914–15, although it lacked a mass following. When Giolitti resigned in 1914, his political system came to an end. He was replaced by the Liberal conservative Antonio Salandra, whose government engaged in secret negotiations with the Triple Entente in March 1915, leading to the Pact of London, which guaranteed Italian intervention within three months. Thanks to the activism of the Nationalists, who were able to stage a series of public demonstrations in favour of intervention in the war in May 1915, parliamentary opposition was successfully neutralized. The Pact was ratified and Italy declared war on Austria-Hungary in May 1915 and on Germany in August 1916.

Just as Giolitti's strategy had resembled, on a much larger scale, Depretis's *trasformismo*, so Nationalism recreated the political climate which had brought Crispi to power under the banner of a unifying authoritarian agenda. There was one crucial difference, however, from Crispi's arrival in government. This time it was not just *trasformismo* that was discredited, but Liberalism itself. By actively encouraging his political opponents and even his own Liberal Party to become entrenched around sectoral/territorial interests, and by allowing the parliamentary system to become equated with cheap compromise, a weak executive and a lack of direction, Giolitti had revealed Liberalism, Socialism and Catholicism as incapable of putting forward a national political programme. The seeds had been sown for a nationalization of Italian political culture outside the Liberal-democratic framework.

Italian Fascism: the creation of a homogeneous national culture?

Two opposing conceptions of the nature of the war and its implications for Italy's domestic as well as foreign politics continued to divide the 'interventionist' front during the conflict. According to people like Salvemini and Bissolati, the war would strengthen the democratic movement and institutions, whereas the Nationalists saw the war purely in imperialistic terms, hoping that it would lead to a more authoritarian state. Inevitably perhaps, given the need for a strong executive to direct the war effort, there was a trend towards the type of state envisaged by the Nationalists. Thus committees made up of representatives of the political, military and industrial establishment were empowered to make decisions behind closed doors. The trend had appeared justified in the face of military setbacks, and social and political unrest at home.

After the First World War the most pressing political issue was how to 'revitalize' Parliament and adjust the political system to the rapid transformation of the country into a mass society. In the South, traditional political alliances appeared shattered: thousands of peasants invaded large estates, asking the government to fulfil promises of land distribution it had made during the war. In northern and central Italy the sharecroppers showed increasing militancy, and strikes and other forms of protest became widespread. Trade-union membership soared. These were not problems unique to Italy. Almost everywhere in Europe existing political systems had to adapt to the deep social changes brought about by the war and respond to the increasing demands for political representation by the working classes. Other countries, however, such as Great Britain, achieved a relatively smooth transition to a post-war settlement. In Italy, the changes were too abrupt to permit such a smooth transition, and the country's political system was too immature to 'absorb' the new divisions, while the decision-making process had shifted further away from Parliament during the war.

Another reason why Parliament was not able to mediate between the various demands put forward by conflicting social groups was that the two political parties which at first most benefited, in terms of members and votes, from the social changes brought by the war – the Socialist Party and the newly formed Catholic Party (Partito Popolare, 'Popular Party') – were not interested in taking the initiative and transforming the old Liberal political system into a parliamentary democracy based on mass parties. Neither wanted to form a coalition government by collaborating with the other, for two main reasons. First, the ideologies of the two parties were incompatible. Secondly, they both spoke largely for a regional constituency, and failed to think in terms of national politics. In 1919 the Socialist Party was the nearest thing Italy had to a modern mass party. Yet even this party was taken unawares by the political mobilization of rural social groups. Furthermore, the Socialist Party had developed a dual nature, being divided internally between a reformist wing, which looked back to the Giolittian system, and a revolutionary wing, which looked forward to a Soviet-style revolution. The Catholic Party, founded in 1919, was also a 'mass' party, at least when compared to the Liberals, but it was even more regionally based than its main rival, and lacked the necessary expertise and cohesion to make Parliament work on a new basis. It was divided into three currents: the left wing, representing the interests of the small landowners and share-croppers of the northern regions; the right wing, representing the interests of the large landowners, whose paternalism was being threatened by the increasing militancy of their share-croppers; and the centre, which spent most of its energy trying to keep the party together. In addition, the Catholic Party did not enjoy the full backing of the Vatican, which considered it both too radical and too secular, thereby depriving it of an important source of legitimacy.

The mutual exclusiveness of the Catholic and Socialist subcultures, and the worsening of the class-based cleavage in both the rural and the industrial sectors, opened the way for Fascism. Mussolini was quick to grasp the potential of the Nationalist programme for achieving political power, but he was also aware of the need to appeal to rural Italy and to respond to the mobilization of both industrial and rural workers. Nationalism was by no means dead after the war. The myth of 'mutilated victory' – in other words, the feeling that Italy was being unfairly treated at the Paris Peace Conference of 1919 – refuelled Nationalist feelings and discredited the Liberal ruling class. The division of public opinion between interventionists and neutralists persisted after the war, keeping alive those right-wing, anti-parliamentary, anti-Liberal groups which had successfully allied themselves with big business before the war.

Mussolini respun the web of these alliances around his own Fascist movement, which had been founded in March 1919. More importantly, in the autumn of 1920, his party developed into a mass party of the right. In the Po Valley, in particular, it broke the Socialists' hold over labour, collaborating with landowners and large tenant farmers, promising support for those middle strata which were seeking upward social mobility, and making a systematic use of violence against recalcitrant labourers. This is known as 'agrarian Fascism', and, interestingly, it was a regional phenomenon. Consciously or not, Fascism exploited the territorial character of its political opponents, and dealt separately with each one. By concentrating on attacking the Socialists and conspicuously sparing the Catholic movement, Fascism could appear as an ally of both the Catholics and the Liberals. When Giolitti briefly resumed office in 1920, he assumed he could safely play the right against the left, and turned a blind eye to Fascist violence. He also formed electoral pacts with both Nationalists and Fascists at the 1921 elections, attempting to revive his old strategy of bringing extra-parliamentary political movements within the Liberal framework. The strategy backfired badly.

The idea of doing away with parliamentary mediation and compromise, of creating a strong authoritarian state bent on imposing national unity through a hierarchical and highly disciplined society, in short the idea of doing away with the Liberal institutions altogether, had become increasingly appealing to some sectors of the establishment. Fascism thus became the successful solution to Italy's post-war crisis. The way it came to power shows that it was to a large extent allowed to succeed by default. The Liberal governments after Giolitti continued to fail to act against its violence, while Mussolini promised a return to law and order. The new Pope, Pius XI, elected in February 1922, distanced himself even further than his predecessor from the Partito Popolare, and appeared to signal his approval of a government which would include the Fascists. Industrialists and landowners viewed Fascism's anti-Socialist tactics with favour. In this context, the famous 'March on Rome' of 28 October 1922, whereby the Fascist 'squads' were to take over control of the city, was an essentially peaceful affair rather than a coup d'état, and the king himself asked Mussolini to lead a coalition government.

Fascism seemed to possess all the ingredients for succeeding in imposing a national culture on Italy. By reintroducing protectionism in 1925, it recemented the socio-economic élites on a long-term basis. By destroying Socialist and Catholic organizations in their respective strongholds (the latter, with similar tactics to those employed in the Po Valley, in 1923–4), it incorporated their followers into its own structures. Thus Fascist unions replaced Catholic and Socialist ones, a Fascist after-work organization was established, and sport and leisure associations became largely a Fascist prerogative. By allying with the Church as a result of the Lateran Agreement of 11 February 1929, Fascism gained legitimacy and neutralized Catholic public opinion. The rift between Church and state was officially over, and the 1929 Plebiscite marked this new phase with the Church openly inviting Catholics to support the régime. Finally, with the introduction of a rudimentary welfare state in the 1930s, Fascism extended the role of the state with the aim of reducing the importance of the Church and making families more dependent on public agencies. And yet its unifying project failed.

There are at least three reasons why Fascism achieved only a superficial homogenization of Italian society and culture. First, economic factors. Following the revaluation of the lira in 1927, there was a partial recession in the late 1920s, followed by the much more serious crisis of the early 1930s. The formation of an inter-class industrial culture, which Fascism had borrowed from Nationalism, depended quite heavily on industrial workers participating in the benefits of industrial expansion, particularly in a regime which ruled out free unions and strikes. Despite disagreements among historians, it seems safe to say that industrial wages, from 1927 up to the mid 1930s, at best remained stable and at worst decreased substantially, leaving workers at most lukewarm towards Fascism and the idea of industrial collaboration for the sake of the nation. Second, the myth of the land and of rural Italy, perhaps incautiously embraced by Fascism, and leading to promises of 'land to the peasants' and highly publicized policies such as the 1925 'battle for wheat' to make Italy self-sufficient in grain production, was increasingly exposed for what it was – just a myth. In particular, the strategy of supporting upwardly mobile small farmers and share-croppers in their quest for land turned sour, again as a result of the recession, with many newly created small landowners falling increasingly into debt in the late 1920s and 1930s. Third, welfare state provisions were only modest in scope and bypassed large sections of society, while the shift to a nuclear family partially dependent on state support was both slow and patchy, allowing social networks and family strategies to remain dominant, and leaving the state in the position of a distant actor.

By 1943 Fascism was totally discredited. A deeply unpopular intervention in the war on the side of Germany and badly fought military campaigns brought down Mussolini in July 1943, after the Allies had landed in Sicily. Following Mussolini's downfall, the king, Victor Emmanuel III, nominated Marshal Badoglio as the new Prime Minister, while the ex-Duce was arrested. Badoglio initiated talks with the Allies, signing an armistice on 3 September which was announced on the 8th, but which was not preceded by any military preparation for war against Germany. Leaving the Italian army in disarray and the population in deep confusion, the king and Badoglio fled to Brindisi, under the protection of the Allies. On 12 September, Mussolini was liberated by the Germans from his prison on the Gran Sasso mountain, taken to Germany, and finally brought back to Italy on 23 September, where he set up a Fascist republic – the Repubblica Sociale Italiana – around Salò, on Lake Garda. The Republic attracted the support of the most fanatical Fascist leaders, and from the beginning was openly and brutally managed by the Germans. The country ended up divided between the South, which was under the Allied military government, and the Centre and North, occupied by the Germans and experiencing a Resistance movement dominated by Communist partisan organizations. This movement was viewed with distrust by the Allies, particularly Great Britain, which favoured continuation with the pre-Fascist moderate Liberal system rather than any radical democratization of the country. Collaboration between the partisans and the Allies was therefore uneasy; as early as 1944, the Allies began preparing for the post-war period, which meant taking seriously into consideration the political future of Italy and especially the possibility of a Communist-led revolution. The ideological conflict within Italy was merging with the ideological conflict between East and West.

Italy's political cultures after 1945

After the collapse of Fascism, Italy's superficial gloss of homogenization disappeared to reveal persisting cultural and structural differences. The old Catholic and Socialist subcultures resurfaced in the north-eastern regions and in the Po Valley respectively, against a process of deterioration of the rural structures out of which they had originated in the late nineteenth century. Such a process had started under Fascism, and was to accelerate in the 1950s and 1960s. In these regions the economic and social structure was undergoing change, while the political culture remained largely unchanged. Even though Socialism in the Po Valley was being increasingly replaced by Communism, the two ideologies performed a similar function, in that each was organized around a territorial network and offered supporters a strong collective identity. The dislocation between structure and culture, however, was more apparent than real. The Catholic and Socialist/Communist subcultures, in fact, not only successfully adapted to socio-economic change, but also actively seconded the aspirations of the rural share-croppers and labourers, by offering them the possibility of social mobility through small-scale, small-business capitalism. The result was a fairly homogeneous socio-economic structure in both regions, accompanied by persisting political and ideological divisions.

After 1945, however, the subcultural and territorial nature of political Catholicism and Communism had become less prominent due to the increasingly national and international roles these two parties and their ideologies were playing. In the case of the Communist Party, participation in the Resistance movement, its organizational role in the southern peasants' agitations of the 1940s, and the abandonment of its anti-clerical tradition, greatly contributed to overcoming the territorial and sectoral limitations of the pre-Fascist Socialist Party. The newly formed Christian Democratic Party also enjoyed a national standing. Unlike the pre-Fascist Partito Popolare, it enjoyed the full support of the Vatican, since it was politically moderate and its leaders had been formed within the ranks of trusted Catholic organizations. It also gained the backing of influential conservative élites, and in the 1950s it replaced the southern landowners and deputies with a centralized party machinery. Italy, at last, appeared on the way to overcoming its regional divisions, with both the Catholic and Communist movements enjoying support throughout the peninsula. Class-based subcultures, on the other hand, were just as strong as in the past. However, in this, Italy was not alone. Indeed, the immediate post-war period in Italy was characterized by a spirit of national consciousness and solidarity, in the name of anti-Fascism. Between 1945 and 1947 the country was ruled by governments of national unity, with the participation of all the anti-Fascist parties, including the Socialist and the Communist Parties. In an atmosphere of compromise and collaboration between the various political forces, a Republic was established in 1946, a Constitution was agreed during 1947, and an electoral system based on proportional representation and universal suffrage was introduced. Yet the general elections of 18 April 1948 were marked by direct confrontation between two electoral and ideological blocks. Communism and anti-Communism, dictatorship and democracy, East and West, anti-clericalism and clericalism (one of the Catholics' slogans was 'Either with or against Christ') dominated the political debate, splitting Italy into two opposing camps.

What made Italy an anomaly compared to other Western European states was the Cold War and the K (Communist) factor. The problem was that the Socialist Party had not evolved into a Social-Democratic party but into a Communist Party enjoying close links with Moscow. In the eyes of the Italian political right and its American allies, the Communist Party was simply a tool in the hands of the Soviet Union, implanted from the outside rather than rooted from within. This had two important consequences. The first was the tacit understanding that the Communist Party had to be excluded from government at all costs. This led to a political system in which there was no alternation in power between two parties or coalitions of parties. The Christian Democratic Party occupied the centre ground of the political spectrum and was permanently in government, in coalition with smaller parties situated either to its right or to its left. The second consequence, closely linked to the first, was that the identification of 'the enemy', compared to the Resistance period and the immediate aftermath of the war, shifted perceptibly from Fascism to Communism. Thus Italy developed a schizophrenic identity and the state became simultaneously the anti-state. Its official culture remained anti-Fascist, celebrating the Resistance, the new republican and democratic institutions, and the new Constitution. The 'covert' culture was anti-Communist and in important respects anti-democratic, bent on preserving Fascist laws and policies, delaying the implementation of the Constitution, making use of Fascist elements in the intelligence services, allying with secret and/or illegal organizations such as the Mafia and Freemasonry. In the 1970s suspicions grew that the state itself – or at least important sections of the state – were behind the so-called 'strategy of tension', consisting of a series of bomb attacks against innocent civilians in public places, which was designed to disseminate disorder and terror in the country with a view to imposing authoritarian rule.

To return to Italy's official and visible culture, it was only with the 'economic miracle' of the late 1950s and early 1960s – when Italian industry expanded at an annual rate of 8 per cent and exports almost doubled – the growth of consumerism, the development of the media and particularly that of television, that a secularized, modernized, standardized society and culture began to take shape. It is indeed possible to view Italy's development between the 1950s and the 1980s as a linear process whereby the subnational boundaries increasingly faded and the integration of the lower classes into the nation-state was finally achieved. The

1970s, in particular, were years of increasing liberalization and secularization of Italian society, with new social and pressure groups demanding greater civil liberties and new rights for women. Divorce and abortion were legalized and new laws relating to the family were passed. Admittedly, the student protests of 1967–8, originating from the failures of the education system but soon turning into a frontal attack against the political system, the industrial workers' struggles for higher wages and rights in the autumn of 1969, as well as 'red terrorism' in the 1970s, were all inspired by revolutionary and anti-capitalist ideologies and do not point to social and cultural integration. Nevertheless, they can also be seen as the last remnant of a revolutionary Syndicalist, anti-parliamentary and anti-Liberal tradition, or, alternatively, as representing confused aspirations for greater democracy. In any case, by the 1980s, the force of protests and agitations had already waned, and the power of the unions had decreased. 'Proletarian' culture had lost much of its appeal, and a new culture based on personal success and individual values had emerged.

In keeping with the linear interpretation outlined above, the decades from 1960 to 1990 would appear to have been characterized by a serious dislocation between the political system, which was blocked because of the Cold War, and the Italian economy and society, which were experiencing great change. After the rigid ideological confrontations and authoritarian style of government of the 1950s, the political system did, in fact, attempt to change, with the 'opening to the left' in 1963, i.e. the transition to centre–left coalitions which included the Socialists. One of the objectives of this transition was precisely to widen the social basis of consensus for the democratic system by implementing a programme of social reforms. There was, however, resistance to the new course in both Italy and the USA, which led to covert operations (such as the threatened coup d'état by General De Lorenzo in 1964) to reverse the political trend towards the left, considered as a dangerous path towards the legitimation of the Communists. In the 1970s the political system again appeared on the verge of substantial changes, when the Communist Party enjoyed a surge in popularity and distanced itself from Moscow, going as far as accepting Italy's membership of Nato. These were the years when Enrico Berlinguer, the leader of the Communist Party, launched the idea of a 'historic compromise' with the Christian Democrats. Again, covert operations intensified and terrorism was used to stop the governmental shift to the left. The use of covert operations in the 1970s shows how long-standing the legacy of the Cold War was in Italy. The 'opening to the left' of 1963, the 'historic compromise' of 1976–9, and the return to centre–left coalition governments in the 1980s, on the other hand, show how that conflict had also given way to a particular *modus vivendi* between the parties, almost like a renewed version of *trasformismo*, defined by Lijphart as 'consensual democracy'.[8] By this term Lijphart refers to a political system where rigid ideological and cultural divisions lead the political forces towards a mutual understanding and an attitude of compromise, which, in turn, leads to political immobilism. It also led to systematic clientelism and corruption, involving hidden networks of power, including Freemasonry and the Mafia.

It is also possible, however, to take the view that Italy's cultural standardization since the 1950s masked the re-creation of regional socio-economic structures and value systems. In a pioneering study, the sociologist Arnaldo Bagnasco identified not one but three Italies: the North-West, characterized by conurbations, large industrial plants and a well-developed services sector; the North-East and Centre, characterized by small-scale industrialization and the persistence of primary and social networks; and the South, externally modernized but economically underdeveloped despite massive state intervention.[9] The North-West presented a more pluralistic and individualistic political culture; the North-East and Centre the resilience of traditional subcultures; the South was still in the grips of a culture of clientelism and patronage.

The end of the Cold War and the ensuing apparent collapse of the traditional ideologies of Catholicism and Socialism/Communism have recently brought great changes to the country, but they have not resolved the basic dilemma outlined above. Is Italy a country which has developed an increasingly homogeneous society and culture, and now needs only to establish a majoritarian political system to end its anomalous status among Western democracies, or, on the contrary, is it still greatly divided economically and socially, and also politically, at least for the foreseeable future?

Beyond the Cold War: Italy in the 1990s

Political developments in Italy since the fall of the Berlin Wall, which freed voters from the perceived need to support the Christian Democratic Party as a bulwark against Communism, do not help us to answer the question outlined above. After the demise of traditional political ideologies, and the dénouement of the Italian state's culture of deception and corruption thanks to the 'Clean Hands' investigation, which unveiled systematic bribes and kickbacks involving political parties and private and public companies, political change has been both rapid and contradictory.

The success of an entirely new party, Forza Italia ('Come On Italy!'), founded by the media tycoon Silvio Berlusconi at the 1994 political elections, would appear to support the interpretation that Italian voters now express their preferences on the basis of party programmes and candidates, rather than ideological allegiances. At another level, it seems however that it is precisely the end of the Cold War and the collapse of traditional ideologies that have exposed the subnational, territorial character of Italy's political cultures. The rise of the regionalist and secessionist Northern League in the north-eastern regions, previously dominated by the Catholic subculture, the continuing success of the ex-Communist Partito Democratico della Sinistra ('Democratic Party of the Left') in the Po Valley and the central regions, the strength of the ex-Fascist Alleanza Nazionale ('National Alliance') in the South, point to persisting political divisions along territorial lines.

The two interpretations outlined above are based upon opposing views of both social and cultural change, yet they are not necessarily in contradiction. We have moved a long way from the idea that economic and social modernization is a uniform process, bringing with it cultural homogenization. Whereas today's mass media and global-communications technologies reinforce both individualism and the development of a national (but also increasingly global) culture, they may also strengthen the local dimension. In other words, globalization will not lead to the break-up of local and regional communities; indeed, subnational boundaries, of a socio-economic as well as of a cultural nature, may acquire a new salience. However, perhaps the time has now come to acknowledge that Italy is not an anomaly in this respect and that a homogeneous national culture is as elusive in Italy as it is in most other Western states, which have to contend with social fragmentation, ethnic divisions, spatial subcultures and differing economic structures.

The question, rather, is whether the subnational cultures need necessarily feed into the political system. The concept of trust can help us understand whether this is likely to happen. As we have seen in the course of this chapter, Italians have derived their interpersonal trust largely from territorial and ideological, indeed quasi-ethnic, feelings of belonging to a community other than the nation-state. When this has not happened, trust has remained restricted to the family, leading to particularism and clientelism. By contrast, the Italian state enjoys a low degree of legitimacy, and relations between the citizens and their political institutions are characterized by a lack of trust. Poor legitimacy of the political system and corruption go hand in hand. Admittedly, regional differences have contributed considerably to this lack of legitimacy; conversely, trust and solidarity vary greatly across the country. Nonetheless, the devastating impact of the Cold War on Italy's quest for national solidarity has perhaps been underestimated. It prevented the democratic state from raising the level of trust in the country and acquiring a new legitimacy.

After the Second World War, Italy, like West Germany, had the opportunity of achieving a successful transition to a Liberal-democratic state, integrating its working classes and gradually reducing territorial imbalances. The creation of a national identity and inclusive citizenship could have stemmed from a genuine commitment to the new republican Constitution. The existence of a strong Communist Party within Italian borders, and the Cold War, prevented any such development. The supranational nature of the political conflict between East and West produced for Italy the paradoxical outcome that its subnational boundaries were artificially strengthened, rather than de-emphasized. Regions which had much in common, in socio-economic terms, such as the North East and the Centre, remained sharply divided politically and ideologically. The South became a battleground between Communism and anti-Communism, until it was 'colonized' by the Christian Democratic Party, which increasingly used the special regional agency set up in 1950 – known as the Cassa per il Mezzogiorno – for clientelistic purposes rather than to promote sustainable economic growth. The state developed a dual identity but pretended that only its official face existed. Citizenship was understood in exclusionary terms. Given the nature of the Italian state during the Cold War, it appears therefore that lack of trust on the part of Italians towards their state was both rational and justified, rather than simply a cultural trait inherited from the past.

Now that the Cold War has finally ended, the Communists have become ex-Communists and the Fascists ex-Fascists, the country has another chance to develop into a democratic state for *all its citizens*. This, however, necessitates an end to the culture of deception on the part of the state, and to cynicism on the part of the citizens, as well as a shared acceptance of clear and transparent democratic rules. Here the signs are somewhat mixed. On the one hand, ideology plays a much lesser role in Italian politics today, and there is a new commitment from various quarters to both economic and political liberalism. Two coalitions of parties have at last alternated in power, the centre–right forming a government in 1994, the centre–left in 1996. The latter was able to take effective measures to reduce the country's excessive deficit and successfully negotiated entry into the European Monetary Union. On the other hand, there has been a certain hastiness in drawing the curtains over the First Republic. More importantly, various attempts by the centre–left government since 1996 to reach widespread agreement for modernizing and revitalizing Italy's obsolete political institutions have so far failed. There is a general consensus that the country has not yet achieved a successful transition from the 'First' to the 'Second' Republic.

Conclusion

Looking back over 140 years of Italian unification, one is tempted to conclude that the whole problem of the creation of a national identity in the face of strong subnational boundaries has been approached in two fundamental ways. The first approach has consisted in the imposition of an authoritarian state (governments of the Historic Right, Crispi's period in office, the First World War and Fascism, and, to a lesser extent, the 1950s). The second approach has consisted of mediation and compromise, often degenerating into clientelism and corruption (governments of the New Left, the Giolittian age, Christian Democratic rule from the 1960s to the 1980s). In the first case, the emphasis was on imposing a national symbolic boundary through the authoritarianism – in the absence of the authority – of the state; in the second, on accommodating existing subnational boundaries. Economic, as well as political, factors appear to have influenced the choice of one or the other strategy. Thus recession and financial constraints seem to have corresponded to an authoritarian approach to politics, while expansion and growth have facilitated compromise. Neither strategy aimed specifically at raising the level of trust in the country. This was attempted in the period immediately following the Second World War, but was thwarted by the outbreak of the Cold War. Now Italy has another chance, but in a climate which lacks the moral imperative of the 1940s and under pressure from various quarters to conceal, rather than learn from, the mistakes of the First Republic. In this context, the therapeutic effects of electoral and institutional reforms may be impaired, and the inertia of traditional approaches to Italy's socio-cultural disunity may yet block the new paths opened by the end of the Cold War.

NOTES

1. Roberto Cartocci, *Fra Lega e Chiesa*. (Bologna: Il Mulino, 1994), p. 50.
2. Robert Putnam, 'La dolce vita is Finally Over', *The Independent*, 10 March 1993.
3. John Davis, 'Remapping Italy's Path to the Twentieth Century', *Journal of Modern History* 66 (1994), pp. 291–320 (p. 320).
4. Ronald Inglehart, *Culture Shift in Advanced Industrial Society* (Princeton University Press, 1990), p. 17.
5. Lucy Riall, *The Italian Risorgimento. State, Society and National Unification* (London and New York: Routledge, 1994).
6. Pamela Pilbeam, *The Middle Classes in Europe 1789–1914* (Basingstoke and London: Macmillan, 1990), p. 278.
7. Franco Gaeta, *Il nazionalismo italiano* (Rome and Bari: Laterza, 1981), pp. 99–128.
8. Arend Lijphart, *Democracies* (New Haven: Yale University Press, 1984).
9. Arnaldo Bagnasco, *Tre Italie* (Bologna: Il Mulino, 1977).

FURTHER READING

Allum, Percy, *Politics and Society in Post-war Naples*. Cambridge University Press, 1973.
Banfield, Edward, *The Moral Basis of a Backward Society*. Chicago: Free Press, 1958.
Bosworth, Richard, *Italy and the Wider World 1860–1960*. London: Routledge, 1996.
Bull, Anna and Paul Corner, *From Peasant to Entrepreneur. The Survival of the Family Economy in Italy*. Providence and Oxford: Berg, 1993.
Chubb, Judith, *Patronage, Power and Poverty in Southern Italy*. Cambridge University Press, 1982.
Ginsborg, Paul, *A History of Contemporary Italy. Society and Politics 1943–1988*. London: Penguin Books 1990.
Hine, David, *Governing Italy*. Oxford: Clarendon Press, 1993.
Levy, Carl, *Italian Regionalism*. Oxford and Washington: Berg, 1996.
Morgan, Philip, *Italian Fascism 1919–1945*. Basingstoke: Macmillan, 1995.
Pasquino, Gianfranco and Patrick McCarthy, *The End of Post-War Politics in Italy. The Landmark 1992 Elections*. Boulder, San Francisco and Oxford: Westview Press, 1993.
Putnam, Robert (with Robert Leonardi and Raffaella Nanetti), *Making Democracy Work: Civic Traditions in Modern Italy*. Princeton University Press, 1993.
Trigilia, Carlo, *Grandi partiti e piccole imprese. Comunisti e democristiani nelle regioni a economia diffusa*. Bologna: Il Mulino, 1986.

3

Questions of language

Unification and the *questione della lingua*

Before the political unification of Italy, Italian was a language used, outside Tuscany and Rome, only by the literate few. Even by these, it was reserved chiefly for writing: in everyday conversation, the great majority of Italians either had to or chose to use one of the dialects of Italy or, in certain areas, a minority language such as French. By the end of the twentieth century, well over 90 per cent of Italians could speak the national language, but most still chose to use dialect or a minority language as well. The process of the diffusion of Italian against a background of continuing linguistic diversity has been a long and difficult one, and it has led to discussions on important cultural and social issues, such as whether the national language should be allowed to develop naturally or should be based on a particular model; how conservative and selective, or tolerant of innovation and variety, it should be; how it was to be disseminated and taught; and, on the other hand, what status should be accorded to languages other than the standard.

In some respects, these discussions have continued the *questione della lingua* which first came to a head in the sixteenth century. In that period a consensus was reached that the literary language of the Italian states should be based on the Tuscan used in the fourteenth century by the indisputably most elegant writers, Petrarch and Boccaccio. This solution was apparently backward-looking, but it proved the most viable and attractive, given the political fragmentation and vulnerability of Italy and the waning cultural prestige of contemporary Tuscany. Tuscan had the added advantage of being structurally more conservative than most other dialects of Italy and therefore relatively closer to Latin, which was known to most educated people. However, the principle of imitation, which had to be adopted even by Tuscans themselves, inevitably proved constricting. From the sixteenth century to the present, consequently, two major problems have underlain debates on the language. One is that many have been reluctant to reject altogether the vitality of the living language by cutting the standard off from spoken and regional varieties of language. Some have argued that a common language should be able to draw on non-Tuscan forms, others that cultivated spoken Tuscan should play a central role in the standard. The lack of popularity of Italian, the gulf between everyday reality and what has been essentially a written or second language, has even led some authors, especially poets and playwrights, to use dialect in their works, sometimes on its own, sometimes side by side with the standard, sometimes in an artificial hybrid language. The other problem concerned the vocabulary of Italian. On the one hand, it was feared that using words and forms which were obsolete in speech would seem ridiculously affected. On the other, changes in cultural and social conditions, especially from the eighteenth century onwards, have raised the question of how much freedom one should have to innovate by borrowing words from foreign languages or by creating new ones.

But unification also brought about an inevitable shift of emphasis in linguistic discussions. Previously, although these had been shaped partly by the political conditions of Italy, they had focused on literature and had concerned only an élite. Once political unity was achieved, however, the debates came to centre not on literary Italian but on the use of the languages of Italy in social contexts. At times they have led to interventions by central and local government. And as language questions have broadened in scope, so they have attracted wider interest. They are no longer merely a matter of debate for academics and literary authors but have become the subject of books, broadcasts and press articles intended for the general public.

From 1861 to 1921

Beneath the political unity of the new Italy lay a profound linguistic disunity. Tullio De Mauro's estimate put the proportion of the nation's twenty-five million inhabitants which could speak Italian in 1861 – the better educated, and natives of Tuscany and Rome – at only 2.5 per cent. This is probably on the low side, yet even Arrigo Castellani's more optimistic assessment put the figure no higher than about 8.8–12.6 per cent, with 9.52 his preferred estimate.[1] Almost all other Italians spoke only one of the language varieties which, north of a line from La Spezia to Rimini and to the east and south of Tuscany, often diverge markedly in pronunciation, grammar and vocabulary from the standard. Most of these varieties are classified as 'dialects', but in the Italian context this term refers to sibling tongues, each descended independently from Latin, rather than to subordinate or debased versions of the interregional standard language (which, as we have seen, itself originated for cultural reasons from a written form of one dialect, Tuscan). Certain other varieties – Sardinian, Friulian and the Ladin of the Dolomites – have even been seen by some as autonomous 'languages' because, while sharing with dialects the crucial characteristic of being used in a relatively restricted area, they have particularly distinctive linguistic features or significant socio-linguistic or cultural prestige. Furthermore, nearly 1 per cent of the population in 1861 belonged to one of the linguistic minorities whose language is used also outside Italy, such as the speakers of French, Occitan and Franco-Provençal in the Valle d'Aosta and Piedmont and of Albanian, Greek and Serbo-Croat in southern Italy.

To acquire knowledge of the standard language would have been beyond the possibilities of many Italians in the 1860s. The main means of access to Italian was still necessarily through the written word. But levels of illiteracy were high: 78 per cent in 1861, 73 per cent in 1871. Literary Italian was remote from everyday life and often too formal to be popular. The education system, which could have given access to both written and spoken Italian, was still limited in its effectiveness. The Casati law of 1859 prescribed four years of free education, but the third and fourth years were compulsory only in *comuni* of over 4,000 inhabitants and, until the Credaro law of 1911, schooling was financed by the *comuni* rather than the state. The Matteucci inquiry of 1864 showed that unification dramatically improved the availability of schooling in southern Italy, but that everywhere absenteeism was high (60 per cent in 1861, 50 per cent in 1871), and that in most places teachers used either dialect or, at best, an Italian influenced by dialect.

The new nation, then, urgently needed a national language. Accordingly, the Minister for Education, Emilio Broglio, set up in 1868 a commission to propose means of 'making more universal, in all classes of the people, knowledge of good language and of good pronunciation'. It had two sections, Milanese and Florentine, and its president was the great Milanese writer Alessandro Manzoni. He had always been impressed by the linguistic model of the French nation, for which Paris provided a common, living tongue, spoken as well as written. In the course of writing and revising his novel *I promessi sposi* ('The Betrothed') between 1821 and 1840, he had concluded that Florence should play the same role in Italy. He rejected the conventional idea that the common language of Italy should be based on the written tradition: for him, a language not in full social use was a dead language. He argued instead that all Italians (not just writers) should adopt in its entirety a living tongue. The choice, he believed, could fall only on the tongue of educated Florentines, because of its prestige and nature, though he was privately concerned that it would be exceptional for the linguistic capital to be separate from the political capital, destined to be Rome. In 1868 he rapidly completed and published an essay *Dell'unità della lingua e dei mezzi di diffonderla* ('On the Unity of the Language and on the Means of Disseminating It'). Florentine usage, he wrote, should be propagated through a dictionary of contemporary usage which would then act as a term of reference for a series of dialect–Florentine glossaries. In an appendix, Manzoni and his two colleagues in the Milanese subcommission proposed to use the education system (which in unified Italy proved to be one of the main starting-points for attempted linguistic reforms) in order to spread living Tuscan, for example by giving preference to Tuscan primary-school teachers and encouraging schoolgirls to learn good language which they would later pass on to their own children.

However, the chairman of the Florentine subcommission, the Genoese priest and educationalist Raffaello Lambruschini, was reluctant to cut links with the past and with the written word. If a dictionary of the living language was to be compiled, he wanted existing dictionaries to be used as its sources. Manzoni resigned from the hopelessly divided commission, but responded to Lambruschini with an *Appendice* (1869) to *Dell'unità*. Here he reiterated his belief that linguistic unity should be based on the usage of a living society and that a new dictionary was the best means both of propagating this usage and of restraining Gallicisms. Broglio's influence ensured the compilation of such a dictionary: the *Novo vocabolario della lingua italiana secondo l'uso di Firenze* ('New Dictionary of the Italian Language According to Florentine Usage', 4 volumes, 1870–97), edited by Broglio himself and Manzoni's Tuscan son-in-law Giovan Battista Giorgini. In practice, however, Manzoni's theories, and measures such as the *Novo vocabolario*, had far less influence than the example of the relatively informal and not rigidly Florentinizing prose of *I promessi sposi*.

Support for Manzoni's ideas did come from writers of an older generation, Francesco Domenico Guerrazzi and Cesare Cantú, and from Luigi Morandi, who became tutor to the future Victor Emmanuel III. Also favourable to Manzoni was Ruggero Bonghi, a colleague on the Milanese subcommission. Bonghi wanted writers to adopt a more accessible and natural prose style, in the Manzonian mould. But he saw that this could be achieved only if the intellectual life of the nation became stronger and culture became more widely diffused. Another who qualified his support for Manzoni was the popular writer Edmondo De Amicis. Although in *L'idioma gentile* ('The Gentle Idiom', 1905) he urged an imaginary youth from his own region, Piedmont, to learn from listening to the everyday conversation of Florence, he also attacked Florentines for using dialect forms and satirized non-Tuscans who made exaggerated use of Florentine pronunciation.

However, with very few exceptions, Manzoni's theories met with outright opposition. For the Jesuit periodical *Civiltà cattolica* ('Catholic Civilization'), the best way of achieving Broglio's aim was to widen the teaching of the existing 'good language' to all classes alongside dialects; the social conditions necessary for the whole nation to adopt a single language did not exist. Luigi Settembrini (1813–76), in a letter of 1868 to Broglio, stressed the crucial point at which Bonghi had hinted: that the spread of a language had to be linked with its use as a medium of culture.[2]

This theme was developed by the great linguist Graziadio Isaia Ascoli in the *Proemio* (Preface, dated Milan, 10 September 1872) to the first volume (1873) of his periodical, the *Archivio glottologico italiano* ('Italian Linguistic Archive'), an essay as influential in defining a new approach to the *questione della lingua* as any previous contribution. Ascoli began by focusing on the first word of the title of the *Novo vocabolario* of 1870. Here the *o* of contemporary spoken Florentine had been preferred to the *uo* of fourteenth-century Florentine which the literary language had adopted and diffused over many centuries. Italy was thus being asked to return once more to Florence in order to adapt what it had taken from the city in the past. However, Italy and Florence did not stand in the same relationship as France and Paris. The example of Germany, on the other hand, showed that a national language did not have to be identified with a single city. But Italy had a double obstacle to achieving a similar linguistic unity: 'low density of culture and excessive preoccupation with form'. Disunity was certainly an evil and, Ascoli agreed with Manzoni, the old ideal of classicism had not helped to overcome it. The new *fiorentinismo*, though, would be harmful to 'the mental activity of the nation' and would only encourage the cult of form.

Another linguist, Napoleone Caix, agreed with Ascoli that a common language had to be based on the common literary tradition allied to 'national thought'. The linguist and critic Francesco D'Ovidio, however, attempted to reconcile the opposing positions: Manzoni was right to call on contemporary Florence to contribute to the diffusion of good Italian, but greater unity would follow political unity and increased 'intellectual and material exchanges', and it could not be imposed artificially but had to be allowed to happen naturally. In 1905, Benedetto Croce, reviewing De Amicis's *Idioma gentile*, dismissed Manzoni's views as backward-looking. Philosophers, he argued, now saw language not as a sign which communicated ideas but as 'the idea or the representation itself'. No single type of language could be declared objectively best; writing well was 'a form of spiritual intensity'. As a Neapolitan, he felt he could not fit markedly Tuscan usage into any spontaneously conceived prose.

The limits to Manzoni's influence can also be seen in the importance which the written tradition continued to have in works of linguistic reference and in education. Giuseppe Rigutini and Policarpo Petrocchi, though supporters of Manzoni, did not ignore the literary language in their dictionaries. Raffaello Fornaciari explained in his *Sintassi italiana dell'uso moderno* ('Italian Syntax of Modern Usage', 1881) that, while the foundation of the contemporary language lay in the Tuscan people, its definitive testimony was provided by writers. He took examples from the fourteenth century onwards and was unwilling to accept such features of 'familiar' spoken Tuscan as the pronoun *gli* for *le*. He also edited, with only minor updatings, his father Luigi's *Esempi di bello scrivere* ('Examples of Elegant Writing', 1829 and 1835) for use in schools. The principle (which had dominated the *questione della lingua* since the sixteenth century) that one should imitate the best authors from the past was supported by the canon of authors which the Coppino law of 1867 prescribed for study after primary school.[3]

Although the first language question to be faced by unified Italy was that of the relationship between Italian and Florentine, past and present, unification brought to the fore two other sets of problems. Firstly, how far should Italian go in accepting new words, many borrowed from French and other languages in adapted or unadapted form, or in tolerating the giving of new meanings to existing words? This problem, much debated by purists earlier in the Ottocento, was aggravated by the sudden need for an everyday national language and by the strong influence of Piedmont in bureaucracy and education. One of several works intended to contain the tide of 'barbarisms' within certain limits, the *Lessico dell'infima e corrotta italianità* ('Dictionary of the Lowest and Corrupt Italian', five editions between 1877 and 1907) by Pietro Fanfani and Costantino Arlía, condemned, for example, the bureaucratic or legal use of *comprensorio* (district) and of the Gallicisms *prestigio* (in the sense of 'authority') and *vidimare* (to certify).

The other set of questions concerned the relationship of the national language with dialects other than Florentine. In the first place, there was the problem, as some saw it, of the growth of non-standard varieties of Italian. The decades up to 1920 brought a gradual expansion in the use of Italian, as a consequence of improved education, migration from country to city as many workers moved from agriculture to factories and offices, emigration, a centralized bureaucracy, military service and the experience of the First World War. By the early twentieth century the proportion of the population which could use Italian of some sort rose to an estimated 50 per cent, although probably no more than 20 per cent used it habitually. Impetus was given to what linguists have baptized *italiano popolare*, a variety (with roots traceable back to medieval times) containing informal features and used by the less educated.[4] But all these new users of Italian were normally also dialect speakers. Interference from local influences, especially in pronunciation and lexis, therefore encouraged the development of regional Italian, in other words regionally marked versions of the national language. There was much criticism of regionalisms, and collections of the various 'errors' committed were compiled. The survey of primary education by Camillo Corradini, published in 1910, showed that, as in 1864, teachers used either dialect or a hybrid language judged 'worse than pure dialect'.

Secondly, in the context of a desire for linguistic unity, how was the existence of dialects to be seen? For some followers of Manzoni, they were 'weeds'. But Carlo Dossi used another horticultural metaphor in order to lament the loss of dialects, 'seedbed of every effective and spontaneous sentence'. Ascoli saw bilingualism in Italian and dialect as a privilege. Francesco De Sanctis spoke in 1883 of how in the previous twenty years the language had taken on the agility and freshness of dialect; for him dialect was destined to become the new 'seedbed' of literary languages. Morandi, Ascoli, De Sanctis (as Minister of Education) and others promoted a positive use of dialects as a resource in teaching 'good language'. The development of dialectology after unification depended not only on European scholarly trends but also on a concern to preserve what was under threat.

Thirdly, there was the question of the use of dialect in literature. In the context of the spoken language, unification began the process of the decline in the use of dialects and of their Italianization; but it did not bring an end to Italy's strong tradition of dialect and plurilingual verse and prose.[5] On the contrary: just as unification acted as a spur to dialectology, so the bringing together of disparate regions without a common spoken language led to a linguistically centrifugal reaction on the part of some authors. Giovanni Verga developed an Italian narrative prose which occasionally included dialect terms but above all imitated the speech patterns of humble Sicilians. Luigi Pirandello still believed in 1921, as he had done in 1890, that Italian did not exist as a spoken language; he was very sparing in using dialect colouring in the Italian of his narrative or theatrical works, but he did write some plays in Sicilian. Dialect was used by several poets: the Neapolitan verse of Salvatore Di Giacomo is the best-known example. Authors who wove dialect words into the fabric of their Italian included the novelists Emilio De Marchi, Antonio Fogazzaro and Federico Tozzi, and the poet Giovanni Pascoli. Italo Svevo used dialect hardly at all, yet on the other hand he refused to give in to criticisms that his prose did not conform with Tuscan. In literature, then, as elsewhere, notwithstanding Manzoni's urgings, the linguistic usage of unified Italy was not (in the phrase which he used of his own novel) 'rinsed in the Arno'.

The Fascist period

In the Fascist era, from 1922 to 1943, there were fewer linguistic discussions than before. In line with Ascoli's analysis, the spread of Italian as a living language was making debates on its desired nature increasingly superfluous. Crocean idealism, with its stress on the expressiveness of language, also discouraged linguistic debate. However, two of the issues already mentioned continued to receive attention, and two which had previously attracted little attention now gained importance. All were linked with one or more aspects of Fascist policy: the nationalist promotion of an *italianità* with Rome at its heart; a totalitarian intolerance of pluralism and an insistence on the subordination of the individual to the centralized authority of the state; and a desire for self-sufficiency ('autarchy') which was deeply tinged with xenophobia. To a much greater extent than at any other time in Italian history, the state attempted, for ideological purposes, to influence language issues by means of laws, ministerial decisions and the manipulation of cultural institutions. Significant initiatives were also taken by individuals who supported the Fascist cause.

The first issue was that of minority languages. In 1919 the proportion of the population which spoke them rose to 2.1 per cent with the annexation of Trentino–Alto Adige and Venezia Giulia. The inhabitants of these regions included speakers of, respectively, a German dialect and Slovene. The Fascist state moved swiftly to attempt to Italianize linguistically both of these territories and the Valle d'Aosta.[6] It was decreed in 1923 that teaching in all primary schools had to be carried out 'in the language of the state'. The purpose of this policy, as Ministers of Education declared explicitly in 1924 and 1926, was to make linguistic minorities 'Italians in sentiment'. The state also imposed the use of Italian in public notices and prescribed or strongly encouraged the Italianization of place names and surnames. The teaching of German was reintroduced in the Alto Adige in the mid 1930s, as a result of Mussolini's rapprochement with Hitler, but linguistic repression in this region left a legacy of deep resentment against central government.

Dialects were another aspect of linguistic usage at odds with the unitary ideology of Fascism. At first the government was tolerant of their cultural status. The primary schools programme introduced in 1923, and drawn up by Giuseppe Lombardo Radice, specified that dialects were to be used as a constant point of reference in teaching Italian. In the 1930s, however, this educational policy was abandoned, partly because of its lack of practical success, and the Ministry of Education began to instruct the press not to publish dialect texts or even to discuss dialects. As one notice to the press in 1931 put the problem, 'Regionalism, and the dialects which constitute its principal expression, are vestiges of the centuries of division and servitude of the old Italy.'[7]

The national pride of Italy was also vulnerable, some felt, where loanwords were concerned. From 1923 onwards a passionate campaign against them was waged by men such as the senator Tommaso Tittoni and the journalist Paolo Monelli. The latter discussed foreign borrowings in his *Barbaro dominio* ('Barbarous Domination', 1933 and 1943). In most cases the words were unadapted French or English ones (*camion*, *film* etc.) with only a few semantic borrowings (such as *esperto* 'expert', *magazzino* 'shop'). Monelli's tone was calmer than that of Fanfani and Arlía in 1877, but his preface revealed his political motivation when it boasted of the 'Fascist clarity' of his campaign, based on the principle that 'strong peoples impose their language'. Up to this time the government had taken only minor protectionist measures against the use of foreign languages in signs and films. But, as relationships with Britain and France worsened, the government campaign gathered strength. Restrictions on the appearance of foreign words in public places, packaging and advertising became much more severe. The government also took up a campaign begun in 1938 by a Florentine writer, Bruno Cicognani, to replace *lei* as a polite form of address with the older *voi*. For Cicognani, *lei* went against the law of grammar and logic and was a testimony of 'servitude and abjection' dating back to the overthrow of the communes by tyrants and reinforced by the usage of Spanish invaders. The Fascist party duly banned *lei* from official correspondence. In 1940 the Accademia d'Italia was charged to find Italian substitutes for loanwords, and as a result a Commissione per l'Italianità della Lingua ('Commission for the Purity of the Italian Language') produced alternative spellings or designations for 1,555 words or phrases. Bruno Migliorini had in 1938 taken a more measured approach, free from xenophobia, in advocating 'neopurism', as he termed the contemporary campaign (distinguishing it from earlier purism, which had opposed neologisms as well as loanwords). While he wished to protect the structure of Italian, he stressed the practical difficulties of replacing or adapting some foreign terms and the need for a 'European linguistic circulation'.[8]

In the same period, standard pronunciation became an issue not only in the context of the recommendations provided in dictionaries and grammars but also in that of broadcasting. In 1939 the state radio organization (EIAR) published a strongly politicized handbook on pronunciation and spelling written by the linguists Giulio Bertoni and Francesco Ugolini. Quoting words of Mussolini on the 'moral' importance of the capital, they identified Rome rather than Florence as the new centre of linguistic unification and recommended 'the beautiful and warm pronunciation of cultured Roman conversation'.

A victim of Fascist repression, the great Communist intellectual Antonio Gramsci had studied linguistics at university, and language remained a central interest during his imprisonment from 1926 until his death in 1937. His prison notebooks contain perceptive pages on the relationships of power which underlay the *questione della lingua*. In notebook

29, of 1935, Gramsci wrote that from the time of Dante onwards the *questione* had been an aspect of the political struggle, in which intellectuals had reacted against the political and economic collapse of Italy and had attempted to strengthen their own class. Whenever the *questione* surfaced, it was a sign that the ruling class was seeking to reorganize its 'cultural hegemony' over the masses; and various phenomena, such as the publications of Monelli, showed that this was happening in his own day. However, it was not until later, after Gramsci's works had been published in Turin (1948–51), that they began to influence the linguistic thought of a new generation of left-wing intellectuals, most notably Pier Paolo Pasolini.

From 1944 to 1999

In the decades after the Second World War, Italian became a truly national spoken language. There was an increased need for communication between people of different origins, since up to the early 1970s there was large-scale migration from the South towards the industrial North-West and from the countryside into towns. The proportion of the working population employed in agriculture fell from 42.2 per cent in 1951 to 11.2 per cent in 1981 and 7.4 per cent in 1995. At the same time, two factors made the national language more accessible. Firstly, a reform of 1962 made eight years of education, up to the end of the *scuola media* at the age of fourteen, free and compulsory. By 1991, the illiterate proportion of the population over six years old had fallen to 2.1 per cent, and to 0.5 per cent for those aged between six and fifty-four. The second factor, the growth of radio and (from 1954) television broadcasting, was even more important, since it affected all parts of the community.

Consequently, Italian (though here the term does not refer to the standard alone but includes regionally, socially and contextually marked varieties of the national language) increasingly took over the role of dialect in everyday spoken communication, as is shown by the figures, from Istituto Doxa surveys, which show the percentages of respondents using Italian or dialect, or alternating between them, in particular situations. Table 1 relates to speech within the family; Table 2 relates to speech outside the home. These national statistics conceal important social and regional variations, with dialect used more by men, the old, the less well educated, in the countryside, in the South and the islands, but also in the Veneto. A survey carried out by the Istituto Nazionale di Statistica (ISTAT, National Statistical Institute), in 1995

Table 1. *Speech within the family*

	1974	1982	1988	1991
Italian only used	25.0	29.4	34.4	33.6
Both dialect and Italian used	23.7	23.9	26.0	30.5
Dialect only used	51.3	46.7	39.6	35.9

Table 2. *Speech outside the home*

	1974	1982	1988	1991
Italian only used	22.7	26.7	31.0	29.9
Italian used more often	12.9	15.2	16.3	18.2
Both dialect and Italian used	22.1	22.0	19.5	29.1
Dialect used more often	13.4	13.1	9.9	10.0
Dialect only used	28.9	23.0	23.3	12.8

suggested that 94 per cent of Italians spoke Italian in some context but that 60 per cent still knew and used dialect. In the home, 44.6 per cent of the sample (some 21,000 families) used Italian always or mostly, 28.3 per cent used both Italian and dialect, and 23.6 per cent used mainly dialect. With friends, 47.3 per cent used Italian, 32.1 per cent used Italian and dialect, and 16.6 used dialect. When speaking to other categories of people, though, the percentage of those using only or mostly Italian rose to 71.5 and that of those using only or mostly dialect fell to 6.8. The linguistic practice of children indicated that Italian would continue to spread: 81.7 per cent of those aged between six and ten spoke Italian outside the circles of family and friends.

Such changes naturally affected the development of both Italian and the dialects. The numbers of those speaking Italian outside the home include a majority which also speaks dialect; there is thus more scope than previously for interference between the two types of language. Because of the spread of Italian as a spoken language, it has also been noted that less formal linguistic usage has become more widely acceptable. The lofty norm based on the literary tradition is being replaced by an *italiano dell'uso medio* (average Italian) or *neo-standard* closer to speech.[9]

Moreover, the decline in the influence of Florence as opposed to that of the industrialized North-West and of Rome (not only the political capital but also the centre of state broadcasting and of the film industry), together with economic and technical innovations, led to the introduction of many new words: regionalisms, neologisms and foreign (now mainly English) borrowings. Just as the expansion of Italian after unification aroused fears about its contamination, so the spread of the language in a changing post-war Italy led some writers to lament that it had become slovenly, anarchic, vulgar, awkward and (especially in official and political contexts) obscure, and to attack the 'permissiveness' of others who felt that the language, far from being in terminal decline, was following a stable evolution. Unadapted Anglo-Americanisms were seen by some as a danger to the health of Italian, though others have judged such concern excessive.[10]

The question of which regional pronunciation, if any, should be regarded as a model became considerably more controversial from 1945. In that year Bruno Migliorini attempted to remove the Rome–Florence rivalry which had grown under Fascism by proposing a reasoned but overcomplicated compromise between the two models. As the Fascist era grew more distant, some reasserted the primacy of Florence. In *La corretta pronuncia italiana* ('Correct Italian Pronunciation', 1965), Carlo Tagliavini argued that, since Florence had provided the written language, cultivated Florentine should also be chosen as a model for speech. In 1966 Giulio Lepschy made a devastating attack on those who considered one local variety of pronunciation, Florentine, objectively more correct than others. His appeal for Italians to be left to speak Italian freely, without normative interventions, led to heated objections from some older linguists (see *L'Italia dialettale* 30 [1967], pp. 181–207). But Lepschy's essay, following explicitly in the tradition of Ascoli and of Croce's review of De Amicis, pointed the way to an attitude more tolerant of regional diversity within Italian. For foreign learners, too, cultivated Florentine pronunciation lost its former high status, and it was suggested that northern pronunciation should be taken as a model because it now had the greatest prestige.[11]

In 1964 Pier Paolo Pasolini began a lecture entitled 'Nuove questioni linguistiche' ('New Linguistic Questions') by asserting that Italy had no true national language. Only the bourgeoisie possessed both spoken and literary Italian. However, he went on to note that technical terms were becoming a common element in his own prose, in the language of politicians and in advertising. He therefore believed that this technological language was tending to create a new linguistic unity at all levels. 'Italian as a national language has been born', he announced, with the new technocratic class of the industrial North, the Turin–Milan axis as he put it, now dominant in place of the Rome–Florence axis which seemed to prevail before. Pasolini's analysis was challenged by many. He rightly sensed a change in the use of Italian, but he both overestimated the importance of its technical component and underestimated the extent to which unity was being achieved on the basis of the language in its traditional form. Early in 1965, Italo Calvino responded to Pasolini's article with two essays in which he called for the use of Italian to be as concrete and precise as possible and warned against the bureaucratic *antilingua* which, on the contrary, preferred the vague to the meaningful.[12] Such feelings of alienation from *burocratese* eventually found an official response in 1994–6, when a project of the Dipartimento della Funzione Pubblica ('Department of Public Administration') aimed to simplify and clarify what to most was a remote and arcane register.

Towards the end of the 1960s, voices began to be raised in condemnation of the linguistic barriers which the education system seemed to set in the path of many who did not have a command of standard Italian. The *Lettera a una professoressa* ('Letter to a Schoolmistress', 1967) by Don Lorenzo Milani accused schools of discriminating against working-class children because they could not express themselves correctly. De Mauro and others appealed in the mid 1970s for a more democratic education which did not look down on non-standard varieties such as dialects. The new *scuola media* syllabus of 1979 duly encouraged their use as a cultural and linguistic resource. In the light of subsequent experience, however, there was a return towards recognizing the importance of a linguistic norm.

Concern that Italian usage fostered another type of repression, discrimination against women, came to the fore in the 1980s. Alma Sabatini's recommendations for schools and school textbooks on 'a non-sexist use of the Italian language' (*Il sessismo nella lingua italiana*, 1987 and 1993) were published as part of a government programme to achieve equality between the sexes. A suggestion which would alter the language itself was that feminine forms should be preferred for professional and similar titles, giving for example *la senatrice, la medica, la professora, la studente* (not *la studentessa*, since the *-essa* suffix can be pejorative). Such proposals will be adopted only if social attitudes change. But the 1995 edition of the authoritative Zingarelli dictionary significantly recommended *l'avvocata* (rather than *l'avvocatessa*), *l'ambasciatrice, la presidente* and so on.

We saw earlier that unification provoked a more pronounced

regionalism in the language of literature. In post-war Italy, against a background of declining use of dialect, and doubtless in reaction to the centralizing oppression of Fascism, there was a similar need to reassess the cultural functions of dialects and of non-standard Italian. Such varieties of language were used to add greater authenticity to portrayals of working-class life, both in Neorealist cinema and in the novels of Pasolini and the Roman tales of Alberto Moravia. Several poets (including, again, Pasolini) used the resources of dialect. On the other hand, De Mauro pointed out that the cinema contributed to the spread of Italian by associating dialect with negative features of society, with oppression and provincialism, and that theatre in dialect is perceived to lack immediacy, since it is most successful in large cities, precisely where the decline of dialects has been strongest. Some major writers saw dangers in the recourse to dialect. Already in 1935 Cesare Pavese had noted in his diary that he had striven to make his work not dialectal but national. His views did not change in the 1940s. Since dialect was now distinct from Italian, one could not turn back without donning a peasant's mask. Dialect was 'subhistory'. One had to run the risk of writing in Italian, thus moving into history; the problem was to invent a 'new vivacity [...] without folklore', i.e. without superficial local colour. Moravia, in 1959, saw the contemporary fashion for dialects as a legitimate consequence of the crisis of cultured language and of the class which spoke it, after the fall of Fascism. But he warned that modern writers were using dialect in an artificial, experimental way, without the spontaneity of the great dialect authors of pre-unification Italy. Calvino condemned the dialect revival as a sign of involution and tiredness. Writers had to devise their own complex language, going beyond the mere 'photographing' of dialects, just as a novel should be 'a definition of our time, not of Naples or of Florence'. However, dialects used for expressionistic rather than naturalistic purposes were a major element in the plurilingual prose of Carlo Emilio Gadda and others. The post-Fascist period also saw the championing by literary critics, foremost among them Gianfranco Contini, of the tradition of *plurilinguismo* (as opposed to a Petrarchan *monolinguismo*) which was seen to stretch from Dante to their own times.

In the 1980s, there was a turning back to dialects in the context of the northern separatist movements. Imitating the Liga Veneta, the Lega Lombarda aimed in its 1982 programme to 'recover the Lombard linguistic heritage and diffuse it through education'. This policy was abandoned in the mid 1980s. But in 1991 fears that dialect would be used as a focus of separatism were raised again. In November a bill on minority languages was approved by the Chamber of Deputies; it did not, however, reach the Senate. The new law would have allowed thirteen such languages to be used in schools, local administration and broadcasting. Its aim was to put into practice the 'safeguarding of linguistic minorities' envisaged in Article 6 of the Constitution and to provide a means of civic expression for all Italians. However, the bill came in the wake of the break-up of the Soviet Union and of Yugoslavia, and among the thirteen languages mentioned were Sardinian, Friulian and Dolomitic Ladin, which are counted by some among the Italian dialects. The vote caused an outcry. Academics and politicians saw the bill as the thin end of a wedge which would destroy Italy's hard-won political and cultural unity by promoting separatists' use of dialects and by hampering the teaching of the national language. Only in December 1999 did the Italian Parliament pass a law on this subject.

The main linguistic problem which faced Italy at the time of unification was the need to provide a common language for a nation which spoke chiefly dialects or minority languages. At the start of the twenty-first century, now that Italian, for all its variety, is firmly established as a unitary national language in writing and in formal spoken contexts, an important question which remains open is the obverse of the earlier one: whether, and if so how, Italy should foster its rich multilingual heritage.

NOTES

1. Arrigo Castellani, 'Quanti erano gl'italofoni nel 1861?', *Studi linguistici italiani* 8 (1982), pp. 3–26.

2. Tullio De Mauro *et al.*, *Lingua e dialetti nella cultura italiana da Dante a Gramsci* (Messina and Florence: D'Anna, 1980), pp. 151–64.

3. Marino Raicich, *Scuola, cultura e politica da De Sanctis a Gentile* (Pisa: Nistri-Lischi, 1981), pp. 122–3.

4. Manlio Cortelazzo, *Avviamento critico allo studio della dialettologia italiana*. III: *Lineamenti di italiano popolare* (Pisa: Pacini, 1976); Giulio Lepschy, 'L'italiano popolare: riflessioni su riflessioni', in F. Albano Leoni *et al.* (eds.), *Italia linguistica: idee, storia, strutture* (Bologna: Il Mulino, 1985), pp. 269–82.

5. Hermann W. Haller, *The Hidden Italy: A Bilingual Edition of Italian Dialect Poetry* (Detroit: Wayne State University Press, 1986) and *The Other Italy: The Literary Canon in Dialect* (Toronto: University of Toronto Press, 1999); Verina R. Jones, 'Dialect Literature and Popular Literature', *Italian Studies* 45 (1990), pp. 103–17; Alfredo Stussi, *Lingua, dialetto e letteratura* (Turin: Einandi, 1993); Emmanuela Tandello and Diego Zancani (eds.), *Italian Dialects and Literature. From the Renaissance to the Present. Journal of the Institute of Romance Studies*, Supplement 1, 1996.

6. Sergio Raffaelli, *Le parole proibite: purismo di stato e regolamentazione della pubblicità in Italia (1812–1945)* (Bologna: Il Mulino, 1983); Gabriella Klein, *La politica linguistica del Fascismo* (Bologna: Il Mulino, 1986), pp. 67–110.

7. Fabio Foresti, 'Proposte interpretative e di ricerca su lingua e fascismo: la "politica linguistica" ', in Erasmo Leso *et al.*, *La lingua italiana e il fascismo*, 2nd edn (Bologna: Consorzio Provinciale Pubblica Lettura, 1978), pp. 111–48 (p. 120).

8. Bruno Migliorini, 'Purismo e neopurismo' (1938), in his *La lingua italiana nel Novecento* (Florence: Le Lettere, 1990), pp. 81–107.

9. Francesco Sabatini, 'L'"italiano dell'uso medio": una realtà tra le varietà linguistiche italiane', in G. Holtus and E. Radtke (eds.), *Gesprochenes Italienisch in Geschichte und Gegenwart* (Tübingen: Narr, 1985), pp. 154–84; Gaetano Berruto, *Sociolinguistica dell'italiano contemporaneo* (Rome: La Nuova Italia Scientifica, 1987), pp. 13–103.

10. For examples, see respectively Arrigo Castellani, 'Morbus anglicus', *Studi linguistici italiani* 13 (1987), pp. 137–49, and Gian Luigi Beccaria, *Italiano antico e nuovo* (Milan: Garzanti, 1988), pp. 215–45.

11. Bruno Migliorini, *Pronunzia fiorentina o pronunzia romana?* (Florence: Sansoni, 1945); Giulio Lepschy, *Saggi di linguistica italiana* (Bologna: Il Mulino, 1978), pp. 77–93; Nora Galli de' Paratesi, *Lingua toscana in bocca ambrosiana* (Bologna: Il Mulino, 1984), pp. 239–45.

12. Oreste Parlangèli (ed.), *La nuova questione della lingua* (Brescia: Paideia, 1971), pp. 79–101; Pier Paolo Pasolini, *Empirismo eretico* (Milan: Garzanti, 1972), pp. 9–28; Italo Calvino, *Una pietra sopra: discorsi di letteratura e società* (Turin: Einaudi, 1980), pp. 116–26.

FURTHER READING

Bruni, Francesco, *L'italiano: elementi di storia della lingua e della cultura*. Turin: UTET, 1984.

Bruni, Francesco (ed.), *L'italiano nelle regioni: lingua nazionale e identità regionali*. Turin: UTET, 1992.

De Mauro, Tullio, *Storia linguistica dell'Italia unita*. 5th edn. Bari: Laterza, 1999.

Grassi, Corrado, Alberto A. Sobrero and Tullio Telmon, *Fondamenti di dialettologia italiana*. Bari: Laterza, 1997.

Lepschy, Anna Laura, Giulio Lepschy and Miriam Voghera, 'Linguistic Variety in Italy', in C. Levy (ed.), *Italian Regionalism: History, Identity and Politics*. Oxford: Berg, 1996, pp. 69–80.

Maiden, Martin, *A Linguistic History of Italian*. London and New York: Longman, 1995.

Maiden, Martin and Mair Parry (eds.), *The Dialects of Italy*. London and New York: Routledge, 1997.

Marazzini, Claudio, *La lingua italiana: profilo storico*. 2nd edn. Bologna: Il Mulino, 1998.

Da Dante alla lingua selvaggia: sette secoli di dibattiti sull'italiano. Rome: Carocci, 1999.

Migliorini, Bruno, *The Italian Language*, abridged and recast by T. G. Griffith. 2nd edn. London: Faber and Faber, 1984.

Serianni, Luca and Pietro Trifone (eds.), *Storia della lingua italiana*, 3 vols. Turin: Einaudi, 1993–4.

Sobrero, Alberto A. (ed.), *Introduzione all'italiano contemporaneo*, 2 vols. I: *Le strutture*. II: *La variazione e gli usi*. Bari: Laterza, 1993.

4

Intellectuals, culture and power in modern Italy

An idea of Italy

On the face of it, contemporary Italian intellectuals have a more prestigious existence than their Anglo-Saxon counterparts. Whether as writers, academics, journalists or film-directors, Italian intellectuals are courted by political parties of all persuasions to add lustre to their slates at election time, and wooed by the media as influential opinion makers. The contact Italian intellectuals have with the institutions of civil society comes from a long tradition going back to the Middle Ages. Indeed, Italian society has consistently relied on its intellectuals, rather than its political class, to supply the nation's agents for social change. When Dante, for example, in his *De vulgari eloquentia* examined the panoply of local dialects to find one on which to base a supraregional language for the peninsula, he turned to the literary idiom of his fellow poets, which seemed to him the only noble and unifying element present in an Italy rife with factionalism.

Dante set a trend that was to be repeated as Italy made its way toward unification in the second half of the nineteenth century. Unlike England and France, Italy had no dominant centre like London or Paris from which political, cultural and linguistic hegemony could be exerted. Instead, Italy had several principalities or city-states, many of which were in competition with each other and split within their own communities. The absence of a dominant centre deprived the country of a stable political leadership, leaving it easy prey for the long period of foreign domination which began in 1494 with the conquest by Charles VIII of France and lasted four centuries. Nevertheless, foreign domination had the positive effect of engendering the beginnings of a national sensibility.

National unity, however, was an idea which remained far more the property of intellectuals than of the political class, and the names that most readily spring to mind as the precursors of a unified Italy come from the world of literature or opera – Dante, Petrarch, Machiavelli, Pietro Bembo, Baldassare Castiglione, Vittorio Alfieri, Ugo Foscolo and Giuseppe Verdi – rather than from the world of politics. Although the idea of a unified Italy began to circulate in intellectual circles after 1494, in concrete terms little political progress was made towards national unity. It was only when the drive toward unification was taken up by the more politically sophisticated Piedmontese Liberals, and in particular by Cavour (1810–61), that Italy as a united nation became a reality. Despite their success, the main agents of the unification process, the enlightened members of the Piedmontese bourgeoisie, did little to set a national trend, and found relatively few emulators outside their region.

In the absence of a dynamic bourgeois class, it fell to intellectuals to provide the impetus Italy needed to modernize itself. This was a role which the intellectuals of the post-unification period accepted with relish; however, it was a role which went beyond the effective powers of any class of intellectuals. In a society lacking agents of political and social change, there was little intellectuals could do, no matter how gifted they were. In addition, they were constrained by two further factors: first, their reluctance to ally themselves with modern society's main agent of change, the political party; and second, their traditional strong allegiance to 'high' culture, the effect of which has been that Italian intellectuals have generally produced texts whose messages have not been, and indeed could not be, appreciated by the nation as a whole, not least because the Tuscan-based literary Italian that the cultural élite had adopted as the national language in the sixteenth century was not the language spoken by the majority of the nation. Lacking the power and influence to exercise cultural leadership, hindered by a bourgeoisie that was unreceptive to enlightened reform, unwilling to bridge the gap between intellectual and civil society, the history of Italian intellectuals' attempts to exert an influence over Italian society is a history of gallant well-intentioned effort, but above all a history of failure.

Intellectuals in the early twentieth century

No Italian philosopher has investigated the failure of Italian intellectuals to bridge the gap between intellectual and civil society more thoroughly than Antonio Gramsci (1891–1937), the Sardinian-born co-founder of the Italian Communist Party (PCI). Written in the prison to which he had been condemned by the Fascists in 1926, his *Prison Notebooks* bear specifically on the intellectuals' function as 'permanent persuaders' within civil society and as agents both for the promotion of change and for the maintenance of the status quo. His analysis of the Risorgimento as a passive revolution, in which the Piedmontese moderates consolidated their power over the whole nation, focused on the radicals' inability to develop a political culture which had relevance for the Action Party's potential supporters in the peasant masses. Instead of arming itself with effective political weapons such as the offer of land reform and a political platform which spoke to the peasants in a language they could understand, the Action Party led by Giuseppe Mazzini (1805–72) stood for an abstract political culture based largely on the calls for unification which had come from Italian literature. Although such writings represented a powerful rallying cry for the intellectuals of the time – the minority who had read them – their appeals had no purchase on the consciousness of the peasantry.

As Gramsci wrote his notes from his prison cell in the late 1920s and 1930s, he must have been thinking of those intellectuals who, in the first decades of the twentieth century, had attempted to reform Italian society. Like Gramsci, though for different reasons, many of these intellectuals – most notably Giuseppe Prezzolini (1882–1983), Giovanni Papini (1881–1956) and others gathered around the influential Florence-based review *La voce* ('The Voice'), together with the philosopher Benedetto Croce (1866–1952) and Piero Gobetti (1901–26) – were deeply disappointed with the Italy that had emerged in the years after the unification process. What particularly disgruntled the *Voce* group was that power in the unified nation had been shifted from the upper to the middle classes. This shift had brought into existence an Italy that was very different from the great nation that the Risorgimento had seemed to promise. Italian culture had invested great hopes in the Risorgimento and saw it as the fulfilment of centuries-long dreams. These dreams, which all centred around a unified Italy's return to its proper status as great world power after centuries of foreign domination, were largely the creation of the literary culture of the pre-Risorgimento centuries which had romanticized the notion of the unified nation. Nevertheless, it was an attractive image; and for a while it seemed that the battles and exploits which had created Italy, and especially the charismatic figures of

Mazzini and Garibaldi (1807–82), gave credence to the idea that dreams were coming true in history. But the Italy that emerged from the Risorgimento, and the modest, myopic ruling class that was in power, seemed to many of the *vociani* to be but pale shadows of the nation that had been envisaged and of the heroes that had created it. Italy was now *Italietta* ('Small Italy') or *Italia vile* ('Vile Italy'), the product of the triumphant vulgarity of Italy's new masters, the lower middle classes and their new found commercial prosperity based on hard work, sacrifice and thrift. Deeply anti-Socialist, an ideology they saw as aspiring to the same mediocrity exhibited by the bourgeoisie, the *vociani* imagined themselves as a revolutionary vanguard, an enlightened élite that rejected all the mediations of bourgeois political life and parliamentary democracy. Rather than seeking representation in existing political parties, the *vociani* sought to create their own party, the 'party of intellectuals', whose aim was to launch (to quote the title of Papini's 1906 article) 'The Campaign for Compulsory Reawakening'.

The *vociani* owed a great debt to their contemporary, the philosopher Benedetto Croce. Their project aimed to return to people the powers of creativity and agency that Croce had theorized in his early writings. In the figure of what Prezzolini called 'Croce's God-man', many of the *vociani* found inspiration for their own assault on the constricting categories of thought and action in which contemporary humankind had been imprisoned. Although he had given his initial support to *La voce*, and reviews like *Hermes* and *Leonardo* which had preceded it, Croce became increasingly impatient with the *vociani*'s drift into a mystical world that bore little relation to reality and, as such, ridiculed his rediscovery of the powers of human agency. The *vociani* had become ever more disenchanted with the 'age of prose' that had followed the heroic Risorgimento 'age of poetry', and looked to Gabriele D'Annunzio (1863–1938) as the poet–seer who would recreate Italy's Golden Age. Consequently, some *vociani*, especially Papini, attacked the staidness of their former ally in the new Futurist review *Lacerba*. Croce survived the attack and went on to outlast the *vociani*. Indeed, the influence his thought has had on Italian culture has made him the most important of all twentieth-century Italian intellectuals. Rather than the *vociani* and the Futurists, it was Croce's example that gave Italian intellectuals the sense of mission which many feared was lacking in the post-Risorgimento period; rather than to Prezzolini and Papini, it was to Croce that Gramsci referred when he spoke of his influence over Italian culture as akin to that of a secular Pope; and it was to Croce that Italy's anti-Fascists turned as an antidote to *La voce* and Futurist-style cultural politics which, with their Nationalism, anti-Socialism, denigration of parliamentary democracy and valorization of the actions of the strong individual, the superman, had, if not created Fascism, then certainly helped to pave its way.

Deeply sceptical about any form of transcendent thought – be it of Christian, Hegelian or Marxist origin – Croce developed a new idealist philosophy that freed human activity from the abstract paradigms in which it had been imprisoned by Positivism, the philosophical orthodoxy of the period. Following the thought of Giambattista Vico, his Neapolitan precursor, Croce viewed humankind as neither tool nor creature of history. Rather, humankind was itself the tool that forged history as its own creation. This newly found confidence in the creative powers of human agency had also been championed at the end of the nineteenth century by one of Croce's precursors, who also deeply influenced the *vociani*, the literary scholar Francesco De Sanctis (1817–83); and it was on the basis of this sense that Croce aimed to rejuvenate Italy. What he had to say obviously struck a chord, as the tumultuous response granted to his *Aesthetics* amply testified. But if this text, published in 1902, made him a crucial figure on both the Italian and European intellectual scene, Croce exerted even greater influence through his review *La critica* ('Criticism'), which he founded in 1903. With this review, Croce and his co-editor, Giovanni Gentile (1875–1944) – with whom he later quarrelled and who became the theorist of the Fascist régime – set out to establish their cultural hegemony over Italian intellectuals. Unlike other reviews, which featured contributors drawn from across the spectrum of Italian intellectual life, *La critica* followed a rigid editorial policy. Almost all the articles were written by either Croce or Gentile, and the infrequent guest contributors all had to toe the review's cultural line. Croce's purpose with *La critica* was avowedly political. Through its columns, he set out to construct a new literary and cultural canon that would renew the Italian tradition and form a new class of intellectuals. To be political, however, did not mean putting culture at the service of politics, and Croce was always adamant that culture was an autonomous activity separate and different from politics, indeed superior to it. At the same time, however, Croce never denied that culture had a political function.

The extent of Croce's influence on Italian culture in the first decades of the twentieth century can be gauged by the array of intellectuals from differing ideological backgrounds who found inspiration in him. If his thought had been an example for the conservative *vociani* in the early decades of the century, in the years after the Fascist attainment of power in 1922 Croce had an equal attraction for many of Italy's young anti-Fascists. Croce's formal leadership of the Italian anti-Fascist movement in the mid 1920s came about with his 'Manifesto of Anti-Fascist Intellectuals', written in response to Gentile's 'Manifesto of Fascist Intellectuals', which had been signed by figures as prominent as Luigi Pirandello (1867–1936) and Filippo Marinetti (1876–1947). However, Croce's influence over young, anti-Fascist intellectuals had deeper roots than the manifesto. It came rather from his belief that the cultural activity resulting from an individual giving expression to his or her creative energies was also political activity; and that free cultural activity was not and could not be subservient to politics. This twin position was enormously attractive to many young intellectuals for whom Croce's thought offered a liberation. In fact, the future leaders of Italy's anti-Fascist movement like Gobetti, Leone Ginzburg (1909–45), Norberto Bobbio (1909–), Vittorio Foa (1910–), Ugo La Malfa (1903–79) and others were set on the path toward anti-Fascism by reading Croce.

Both a great admirer of Croce and his sternest critic, Gramsci was among the first to realize the implications of Croce's cultural politics and how it drew intellectuals into the orbit of the moderate Liberal Party. Croce was not as disingenuous as the *vociani* had been in believing that mediation between politics and culture could be sidestepped. The bridge between culture and politics that Croce designed was the Liberal Party, of which he became President and which he saw as the party of men and women of culture. Croce's Liberal Party was no ordinary political party: for one thing, it had no party line, policy being determined on a case-by-case basis as a result of the creative cultural activity of the party's militants. This, of course, left a great deal of room for manoeuvre. But this was Croce's point, and the source of his party's attractiveness. Yet this apparently freehand approach to politics had its pitfalls. In the early 1920s, for example, it led Croce to welcome Mussolini's Fascist government as the necessary short-term shock treatment Italy needed to defuse the threat posed by the left. In Croce's scenario, Fascism was to take a back seat once its immediate task had been accomplished, and return power to the traditional party of government, the Liberals. Instead, in the worst misjudgment of Croce's career, Fascism stayed in power until 1943.

Gramsci detected the profound conservatism lurking behind Croce's cultural politics. For Gramsci, the centre of the political spectrum which Croce claimed was proper to the Liberal Party was not a centre at all. Rather, it was a deeply entrenched moderate position that masqueraded as an ideologically neutral centre. The effect of Croce's cultural politics was to construct intellectuals who adhered to his thought as Liberals, at the very moment they imagined they were exercising their free creativity. If the moral and intellectual leadership of society was in the hands of moderate Croceans, argued Gramsci, then in order to further the progress of the working classes it was necessary to develop an alternative cultural politics which would exert the same power of attraction over Italian intellectuals as Croce's had done. The traditional figure of the intellectual – one like Croce who appeared to speak the value-free language of culture, but who in reality was the mouthpiece of established class and ideological positions – had to be replaced by a new figure, the 'organic' intellectual, drawn from the working classes and who spoke for his/her class's interests.

In Gramsci's thought, it is intellectuals who lay the cultural foundations on which moral and intellectual leadership are established in society. This cannot be the task of a small, isolated group; and, for Gramsci, intellectuals are not only people engaged in the academic or writing professions, but all those figures who have attained a certain position within civil society, who promulgate an opinion or world-view, and who are thus in some way permanent persuaders engaged in the formation of consciousness. Teachers, of course, are intellectuals; but so are clerics, doctors, veterinarians, journalists, even barbers insofar as they contribute to the formation of a given society's world-view. What was lacking in Italy, and had been lacking at least since the Risorgimento, Gramsci claimed, were groups of intellectuals who represented the interests of the potentially revolutionary sectors of Italian society, the working class and the peasantry.

A great deal of the inspiration for Gramsci's thinking on the new organic intellectual came from his experiences with the factory councils in Turin between 1919 and 1920. These were worker-run councils that had taken over the management of some factories and offered a model of an Italian worker-run state. Despite their limited impact outside Turin, the factory councils also had a lasting effect on a young Liberal intellectual, Piero Gobetti. Unlike other Liberals, Gobetti was convinced that the new protagonists of post-First-World-War Italy would be the members no longer of the bourgeoisie, but of the working classes. For

Gobetti, the bourgeoisie represented a moment of inertia in the course of a society's political development, and so could not supply its dynamic motor. In the Turin factory councils Gobetti saw the work ethic, sense of sacrifice, and personal responsibility which the Italian bourgeoisie lacked, but which would enable the working class to become an effective agent of change in Italian society as a whole.

The Italian bourgeoisie, however, was less than enthusiastic about the insurrectionary climate that marked the years following the end of the First World War, and of which the factory councils had been a product. Indeed, to a great extent it was the Italian bourgeoisie's fear of the workers' movement that had paved the way for the coming to power of Fascism. In the way it treated intellectuals, the Fascist regime was very much a two-headed beast. On the one hand, it ensured that its most outspoken opponents were silenced, as with Gramsci, by sending him to prison; or, as with Gobetti, by beating him up to such a degree that he died of his injuries in Paris; or by forcing them into exile abroad, as with Carlo (1899–1937) and Nello Rosselli (1900–37), who were murdered in France on Fascist orders; or, as with Carlo Levi (1902–75) and Leone Ginzburg, by sending them into involuntary exile in the remote regions of Southern Italy. On the other hand, the régime did relatively little to harass Croce and left him isolated rather than attempting any punitive treatment. By the mid 1920s, when Croce finally rejected Fascism, he had become such a well-known international figure that his name alone served him as a shield against any possible retaliation. Furthermore, the régime had everything to gain from leaving him in relative peace, as it could thus project abroad an image of tolerance.

The Fascists were well aware of how culture could be harnessed to the régime's political aims. Indeed, they controlled newspapers, the radio, cinema, and the free time of Italian citizens, this latter through the régime's network of workers' leisure-time organizations known as Dopolavoro ('After Work'). Yet, despite these measures, it would be a mistake to assume that Fascism invaded all spheres of cultural life, that Italians were coerced into dancing to the régime's tune, or that they were force-fed an undiluted diet of political propaganda. For every attempt by the Ministry of Popular Culture (known as Minculpop) to nationalize the masses and foster an Italian consciousness in line with the régime's aims, there were countless US-made films shown in the nation's crowded cinemas, including Mickey Mouse who was, it seems, a particular favourite in the Mussolini household.

Intellectuals and the Communist Party

Gramsci stressed the importance of binding the masses to a political project, and he envisaged the PCI spreading cultural-political messages to the masses through the mediation of organic intellectuals. Implementation of Gramsci's scheme, however, had to await the fall of Fascism, during the hegemony of which the PCI, whose leadership was in exile in Moscow, had been forced into clandestine activities. Despite its proscription under Fascism and its losses in personnel during the twenty-year régime and in the anti-Fascist Resistance movement of 1943–5, which it in great part led, the PCI, together with the moderate Catholic party, Christian Democracy, became the dominant player on the post-war Italian stage. Intellectuals were drawn in great numbers to the PCI, and for a while it seemed that the party, or at least the left, had a monopoly over cultural activity in Italy. This occurred not because the PCI took draconian measures to silence its ideological adversaries, but because, after Fascism, it had become problematic to take up a conservative political and cultural agenda, a major consequence of which was the almost total disappearance of a Liberal voice from Italian culture and politics of the immediate post-war period.

Even if intellectuals were drawn to the PCI in great numbers, the question of the relationship between culture and politics that the *vociani*, Croce, and Gramsci, had attempted to settle remained open. Perhaps the clearest illustration of the tension between the two spheres is provided by the short-lived, but nevertheless influential, literary and cultural review *Il politecnico*. Founded in 1945 and edited by the Communist intellectual and writer Elio Vittorini (1908–66), the review set itself the task of broadening the nation's horizons and supplying it with an effective culture that would inform its political life – effective, because never before had culture been part of everyday life, nor had it ever had a civilizing effect on human beings and afforded them protection against the worst excesses of history, such as Fascism. Vittorini aimed to give culture real power in the world; yet, at the same time, this necessitated some accommodation with politics and political parties. It was the failure to find a middle way between intellectual freedom and party discipline that proved to be the review's undoing. Vittorini's insistence that culture be autonomous complicated his allegiance to the PCI, provoking the anger of the party leader Palmiro Togliatti (1893–1964), who had originally welcomed *Il politecnico*. For Togliatti, in particular, the review had promised to be a useful tool in the construction of the PCI's cultural hegemony – Gramsci's precondition for assuming the leadership of society. To Togliatti's claim that integrating their cultural activity with the party's needs did not automatically mean that intellectuals' autonomy was sacrificed, Vittorini replied reaffirming that autonomy was a precondition for culture's political role.

Togliatti's disagreement with Vittorini was as much aesthetic as it was political. Having identified Realism and Neorealism as the literary genres that would best represent the values of class solidarity and commitment for which the post-war PCI stood, Togliatti had little time for *Il politecnico*'s tendency to promote, alongside Italian Realist artists, a literature that was more formally experimental and which drew on European and American influences. Indeed, it was the question of the nation which informed Togliatti's attack on Vittorini. Rather than being insurrectionary, the cultural policy pursed by the PCI in the immediate post-war years promoted the idea of interclass, domestic solidarity. The PCI was anxious to create an image of itself as a reliable, patriotic force whose activities during the Resistance on behalf of the Italian nation had shown that it had the interests of the nation at heart.

Yet, despite the PCI's unquestionable power in the cultural sphere, the extent to which the party's intellectuals influenced Italian civil society is highly debatable. It has been argued that the PCI exercised a greater power of attraction over intellectuals than over civil society. The result of the 1948 general election, a landslide victory for the anti-Communist Christian Democracy, seems to bear this out. The PCI, portrayed in election propaganda as a political force whose ideology was incompatible with Italian society, was defeated on the very terrain of reliability and patriotic values on which it had attempted to build its post-war house. Although the PCI was hampered by the massive injection of American funds into the Christian-Democrat campaign and by a vicious propaganda war, the Catholic election victory sent the clear message that moderate, Catholic intellectuals held more sway over Italian civil society than their Communist counterparts.

One of the reasons why PCI intellectuals, and the party's cultural policy in general, had a limited impact on Italian civil society can be traced to the party's attitude to culture. The PCI's main allegiance was to 'high' culture, and many party intellectuals, thanks to their perception of its pernicious role under Fascism, were deeply suspicious of what they considered to be the conservative agenda lying behind mass culture.

These attitudes had two effects, one positive, the other less so. First, through its network of book clubs, popular libraries, film clubs etc., the PCI brought 'high' culture, literacy, personal dignity, and an enhanced sense of self to many Italians who had not been well served by the state's education system; at the same time, the emphasis on 'high' culture meant that the PCI had little influence over those sectors of Italian society whose cultural demands were primarily satisfied by forms of mass culture. And when in the late 1970s and 1980s, following the deregulation of television, the diet of mass culture available to Italians increased dramatically, the party found it difficult to react appropriately.

Intellectuals and culture in a changing Italy

The political role of the intellectual underwent a profound change as the post-war period progressed. If, in the optimistic atmosphere of the post-war years, many left-wing intellectuals sought to forge alliances with the working class, as time passed it became increasingly clear that the working class was a problematic ally. During the 1960s, as prosperity increased and memories of post-war economic hardships receded, so too did the revolutionary option. Far more than intellectuals, workers seemed basically content with their lot and, despite intractable structural inequalities, showed little inclination for change. As a result, committed intellectuals turned their attention to new concerns. In particular, on the one hand, they sought Italy's (and Europe's) missing revolution in geographically distant places like China and Africa; more generally, they focused on the superstructural elements of civil society, like language and literature, which shaped consciousness and perception. If language was one of the vehicles for the bourgeois codes which had conditioned the working class, it was only by revising those codes that the preconditions for change could be created. This conclusion had radical consequences: intellectuals no longer needed the working class as a direct ally. They were free to carry out their work independently; and the kind of writing encouraged was of a far more experimental nature than the Neorealist texts sanctioned by the PCI – a kind of writing, in fact, that had little meaning for a mass readership.

The events of 1968 brought intellectuals back into the kind of contact with civil society that had seemed lost a few years earlier. A fertile terrain for the revolt of 1968 had been created by the Vietnam war, the cultural revolution in China, events in France, the pontificate of John XXIII and the Second Vatican Council which encouraged more direct contact between Catholics and civil society, and domestic circumstances such as the increased demands made on factory workers. Above all, the 1968 revolt was the revolt, against their cultural and political parent-figures, of a younger generation, the *sessantottini* ('sixty-eighters') as they called themselves, many of whom were born in the post-war years. In the Italian context, this meant a revolt against both the Catholic and Communist cultures, neither of which had been able to meet the demands of the new constituencies emerging within Italian society – the women's, gay, and ecological movements, for example. The cultural needs of such groups were catered for by alternative circuits of bookshops, publishing houses and film clubs. These counter-cultural groups also began to have a direct effect on civil society. Although they were unable to put the structural bases of economic power into question, they succeeded in bringing about radical changes in Italian society. First, young people managed to carve out an identity for themselves from within the counter-culture. Culture became less associated with an external aspect of life to which one had or did not have access, and more with a lifestyle that was defined by the shared beliefs, tastes, language, spaces, clothes, and political world-view of group members. Second, the counter-culture changed the mode of cultural communication through networks of small radio stations and the confessional style of their typical format, the phone-in programme. Third, some of the counter-culture's theorizing, like the women's movement's assertion that the private was political, entered the discourse of mainstream society and had deep-seated effects on personal relationships. Finally, the deregulation of radio and television in 1975, and the passing of legislation permitting divorce and abortion would probably not have occurred, or possibly only much later, without the pressure exerted by the counter-culture.

Another lasting effect of 1968 was the deep changes it brought about in the forms of cultural mediation. In the post-1968 period, and increasingly up to the present, Italian culture has become less bookish and print-dominated as radio and especially television have become the privileged means of communicating with large numbers of people. Indeed, to be an influential intellectual in the Italy of the 1990s meant to have mastered the new media. And in the case of left-wing intellectuals, it meant overcoming their deeply rooted reticence towards such media. Two intellectuals, originally from similar ideological backgrounds, but who have gone in opposite directions, Walter Veltroni (1955–) and

Giuliano Ferrara (1952–), owe much of their influence to their dexterity with the new modes of communication. Veltroni is a young, telegenic intellectual whose political formation took place in the PCI, but who has come to the forefront of Italian political life as a leading light in the Democratic Party of the Left (PDS) and as General Secretary of the Democrats of the Left (DS), the new names the PCI has given itself since the fall of the Berlin Wall. His cultural formation, however, is strongly US-influenced and shows the kind of appreciation of popular culture which is comparatively rare in a left-wing intellectual. As editor of the PDS, and formerly PCI, newspaper *L'Unità*, for instance, Veltroni boosted circulation by including with the newspaper cassettes of popular films and card collections of famous footballers.

The son of a PCI official, Ferrara worked full-time as a salaried administrator in the party's Turin headquarters. However, he left the PCI to join the Italian Socialist Party, which in the 1980s was dominated by Bettino Craxi (1934–2000) and was following an anti-PCI line. After a few years with the Socialists, during which he became a well-known presence on Italian television, Ferrara joined Silvio Berlusconi's new party *Forza Italia*, which was named after a well-known football slogan. In fact, it is on Berlusconi's television channels that Ferrara has become known nationally. Ferrara is an interesting figure for two reasons. First, he has willingly embraced every opportunity the media have made available to him, even that of US-style 'trash' television, to communicate with a large audience in a simple, direct, mainly pro-Berlusconi language which has few precedents in either Italian broadcasting or politics. The second reason is that he has consciously styled himself as the exemplary figure of the modern Italian intellectual, who knew when to leave the sinking ship of Communism and ally himself with what he saw as the more modern, enlightened, Liberal-leaning forces represented by Craxi and Berlusconi.

In fact, the emergence of a generation of neo-Liberal intellectuals in the 1990s, many of whom have made the move from the left to the centre of the Italian political spectrum, represents something very new: namely, a challenge to the hegemony which left-wing intellectuals have generally enjoyed in the years since the end of the Second World War. Indeed, Liberal intellectuals have not only attacked the cultural and political bases on which Italy's First Republic was built, but have also suggested that the hegemony enjoyed by the left in the post-war period has been to the detriment of the nation as a whole. This latest development in Italian cultural life would not have been possible without the collapse of the Berlin Wall and its attendant ideological ramifications. Now that Communism had finally been discredited – Liberal intellectuals reasoned – it was high time that Liberalism, the forgotten ideology of post-war Italy, made a comeback.

The active presence of high-profile Liberal intellectuals meant that the 1990s were a time of great intellectual antagonism in Italy. This marked a radical change from much of the post-war period, based as it was largely on the common experience and values of the Resistance and anti-Fascist struggles. In the Italy of the 1990s, however, a far more abrasive cultural battle was fought out, the main terrain of which was Italy's post-war First Republic, judged by Liberals to be little more than a manifestation of Communist hegemony in deed if not in name. The attack Liberal intellectuals have mounted on post-war Italy has taken two directions: first, a concerted attempt to discredit the Italian Resistance and anti-Fascist movement on which both Togliatti's post-war PCI and the First Republic based their claims to legitimacy; secondly, an equally concerted attempt to suggest that Fascism had not been the disastrous experience left-leaning intellectuals had typically depicted. In the first case, the figure of the partisan has been redescribed as no longer the patriotic hero, but a machine-gun-toting terrorist meting out indiscriminate and ideologically driven retribution; and Togliatti, one of the father-figures of the First Republic, has been portrayed as indifferent to the fate of Italy and Italians, a slave to Moscow, where his ultimate loyalties lay. In the second case, Fascists have been redescribed as brave soldiers who fought for what they thought were the best interests of their country. At the heart of this still ongoing debate lie patriotic values: those of the Communist and post-Communist left are being called into question, those of the Fascist right are being reaffirmed.

To non-Italian eyes, the campaign to discredit the only Italians to come out of the Second World War with any credit and to relegitimate a particularly obnoxious Fascist régime may appear incredible. Closer inspection of the terms of the debate reveals that what is at stake is less Fascism and the Resistance as such than the function that these two crucial twentieth-century experiences have assumed for Italian culture and politics. The real quarry of Liberal intellectuals is what they see as the thoroughly negative role that the PCI-dominated left has played in post-war Italy: hence their attempts to destroy the anti-Fascist legacy, the PCI's main source of legitimacy. The main charge that neo-Liberal intellectuals level at the PCI is that it exploited its position within Italian society, through its leadership of the Resistance movement, to install a régime of left-wing cultural hegemony in the post-Second-World War nation, from which all non-PCI aligned intellectuals were excluded. The exclusion of Liberal intellectuals from Italy's corridors of cultural power – neo-Liberals argue – has had the detrimental effect of depriving Italy of the kind of dynamic, Liberal free-market culture which in the wake of Thatcherism, Reaganism and the collapse of the Berlin Wall has proved itself victorious in Western and Eastern Europe and Asia.

Yet talk of a left-wing cultural régime orchestrated by the PCI on orders from its masters in Moscow is clearly a mystification. It is difficult to imagine how a party which had never been in government until 1996, even allowing for its period of collaboration with the DC in the 1970s, could ever exercise such a tight stranglehold on Italian cultural life. Although the PCI certainly had a great influence on cultural matters through its control of newspapers, weekly and monthly magazines, publishing houses, and radio and television stations, as was only natural for a party which had a strong grassroots organization throughout most of the country and consistently polled around 30 per cent of the vote, that influence never amounted to anything resembling a monopoly. Indeed, the historian Renzo De Felice (1929–95), who dedicated much of his life to a huge and controversial study of Fascism, and who is the intellectual figure most often put forward as a victim of Italian left-wing cultural hegemony, published his many volumes with prestigious publishing houses, was appointed to an important Chair at the University of Rome, and founded an influential school of historical research. It is certainly true that many PCI intellectuals disagreed publicly and violently with De Felice's analysis of Fascism, especially his claim that Fascism enjoyed the consensus of vast sections of Italian society, and that many of their objections stemmed from a reluctance to consider the experiences of Fascism and the Resistance in anything other than the starkest of black-and-white terms. But such reluctance to revise entrenched positions constitutes cultural myopia rather than censorship. Indeed, the first revisions of the overly simplistic and entrenched versions of the Fascist and Resistance experiences that dominated left-wing culture in the immediate post-war years were produced by historians like Luisa Passerini (1941–) and Giovanni De Luna (1943–) who came from the broad area of the Italian left.

Even though the making of predictions is not an exact science, it seems likely that the revision of recent and not-so-recent Italian history will be the terrain on which the cultural and political battles of the near future will be fought. The outcome of these debates will depend, on the one hand, on how well left-wing Italian intellectuals are able to defend Italy's anti-Fascist legacy and to update it, making it relevant to younger generations for whom the Resistance is fast taking on the status of forgotten ancient history; on the other, on how well Italian Liberals fare in their project to delegitimate the anti-Fascist basis of Italy's First Republic and create conditions amenable to the birth of a Second Republic in which the Italian right can play the cultural and political role which, in their eyes at least, it had been denied by the left-dominated Italy of the post-war years.[1]

NOTES

1. A longer version of this chapter is forthcoming in *The Italianist* 21 (2001).

FURTHER READING

Adamson, Walter, *Avant-Garde Florence: From Modernism to Fascism*, Cambridge Mass. and London: Harvard University Press, 1993.

Asor Rosa, Alberto, 'La cultura', in *Storia d'Italia*, vol. IV-ii. Turin: Einaudi, 1975, pp. 821–1664.

Croce, Benedetto, *Estetica come scienza dell'espressione e linguistica generale*, 9th edn. Bari: Laterza, 1950.

De Luna, Giovanni, *Storia del Partito d'azione*. Milan: Feltrinelli, 1982.

Forgacs, David, 'Cultural Consumption, 1940s to 1990s', in D. Forgacs and R. Lumley (eds.), *Italian Cultural Studies*. Oxford University Press, 1997, pp. 273–90.

Gobetti, Piero, *La rivoluzione liberale*, ed. E. Alessandrone Perona. Turin: Einaudi, 1964.

Gramsci, Antonio, *Gli intellettuali e l'organizzazione della cultura*. Turin: Einaudi, 1949.
    Il Risorgimento. Rome: Editori Riuniti, 1971.

Jacobitti, Edmund, 'Hegemony Before Gramsci: The Case of Benedetto Croce', *Journal of Modern History* 52 (1980), pp. 66–84.

Lumley, Robert, 'Challenging Tradition: Social Movements, Cultural Change and the Ecology Question', in Z. Barański and R. Lumley (eds.), *Culture and Conflict in Postwar Italy*. New York: St. Martin's Press, 1990, pp. 115–36.

Passerini, Luisa, *Fascism in Popular Memory: The Cultural Experience of the Turin Working Class*. Cambridge University Press, 1987.

Sapegno, Maria Serena, '"Italia", "Italiani"', in *Letteratura Italiana*, vol. V. Turin: Einaudi, 1982, pp. 169–221.

5

Catholicism

Introduction

In the last hundred years the Church of Rome has formulated two great projects defining the Christian presence in society: those of Popes Leo XIII (1878–1903) and John XXIII (1958–63). The former was determined by the need to come to terms with the new situation created by the French Revolution; the latter was provoked by the need to adjust to the momentous changes which had taken place since the Second World War. Both projects represented major changes in the orientation of an institution that has always preferred to claim continuity rather than admit change, that 'sees restoration where others see revolution'.[1] The projects focused, in the first case, on establishing the bases for a Christian reconquest of a hostile world; and, in the second case, on changing the Church's approach to an outside world no longer conceived as fundamentally hostile, hence one with which it could enter into dialogue.

The significance of these projects for Italian Catholic culture is obvious in view of the authority of papal pronouncements in the production and propagation of Catholic doctrine. It is well known that the Marxist critic Antonio Gramsci discussed the Catholic Church as an ideological apparatus with its own institutional grassroots structure (parishes and dioceses) and cadres (clergy) whose task was to guide and instruct the faithful about their place in the world. This was traditionally achieved, first, in a largely didactic manner through liturgical activity (sermons, catechism) to ensure that the simple verities of the faith were continually reaffirmed; and, second, by controlling the orthodoxy of intellectual expression through disciplinary measures such as excommunication.

The Church's doctrinal activity suggests that discussion of Italian Catholicism needs to attend to three areas: Church teachings, grassroot Catholic understandings, and the interconnection between the two. These areas will be examined in terms of the two projects outlined above.

Leo XIII and the Christian reconquest

Papal teaching and instrumentalities

The French Revolution broke the Church of Rome's traditional link with the states of the Ancien Régime and, hence, its identification with pre-revolutionary societies. It was responsible for the complete laicization of the state and public life for the first time in the history of Christian Europe, and so for the complete separation of Church and state. With the advent of Liberalism as the main ideology of the new rulers of Europe, the Catholic Church found itself in a hostile environment. The situation was worse in Italy than in other European countries because the newly unified state occupied the Papal States (1860–70), thereby depriving the Church of its temporal power. Pope Pius IX (1846–78) refused to accept this *fait accompli*, and the resulting Roman Question (that is, the conflict over the territorial sovereignty of the Holy See) was to determine the Church's largely hostile relations with the Italian state for the next fifty years, until its resolution in the Lateran Pacts of 1929.

The Church's reaction to a hostile outside world was to condemn it. For Pius IX and his successors, Liberalism was the very negation of Christianity since it put humanity in God's place. It constituted an even greater threat than Protestantism, because it was presented as the bearer of a total civilization superior to Christianity. Thus, the Popes viewed Liberalism as a mortal enemy, the more so since the Church of Rome considered itself not only as the one true Church, but as the perfect society. This explains Pius IX's intransigence, expressed in the formula 'There can be no compromise with this world-order', and his condemnation of the secular world as iniquitous in the *Syllabus errorum* (1864).

Leo XIII (1878–1903), however, while maintaining the intransigence of his predecessor in temporal and doctrinal matters, realized that simple rejection and condemnation were insufficient if the Church was not to lose its influence over people's minds and over society. To ensure that this did not happen, it had to offer an alternative vision of society. This required the Church coming to terms with its new situation in the world; however, this was not to be done at any price because the Church's principles encompassed eternal truths. The strategy adopted was simple: combine maximum doctrinal rigour with extreme realism. This meant defending Church principles while taking advantage of the political opportunities offered by secular régimes.

Moreover, since the Church saw modern society as a counter-church, the solution was to develop itself as a counter-society. Indeed, many influential Catholics harboured the belief that eventually modern society would be forced to recognize the error of its ways and once again embrace the Church. In the meantime, Leo's great project, which he pursued methodically throughout his pontificate in nine major encyclicals (letters addressed to clergy and faithful stating official Church doctrine), was to prepare the Church to regain its former dominant position. The tools for achieving this were essentially two: teaching and organization. The aims were to restore the philosophical basis of Catholic teaching while setting out its practical implications in terms of lay action for modern society (social doctrine), and to propagate this teaching (mass confessional associations).

Although more of a practical man than a theoretician, Leo XIII understood that all institutional activity required a basis in a coherent body of knowledge. Thus, in his first encyclical (*Aeterni Patris*, 1879), he restored Thomism – the Scholastic philosophy of St Thomas Aquinas (1227–74) which harmonized faith and reason – as the Church's official philosophy. He thus emphasized the continuity of Christian teaching and traditional Catholic identity. Leo's exaltation of the perennial significance of Thomism was proof that Catholicism had a complete, philosophically based doctrine capable of confronting its modern ideological rivals on their own ground, that of understanding the world. The doctrinal certitudes announced in a long series of papal encyclicals by Leo's successors reinforced Catholic identity, while at the same time furnishing an explanation for the unhappy state of modern society: present ills were the result of loss of faith and the consequent abandonment of Christian principles.

Thomism also provided a philosophical structure through which political and ethical questions could be posed and analysed. God was rational and purposive and the natural world was made in his image; humanity's role was to live in harmony with nature; belief and reason were not contradictory, but merely two different ways of knowing truth. Indeed, the Thomist vision of a hierarchical and ordered world, beginning with God and proceeding through a series of gradations of Being which placed humanity in a unique position as the link between heaven and earth, was given intellectual substance in the famous theory of natural law organized in terms of three levels: divine law, natural law and human positive law. The dictates of each level needed to be in accord for social harmony to be achieved.

In addition, the Thomist framework provided a way for dealing with change and the political pretensions of the Church's ideological rivals. This was the doctrine of 'indirect sovereignty' based on the separation of the spiritual and temporal, but with the primacy of the former. This distinction provided the basis of the so-called 'thesis and hypothesis' theory which distinguished between authoritative pronouncements (theses: to be obeyed in all circumstances) and other pronouncements (hypotheses: modifiable if necessity demands) in expounding the Christian message. The significance of this doctrine was that it permitted the Church to adjust to change without altering any fundamental principle, and so opened the way to acknowledging some of the values of modern society. The doctrine of 'indirect sovereignty' had a further aspect. Since divine law was superior to natural law, the Church claimed the right to intervene in those areas of the temporal sphere involving moral questions, which meant virtually all areas of contemporary life. Indeed, in his encyclical *Quas primas* (1925), Pius XI (1922–39) asserted not only the spiritual dimensions of this moral leadership, but also its socio-political dimensions, announcing a programme of Christian restoration. Unsurprisingly, such papal pretensions were a source of potential conflict with lay governments.

Finally, the restoration of Thomism furnished a pedagogical method for the propagation of the Christian message. Leo's encyclicals made a successful ideological appeal to the faithful. They inspired mobilization among the lower clergy which led to the creation of those associations that were to constitute a mass social movement in the new century, the Italian Catholic movement. It was in the nascent parish circles that the encyclicals were discussed, thereby ensuring their influence on Italian Catholic culture. The basis of Catholic social doctrine, as expounded in Leo's great encyclical *Rerum novarum* (1893), was the famous medieval organicist conception of human society, whereby society was a divinely ordained moral organism in which each part had a special role to play in securing the well-being of the whole. As Leo XIII put it: 'nature wishes the two classes in civil society to find harmony between themselves and the equilibrium that results. The one has an absolute need of the other;

neither capital without labour, nor labour without capital. Concord creates the beauty and order of things; whereas perpetual conflict can only bring confusion and barbarity.' The Church's task was to promote this social concord by laying down the duties of each class based on justice. Catholic social doctrine propounded the pacific acceptance by each group of its natural and rightful place in society, and the faithful execution by each of its duties as established by the Church: 'that the masters accept the need to be good masters and the servants accept their subordination'.[2] As a result, the Church could claim to be the guardian of workers and employers alike.

Private property, the family and work were the three interconnected pillars of the Church's social doctrine. They too were a product of Thomist natural law and of its belief in humanity's privileged relationship with God. From this stemmed two important consequences: humanity's absolute and rightful domination over nature – this was the principal distinction between humanity and the animal world – and the essential equality of all human beings in the social and economic spheres. The domination that humanity has over non-human elements, deriving from its capacity to reason, is the basis of the right to property. This right fulfilled the fundamental need of humanity to express its own dignity and freedom through the family and work. However, enjoyment of the right was limited by its social aspect: the basic equality of all human beings. Hence, the Church's social doctrine explicitly rejected both Liberal capitalism and Marxist Socialism. Moreover, it specifically encouraged class harmony by endorsing the natural right of the workers to a just wage while stressing the Christian obligations of the employer. It proposed a régime of corporations of employers and workers which were to be self-regulating, but co-ordinated by the state. How this co-ordination was to be achieved was crucial, because it was the key to the social harmony which the Church's 'corporatist' régime was intended to secure. Other moral aspects derived from the social doctrine's natural-law approach were the protection and encouragement of the family as the most direct expression of humanity's nature; and, last but not least, the principle that there is no authority except from God (*Immortale Dei*, 1885).

Turning to the organizational aspect of Leo XIII's project, the Church formulated two major responses to the problems posed by its position in a hostile world. The first was to centralize power and authority in the Holy See and in the person of the Sovereign Pontiff. This had already begun under Pius IX, and became the central theme of the First Vatican Council (1870), which proclaimed the dogma of papal infallibility in doctrinal matters. It was followed by the publication of the Code of Canon Law under Benedict XV in 1918, which set out the rules governing the behaviour of Catholics. The purpose was to ensure uniformity of action within the Church, and to secure the strict obedience of the faithful and clergy to their bishops and of the bishops to the Pope. The second response was what has been called 'the appeal to the laity', namely, exploiting the opportunities offered by the new secular régimes, specifically the possibility of mobilizing the faithful in civil society outside the state sphere. 'The appeal to the laity' amounted to the Church's sponsoring of large-scale organizations in which and through which the layperson was called actively to support the Church by defending and extending its mission in the world. Lay mobilization assumed a wide variety of organizational forms: religious, social, economic and, eventually, political.

The Pope who developed this second response and made it the basis of his strategy of 'Christian reconquest' was Pius XI. For him, Catholic Action, the mass organization of lay Catholic militants founded in the late nineteenth century, was the principal instrument for the propagation and achievement of Christian principles in individual, family and social life, but always under strict clerical control. We should perhaps add that Pius XI's predilection for Catholic Action should probably be explained in terms of the specific circumstances of his pontificate (1922–39, i.e. during the Fascist régime), when all non-Fascist organizations except Catholic Action were banned. It was allowed to survive, under the 1929 Lateran Pacts, with a role limited to educational and religious activity. Indeed, it not only survived but prospered, with membership expanding throughout the 1930s to constitute a mass force of two million people, disciplined and obedient, at the Pope's command ('The Pope's Army').

In addition, as part of his aim to secure the Kingdom of Christ on earth, Pius XI frequently expressed his views on various social issues, such as the family and education, to assert the Church's position in particular when these matters were neglected or opposed by secular governments. However, it was his successor, Pius XII (1939–58), who, in the 1940s and 1950s, stressed the role of papal teaching in the 'reconquest' strategy. He discoursed on every topic, thus giving the impression that Catholic culture was complete in itself and able to provide doctrinal orientation in every branch of knowledge and in professional matters.

Ideological concerns and propagation networks

Analysis of devotional literature indicates a number of ideological concerns which remained largely unchanged from the unification of Italy right down to the Second Vatican Council (1963–5). The major concerns were the value of private property, the family and the subordination of women, the myth of the land, the acceptance of one's social station and the virtue of obedience, and the castigation of atheists, Communists and sinners. The purpose of this literature was to propagate the papal message that there was no moral alternative to the Christian way of life.

Private property operated as a moral value on two levels. For the wealthy, their property confirmed that they were among the 'privileged', and hence that they had a responsibility to husband it with care. For the poor, lack of property was proof of their humble station, and hence of the need to practise humility, which was likely to secure their salvation in the afterlife. Alongside property was the family, which was the natural condition for both men and women (and so willed by divine law); it determined, moreover, the very different, but complementary, roles of men and women: he, the lord and master; she, the maid and servant. The purpose of marriage (and the family) was to collaborate with God in perpetuating human life. A woman's role was that of mother and husband's helpmate, with the attendant virtues of modesty, submission and sacrifice. The role model was Mary, who suffered silently and with dignity. For women, there were no Christian virtues outside the family.

The myth of the land as the source and depository of all Christian and civic virtues was an even more significant ideological theme. Peasant society represented a fundamental point of reference for the identification of ethico-religious and political values (Nature–Man–God). During the course of the nineteenth century, Catholic apologists transposed the Enlightenment myth of the 'noble savage' into the ideology of the 'noble peasant' – last refuge of sound customs and the true faith.[3] It was this myth that led the ecclesiastical hierarchy to condemn industry and urbanization as the source of spiritual and material degradation. Two other Catholic themes were linked to the myth of peasant society: the acceptance of one's station in life and the supreme virtue of obedience to God's will. Not only were they a call to support the social status quo and reject secular ideologies, they also constituted a command to obey the Church as an institution and to regard its leader, the Pope, as the only true interpreter of God's will.

Finally, the notion of obedience reappeared in the castigation of atheists, sinners and revolutionaries, for whom eternal damnation was promised. Since the Counter-Reformation, dechristianization had been considered by the Church as a direct consequence of the Reformation which was deemed the work of Satan. The revival of the notion of the works of the devil to explain modern civilization led to the widespread use of apocalyptic language. Since 1917, but above all during the Cold War, Communism had been the specific target of these ecclesiastical condemnations. Moreover, the association of the devil, atheism and revolution with urban civilization enabled the Church to weave its major themes (the land, family and labour) into a coherent ideological product: 'peasant civilization' with its nostalgic appeal to a past 'golden age'.

Before examining the views of the faithful, it is worth outlining the networks that propagated Catholic culture in the pre-Second Vatican Council period. Catholic institutions were both numerous and widespread. First, there were the ecclesiastical territorial institutions which in the 1950s comprised a clerical population of a quarter of a million, of whom 65,000 were bishops and priests who ministered to the faithful in 282 dioceses and 25,000 parishes. Secondly, there were the Catholic associational networks which embraced some 10 per cent of Italians: Catholic Action itself in the 1950s numbered over three million members in 80,000 groups. Together with its dependent bodies, Catholic Action was numerically the largest private organization in the country. To this, one can add the more autonomous professional bodies, all founded in the immediate post-war period, like the Farmers' Confederation (one and a half million families, representing seven million people in 13,000 sections); ACLI (Association of Catholic Workers – one million members in 6,000 branches); CISL (Trade Union Confederation – two and a half million members); and the Christian Democratic Party (one and a half million members in 12,000 branches, and some eleven million voters). Thirdly, there was the Catholic press which controlled some 1,800 publications with an overall circulation of sixteen million copies, more than half the magazine sales in Italy. Lastly, given that the Christian Democrat Party was continuously in power, the Church could count on public instutions (schools, radio and television) to spread the precepts of Catholic culture.

The orientation of the faithful

The faithful generally assimilated the themes outlined above; however, in certain circumstances, there were subtle interpretations whereby the 'official' arguments were stood on their head or simply rejected. The process and extent of reinterpretation depended on the role of the Church in local society. In the Lombardo-Veneto of the 1950s, where local society was strongly integrated around the local parish, Catholic culture had become the local mass culture. On the other hand, in the South in the same period, where local society was in an advanced state of transformation, reinterpretation was more widespread. One needs only recall the spread of Protestant sects in the South since the start of the century.

Studies of the 1950s point to the direct reproduction by the faithful of the messages contained in clerical discourse. The repetition of catchwords and ready-made phrases confirm the themes already outlined: the family, labour, acceptance of one's station, obedience to the Church. For example: 'Teaching religion makes us good Christians, good labourers and good men, honest and devoted to our families' (peasant); 'Religion helps us to endure the sad adversities of life' (mechanic); 'Religion is a faith, believing what the priests tell and have told us and what we have learned from Scripture' (housewife).[4] An analysis of 1950s political stereotypes has persuasively shown that in the Lombardo-Veneto three sets of messages predominated: religion–Church, labour–social justice and fatherland–freedom.[5] They mirrored the stereotypes of Catholic culture, and determined mass attitudes towards political parties. In the words of one respondent: 'Occupation peasant. I am ignorant of politics. I observe the Ten Commandments and I vote for the Christian Democrats.' The DC was the most popular party because it was viewed positively with regard to religion and patriotism, even though it was perceived negatively with regard to labour–social justice. The Communist Party lost because, although it was judged positively on social justice, it was condemned for its atheism. However, where the Catholic cultural message was more problematic, for instance in secularized and working-class areas, more critical attitudes were found. These tended to take one of two forms: either total rejection in the form of anticlericalism, or an acceptance of the Catholic cultural framework, while turning the judgments implicit in the 'official' interpretation on their heads. For example: 'The DC should be less accommodating and ensure greater respect for the laws which help smallholders and the less well-off' (clerk). Thus, even in cases where religion was not the sole factor determining the influence of Catholic culture at the grassroots, it remained nonetheless a significant one.[6]

Historians have commented on the Church's role in determining the political and cultural orientation of the majority of Italians in the Fascist and Cold-War periods. The reason for this, it is claimed, lay in the centralism and discipline imposed on the Church by Leo XIII and his successors. Discipline was such that the behaviour of ordinary Catholics faithfully followed the clergy's instructions. The lines of communication were very efficient: papal pronouncements were discussed in the most authoritative Catholic journals, and popularized in thousands of parish magazines and bulletins and, above all, in the sermons of parish priests.

John XXIII and the People of God

The Church's dream of the Christian reconquest of Italian society was shattered as much by the development of that society as by the triumph of rival ideologies. Indeed, by the 1960s Italy was no longer a Catholic country, in the sense that practising Catholics were a minority – a fact which the divorce and abortion referendums of 1974 and 1981 respectively were to confirm. Pope Leo XIII's and his successors' project of the Church regaining its hegemony over Italian society through its appeal to the people was no longer viable.

The Pope and the Council

John XXIII's pontificate (1958–63) and the Second Vatican Council (1962–5) which he called mark something of a break in the Church's recent history. This was the result more of 'witness' – John XXIII's whole conception of being Pope – than of doctrinal revolution. As he declared in his 1961 encyclical *Mater et Magistra*, 'a social message is not only to be proclaimed, but is also to be put concretely into practice'. The new Pope saw his role as that of the 'Good Shepherd'. He believed in the essential goodness of humanity, but he was also aware of the crisis threatening the Church because it was losing contact with ordinary men and women, who consequently were turning away from God. It was his firm intent that contact be renewed. Hence the Pope's surprise decision to call the Council and his pastoral activity as Bishop of Rome. This aim was evident above all in his Gospel message of hope and co-operation: he preached the language of mercy and reconciliation rather than that of reprobation, used by his immediate precedessors. This approach reached its climax in his last and most celebrated encyclical, *Pacem in terris* (1963), which was addressed – an absolute novelty – to 'all men of good will' and not just to the episcopacy, clergy and faithful. While following orthodox Catholic doctrine, imputing the present crisis in the world to its having forsaken God, the encyclical nonetheless emphasizes the distinction between 'error and the erring' (the non-believer 'is above all always a human being and retains [. . .] his personal dignity') and the need for dialogue with other currents of opinion, even with those with whom the Church disagreed on fundamentals. The justification for such behaviour was an acute historical intuition, namely, that false doctrines regarding mankind's nature, origin and purpose should not be confused with the political movements that found inspiration in them.

During the first session of the Council, a change in the direction of the Church corresponding to John XXIII's vision appeared to be a real possibility; however, none of the proposed constitutional documents was voted on and the Pope died before the second session opened. Although his successor, Paul VI (1963–78), was committed to the spirit of the Council, he was much more cautious and concerned with doctrinal continuity, so that some of the Council's innovatory impact was blunted. Despite the compromises, however, two documents, *Lumen gentium* and *Gaudium et spes*, remain important for their innovatory thrust.

Lumen gentium was the Church's new dogmatic constitution and went beyond the earlier Tridentine hierarchical conception of Church authority, revalorizing the contribution of all its members. The chapter defining the Church as the 'People of God', that is embracing believers and unbelievers alike, was significantly placed before the one setting out the Church's hierarchical structure. Moreover, the constitution proposed a more active role for the laity than hitherto, speaking of a 'common ministry of the faithful' in addition to the 'official or hierarchical ministry'. It reconfirmed, nonetheless, the doctrine of papal pre-eminence.

Gaudium et spes was the document that originated from John XXIII's concern that one of the Council's principal tasks should be to respond to the world's problems and hopes: poverty, liberation and peace. It was presented as the Magna Carta of the Church's social teaching: the pastoral constitution of 'the Church in the contemporary world'. Its existence was an authentic novelty; however, owing to the difficulty the Council had in its final session in reconciling the new perspectives with traditional views, it was both long, complex and convoluted. For example, in the first part, it proclaimed basic human rights, including respect for the freedom of conscience of the 'erring' and the fundamental equality of all human beings and their opinions; but in the second, it repeated the traditional views on the family, marriage, divorce, birth control and abortion. In this way, doctrinal continuity was safeguarded, while leaving the way open for dialogue between believers and non-believers. Such an approach, however, frustrated the Council Fathers who believed that a deeper inquiry was necessary if the Church was to appreciate the demographic, economic, social, and not just the moral, implications of its family doctrine.

What needs to be emphasized is that the Council proposed the premises for a radical change in the Church, but it lacked both the time and the power effectively to overcome the mentality of the Vatican administration. Indeed, John XXIII's intuition of the relevance of the Gospel message to the modern world was more a change of style than a real project. In action, it caused tensions; and his successors, fearful of the consequences, endeavoured to limit the Council's impact. Indeed, both Paul VI and John Paul II (1978–) increasingly blamed the overt crisis of the Church in the 1970s and 1980s on the Council. Thus, as early as 1972, Paul VI claimed that the Council had not produced the sunny day that it was legitimate to expect, but 'a day of clouds, storms, and darkness'. Despite such reservations, the Church has made an effort to adapt itself to the needs of the post-Conciliar world, above all by increasingly emphasizing the ethical, rather than the purely religious, dimension of the Christian message. Thus, papal pronouncements have attempted not only to demonstrate that Catholic moral commandments contain valid responses to the problems of contemporary society, but also to present them in a persuasive manner: no longer dogmatically, but problematically. Thus, John Paul II, in his encyclical *Centesimus annus* (1991), weighs the pros and cons of capitalism as the best possible economic system, recognizing its virtues, recalling its vices and eschewing all sweeping judgments.[7]

Pluralism and dialogue

Despite the surprise and general hostility of the Italian episcopacy, the impact of John XXIII's pontificate and the Second Vatican Council was quite dramatic. By liberating latent cultural tensions and energy, it brought the crisis of Catholicism into the open. The changes produced by the 'Catholic reformation of the Sixties' passed through three phases which coincided with the three succeeding pontificates. The first phase

(1963–5) was more or less responsible for the liquidation of the project of Christian reconquest of Italian society, at least in Pius XII's version of a hierarchically organized militant Church. Pluralism and dialogue, as signalled in John XXIII's actions and encyclicals, were the order of the day. The second phase (1965–76: Paul VI) was dominated by Catholic dissent; spontaneous development of grassroots communities; crises of the clergy (decline in vocations, exodus from Holy Orders) and of official Catholic collateral organizations; and the formation of opposition movements, like 'Cristiani per il socialismo' or local ecumenical movements. The third phase (since 1978: John Paul II) has been something of the calm after the storm and has seen the Church attempting to reconstitute unity around the Pope's charismatic figure.

From the point of view of grassroots cultural shift, the second phase is of particular relevance. The religious and cultural crisis that the Second Vatican Council released (coinciding with the upheavals of 1968) undermined the organizational viability of the official Catholic collateral associations, resulting in confusion, splits and the dissolution of numerous local associations. Membership of Catholic Action and other associations declined by two-thirds in the five years from 1966 to 1971. Indeed, the result in 1969 was a new statute for Catholic Action founded on the so-called 'religious choice', that is a purely apostolic commitment to the Church's pastoral mission. The development, on the other hand, of a whole series of spontaneous groups led to loss of Church credibility, protest against the ecclesiastical hierarchy, and a general fragmentation, both organizational and cultural, of the hitherto disciplined Catholic movement. Catholic dissent reached its peak in the mid 1970s with the vote in favour of divorce in the 1974 referendum. However, the failure of the protest groups to change the world pushed them towards mysticism, which enabled the Church authorities to regain some measure of institutional control over cultural dissent in the religious sphere. This was achieved in two ways: first, by the systematic elimination of dissent towards Church authority; and secondly, through the recovery of part of the innovatory experiences in a spirit of give and take (acceptance of certain criticisms of the Church concerning submission to Church authority).

Research in the 1970s identified four major cultural areas within Catholicism.[8] The first, 'Traditional Catholicism', corresponded to the pre-Conciliar Catholic culture outlined above, and had its touchstones in the words 'religion', 'charity', 'Christianity', 'spirit' and 'Catholic', which expressed the thematic contents of the now minority, rural Catholic tradition.

The second was 'Progressive Catholicism', which can be defined as the official culture of the Second Vatican Council, and whose vocabulary comprised the key words 'community', 'service', 'path', 'choice', 'testimony', 'liturgy', 'catechism', 'Gospel', 'love' and 'communion'. 'Progressive Catholicism' owes much to the French Catholic philosopher Jacques Maritain and his book *L'Humanisme intégral* (1936), which argued the case for the autonomy of Catholics in the temporal sphere where the faithful should be free to bear witness according to personal conscience.

The third area was 'Modern Extra-Ecclesiastical Catholicism' which was tendentially heterodox and made up of groups that had broken with the Church, initially on the grounds of class. Key words in their vocabulary were: 'friendship', 'experience', 'person', 'friend', 'personal', 'together', 'achieve', 'need'. They were the groups most profoundly affected by the post-1968 experience, and which formed 'Cristiani per il socialismo'. The interaction of this experience with traditional Catholic culture was responsible for the so-called 'spontaneous Catholic associationism' that characterized the 1970s. This form of Catholicism stressed the fraternal (or horizontal) relationship instead of the traditional vertical relationship of authority between clergy and laity – a development that Pope John Paul II has gone out of his way to quell.

The fourth tendency was 'Intransigent Catholicism', which was that of the hardline militants, particularly associated with Comunione e liberazione, who were well organized and hostile to all forms of 'progressive Catholicism'. Its vocabulary included such key words as 'man', 'neighbourhood', 'reality', 'world', 'social' and 'political'. The main thrust of this group was to see the Gospel message in purely political terms that could be implemented in a lay context.

The second and third groupings were more widespread, at least among the young, than the first and the fourth. Further, the latter were stronger in central Italy (including Rome) and the South than in the North. By the 1990s, the Catholic cultural area seemed to have stabilized. For example, Garelli identified two groups: what he called the 'Catholic majority' (some two-thirds of Italians who accept the generic definition of 'Catholic'), and the 'Catholic minority'' (perhaps one-third, who are intensely religious, of whom one-tenth belong to groups, movements or associations).[9] Thus, while 80 per cent of Italians believe in a Christian God, the quota that actually believes in specific Catholic precepts is dra matically lower (fewer than 30 per cent). The significance of the distinction is twofold: first, the proportion of 'committed Catholics' that recognizes and obeys the precepts is half that of 'generic Catholics'; secondly, the proportion of 'committed Catholics' who believe that not following certain precepts, above all in the field of family and sexual morals, which papal teaching continues to stress is not a mortal sin, is substantial (about 35 per cent). This breakdown in the system of Catholic moral beliefs has been attributed to a process of deregulation aided and abetted by the Church itself and 'consisting in the progressive neglect of the repertory of indications given to those – the clergy – whose task was once that of ensuring compliance in moral behaviour, above all in the field of sexual and family ethics.'[10]

Conclusion

The great change in Catholic culture after unification resulted from a change in the project of defining the Christian presence in Italian society: it is no longer a militant movement seeking to reconquer a monopoly position for the Church, but rather a plurality of groups in dialogue with other cultural movements, promoting peace and good will for all conditions of persons. Indeed, it can be argued that the passage of Catholicism from an institutional centre of social aggregation in Italian society to a largely cultural area has paradoxically come about as much as a result of the Church's action as against its will. However, one thing the Church has not abandoned is its dogma: the claim to universal truth. In his encyclical *Veritatis splendor* (1993), Pope John Paul II is explicit: all modern philosophies are false – Liberalism and Socialism, but also Rationalism in all its forms, Naturalism, Pantheism, Positivism, Materialism, etc. – for the very simple reason that 'by the will of Christ, the Catholic Church is the master of the truth; its function is to express and teach the authentic truth at the same time as proclaiming and confirming, by virtue of its authority, the principles of the moral order that follow the very nature of man.' However, this claim has been increasingly rejected by a majority of Italians, because the simple moral principles dictated by 'the commandments of divine and natural law' are increasingly at odds with the contradictory experience of life in a postmodern society. A measure of this changed attitude is the disappearance, with the Cold War, of the Christian Democrat Party after almost fifty continuous years in power.

NOTES

1. N. Ravitch, *The Catholic Church and the French Nation* (London: Routledge, 1980), p. 135.
2. The two passages are quoted in Giuliano della Pergola, 'Le ideologie dei cattolici italiani dalla questione operaia a Cristiani per il socialismo', in Fernando Vianello *et al.*, *Tutto il potere della DC* (Rome: Coines Edizioni, 1975), pp. 109–55 (pp. 114 and 116).
3. See Carlo Prandi, 'Alle origini moderne dell'egemonia. "Religione" e "popolare" in Italia tra XVIII e XIX secolo', in G. Guizzardi (ed.), *Chiesa e religione del popolo* (Turin: Claudina, 1981).
4. The first two quotations from Percy Allum and Ilvo Diamanti, *'50/'80: Venti anni* (Rome: Edizioni Lavoro, 1986), pp. 120–1; the last from Percy Allum, *Politics and Society in Postwar Naples* (Cambridge University Press, 1973), p. 269.
5. Ilvo Diamanti, 'La filigrana bianca della comunità. Senso comune, consenso politico, appartenenza religiosa nel Veneto degli anni '50', *Venetica* 6 (1986), pp. 55–81.
6. Ibid., p. 67.
7. See E. Pace, *L'unità dei cattolici in Italia* (Milan: Guerini e Associati, 1995), p. 125.
8. See della Pergola, 'Le ideologie'; G.-C. Milanesi (ed.), *Oggi credono così*, 2 vols. (Milan: Elledici, 1981); G.-C. Quaranta, *L'associazionismo invisibile* (Florence: Sansoni, 1982).
9. F. Garelli, *Religione e chiesa in Italia* (Bologna: Il Mulino, 1991).
10. Pace, *L'unità dei cattolici*, p. 127.

FURTHER READING

Alberigo, G. and A. Ricciardi (eds.), *Chiesa e papato nel mondo contemporaneo*. Bari: Laterza, 1990.
Guizzardi, G., 'The "Rural Civilization". The Structure of an Ideology of Consent', *Social Compass* 23 (1976), pp. 197–220.
Miccoli, G., 'La Chiesa e il fascismo', in G. Quazza (ed.), *Fascismo e società italiana*. Turin: Einaudi, 1973, pp. 185–208.
Magister S., *La politica vaticana in Italia, 1943–1978*. Rome: Editori Riuniti, 1979.
Martini, G., *La Chiesa negli ultimi trent'anni*. Rome: Studium, 1977.
Nichols, P., *The Politics of the Vatican*. London: Pall Mall, 1968.
Poggi, G.-F., *Catholic Action in Italy*. Stanford University Press, 1967.
Poulat, E., 'L'Eglise romaine, le savoir et le pouvoir', *Archives de sociologie des religions* 37 (1974), pp. 5–21.

6

Socialism, Communism and other 'isms'

Before the second half of the nineteenth century, there was no Socialist movement in Italy, for the conditions that would enhance its development had yet to come into being. Socialist concerns for justice and equality were not lacking in the writings of reformers and patriots of the eighteenth and early nineteenth centuries, but they remained, with few exceptions, universal ideals largely untested in concrete, historical arenas of struggle.[1] It was not until the Risorgimento had borne the fruits of Italian unity, providing the stimulus and the basis for the development of capitalism on a national scale, that the Socialist movement could find its channels of political development and ideological growth.

The Italian Socialist Party was formed at the time of the Second Congress of the Italian Workers' Party, held in Genoa in August 1892. The principal decisions taken included the definitive separation between Anarchists and Marxists, and the constitution of a party with a distinctly proletarian base and committed to Marxist principles. The programme voted in 1892 would remain the party's official platform until 1919. It proclaimed as its end 'the socialization of the means of work [. . .] and [the] collective control of production' which could only be achieved by the 'action of all the proletariat organized in a "class party"'.[2] The main currents operative in pursuing some or all of these objectives were essentially three: Marxism, Reformism and Syndicalism. Bakuninist Anarchism, which preached the abolition of the state, had a discrete following mainly in Southern Italy and constituted an important moment in the party's prehistory. Its defeat in about 1880 signalled the birth of a modern Socialism, based on reason and the political growth of the working class; its legacy, however, would not be erased completely from the party's history, as the tactics of Syndicalism and, later, 'Mussolini-ism' would bear ample testimony.

Marxism

While Marxism had been known in Italy since 1848, it took hold among Italian intellectuals only in the late 1880s. The cultural environment in which it was diffused was largely Positivist and anti-clerical. The philosopher Antonio Labriola and the future leader of the Socialist Party, Filippo Turati, were its principal spokesmen. Labriola propounded what is commonly referred to as 'orthodox' Marxism: a doctrine, based in the Hegelian dialectic, that reiterated Marx's original views on the inevitable overthrow of capitalism by violent revolution. Although Labriola's orthodox position would have a lasting influence on the Socialist movement, it would be overshadowed by the much less radical and more practical positions held by Turati, which left open the question whether violent revolution was necessary and inevitable, while still adhering to the tenets of an evolutionary Socialism. Turati's brand of Socialism, from which the party took its organizational impetus, maintained that, in order to gain power, the workers had to engage in an organized *class* struggle in the *political* arena, that is, in relation to the then dominant Liberal governments and within the parliamentary system. This position set the stage for the battles between reformists and revolutionaries that would impair party unity for decades to come.

Reformism

Like Marxism, Reformism in the Italian context branched from left to right in its approach to Socialism, that is, from positions that remained anchored to the Marxist principle of revolution, while emphasizing the political development of the working class and proletarian reforms, to those which were collectivist, but not, strictly speaking, Marxist. This latter orientation preached the conquest of political power by the working class through elections and reforms, while rejecting all insurrectional activity. These ideas had been instrumental in the formation in 1882 of the Italian Workers' Party and played a crucial role in the development of the Socialist programme. Alongside such reformism developed the revision of Marxist doctrine inspired by the work of Eduard

Bernstein, which brought the idea of 'Socialism-by-degrees' to its logical consequences. For the German Social Democrat Bernstein, capitalism had become too strong to collapse either under the weight of its internal contradictions or by the pressures applied to it by the workers' movement, while class distinctions were seen to be less and less binding. Hence the only road that could lead to Socialism was transformation within the structure of the capitalist state.

Bernstein's Revisionism, which negated both the Marxist dialectic (according to which the more capitalism exploited the proletariat, the more the proletariat was in a position to organize itself into a revolutionary force capable of 'expropriating the expropriators') and the autonomy of the working class, was an attack on Marx from the right. Its impact on the Socialist movement consisted much less in its concrete appeal than in its having created the theoretical premise from which a more influential form of Revisionism from the left would develop. For, if the concept of class struggle was no longer valid, where did Socialism, as a class-oriented political party, find its justification? The Syndicalist movement, whose principal theoretician was the Frenchman George Sorel, would emerge at this very moment, when Socialism began moving towards accommodation with Liberal political institutions.

Syndicalism

Denouncing all compromise with bourgeois politics, Syndicalism maintained that only the trade unions could guarantee the autonomy of the working class. From within the trade unions, the workers would wage their battles against the capitalist enemy by means of their most powerful weapon, the general strike. The general strike, in Sorel's view, was not a practical expedient but rather a myth of 'creative violence' which he equated with *the* Revolution. The deliberate impulsiveness of revolutionary Syndicalism, the emphasis it placed on the force of 'willing' (voluntarism), became instrumental in the birth and growth of Fascism.

On the whole, the extremes of Revisionism and Syndicalism were rejected by the Socialist Party, while orthodox Marxism, accepted as economic theory, remained until 1912 in the background of the party's politics. Genuine Socialist revolutionary work was that performed on a daily basis in the factories and co-operatives; it sought the progressive erosion of bourgeois hegemony through practical means. And in sharp contrast to Syndicalism, Socialism was not the expression of a revolutionary will to power to be harnessed and directed by the party, but rather the end of an evolutionary process.

Socialism during the Giolitti ministries

The party, from its foundation to 1926, when it was forced by Fascism to leave Italy, developed in tandem with the national state, as a response to Liberal politics at home and in the international arena. Having survived persecution under the Crispi and Pelloux governments, it gained in strength, unity and adherents. However, during the Giolitti ministries (1901–14) it split irreparably along ideological and political lines. Giolitti's attitude toward Socialism was one of astute compromise. He supported the representation of workers' organizations and promoted a series of 'Socialist-like' reforms, including public-health legislation and subsidies for the co-operatives, in an attempt to make the working classes more receptive to Liberal politics. The party, in the light of Giolitti's politicking, had difficulty in charting a clear course. In order to avoid disintegration, it embraced the contradictory distinction between minimum and maximum programmes, the former geared to reform, the latter to revolution. This position gave rise to the policy of integralism, which was born from the alliance of Syndicalists and centrists, and attempted to negate the contradiction between violent revolution and reform simply by combining the politics of long-range goals and short-term gains. In 1903, the Socialists joined the government, despite the dissension of the Syndicalists who, a year later, manoeuvred a general strike, the effect of which on Socialism was that it abandoned integralism, expelled the Syndicalists, and returned to the moderate, reformist leadership of Turati.

In 1911, in competition with England, France and Germany over economic rights in North Africa, Italy declared war on Turkey over Libya, which belonged to the Turkish Empire. The party under Turati's direction, amid the notable growth in national prosperity, had been on a course between outright collaboration with Liberalism, a position supported by Leonida Bissolati and Invanoe Bonomi, and orthodox (revolutionary) Marxism, whose leader was Costantino Lazzari. The war moved the party decisively to the left. With the advent of an imperialist war, it was no longer possible to justify reconciliation with the bourgeois parties. Among the rank and file, the opposition to the war was immediate. Against the right's cry for unity at any cost came strikes and numerous instances of organized disruption.

Mussolini

The second Party Congress of Reggio Emilia (1912) has rightly been viewed as an important turning-point for Italian Socialism. It was at this Congress that Benito Mussolini made his first major public appearance. Mussolini had sensed that times had changed and that the anti-reformist battle could be fought not from the margins but from the centre of the party. In reality, his anti-reformist polemics conveyed no new messages with respect to what the Syndicalists had been preaching for years. What was new was the fiery style with which he condemned a large variety of adversaries, but especially Giolitti and the party's collaborationist wing. When the dust had settled, the party had voted out Bissolati and Bonomi and forced Turati, again for the sake of unity, to compromise with the new revolutionary leadership.

It was plain from the start that Mussolini had little in common with veteran revolutionary Socialists. His vehement campaign against Giolitti had no equal, even among the Syndicalists and the most intransigent of revolutionary Marxists, and his ability to excite and mobilize the masses clearly set him apart from any other politician of his time. He differed from the Anarchists in that he was not an idealist, and from the Syndicalists because his disruptive tactics were devoid of mythicizing fervour. Rather, those tactics were guided by an ideological fluidity that made it possible to adapt them to different situations. What remained constant in Mussolini's invectives, however, was his hatred for parliamentary government and the Liberal state which he strove to undermine. To further this goal, Mussolini, as editor-in-chief of the party newspaper *Avanti!* ('Forward!'), persuaded Socialism to open its doors to the petty bourgeoisie and the subproletariat which until then had been active on the fringes of the workers' movement. He supported the organization of 'red blocs' whose purpose was simply to promote turmoil. Under Mussolini's leadership, Socialism had become a vehicle for the agitation and disturbances that culminated in the 'Red Week' of June 1914. In many respects the party took on an avant-garde character, similar to that of the Futurist Party which, motivated by a need to engage in concrete social struggle, also participated in street rallies and riots.

Although the general strike and insurrectional activity were short-lived, it emerged from the ensuing regional elections that the Socialist move to the left had a solid base. However, there was no revolution in sight. Order had been restored, as doubt reigned on both sides. The left was uncertain as to whether the proletariat had either the maturity or the ability to carry out a revolution, while the bourgeoisie appeared passive and undecided on how to respond to such a threat. Mussolini once again took advantage of the situation. He saw that the workers' movement was not prepared to go the full distance, but also that the Liberal state was unwilling to act forcefully in stopping the strikes and protests. Heeding the reactionary fervour building up within the bourgeoisie, he continued his call to revolution, but now it was not a particularly 'Socialist' or 'proletarian' revolution he expounded, but rather just 'revolution'.

Italy entered the First World War on 15 May 1915. At first the party, now back in the hands of Turati, preached 'neither collaboration nor sabotage', but as the war intensified, this position changed to one of wholehearted support for the Italian forces. Such enthusiasm came to an abrupt end in the autumn of 1917 with the defeat of Italian forces at the battle of Caporetto. Shortly thereafter news of the Russian Revolution reached Italy.

Socialism after the Russian Revolution

In the wake of these two crucial events, the party's left wing once again mobilized. The time was ripe for revolution and the Russians had provided the model. Lazzari and Nicola Bombacci urged the Italian troops to fight not against the enemy but against their own government. However, the soldiers, although sick of the war, could not, for the lack of a unifying ideological message and practical organization, be incited to overthrow the capitalist state.

Until 1918, the Socialist Party had been held together by virtue of such paradoxical ideological formulations as 'the party has to be reformist in order to be revolutionary and revolutionary in order to be reformist',[3] thereby eliminating the extremes of left and right in order to promote a functional unity. Now the great historical events called for clarity and resolve among the opposing factions. The time of debate and compromise had past. Socialism had to decide not only what it wanted but what it could and should pursue. In Russia, the Bolshevik revolution had transformed Socialist ideology into a reality; it was no longer possible to adhere to a programme which supported furthering Socialism through the existing organs of government. Given that the programme agreed upon in Genoa in 1892 had been rendered obsolete by historical events, it was necessary to set a different course.

In October 1919, the party met in Bologna to draft a new political agenda. The ideology that prevailed was neither reformist or ultra-revolutionary, but rather that of the 'maximalist electionists' which constituted a centre position within the party. It defended both the use of violence as a means of achieving power and the furthering of the principles underlying the Communist revolution in Russia from within the capitalist state. In contrast to the programme of 1892, which was based on the idea that pressure could be exerted on the ruling classes to accept Socialist policies, the new objective of the party was to create a state within the state as a means of ending bourgeois rule. For Italian Socialism this was both too little and too much. Although the new programme placed its emphasis on revolution, it also opted to work within the parliamentary system to create the conditions for bringing about the revolution. Therefore, in practice, it was much less a departure from reformist policies than it seemed in principle. At the same time, it also prevented the party from moving Liberal politics definitively to the left by taking hold of the government, since this would have entailed an alliance with the newly formed Popular Party, the first Catholic political party in Italy, led by the Sicilian priest Don Luigi Sturzo.

It is fair to say that, for the sake of party unity, Socialism missed its chance in 1919, either to overturn or to reform the capitalist state. There is no doubt that, in the aftermath of the war, Italian capitalism was under siege and – it appeared – on the verge of collapse. Strikes paralysed every sector of the economy; inflation ran rampant, demobilization left a whole generation of servicemen without a sense of purpose or a place in society, the treaty of Versailles took away the promised spoils of victory. But the 'revolution' which would put an end to the chaos was of a kind the Socialists could neither imagine nor effectively combat. It was a 'revolution' of 'reaction', generated in defence of bourgeois privilege, against proletarian demands, by a host of outcasts from the Liberal state. It crystallized in the Fascist coup d'état of October 1922. Under the guidance of Mussolini, it was able to use the debris left by the war to good advantage. Financed by landowners and big industry, the Fascists broke up strikes and conducted a series of punitive raids against local Socialist headquarters. Their strategy was simple and straightforward: do whatever was necessary to prevent a proletarian revolution.

The Communists

The Socialist Party now had to wage a physical battle against Fascism for which it was unprepared, while at the same time it had to decide how to respond to the well-organized Communist movement that had grown up in northern factories, especially in Turin. To force the party's hand even more, there came from Moscow the famous list of Twenty-One Points, conditions that had to be fulfilled by any party wanting to belong to the Third International. In essence, Moscow demanded that the party abandon its desire for unity and thus purify its ranks of all bourgeois and patriotic elements. The party held a special Congress at Livorno in January 1921 to vote on the matter. It resulted in the Communists, who unconditionally supported Moscow's Twenty-One points, leaving the party and founding the Italian Communist Party (PCI). The schism dealt a lethal blow to the Socialist movement, dividing allegiances throughout the country at both the political and trade-union levels. Henceforth, the history of Socialism in Italy would be marked by the relationship between two political parties, inspired by the same social ideology, which would represent the interests of more or less the same constituency.

The newly formed Communist Party was faced with the difficult task of creating a foundational ideology, which included defining its position in relation to the Socialist Party and to the Third International. Its architect was the most important Marxist thinker of the twentieth century, Antonio Gramsci. The Communist Party, as conceived by Gramsci, was the revolutionary party of the working class, actively engaged in uniting the masses and linking them integrally to the international Communist movement. The party's aim was to bring about a real revolution in opposition to the failed revolution of the Risorgimento. The ideological tension between Communism and those positions within Socialism against which it waged battle would be lessened not by rejecting them outright, but rather by historicizing them: that is, by showing, as Gramsci did, that what was once vital in them had now found its place in history within Communism. In relation to the party as such, Gramsci argued that it alone was the repository of Communism's moral and ethical substance and that, therefore, it was the guiding force of the Revolution. Hence the Communist Party, with Gramsci as its undisputed intellectual leader, took its distance from a now irreparably fragmented Socialist movement. It was inspired by a deep idealism and by the belief, supported by the Russian Revolution, that it was on the correct side of history.

Against Fascism

After the Livorno Congress, the Socialist Party had to wage its fight on two fronts: against the Communist heretics and against the strategic violence of Fascism which, in 1921, had intensified its raids against strikers and 'Bolshevik' strongholds, preparing the ground for its takeover of the government a year later. The fate of Socialism had been decided; the reasons for its failure can be best summed up perhaps in the words of Pietro Nenni, a future party leader: 'A revolution announced every day and every day postponed ends by being a beaten revolution. And slavery awaits the beaten.'[4] This rather simple assessment cuts to the heart of the matter. Socialism both defeated itself and was defeated because it was a party of intellectuals and politicians, skilled in debate, for whom 'revolution' was nothing more than a concept or, at best, a strong belief; it was defeated because it lacked both the will and the means to translate that concept into a practical means of waging an all-out physical (and moral) war against its adversaries; and it failed because it underestimated the will and the power of its enemies to do whatever was necessary to combat the threat it posed.

The Communist Party also had its part to play in the Socialist defeat. As far as it was concerned (at least initially), Fascism was nothing more than a pause in the march of history; it thus expended most of its energy in attacking what was left of the Reformists and Maximalists who, after the split and the Fascist coup, had regrouped in the Partito Socialista dei Lavoratori Italiani and the Partito Socialista Massimalista. Of these two configurations, the latter, having abandoned any attempt at compromise with the international Communist movement, directed its attention to impugning the intimidation and violence with which Fascism controlled parliament in the wake of the March on Rome. Its most eloquent spokesman was its secretary, Giacomo Matteotti, whose name became a symbol of anti-Fascism and of courage in the defence of Socialism and democratic government. After a virulent, extemporaneous attack on Fascism in the Chamber of Deputies, Matteotti was kidnapped and murdered in June 1924 by a squad of thugs commissioned by

Mussolini. The events that followed resulted in the defeat of parliamentary democracy and the beginning of Fascist dictatorial rule.

Matteotti was the first Socialist to understand the true nature of Fascism. His assassination marks the passage to a new Socialist orientation, one defined by a broadly anti-Fascist ethical base. The time had come for Socialism to abandon the ideals and myths on which the party was founded and enter into a new age with a new generation of minds as its spiritual and political leaders. Of the new, young, and distinctly anti-Fascist intellectuals who came to the forefront in the wake of Matteotti's death, two stand out for their courage, intelligence and moral commitment: Piero Gobetti and Carlo Roselli, both of whom were also killed by Fascist thugs. Gobetti was only twenty-four when he too was sentenced to death by Mussolini. A friend and associate of Gramsci in Turin, Gobetti was a brilliant and indefatigable journalist. In 1922, he founded the *Rivoluzione liberale*, a paper which expounded his ideal of an open-minded Communism devoid of dogma and receptive to anti-Fascists of all beliefs. His broad-based brand of anti-Fascism was, for its time, a utopian dream whose appeal remained strong for a few decades.

Like Gobetti, Carlo Roselli was another young Liberal intellectual who believed that Fascism could be defeated only through a revival of Socialism. He, however, was much more pragmatic and political than Gobetti. His was a Socialism whose principal task was to defeat Fascism through a resurgence of what was best in the Liberal and Republican heritage. Exiled in Paris, Rosselli created the Giustizia e Libertà group through which he voiced his idea of a liberal Socialism. 'Justice and Liberty' gradually took on the features of a political party, and, after the war, its adherents went on to form the Partito d'Azione ('Action Party'). Rosselli, with his brother Nello, would be murdered by Fascist agents in 1937.

The post-war period

In late 1925, after an unsuccessful attempt on Mussolini's life, Fascism put an end to what was left of democratic liberties in Italy. Socialists and Communists alike were either imprisoned, if not killed, or had to live in exile until 1943. During the intervening years much happened to determine the character of post-war Socialism. New leaders came forth to mend the rift between the two Socialist parties in a united front against Fascism, and it seemed possible, briefly, that the common enemy could also bring the Communists back into the fold. Pietro Nenni, who became the secretary of the newly reunited party in exile and the editor of the *Nuovo Avanti* ('New Forward'), was particularly instrumental in the unitary movement and in establishing ties with the Communists. Giuseppe Saragat was another new face who would become prominent in the party after the war. Saragat was a Liberal who came to Socialism after a career in banking. His objective, which he developed from an excellent knowledge of English Socialism, was to achieve a Socialist economy through parliamentary means. His was a Socialism based solely on economics, completely devoid of class hatred and revolutionary ideals.

Post-war Socialism would also draw on the distinguished history of the Italian partisan movement, particularly on the Resistance to Nazi rule over Northern Italy, in which both Communists and Socialists played the most decisive part. The Communists, who suffered the greatest repression under Fascism, formed the Garibaldi Brigades, and were the largest single political component of the Resistance. The Socialists came second under the banner of the 'Justice and Liberty' Brigades of the Action Party, which incorporated adherents to different Socialist and radical groups.

The relative unity achieved by the Socialist movement during exile and the Resistance was quick to dissolve after 1944. In the war's aftermath, the reconstituted party began a new course with the hope of having learned the lesson of past errors. Like the Partito d'Azione to its right and the Communists to its left, it supported the republic and was willing to work within the structures of democratic government to further its goals. Up until 1947, the pact that it formed in exile with the Communists remained intact. But as the relations between Soviet Russia and the Western powers deteriorated, the friction between Socialists and Communists intensified. The right wing of the party, led by Saragat, opposed unity of action with the Communists and eventually broke away to form the Partito Socialista dei Lavoratori Italiani ('Italian Workers' Socialist Party'), which in 1947 became the Italian Social Democratic Party. Ultimately, it came down to making a choice between Soviet Russia and the United States, which was busy financing the nation's reconstruction. Saragat and his followers chose what can be called the capitalist way to Socialism, that is, first the creation of wealth through the development of industry and agriculture, then the reform of institutions along Socialist lines. However, the majority of the party, now bearing the name of Partito Socialista Unità Proletaria (PSIUP, 'Socialist Party of Proletarian Unity'), remained faithful to the positions outlined by Nenni which stressed, if not unity, at least co-operation with the Communists. But as the Cold War developed, it became more and more difficult to carry out such a strategy. Expelled from the government in 1947, the Socialist and Communist Parties began fighting each other again, and by the end of 1948 the alliance between them had for all practical purposes completely dissolved. The elections of April of that year, in which both Communists and Socialists lost badly, left the Socialist Party in shambles. From this point on, with the implementation of the Marshall Plan and the Stalinization of the Soviet Union, the Socialist Party began its tormented journey towards the centre of Italian electoral politics, surrendering much of its rich heritage to the Communists.

Communist Party membership grew considerably in the late 1940s and early 1950s. It also brought within its sphere of influence numerous allied associations such as the Unione delle Donne Italiane ('Union of Italian Women') and the Lega delle Cooperative ('The League of Co-operatives'), which contributed to strengthening its position on the left. However, on account of the Cold War, and the absolute majority enjoyed by the Christian Democrats in parliament, the party was forced to the margins of Italian political life. Its isolation was the result of a concerted effort on the part of the government, helped by American money, and the Vatican. Part of this strategy involved the creation of non-Communist trade unions. Next to the largely Communist CGIL (Confederazione Generale Italiana del Lavoro, 'General Italian Confederation of Labour', created in 1943) rose the Social Democratic and Republican UIL (Unione Italiana del Lavoro, 'Italian Union of Labour') and the Catholic CISL (Confederazione Italiana Sindacati Lavoratori, 'Italian Confederation of Workers' Trade Unions'). These new politically oriented labour organizations, which had difficulty working together, considerably weakened the workers' movement, and as a result the influence of the Communist Party on labour. In 1949 the Church too contributed directly to intensifying the Cold War by excommunicating all Marxists. Isolation was also furthered from within the party, as its intellectuals reacted against the controls imposed on their ideas by the Soviet Union through the agency of the Party's Commissioner of Cultural Affairs, Emilio Sereni. A typical example of the strained relations between the party hierarchy and its intellectuals is the case of *Il politecnico*, a review founded by the novelist Elio Vittorini in 1945 with the purpose of initiating a debate on the meaning of culture. The journal hosted the writings of many Communist intellectuals who were active in the Resistance; its general goal was to bring Italy up to date on the development of European and American culture. This meant, in effect, the liberalization of party positions with regard to non-Marxist cultural practices. Vittorini's defence of the literary and artistic avant-garde, his open window on American culture and his rejection of Zhdanovism were repudiated by Palmiro Togliatti, one of the founders of the PCI and the chief architect of its policies throughout the Cold War period. *Il politecnico* was forced to close in early 1947 for the lack of party support. By 1950, although few intellectuals actually defected or were expelled from the party, dissatisfaction with its cultural politics was widespread. Only in 1951, when Sereni was replaced by Carlo Salinari, did tensions between intellectuals and the party hierarchy ease somewhat.

In the early 1950s, the PCI was controlled by Luigi Longo and Pietro Secchia, both old-guard Stalinists. Togliatti was not prepared to wage an effective war against the right wing of his party. After having survived an assassination attempt by a lone fanatic in 1948, he was almost killed two years later in a car accident from which it took him over a year to recover. But with the death of Stalin in March 1953 and the subsequent de-Stalinization of the USSR, Togliatti's moderate internal politics took hold once again. Giorgio Amendola replaced Secchia as head of the party's internal apparatus, while Togliatti, in the wake of Khrushchev's speech on Stalin's crimes (February 1956), attempted to steer a course between attributing Stalin's excesses to an excess of personal power and proclaiming the soundness of the Italian bureaucratic model.

Togliatti's politics of loyalty and independence with regard to the USSR were dealt a severe blow in October 1956 with the Soviet invasion of Hungary, which led to an extensive exodus of militants from the international Communist movement. Within the PCI, most of the leaders supported the Russian invasion, but numerous intellectuals left the party and disillusionment was widespread among the rank and file, especially in the South among peasants and workers whose faith in the Soviet Union was previously strong. It was estimated that some 400,000 members defected between 1955 and 1957.[5] Yet the party remained substantially intact, while outside of it developed currents of dissidence expressed in such journals as *Opinione* ('Opinion'), *Passato e presente* ('Past and Present') and, later, in the 1960s and 1970s, *Quaderni piacentini* ('Notebooks from Piacenza'), which became a major forum for the New Left. Although the rift between dissidents and the party hierarchy was widened by Togliatti's refusal to criticize the USSR, it was clear that, after the watershed events of 1956, the PCI had to become – and in fact became – more autonomous and Eurocentric in its outlook, less committed to

Communist orthodoxy and more liberal in its cultural politics, despite Togliatti's loyalty to Moscow.

The effect of 1956 on the Socialist Party was equally significant. The Russian invasion of Hungary, which the Socialists condemned outright, marked the end of the PSI's united front with the Communists. Henceforth it would act alone to fashion its own destiny in alliance with the Christian Democrats who, after the elections of 1958, with the emergence of Amintore Fanfani and Aldo Moro as party leaders, became committed to an opening to the left. The alliance was also made possible by the more liberal climate in Washington brought about by the Kennedy administration, by the liberalization of the Catholic Church at the hands of John XXIII, and by the 'economic boom' then taking hold, which prompted big business to support the move to the left. The Italian industrial giants believed that by assimilating the Socialists into the government they would be blocking the progress of the Communists. The centre–left coalition, however, was not successful. The struggle between the left and right factions within the Socialist Party and the general conservative reaction to the Catholics' move to the left weakened it considerably. The national elections of April 1963 proved, in fact, that the alliance would be less of a solution to the country's political problems than was expected, as significant losses were registered by both the Christian Democrats and the Socialists, while the Communist Party moved from 22 to 25.3 per cent of the vote.

In the summer of 1964, during a trip to the USSR, Togliatti died of a stroke. His death brought to an end the absolute rule of the party's old guard. Luigi Longo, a supporter of Togliatti's 'middle way' policies, took over as Party Secretary, but his role was generally that of a caretaker. Younger Communists, such as Giorgio Amendola and Pietro Ingrao, both sensitive to the realities of Italy's neo-capitalist economy, took important leadership roles within the party, respectively on the right and on the left. Amendola's position was that the country's opening to the left had failed. He believed that, with the imminent collapse of the centre–left alliance, the Socialists would be in a position to reunite with the PCI to form a new left-reformist bloc to correct the inequalities in Italian society. Ingrao, by contrast, did not believe that the party should abandon its Socialist principles in favour of democratic reformism, and saw the centre–left alliance as an attempt to integrate the working-class movement into the capitalist system. In his view, the party, on the one hand, had to react aggressively to reformism by taking charge of worker radicalism in the factories, and, on the other, to become more democratic internally. At the Party Congress held in January 1966, it became clear that Ingrao's supporters were in the minority; the party leadership, Longo and Enrico Berlinguer, regarded Ingrao's brand of radicalism as dangerous to the party's internal structure. Amendola, for his part, was forced to revise his reformist position. The party seemed impervious to the demands of a new culture of young workers and students which would make itself heard in the late 1960s. The moderate direction it would take was clearly marked by its acceptance of the Common Market and its support of the new Dubček government in Czechoslovakia. In 1969, the party publicly opposed the Soviet invasion, while its New Left group, headed by Ingrao and inspired by the spontaneous action of the workers in Prague, founded Il Manifesto group and a daily newspaper of the same name which supported the development of grassroots student and workers' organizations and the democratization of the party's internal operations. Il Manifesto was not the only revolutionary group that came into being after the Autumn of 1968, but it was the one that lasted the longest. In the early 1970s it tried to unite the extra-parliamentary left in a platform of non-violent, yet militant radicalism; having failed to do so, it formed Democrazia Proletaria ('Proletarian Democracy') with other dissidents on the left. The newspaper continued publication into the 1990s.

The 'historic compromise'

By 1970 the Communist Party had completely abandoned the principles of revolutionary change on which it was founded in 1921. While it was still committed to the realization of a Socialist society, it no longer believed in the idea of the dictatorship of the proletariat. The roads to Socialism, as Czechoslovakia and China had shown, could be varied, and the Soviet model was no longer useful in the industrialized West. Instead, the party maintained that in order to succeed in realizing Socialist principles it was necessary to work within the parliamentary system and in coalition with other political parties. Such a change in Communist ideology made possible what became known as the 'historic compromise', an initiative taken by the party to safeguard against the possibility that the reaction under way against the student and worker protests would lead to a rightist coup, similar to the one that brought down Allende in Chile. Its architect was Enrico Berlinguer, elected Party Secretary in 1972. The 'compromise' involved forming an alliance with the Christian Democrats based on what Berlinguer believed were compatibilities in their moral systems, chiefly their common opposition to the wholly materialist and consumerist nature of late capitalism. Through such an alliance, Socialism, Berlinguer argued, could be achieved. It is generally acknowledged that Berlinguer's arguments were flawed because they were based on an unrealistic appraisal of the Christian Democrat Party which represented the capitalist and conservative forces the 'compromise' intended to combat.[6] It is understandable that the 'historic compromise' was regarded by many on the left as the assimilation of the party by the neo-capitalist hegemony. The bargaining with the Christian Democrats, as well as the party's overtures to the Social Democratic and Communist parties of Western Europe, in an effort to build Socialism through large-scale reforms within the capitalist system, were no small factors in accounting for the disaffection with party politics which led to the political terrorism on the left that characterized the 1970s. Moreover, the party endeavoured to show the electorate that it was committed to the parliamentary system and a defender of law and order. It supported repressive police measures against the student movement and the groups that formed the extra-parliamentary left; in so doing, it unwittingly promoted the conditions for Red terrorist violence.[7]

The party's move to the right, supported by its new, non-revolutionary image, succeeded in attracting large numbers of young middle-class voters. The PCI made large gains in the local elections of 1975, and in the national elections of the following year it received 34.4 per cent of the vote, an increase of 7.2 per cent over the previous election, a mere 4.3 per cent less than the Christian Democrats and 24.8 per cent more than the PSI. With such a strong show of popular support, the party gained considerable bargaining power which translated into a number of committee chairs in the Chamber of Deputies and in the Senate, and in the election of Pietro Ingrao as Speaker of the Chamber of Deputies.[8]

The Craxi years

If 1976 witnessed a remarkable rise in the appeal of the Communist Party, it also marked the start of the period known as 'gli anni di piombo' ('the years of the bullet', 1976–80) as Red terrorist activity reached its all-time high. Among numerous political killings and 'kneecappings', the most infamous terrorist event was the kidnapping by the Red Brigades in March 1978 of Aldo Moro, President of the DC, and his 'execution' at their hands two months later. Moro was a left-leaning Christian

Democrat and strong advocate of co-operation with the Communists. His lifeless body was found in the boot of an abandoned car on a street midway between the DC and PCI headquarters, stressing the political symbolism of the kidnapping. On the matter of negotiating with the terrorists for Moro's life, the Communists were intransigent in their policy of 'no compromise', while the PSI, now under the leadership of Bettino Craxi, were in favour of an exchange of prisoners. The Christian Democrats, although divided, also chose to stand firm. The state's refusal to negotiate marked the beginning of the end of terrorist activity in Italy. Although the killings continued into 1980, the Red Brigades had lost all the support they might have had among militant workers and students, becoming more and more isolated, and finally succumbing to the anti-terrorist offensive of General Carlo Alberto Della Chiesa.

The electoral success of the 'historic compromise' was short-lived. From an ideological standpoint, the party had entered into the political establishment, but it did not gain entry into the government. For, with Moro dead, it had no strong Catholic advocate to help combat the influence exerted by the United States on the Christian Democrats to prevent Communist participation. The PCI would never again win such a high percentage of the vote as it did in 1976; its numbers would gradually diminish in the face of the growing appeal of the Radical Party on the left and the newly organized Socialist Party on the right which, under Craxi's leadership, had discarded all traces of its Marxist heritage in favour of Social-Democratic programmes, designed to gain the support of a rising professional class of businessmen and bureaucrats who were interested more in individual gain than in collective welfare. Craxi's Socialist Party, now allied with the Christian Democrats, went on to establish itself at the centre of Italian politics. In wake of the scandal regarding the P2, a clandestine Masonic lodge engaged in subversive anti-Communist activity, which embarrassed and demoralized the DC, and with the PCI licking its wounds from the defeat of the 'historic compromise', in August 1983 Bettino Craxi became the first Socialist Prime Minister of Italy.

While the Socialists, fuelled by Craxi's political skill, became in the 1980s a dominant force in Italian politics, the Communist Party, owing to the decline of Communism in the West but particularly to its inability to renew its political ideology after the death of Berlinguer in 1984, faded into the background. The collapse of Communism in the Soviet Union and in Eastern Europe put an end to all hopes for the party's resurgence. In 1990, the Partito Comunista Italiano, the largest

Communist Party in the West and the force behind the economic progress made by the working class after the defeat of Fascism, was dissolved. Its more moderate members went on to form the Democratic Party of the Left (PDS). The end of the Cold War also created the conditions for the demise of Craxi's Socialist Party. Since it was no longer possible to exploit the fear of Communism, there was no need to create a safe anti-Communist majority, and in the midst of a nationwide campaign to crack down on political corruption, Craxi, along with other prominent politicians and Socialist Party members, was convicted of receiving billions of lire in illegal bribes. He escaped to Tunisia, pending appeal against his eight-year prison sentence.

The success of the PDS in the elections of 1992 and 1994, together with that of the Rifondazione Comunista, which housed those members of the PCI who opposed the change in symbols and ideology, showed that Communism was not yet ready to disappear from the Italian political spectrum, as it had been prophesied. Instead, it was the Socialist Party, devastated by the corruption scandals, which passed out of sight.

NOTES

1. Renato Zangheri, *Storia del socialismo italiano* (Turin: Einaudi, 1993), vol. I, pp. 9–18.
2. Cited in Wayland Hilton-Young, *The Italian Left* (Westport, Conn.: Greenwood Press, 1975), pp. 28–9.
3. Gaetano Arfé, *Storia del socialismo italiano* (Turin: Einaudi, 1965), p. 253.
4. Hilton-Young, *The Italian Left*, p. 133.
5. Paul Ginsborg, *A History of Contemporary Italy* (London: Penguin Books, 1990), p. 207.
6. Ibid., p. 357.
7. Ibid., p. 381.
8. Alexander De Grand, *The Italian Left in the Twentieth Century* (Bloomington and Indianapolis: University of Indiana Press, 1987), p. 157.

FURTHER READING

De Felice, Renzo, *Le interpretazioni del Fascismo*. Rome and Bari: Laterza, 1970.
De Grand, Alexander, *Italian Fascism*. Lincoln: University of Nebraska Press, 1985.
Spriano, Paolo, *Storia del partito comunista italiano*. Rome: Editori Riuniti, 1969.
Tasca, Angelo, *Nascita e avvento del fascismo*. Florence: La Nuova Italia, 1950.
Vialiani, Leo, *Il partito socialista nel periodo della neutralità*. Milan: Feltrinelli, 1963.
Zangheri, Renato, *Storia del socialismo italiano*. Turin: Einaudi, 1963.

7

Other voices: contesting the status quo

Introduction

No word occurs more frequently in any discussion of Italian affairs than 'anomalous'. Italy is conventionally held to be anomalous in many spheres: in the nature of its party system; in the democratic but one-party government which held power throughout the life of the First Republic; in its inability to suppress the systematic use of violence in its territory and to secure for the state what Durkheim termed a 'monopoly of violence'; in its incapacity to construct trusted and efficient institutions; in the mixture of covert and public forces by which the country has been governed; and, underlying all of these, in its idiosyncratic attribution of legitimacy. The process of gaining and conceding legitimacy was, for Max Weber, fundamental to the acceptance of the operation of power in any body politic. Legitimacy is the validation and normalization in a given time and culture of the right to rule. Since it exists at the level of perceptions, ideas, ethics and culture, legitimacy is a relative notion subject to change, not an objective standard to be weighed empirically. Nor is it an absolute, transcendent concept which remains unaltered in time. The self-image of individuals or groups in society alters, and with it the limits of their willingness to underwrite the legitimacy of a particular system of governance. It is a mere cliché to assert that women in the 1990s do not see their social role in the same terms as did their forebears and that, as a consequence, the nature of the polity which they are prepared to view as legitimate has inevitably undergone change. The same is true, if in less dramatic form, of other constituent parts of the Italian body politic.

Every state is an arena of competing voices and interests, whose rivalry will be settled, in a Lockean liberal democracy, inside an accepted framework of law and within given institutions. Such a settlement is not always possible, as the concession of certain demands in unmodified form would shatter the existing social contract. The nature of dissent from the status quo has varied throughout Italian history, with some dissident groups denying all validity to the existing system, and others, more modestly, complaining only of their own exclusion. Not all those who *de facto* dispute the state's monopoly of legitimacy do so in the name of a rival ideology. For many Italian citizens, the state produced by the Risorgimento settlement was, and would remain, either 'absent' or an adversary. Distrusted by its subjects, the Italian state has had to contend with an animus towards it which has no parallel among other European nations. The celebrated words of d'Azeglio – that once Italy had been made, it was time to make the Italians – underlined this lack of popular cohesiveness.

Strong regional identities militated against the sense of nation. As late as the 1960s, Danilo Dolci found Sicilian peasants who had never heard of Italy, while Antonio Gramsci branded the Risorgimento a 'failed revolution' which had been unable to construct a 'national-popular' culture. In Gramsci's analysis, the culture of the new Italy had failed in one fundamental purpose, that of forging a complex of values capable of welding together a society and making it what Benedict Anderson would later term an 'imagined community'.[1] The refusal of federalism during the Risorgimento, the imperialist adventures in Libya, the intervention in the First World War, Mussolini's attempted suppression of dialects, were all attempts to make an Italy which had never been willed into full being. On the other hand, dissident voices were heard throughout the period. The history of 'other voices' in the post-Risorgimento period is the history of one side of a multi-faceted struggle between those who wished to make, and those who wished to un-make, or re-make, Italy.

This chapter aims to study the views of groups and movements which, explicitly or implicitly, at different times and in contrasting ways, contested the legitimacy of the prevailing status quo in the Italian state or in Italian civil society. Discussion will be focused on such diverse bodies as the Catholic Church, which over the course of a century moved from a position of exclusion to one of dominance, and subsequently to a position as no more than one of several influential power blocs in society; the mafia, which can be seen as a state within a state; the extra-parliamentary left and terrorist groups which sought to overthrow the existing structures of society; the various regional Leagues in Northern Italy which aim to undo the Risorgimento; and, perhaps most crucially, the women's movement.

Church and state: the cold war

In strictly historical terms, the first and strongest of the voices of the excluded was the voice of the religion to which the majority of Italians proclaimed their allegiance. At its foundation, the state encountered a denial of legitimacy from the Church. On the seizure of Rome in 1870, Pope Pius IX declared himself a 'prisoner in the Vatican' and with the Papal Bull *Non expedit* forbade Catholics to participate in the affairs of state. The secular, anti-clerical nature of the dominant Liberal Party left the forces of Church and state drawn up for their own 'cold war'. The Church's opposition declined over the years only because it saw more pernicious enemies on the horizon. The Gentiloni Pact (1913), drafted by the Catholic Count of that name, was an accord between Catholic laymen and certain Liberal candidates which upheld the idea of the family and proclaimed hostility to divorce. Catholics were allowed to vote in the elections held that year, but only for candidates who aligned themselves with the pact.

Don Luigi Sturzo's Partito Popolare ('Popular Party'), founded in 1919 and suppressed by the Fascists in 1926, was the first genuinely Catholic party, but it encountered the hostility of the Vatican. Only with the formation of the Democrazia Cristiana (DC), the Christian Democrat Party, in the immediate aftermath of the Second World War, was a Catholic party established with the Church's benediction. The subsequent domination of the state by that party makes it easy to forget that the entry of the Catholic masses into political life, and the accession of their representatives to power, was a revolution in itself. The state which had been the enemy was now in captivity; the excluded were now the masters. Between the elections of 1947 and 1992, the DC was able to exercise its version of one-party rule. Its value for its more powerful allies was that it made Italy a bulwark against Communism; however, this strength was also a weakness. Once the Berlin Wall crumbled, so too did the DC and the régime it headed.

Initially, the DC split into two principal parts: the Centro Cristiano Democratico ('Democratic Christian Centre'), which allied itself with

Berlusconi and the right, and the left-leaning Partito Popolare; but there were schisms in both camps. The situation was further complicated by the announcement in February 1998 by the former President, Francesco Cossiga, that he was to form his own party. The Union for the Defence of the Republic (UDR), however, was not conceived as an exclusively Catholic grouping. The 'single party for all Catholics' has vanished and will not be revived.

The disintegration of the post-war Catholic bloc had been under way at least since the 1974 referendum on divorce, but the new position of the Church vis à vis the state is undoubtedly the main change between the political life of the First and Second Republics. This change may bring closer to realization the hopes of enlightened Risorgimento politicians, such as Sidney Sonnino, who aspired to a situation where the voice of the Church was neither unheard nor dominant. The three democratic régimes which have held power since unification correspond to three phases in the relationship between Church and state, and in the measure of legitimacy accorded by the former to the latter. Under the Kingdom of Italy, with the Liberal Party supreme, Catholics were excluded, or excluded themselves, from the exercise of power, and in turn denied legitimacy to the secular state; under the First Republic, with the Christian Democrats in the ascendancy, Catholics enjoyed a position of supremacy; under the Second Republic, Catholics are part of the structure of power, but without special privileges. This mutual concession of legitimacy represents an equilibrium not previously attained.

Power sharing with the mafia

During the First Republic, the Christian Democrats ruled in open coalition with other parties of the centre–left or centre–right, but also practised a covert version of power-sharing with more sinister forces. The exact course of this collaboration cannot, of its nature, be satisfactorily chronicled; however, historians and journalists have done much to uncover the co-operation between ministries and masonries – the most famous being the P2 Masonic Lodge of Licio Gelli – as well as between elected politicians and subversive right-wing, neo-Fascist organizations. Connivance with Italy's organized crime syndicates is, or was, of a different order, if only because these organizations have a social base which the Lodges and the terrorist cells never had.

Power-sharing with organized crime syndicates like the Sicilian mafia, the Neapolitan camorra and the Calabrian 'ndrangheta had the paradoxical effect of heightening the legitimacy of these bodies while lessening that of the body politic. The distrust in which the state was held was increased by the knowledge that, while its public figures proclaimed their dedication to ideals of justice and equity, the state was actually run by a continual infringement of these values. The cohabitation with the mafia and organized crime, already apparent in the immediate post-1860 period, meant that corruption and the toleration of violence were intrinsic to the exercise of power in large parts of Italy.

The mafia does not proclaim anything so abstract as an alternative philosophy, but it does embody a different voice and an alternative view of honour, wealth and power. Scholars of mafia activity from Henner Hess to Pino Arlacchi, as well as such *pentiti* (ex-mafiosi turned state evidence) as Tommaso Buscetta, have enabled a code of mafia belief and practice, and a hierarchy of mafia values, to be drawn up. The mafia must be viewed as being, in the anthropological sense, a culture. For some observers (notably Hess), the mafia was never more than that. The debate over whether the mafia was a hierarchical organization or something more amorphous can be taken to have been definitively settled by Buscetta's revelations. The mafia has indeed a structure of command, as even such previous opponents of this viewpoint as Pino Arlacchi have recognized.

Nevertheless, the fact that some commentators were mistaken in asserting that the mafia was an *exclusively* cultural entity, to which one belonged by osmosis, not by initiation, cannot be taken as refutation of the existence of a mafia culture, or counter-culture. The mafia represents a degenerate form of the culture of Sicily, itself the product of centuries of conquest by invaders. When power in the state is held by outsiders, the tendency everywhere is to turn inwards, to trust only those linked by blood or adherence to common customs. The family became the only unit accorded unquestioning trust by Sicilians, so that, in Leonardo Sciascia's much-discussed *mot*, 'the family is the state of the Sicilian.' This view of the family and the state was only one among many instances of the failed meeting of minds between North and South which followed the Risorgimento. Piedmontese law, imposed on Sicily after the 1860 landing at Marsala, was founded on a notion of the state derived from the French Revolution and from European Liberalism. The historical and cultural inheritance of the nineteenth-century proto-mafiosi, on the other hand, was formed by their experience of an island familiar only with rule imposed by force and, consequently, of a state denied all legitimacy by those who regarded themselves as its subjects and not its citizens. The cult of the family in such circumstances easily degenerated into the 'amoral familism' which Edward Banfield identified, and deplored, as cause and symptom of the mafia.[2]

In Sciascia's view, Sicilians, whether mafiosi or not, had experienced the state only as repression, law only as the arbitrary whim of the despot and reason only as cunning. However, for trying to explain – not defend – the attitudes of his fictional mafia boss in *The Day of the Owl*, don Mariano Arena, Sciascia was attacked after his death and accused of being bewitched by evil. Paradoxically, one of his detractors, Pino Arlacchi, had also delved into the cultural hinterlands of mafia behaviour, pointing out that, unlike what occurred in developed capitalist societies, the notion of honour was the basic unit of currency in a mafia culture. Other observers have underlined the fundamental importance of the cultural concept of *omertà*, deriving from the Latin *homo* (man), which has declined from its original connotations of maleness, or manliness, to indicate the iron code of silence to be maintained by Sicilians in any dealings with the Law. This practice may have originally represented an imperative of any conquered people in the face of overlords, but it came to underwrite mafia power. None of these considerations implies, as Buscetta has done, that there ever was a golden age of a Robin-Hood mafia, but they are a recognition that there is a specific mafia mindset which positively sanctions deviation from conventionally accepted norms in a way the outlook of ordinary criminals does not. Making all allowance for mendacity and hypocrisy, the statement from mafia boss Genco Russo to Danilo Dolci that he spent his time resolving disputes is an expression of the enduring reliance on interpersonal contact which is the reverse side of the widespread distrust of state institutions.[3]

In the three phases of its development – rural, urban and entrepreneurial – identified by commentators, the mafia has presented a challenge to the monopoly of violence which was, for Durkheim, the fundamental right and duty of the state. Only in the 1990s did the mafia find itself under sustained assault. The greater vigour of police and magistrates in pursuing the mafia is itself a symptom of the changed status and diminished legitimacy of the mafia in the eyes of Sicilians themselves. The 1990s Cosa Nostra had more in common with other forms of international gangsterism than with earlier versions of the mafia, and no longer had those ready links with its social roots which were once part of its being. Its contemporary power is based on the inculcation of fear, not on an interclass, Sicilian solidarity. Its cultural legitimacy is at an end, although that does not mean that its power has been smashed, since the mafia is still a financial power and an armed force. Culture or not, the mafia was and is also a barbaric, exploitative, violent organization whose legitimacy derived in part from the exploitation of *sicilianismo*, a self-interested, quasi-nationalistic ideology which saw in any attack on aspects of Sicilian life, including its organized criminality, an offence against Sicily itself. The Christian Democrat Party, cultivating its own self-interest, made routine use of the mafia to 'encourage' voters to support it and, in return, facilitated the one process which was of genuine interest to the mafia, the accumulation and maximization of wealth. The relationship was an alliance between two (almost) equal forces, a meeting of two cultures, and not the relationship between feudal lord and vassal. It will be interesting to see how the mafia will adapt to the political realities of the Second Republic.

Remaking Italy: the terrorist strategy

The terrorism which affected Italy in the 1970s and early 1980s was fractured and fissured, not only in that Italy faced parallel, simultaneous campaigns of the right and left, but also in the sheer variety of formations operating on both sides. Tullio Barbato counted over 180 distinct groups at the height of the campaign.[4] The terrorist campaign itself can be regarded as spanning the years from the neo-Fascist bombing of the Banca Nazionale dell'Agricoltura in Milan, on 12 December 1969, to the kidnapping by the Red Brigades of General Dozier, on 17 December 1981.

Leaving aside considerations of political morality, the terrorists must be numbered among those who aimed to unmake and remake Italy. They too made a claim to legitimacy based on an inheritance of ideology and mythology from Italy's past. In the case of the neo-Fascist groups, the genealogical line is clear. The 'strategy of tension' was a replay of the campaign of violence practised by Mussolini's *squadristi*. The objective was to create chaos, so arousing demands for the appointment of a 'strong man' to restore order. The P2 Masonic Lodge, presided over by Licio Gelli who was one of Mussolini's henchmen in the Duce's last days, played a significant part in organizing the campaign, highlighting the continuity between late Fascism and its 1970s version. The relationship of the left-wing groups to Italian history was more complex. Their primary source of myth was the Resistance. Giangiacomo Feltrinelli's GAP (Gruppi di azione proletaria, 'Groups of Proletarian Action'), the first of the groups to be formed, presented themselves as a reconstitution of the partisan group with the same initials, and gave as their aim the defence of Italy from reversion to Fascism. Resistance practice provided justification for acts of violence and murder which would have been dismissed as 'adventurism' in orthodox Marxism-Leninism. While the jargon-laden communiqués talked of the power of systems such as the 'SIM', the Imperialist State of the Multinationals, their victims were individual journalists, magistrates and industrialists.

The terrorists were the product of Italian history and society. Attempts to demonstrate that they were willed into being by the *fiat* of the Kremlin or of the Pentagon have been unsuccessful. In the short term, their roots were to be found in the disaffection and militancy which flowed from the 'events of May' 1968 in Paris and from the 'hot autumn' in Italy the following year. The political commentator Giorgio Bocca pointed to deeper roots when he coined the designation *cattocomunisti*, 'Catho-communists',[5] to indicate the mixture of Marxist politics and the absolutist ethic of Catholicism in terrorist ideology. Both of these were part of the Italian heritage, and both Church and party had, at some stage, denied the legitimacy of the state. Although disowned by the Italian Communist Party (PCI), the Red Brigades inherited a myth of revolution from the unreformed, pre-Berlinguer PCI. From the *svolta di Salerno*, the 1944 declaration in which the Communist leader Palmiro Togliatti announced that he would accept the rules of parliamentary democracy, through a gradual process of internal 'destalinization' to the 1968 condemnation of the invasion of Prague and the break with Moscow, the PCI followed its own determined path towards the acceptance of Liberal, pluralist democracy. The party, however, had a tendency to deny rather than confront its own past. It was established PCI leaders – Ingrao, Secchia, Amendola – and not New-Left theorists who had advocated 'revolution not reform'. Left-wing terrorists in the 1970s were able to maintain that their campaign of violence was 'revolutionary' and in keeping with authentic Communist traditions which had been betrayed by the clique of class-collaborators surrounding Enrico Berlinguer.

The terrorists were dismissed by Umberto Eco as nineteenth-century relics, unaware of the nature and complexity of twentieth-century power.[6] The truth of Eco's scornful analysis was demonstrated by the curious respect for the Italian state shown by the Red Brigades. The dispersal of power, characteristic of globalization, seems to have escaped them, as did the weakness and incompetence of the Italian state. The encounter in captivity between the former Christian Democrat Prime Minister, Aldo Moro, and his kidnappers is illuminating for the clash it dramatized between pure ideology and the pragmatic belief in politics as management which was the quintessential DC genius. For Moro – imbued with the refusal of idealism, the distrust of reason divorced from tradition, and the quasi-pessimism which underlies all conservative thought from Burke and de Maistre onwards—the task of governance consisted in compromise, in unending negotiations, in continuity viewed as a value in itself. Moro was the object of Pasolini's scorn[7] for his famously tortuous prose which led him on one occasion to adopt the meaningless phrase about the PCI and the DC being on two 'converging parallels'; yet he was also the architect of the agreement which brought the PCI into the area of government. The Moro kidnapping, viewed at the time as the supreme proof of the strategic genius of the Red Brigades, actually marked the point at which their self-belief began to wane and their voice lost credibility.

The Leagues and the anti-Risorgimento

The declared and explicit project of the Northern League is to reshape and remake the Italian state produced by the Risorgimento. One of the central debates among the leaders and thinkers of the nineteenth-century unification process was whether the new Italy should break with its diversified past, whether power should be centralized or devolved, whether Italy should be a unitary or a federal state. The unitary line, promoted by Cavour (1810–61), was victorious over the federalist policy promoted most strongly by Carlo Cattaneo (1801–69). Umberto Bossi, the charismatic leader of the movement, has carefully constructed a lineage for the League aimed at presenting it not as threateningly novel and iconoclastic, but as the natural heir to a tradition. Apart from acknowledging a debt to Cattaneo, he has identified the League, in its opposition to constituted power and to corruption, as the heir of the Resistance; he has chosen the medieval Lombard *condottiere* Alberto da Giussano as the emblem to be carried on all League banners, and made the small town of Pontida, where the thirteenth-century Lombard *comuni* took an oath to resist the German Emperor Barbarossa, the venue for the League's grand ceremonial gatherings.

Paradoxical though it may be, Mack Smith's definition of Cavour as a 'conservative revolutionary'[8] could be applied to Bossi, who is radical in politics but conservative in economics. The economic policies of the League are those of the New Right in Europe and North America; it adheres to market economics with Thatcherite fervour, has led a fiscal revolt against high taxation and advocates the reduction of state power. The Northern League has no overall political ideology distinct from the federalist proposal, but in Italian politics that approach is genuinely radical. The electoral success of the League compelled other parties, at least for a time, to re-examine their constitutional priorities. The anomaly is that the voice advocating federalism speaks with the accents of the rich, powerful North and not those of the poorer South. Apart from Cattaneo, previous advocates of federalism, such as the Sardinian Emilio Lussu (1890–1975), were from the Mezzogiorno, and were anxious to redress an asymmetry of power and privilege. The League did not create Italy's North–South divide; however, especially in its earlier phases, it unscrupulously adopted an anti-Southern, quasi racist rhetoric, and its policies accentuate rather than lessen difference.

At their formation, the Venetian and Lombard Leagues benefited from the disdain in which the Italian state and the traditional parties were held. Founded in April 1984, the Lombard League has grown with a rapidity which is probably without parallel in European politics. In 1987 it won 3 per cent of the vote in Italy overall, which gave it two seats in the Italian parliament. In February 1991, it united with other Leagues in Northern Italy to form the Lega Nord, which took 8.2 per cent of the vote nationwide in the 1992 elections. In 1994, after elections which it fought in an acrimonious alliance with Silvio Berlusconi's Forza Italia, members of the League entered government, but Bossi quickly withdrew from the coalition, bringing down Berlusconi's administration. Some members left, but the League confounded its critics by its strong showing in the 1996 elections.

The fundamental policies of the League have altered in keeping with Bossi's mercurial character. Initially, the League sought a federal solution to the impasse of Italian politics, but was concerned only with securing for Lombardy a financially autonomous status which would free it of the burden of contributing to less developed regions. By the early 1990s, this policy had shifted to one of overall federalism with a division of Italy into three macro-regions: the North or Padania, the South or Mezzogiorno and the Centre, which had no settled name. In 1995, Bossi announced that federalism was not enough and advocated the secession of Padania. The referendums on devolution in Scotland and Wales caused further alteration in policy, and at the Congress in Varese in July 1999, he declared that the League was aiming for 'devolution, Scottish-style'.

Internal tensions and contradictions within the Northern League came to the surface in the late 1990s. Padania as such had no history, no common memory, no culture of the sort the Lombards, the Piedmontese and the inhabitants of the Veneto claim for their own regions. These localist feelings were particularly strong in the Veneto, whose Liga Veneta was founded before the Lega Lombarda, and where the Northern League had had its strongest showing in the 1996 elections. Fabrizio Comencini, leader of the movement, had never hidden his doubts over Bossi, and in autumn 1998 he denounced him as a tyrant and a traitor. In the ensuing fracas, he led the Liga Veneta out of the Northern League, and declared that the former would struggle for the autonomy of the Veneto alone.

The Northern League can claim the principal credit for ending the discredited and corrupt régime of the First Republic. Bossi succeeded where the left-wing groupings of the 1960s and 1970s failed. He established a force which was electorally credible, which appealed to voters disillusioned with the status quo but distrustful of any alternative which appeared socially and politically too revolutionary. For a time, it seemed that the League and the magistrates involved in the *mani pulite* ('clean hands') anti-corruption drive were two sides of a pincer movement; both attacked the old parties, the magistrates in the name of the law, the League in the name of a new order. Although Bossi later turned on the magistrates, it was no accident that both the League and the magistrates most involved in incriminating the old order were based in the same city. The history of the new Republic, whatever form it eventually takes, had its origin in Milan. However unlikely the prospect of the political dissolution of Italy may be, the success of Bossi does demonstrate the continuing fragility of the cultural unity of the Republic, and the discordance of the voices still heard inside it.

Feminism

The demand for women's rights – the vote, civic and legal equality – has consistently challenged Italy's unitarian and democratic credentials. Church and state have both sought to stabilize society by emphasizing the family and women's role within it. If the strength of traditional patriarchal culture meant a comparatively forlorn movement for emancipation in the early years of the new state, the political crises of the

1960s and 1970s, on the other hand, led to the emergence of one of the West's most forceful Feminist movements. A dual stress on philosophical theory and political praxis stressed women's legitimate position within the institutions of the state, while radically questioning the misogynistic structures of power.

Unification

The ambition of the Risorgimento as conceived by Giuseppe Mazzini (1805–72) was both to create a new nation-state and to bring about the social and moral regeneration of all its citizens, including women. Mazzini's patriotic notion of political freedom and national unity was predicated on releasing women from ignorance and servitude. The united nation, modelled on the family, required the social, civil and political emancipation of women as well as of working men. However, Mazzini's idealism and his familial metaphor suggest not a departure from, but a reaffirmation of, women's traditional roles; as 'mothers to the nation' they should distance themselves from the moral and intellectual squalor which prevented them from playing their full part in the new Italy.

The reality of most women's lives was much less inspiring. While the condition of women in the new state varied somewhat between regions, their disadvantageous economic, political and juridical status was reinforced by the new national legal code. A wife was not permitted to administer her own property or to have a bank account without her husband's permission. She had few rights with regard to her children, while the prevailing morality led to a notorious double standard, reinforced by the law, in sexual matters: women could swiftly be accused of adultery, while a patriarchal notion of honour left largely crimes of passion committed by men unpunished. Yet women contributed substantially to the Italian labour market, employed in textiles and silk production, spinning and weaving, as well as agriculture, for a fraction of the male wage and in largely unregulated conditions. Illiteracy levels, high across the nation, were worse for women. The new nation clearly needed a more educated workforce – however rudimentary that education – and jobs such as schoolteaching and telegraph operating soon became filled by girls from the lower and middle classes. While exact statistics are unobtainable, it is hard to overestimate the scale of women's work, whether in the fields, the factories, schools or the home. It is arguable that the modest industrial revolution achieved by Italy was rooted in exploitative working conditions for women. There was a vast gulf between their contribution to the nation through work and the minimal rights accorded them by the state.

The questione femminile

Feminism emerged later in Italy than in Britain or France, where political and industrial revolution had profoundly shaken the *anciens régimes*, or the USA, where the anti-slavery movement had led to a parallel analysis of the condition of women. Early philanthropic interventions on behalf of women in Italy, in the second half of the nineteenth century, aimed to improve standards of education for girls and combat illiteracy, and many of these early emancipationists had their intellectual and ideological roots in Mazzini's moral and secular Republicanism. The *questione femminile* gathered momentum as women gained experience in the new factories that were becoming established in northern cities, while the Italian Socialist Party, which returned its first candidate to Parliament in 1892, began to organize in favour of workers' rights. A range of positions began to develop around the new term 'Feminism', which entered Italian usage through women's magazines such as *La donna* ('The Woman'). Indeed, 'the introduction of the term and its widespread use indicates a significant shift: feminism is of its very nature extraneous to the various political formations.'[9] While Radical, Socialist and Catholic Feminists differed over questions affecting the family, such as divorce, all agreed on the need for improved access to education and to the professions, for the issue of prostitution to be addressed, for working conditions to be regulated, and for some form of maternity leave to be conceded.

The question of suffrage

With the development of the industrial infrastructure in Italy, changing patterns of work coincided with the rise of left-wing movements such as Anarchism and, more importantly, Socialism. As women flowed into the new factories, so they began to be conscious of a double exploitation both at work and in their social and domestic roles. Yet the demand for suffrage caused the fledgling Socialist Party an acute dilemma. Turati's closest female associate, Anna Kuliscioff, persistently reminded the party of the gender equality envisaged by Marxism. Turati could hardly oppose votes for male workers in the new factories, but to support votes for women was considered politically too dangerous, a move which might not only hand votes to less progressive parties, but which might also be greeted with less than enthusiasm by Socialist supporters. Early industrial workers sought a level of wages with which to support the family, not emancipation which they feared would destroy it. Italian suffrage remained extremely narrow until well into the twentieth century, when, in 1913, Giolitti massively expanded the vote at the time of the Gentiloni pact, a manoeuvre designed largely to end the Catholic boycott of the new state. But suffrage still did not extend to women. While some Catholics over the next few years were to make common cause with Luigi Sturzo's Partito Popolare – one of the few strands of Italian politics, together with small groups of Liberals and Feminists, to endorse women's suffrage – the Vatican remained implacably hostile.

Other Feminisms

Other Feminists, such as Anna Maria Mozzoni (1840–1920), adopted a different strategy from Kuliscioff's, arguing for the question of women's emancipation to be considered apart from trade-union and class discourse. For Mozzoni – political activist, writer and indefatigable promoter of women's rights and suffrage – Feminism should retain its own agenda and not be subsumed within a wider struggle. Mozzoni analysed women's social, economic and juridical inferiority, arguing, as had Mazzini, for the Risorgimento to be made complete by the absorption of women into the modern progressive state through education, work and the introduction of divorce. She battled for equal pay as early as 1863, translated John Stuart Mill's *On the Subjection of Women* in 1870, and was a leading contributor to the journal *La donna*, founded by Adelaide Beccari in 1869, which brought together women whose demands for emancipation were based on Mazzinian ideals of humanity and equality. Post-unification Italy, however, was largely hostile to women's issues and the demand for emancipation. The country's drive to modernize was fettered by an increasingly stagnant economy. Mozzoni, like Sibilla Aleramo, sought to arouse the middle-class female consciousness and to separate bourgeois women from an exclusively domestic role, even while the torpor of the Italian economy and the weight of tradition left little possibility for the expansion of women's work into the professions. The failure to win suffrage in 1912 was a serious defeat, and the emancipationist movement died away with the onset of war and the subsequent rise of Fascism. Once again, the *questione femminile* had been swallowed up by more powerful political forces predicated on the oppression and exclusion of large sections of the nation.

From Futurism and Fascism to the New Feminism
With the failure of the battle for the vote – never as vigorous and subversive as in America or Britain – few new voices were to be raised to assert women's political or civil rights. Marinetti's Futurist movement showed early promise with its virulent attack on the family, on traditional bourgeois culture, and on all the archaic underpinnings of Italian society; however, it was to prove itself as misogynistic as Fascism. Meanwhile, many early Feminists, such as Teresa Labriola, found that nationalist sentiment brought them closer to Fascism than to Socialist Feminism. Fascism had claimed to succeed where the Risorgimento had failed, in creating a united and powerful nation-state able to compete on the international stage. Fascist ideology parallelled Catholic traditionalism in its promulgation of the woman as wife and mother; and the Lateran Pacts of 1929 sealed the mutual interests of Church and state in the limited definition of women's roles. Yet the exalted cult of motherhood concealed the shortcomings of an economy where cheap female labour would not be sacrificed for ideological principle. Mussolini's battle for population growth failed. Barring women from the higher echelons of the professions affected limited numbers and masked shifting work-patterns; indeed, more rather than fewer women entered the labour market – a young, largely unskilled and badly paid workforce which, on marrying, returned to the home.

With the fall of Mussolini and the drama of the Resistance, women once more entered the body politic. Historians still debate the extent to which the Resistance afforded a space to develop an alternative, female vision of social politics; however, it was without doubt women's contribution to the Resistance that finally led to their participation in elections, local in 1946 and national in 1948. There were those on the left, however, who blamed women, supposedly politically naive, priest-ridden and easily manipulated, for the emergence of the DC as the most powerful political force.

While the powerful Italian Feminist movement in the late 1960s and 1970s had clear parallels elsewhere in Europe and the United States, once again Italy's singular situation lent its organization and its discursive practices specifically national configurations. The polarization of post-war Italian politics left women little space between a Christian

Democrat Party increasingly reliant on the social control offered by the Church, and a strong left which functioned as a near-autonomous local culture and was, at best, ambivalent about emancipatory politics. The reformist UDI (Unione Donne Italiane, 'Unon of Italian Women'), affiliated to the PCI, kept women's issues on the agenda, and a slowly expanding bourgeois female culture found expression in women's magazines, some of which began to express overtly Feminist ideas. The new consumer society, the breakdown of social formations as people moved in search of work, and the rapid expansion of educational opportunity led increasingly to dissatisfaction with traditional roles and expectations.

The crisis of traditional parties in the early 1970s created political space for social movements and facilitated the politicization of civil society. Feminism grew out of the student protests of 1968 and the subsequent workers' movement, outstripping both in longevity and effectiveness. The traditional marginalization of women led to highly politicized groups of radical women operating on the borders of, or outside, orthodox politics. Communist women, for example, looked with suspicion upon consciousness-raising as an élitist political practice – a bourgeois phenomenon, not a strategy to be taken up in the class struggle. At the same time, some of Feminism's most biting analyses were of left-wing political organizations which replicated rather than challenged the patriarchal structures of the Church and the Catholic political parties. This was a break from the moderate reformism of movements such as the UDI. Class-based political analysis was dismissed as inadequate and hostile to women's interests. Women operated within and alongside political parties, while simultaneously setting up their own autonomous formations which were structured on a loose federal, rather than national, system.

The achievements of the new Feminism were considerable. Women were able to organize on a large scale, unlike earlier movements which had never achieved mass support. These achievements included a national plan for nurseries and family-planning clinics. Improved rights in the workplace included equal pay for equal work, paternity leave and five-month maternity leave, while reform of family law gave women equal authority within the family. Some Feminist groups sought to politicize the question of housework, demanding a salary for housewives. Legal reform also included the repeal of the legislation on rape, whereby a marriage of 'reparation' effectively cancelled out the crime, thereby placing enormous pressure on women not to pursue their complaints through the courts. The Movimento di Liberazione della Donna ('Movement for the Liberation of Women', MLD), affiliated to the Radical Party, demanded contraception, free medical services and the end of discrimination on the grounds of gender. Two major issues, however, deemed almost untouchable by earlier activists, united the various strands of Feminism: maternity and the family, presented in the 1970s in terms of the availability of divorce and the right to abortion.

The need to appease the Church had kept the question of divorce off the political agenda. Finally introduced in 1970 by the Radical Party, the divorce law found consensus across the political spectrum, excluding the DC. The MLD was active in promoting the law, and the campaign constituted the first focus for concerted Feminist intervention. The referendum of 1974 was equally significant, with mass demonstrations and campaigning by a now confident Feminist movement. The upholding of the divorce law marked the abyss between popular lay opinion and the repressive political culture of the DC; it also highlighted the caution of the Communists, who had no wish to be branded as the party which wanted to destroy the family.

The campaign for abortion, as well as being the single issue which united all aspects of Feminist opinion in Italy, similarly placed women on the front line between traditionalism and a modern, secular society. The huge pro-abortion rallies established Feminism as a radical force which cut across traditional class and political lines, while women's new willingness to reveal the sore of clandestine abortion exposed the reality of women's lives. The MLD campaigned for abortion and easily collected the 500,000 signatures required to trigger a referendum, thus forcing the issue on to the political agenda. Abortion was finally legalized in 1978, albeit with a number of important restrictions, and a later referendum to abolish 'Law 194' regulating and permitting abortion was convincingly defeated.

As a powerful grassroots organization with strong political links, Feminism brought about swift reform of an archaic political and legal system. Having changed the law on divorce and abortion, the mass campaigns and rallies of Feminism were largely at an end, and the women's movement returned largely to its former loose, fragmented structure. It turned its attention to a more reflective, theoretical exploration of sexual difference, not content to rest with the belated admission of women to specific areas and rewards of work and representation. As early as 1966 a manifesto produced by the Milan-based Demau group had renounced emancipation and the conventional objective of female integration in favour of an exploration of sexual difference. Unlike earlier forms of Feminism, Neo-feminism implicitly challenged rather than upheld the legitimacy of the state. Even while it remained rooted in political activism, demanding equality before the law, the new Feminism also sought to understand the significance of gender as a linguistic and philosophical category, and to seek alternative forms of personal and social relationships. Italian feminism, eclectic in its outlook and in its sources, seeks to bridge the gap between a theoretical, philosophical analysis and active political engagement.

Gradually the centre of attention shifted from the relationship with the (male-dominated) institutions to developing new ways of living which would be woman- rather than man-centred, where relations between women rather than between the sexes became the dominant focal point. Equality is dismissed as a goal, on account of its inherent tendency to assimilate women's difference into the male preconceptions of the world: sexual difference requires a shift in thought and in language in order to accommodate a double perspective. In practical terms this led to the establishment of women's cultural centres, most famously the Centro Culturale Virginia Woolf in Rome, and of separate academic syllabuses and courses of study as well as separate cultural spaces, including women-only theatres and publishing houses. For women to take each other as reference points meant much more than embracing lesbianism as a political and ethical, as well as a sexual, choice. The dynamic separatism of *affidamento*, or 'entrustment', whereby one woman sets out consciously to relate both her public and private self to another woman, was rooted in the desire not only to produce a supportive network, but also radically to rethink a system which took the male as its formative paradigm. This move was closely related to the analysis of maternity. The traditionally oppressive, static mother was rejected in favour of a mother-figure who would offer a more dynamic possibility for achieving one's potential and more open-ended relationships between women.

Practical as well as theoretical, Italian Feminism embraces both functional change and theoretical reflection. After two decades of Feminism, women are active in all areas of cultural, social and political life. Nonetheless, the collapse of the First Republic was largely unaffected by the women's movement. The proportion of female deputies in the Italian parliament has still to rise above ten per cent, while quota systems in local elections have proved extremely controversial. Italian society and culture remain irreducibly male-dominated, despite the dramatic success of a number of individual women writers and the high profile of a handful of women politicians. Italian Feminism at the beginning of the twenty-first century no longer has the clear objectives of the 1970s, although equal opportunities and the tackling of sexual harassment and violence are still on the agenda. Nonetheless, the impact of Feminism is felt in every area of social, cultural and family life, and in modes not always registered by the cold statistical measurements of orthodox politics.

NOTES

1. Benedict R. Anderson, *Imagined Communities: Reflections on the Origins and Spread of Nationalism* (London: Verso, 1983), pp. 23–45.

2. Edward C. Banfield, *The Moral Basis of a Backward Society* (New York: Harcourt Brace, 1958).

3. Danilo Dolci, *Sicilian Lives* (London: Writers and Readers, 1981), pp. 67–8.

4. Tullio Barbato, *Il terrorismo in Italia* (Milan: Bibliografica, 1980), p. 35.

5. Giorgio Bocca, *Il terrorismo italiano 1970–1978* (Milan: Rizzoli, 1978), p. 7.

6. Umberto Eco, *Faith in Fakes* (London: Secker and Warburg, 1986), pp. 113–19.

7. Pier Paolo Pasolini, *Scritti corsari* (Milan: Garzanti, 1975), pp. 45–7.

8. Denis Mack Smith, *Cavour* (London: Weidenfeld and Nicolson, 1985), p. xi.

9. Franca Pieroni Bortolotti, *Alle origini del movimento femminile in Italia, 1848–1892* (Turin: Einaudi, 1963), p. 17.

FURTHER READING

Arlacchi, Pino, *La mafia imprenditrice*. Bologna: Il Mulino, 1983.

Birnbaum, L. Chiavola. *La liberazione della donna: Feminism in Italy*. Middletown, Conn.: Wesleyan University Press, 1986.

Chiarante, Giuseppe, *La democrazia cristiana*. Rome: Editori Riuniti, 1980.

Cicioni, Mirna and Nicole Prunster (eds.), *Visions and Revisions: Women in Italian Culture*. Oxford: Berg, 1993.

De Giorgio, Michela, *Le italiane dall'Unità a oggi*. Rome and Bari: Laterza, 1992.

Diamanti, Ilvo, *La lega*. Rome: Donzelli, 1993.

Duggan, Christopher, *Fascism and the Mafia*. New Haven, Conn.: Yale University Press, 1989.

Falcone, Giovanni, *Cose di Cosa Nostra*. Milan: Rizzoli, 1991.

Hess, Henner, *Mafia*. Rome and Bari: Laterza, 1973.

Kemp, Sandra and Paola Bono (eds.), *Italian Feminist Thought*. Oxford: Blackwell, 1991.

Kemp, Sandra and Paola Bono (eds.), *The Lonely Mirror: Italian Perspectives on Feminist Theory*. London: Routledge, 1993.

Spadolini, Giovanni, *Giolitti e i cattolici 1901–1914*. Florence: Le Monnier, 1960.

8

Narratives of self and society

11 May 1860. Garibaldi lands at Marsala, Sicily, and opens the way for the unification of Italy under Victor Emmanuel II of Savoy, the 'galantuomo' King.

> [The Prince] opened the newspaper. 'On May 11 an act of flagrant piracy was effected through the landing of armed men on the Marsala coast. Subsequent reports have clarified that the band numbers about eight hundred, and is commanded by Garibaldi' [...] The name of Garibaldi troubled him a bit. That adventurer, all hair and beard, was a pure Mazzinian. He would cause trouble. 'But if the *Galantuomo* [King] has let him come down here it means he's sure of him. They'll bridle him.'[1]

The novel is indeed the modern artistic form of the bourgeoisie, but there is no law prohibiting aristocrats from writing in another class's style; so, almost exactly a century after the unification of Italy, a Sicilian prince, Giuseppe Tomasi di Lampedusa (1896–1957), wrote a very successful and revealing novel, *Il Gattopardo* ('The Leopard'‡, 1958) about the events that led to the decline and eventual demise of the aristocracy. Modelled on the author's grandfather, the protagonist of the book, Prince Fabrizio Salina, witnesses those events with the wisdom and detachment of his age and with a historical and sociological insight that makes him support his nephew, Tancredi Falconeri, when the latter joins the *Garibaldini* – 'If we want everything to stay as it is, everything has to change' (p. 24), he tells his worried uncle – and when he wants to marry the beautiful bourgeois Angelica Sedara instead of Concetta, the prince's own daughter.

Il Gattopardo is perhaps the most conspicuous example in modern Italian literature of a historical novel – a genre which, in the wake of Ugo

Foscolo (1778–1827), Alessandro Manzoni (1785–1873), Ippolito Nievo (1831–61) and Giuseppe Rovani (1818–74), not to mention the popular success of Massimo d'Azeglio (1798–1866) and others, has occupied a prominent position, accompanying the rise of the new state with narrative sagas that have effectively inserted individual or family stories within the historical context of national development. Undoubtedly, Manzoni is the writer who is the father of modern Italian fiction. His *I promessi sposi* ('The Betrothed'‡, 1827–40) is the single work that has exerted a crucial influence not only on the historical novel, but on the Italian novel in general, and not only in the first half of the nineteenth century, but also well into the twentieth. After Manzoni's Lombardy (depicted under a seventeenth-century Spanish rule that recalled the contemporary Austrian domination), the region that gained literary pre-eminence was Sicily: novels dealing with the aftermath of the Risorgimento in the island have played a particularly significant role.

Giovanni Verga (1840–1922) was interested not so much in historical novels as in a great naturalistic-style cycle, *I vinti* ('The Vanquished'), of which only two novels were completed. Yet these contain pages on history that, together with their descriptions of Sicilian landscapes and characters, and with the more explicitly historical novel *I Vicerè* ('The Viceroys'‡, 1894) by his contemporary Federico De Roberto (1861–1927), established a kind of Sicilian code of historical-novel writing which had to be followed (either in acknowledgment or rejection) by later writers such as Luigi Pirandello (1867–1936), himself a Sicilian. When he decided to paint the large historical fresco of *I vecchi e i giovani* ('The Old and the Young'‡, 1913), Pirandello followed some of Verga's and De Roberto's images, themes and ideas in outlining the historical reasons for the disillusionment of an entire generation and an entire region after the failures of the Risorgimento.

Certainly, Tomasi di Lampedusa drew upon these predecessors when he wrote *Il Gattopardo*. The historical and social picture he presented is so persuasive that it overshadows the portrayal of his protagonist. The supple and ornate language in which he composed his elegy for a lost age, as well as his perceptive insights into the nature of class struggle and historical causality, were not sufficient, at first, to outweigh the conservative implications of his world-vision in the eyes of many intellectuals. The Italian language was enriched by a new word, *gattopardismo*, which stood (and still stands) for the ability to change sides in politics without effecting any real, meaningful change on society. It was against

Lampedusa's conservatism that Leonardo Sciascia (1921–89) – who was to be the author of such historical novels as *Il consiglio d'Egitto* ('The Council of Egypt'‡, 1963) and *Morte dell'inquisitore* ('Death of the Inquisitor'‡, 1964) – reacted with a novella, 'Il Quarantottu' ('The Fortyeight', 1958), that was immediately received as a progressive response to *Il Gattopardo*. Against the same historical background of Garibaldi's landing in Sicily, the character Ippolito Nievo, the Romantic novelist who actually was a member of the Garibaldi expedition, becomes the spokesperson for all those Sicilians who do not speak out but who, despite the odds, treasure dignity and justice in their hearts. Similarly, in a luxuriant and refined language, *Il sorriso dell'ignoto marinaio* ('The Smile of the Unknown Sailor', 1976) by Vincenzo Consolo (1933–) portrays the social struggles of poor Sicilian workers and peasants, mostly from the viewpoint of a Liberal aristocrat, Baron Mandralisca. In all these novels Sicily is the microcosm in which a crucial period of Italian history is played out.

In other novels, the Risorgimento is part of a broader picture, as in *Il mulino del Po* ('The Mill on the Po'‡, 1940), by Riccardo Bacchelli (1891–1985) or is shunned altogether. Luigi Malerba (1927–) deals with the Middle Ages in *Il pataffio* ('Pastiche', 1978 – the title refers to the plot as well as to the language) and with Papal Rome in the sixteenth century in *Le maschere* ('The Masks', 1995). Sicily in the eighteenth century is the setting for Dacia Maraini's (1936–) *La lunga vita di Marianna Ucria* ('The Long Life of Marianna Ucria'‡, 1990) and in the early nineteenth century for *Le menzogne della notte* ('Night's Lies', 1988) by Gesualdo Bufalino (1920–96). Seventeenth-century Piedmont is the setting for Sebastiano Vassalli's (1941–) *La chimera* ('The Chimera', 1990), a beautiful novel that, following and renewing the Manzonian model, is also a microhistory dealing with a young girl who is falsely accused of being a witch and burnt at the stake. And an old sexton chronicles the life of a tiny Istrian parish from the Hapsburg Empire to Italian rule and the Yugoslav takeover in *La miglior vita* ('The Best Life', 1977) by Fulvio Tomizza (1935–).

A peculiar feature of Italian literature is the use of art history as the subject-matter for historical novels and short stories. Thus, *Artemisia* (1947‡), by Anna Banti (1895–1985) is an intriguing identification of the writer with the seventeenth-century painter Artemisia Gentileschi; and, like a modern Vasari, Neri Pozza (1912–88) brings back the splendours of Venetian Renaissance art and culture in *Processo per eresia* ('Trial for Heresy', 1970) and *La putina greca* ('The Little Greek Girl', 1972) through the everyday humanity of a number of artists, from Lotto to Titian, and through the distinct stylistic features of the dialect.

History can also be made the subject of a novel in other ways. Elsa Morante's *La storia* ('History'/'The Story'‡, 1974) thematizes the vicissitudes of a group of humble characters during the Second World War, the Resistance and the Holocaust. It aspires to an epic grandeur; however, the lasting impressions that readers carry away are of such figures as the mother Ida Ramundo, the small child Useppe and the intellectual Davide Segre – all of them *victims* of history.

More recently, Umberto Eco (1932–) has drawn on the genre of the historical novel to create three bestsellers, *Il nome della rosa* ('The Name of the Rose'‡, 1980), *Il pendolo di Foucault* ('Foucault's Pendulum'‡, 1988), and *L'isola del giorno prima* ('The Island of the Day Before'‡, 1994). Dealing respectively with religious power struggles during the Middle Ages, an international plot which also dates back to the Middle Ages but reaches forward to involve contemporary terrorism, and geographical explorations during the seventeenth century, these three books are historical novels only on one level. They are better understood as encyclopaedic works in which the author's erudition and fantasy, as well as his semiological, philosophical and narratological interests, combine to form fictional worlds that are as much historical as they are projections of the present.

In little more than a century, the course of the Italian historical novel has been, first, to accompany the emergence of the national state, and then to transcend both regional and national boundaries to become cosmopolitan and marketable worldwide.

20 July 1866. The Italian fleet is defeated at the battle of Lissa in the Adriatic Sea by the Austrian Navy.

> In that group, instead of the fallen donkey, there were two sailors, with their sacks on their shoulders and their heads bandaged [. . .] They said that a great naval battle had been fought, and that ships as big as Aci Trezza had drowned, packed to the gunnels with sailors; in sum, a world of things which made them seem like those who told the story of Roland and of the paladins of France down at the waterfront in Catania, and people stood listening straining their ears, thick as flies.[2]

During its first years as a unified country, Italy had to overcome numerous difficulties that had to do partly with international recognition – in 1866 it reclaimed the Veneto from the Hapsburg Empire, and in 1870 the Vatican lost the protection of the French, so that Rome finally became the capital of the Kingdom – but mostly with the variety of the economic, social and cultural conditions present in its territory. Such conditions explain the pedagogical fervour of two famous narrative texts for children, *Le avventure di Pinocchio* ('The Adventures of Pinocchio'‡, 1883,) by Carlo Collodi (1826–90) and *Cuore* ('Heart'‡, 1886) by Edmondo De Amicis (1846–1908), both of which extended their influence well beyond the 1880s into this century; and even a cookbook, the affable *La scienza in cucina e l'arte di mangiar bene* ('Science in the Kitchen and the Art of Eating Well'‡, 1891) by Pellegrino Artusi (1820–1911), contributed greatly to the unification of culinary customs and terminology. Many writers devoted their attention and their fictional representations to the nation's regional differences, which became a characteristic trait of the literary movement called *verismo* (from 'il vero', the truth). Its poetics were expounded and practised especially by two Sicilian authors and friends, Luigi Capuana (1839–1915) and Giovanni Verga.

The technique of narrative impersonality was especially important for the poetics of *verismo*. Patterned after the French Naturalists' documentary and scientific tenets, it was masterfully used by Verga in numerous short stories dealing with poor Sicilian peasants (one of these stories became a famous opera, Pietro Mascagni's *Cavalleria rusticana*) and in his major novels. *I Malavoglia* ('The Malavoglias'‡, 1881) recounts the life of the Malavoglia family in the village of Aci Trezza through an anonymous narrative voice that can be identified with the spirit of the village itself – the speaking community from whose point of view all events are perceived and narrated: thus the battleships are 'as big as Aci Trezza', and they had 'drowned' in the battle. But such a narrative voice should be identified more precisely with language itself, the spoken language – for example, in the constant use of prosopopeia, of which the 'drowned' ships are but an instance. The result is a truly epic, yet humble narrative, in which the impersonality of the narrative voice does not prevent pathos while providing the objectivity necessary for multiple viewpoints and voices. It is the same technique that, many years after Verga, Virginia Woolf, a mistress of Modernism, was to use in *To the Lighthouse* (1927).

Verga's other major novel, *Mastro-don Gesualdo* (1889‡), has a broader scope. It portrays the ascent of Gesualdo Motta, a self-made man who rises from poverty to riches and marries into the aristocracy, only to be left to die alone in his mansion. Here impersonality functions with the same objectivity and multiplicity as in *I Malavoglia*, but with two major differences: it no longer represents a community, and the narrative voice dialogues with the characters and corrects, comments on or undermines their words. Through this particular use of impersonality Verga again shows his modernity and sets an intriguing precedent for the works and the viewpoints of writers such as Luigi Pirandello and Italo Svevo.

However, in terms of literary history, Verga's legacy was mostly tied to the objective representation of humble realities within well-defined local boundaries. Such a legacy developed even in authors like Antonio Fogazzaro (1842–1911), who was interested (*à la* Manzoni) in ethical and religious problems and dealt with the middle class and the provincial aristocracy of the Valsolda in *Piccolo mondo antico* ('The Little World of the Past'‡, 1896), and Federigo Tozzi (1883–1920), whose lower-middle-class characters live out their dramas, narrated with psychoanalytic sensitivity, in Siena and the surrounding Tuscan countryside in such anti-Naturalistic novels as *Con gli occhi chiusi* ('With Closed Eyes'‡, 1920) and *Tre croci* ('Three Crosses'‡, 1920).

The influence of Verga and *verismo* can be traced well into the twentieth century. *Maria Zef* (1937‡) by Paola Drigo (1876–1938) is the gripping story of family incest and the rape of a very poor girl, set in the mountains of Carnia-Friuli; *Zebio Cotal* (1958) by Guido Cavani (1897–1967) and *Casa d'altri* ('The Others' House', 1952) by Silvio D'Arzo (1920–52) deal with the life of destitute persons in the Emilian Apennines; Fulvio Tomizza's *Materada* (1960) portrays the rugged destinies of Istrian villagers. The modes of *verismo* can even be noted in the dry and almost minimalist style of the best among the many books by Carlo Cassola (1917–87): *Il taglio del bosco* ('Timber Cutting', 1954) or *La ragazza di Bube* ('Bube's Girl'‡, 1960). The minute and detailed realism of Giorgio Bassani (1916–2000), on the other hand, should be traced back to a classical model such as Manzoni's, notwithstanding its 'localism'; his works are collected under the title *Il romanzo di Ferrara* ('The Novel of Ferrara', 1980)

16 February 1883. Funeral of Richard Wagner.

> The corpse was there, enclosed in its crystal coffin; and next to it, standing, was the woman with the face of snow [...] The silence was acute, and they [the six pall-bearers] did not bat an eyelid, but a violent grief wounded their souls like a squall and shook them violently down to their deep roots [   ] An infinite smile illuminated

the face of the laid-out hero: infinite and distant as the rainbow of the glaciers, as the glare of the seas, as the halo of the stars [. . .] The profound silence was worthy of Him who had transformed the powers of the Universe into infinite song for the religion of men.[3]

Certainly the funeral of a great composer can take on emblematic overtones and become the symbol of an entire age, especially if it is described, as in *Il fuoco* ('The Fire'‡, 1900), by another emblematic figure like Gabriele D'Annunzio (1863–1938) for his own artistic purposes – against the backdrop of Venice, the city that he made the capital of Decadentism in the collective imagination of his time (it is enough to think of Thomas Mann).

The description of Wagner's funeral has in fact many characteristics of Decadentism: pretentious language (including the use of capital letters), grandiose nature similes, sublime passions, noble sentiments; the celebration of an artist as hero (and 'hero' is always associated with the Nietzschean notion of 'superman'); the pre-eminence of music, theatrical music to be precise, as an indication of the fusion of the arts, and of art and life – D'Annunzio's own ideal and world-view –; the culturally and historically precise choice of Wagner (not Verdi!) – a clear indication that certain aesthetic ideas dear to the author were European, and not just Italian, in scope.

D'Annunzio's Decadentism was an exacerbation of Romantic tenets and tastes, filtered through his omnivorous erudition that extended from the Italian Renaissance and Baroque artists to French and English Symbolist poets and writers, from German philosophers to Russian novelists. The celebration of Wagner in *Il fuoco*, at the end of a novel whose female protagonist is the thinly disguised actress Eleonora Duse, follows that of the aesthete in *Il piacere* ('Pleasure'‡, 1889) and the political leader in *Le vergini delle rocce* ('The Virgins of the Rocks', 1896).

D'Annunzio loved experimentation, and as an accomplished image maker (he called himself 'l'imaginifico') he did not hesitate to pattern his stylistic choices on medieval religious texts (for their archaic vocabulary and mystic inspiration), as well as on the contemporary linguistic games of the *scapigliati*, the 'dishevelled' avant-garde writers, such as Cletto Arrighi (1830–1906), Giovanni Faldella (1846–1928) or Carlo Dossi (1849–1910); he was equally interested in the morbid themes of some of Iginio Ugo Tarchetti's stories, such as *Fosca* (1869). As image maker, he was tremendously conscious of the expectations of his audience, and in an age in which the mass media were still limited to a small portion of the population, he certainly succeeded in reaching it, and in fulfilling the sentimental and aesthetic needs of the bourgeoisie, to whom he proposed aristocratic and sublime models.

His influence was enormous, far-reaching and long-lasting. (E. M. Forster, to name but one, was still fascinated by him even on the eve of the Second World War.) It was most powerful in poetry, but it should not be underestimated in narrative prose, in the theatre, in fashion, in politics; Mussolini learned much from him, admired him, used him, and finally kept him at a distance in an elaborate villa on Lake Garda. Certainly, Eugenio Montale's statement that in order to be a modern poet it is necessary to have 'passed through' D'Annunzio is valid too for the novelist. It is no wonder that James Joyce was fascinated by D'Annunzio's rich style studded with verbal inventions, regardless of the fact that, as his friend Ettore Schmitz (who wrote under the pseudonym Italo Svevo) would point out to him, the writer's meaning often remained elusive. In the first three decades of this century, Massimo Bontempelli (1878–1960) owes much for his 'magic realism' to the Dannunzian penchant for the irrational and even the mystical, as does Grazia Deledda (1871–1936), who, in 1926, received the Nobel Prize, when she was honoured for her novels of her native Sardinia (the regional theme is of course a legacy of *verismo*; her island's primitive and superstitious customs would appeal to D. H. Lawrence and to Elio Vittorini). In turn, the 'magic' of magic realism can be seen as a precedent for the fantastic inventions of writers as diverse as Dino Buzzati (1906–72), Tommaso Landolfi (1908–79) and Anna Maria Ortese (1914–), while Alberto Savinio (1891–1952) remains in a decidedly Surrealist area.

Without D'Annunzio's taste for an elaborate and hyperliterary vocabulary, it would be difficult to understand Emilio Cecchi (1884–1966), whose 'art prose' distilled the aestheticization of experience for an entire generation, as well as the works of later writers like Carlo Emilio Gadda (1893–1973), Antonio Pizzuto (1893–1976), Gesualdo Bufalino (1920–96), Giorgio Manganelli (1922–90), Luigi Meneghello (1922–) and Alberto Arbasino (1930–), who are all remarkable for their linguistic refinement and experimentation. And while Elsa Morante (1912–85) wrote her novels, from *Menzogna e sortilegio* ('Deceit and Sorcery'‡, 1948) to *Aracoeli* (1982), with luxuriant images and metaphors, her vision of the world is the very antithesis of D'Annunzio's: her characters, like the young narrator of *L'isola di Arturo* ('Arturo's Island'‡, 1957), a true masterpiece, are anti-heroes.

24 May 1915. Italy enters the First World War.

> 26 June 1915. The war has reached me! I who used to listen to the
> stories of the war as if it were a war of other times about which it was
> amusing to talk, but about which it would have been foolish to worry,
> here I happened to be in the middle of it, surprised and at the same
> time astonished that I had not realized before that sooner or later I
> had to become caught up in it. I had lived quite calmly in a building
> whose ground floor was burning and had not foreseen that sooner or
> later the whole building together with me would be immersed in
> flames.
>
> The war grabbed me, shook me violently like a rag, deprived me in
> one go of all my family and also of my administrator.[4]

The mature Zeno Cosini, the protagonist of *La coscienza di Zeno*
('Zeno's Conscience'‡, 1923) by Italo Svevo (1861–1928), who is telling the
story of his psychoanalytical treatment and of how he was affected by the
war, is a major representative of the modern anti-hero. His 'conscience' is
the sum of many incongruous fragments that laboriously and hilari-
ously make up a unified self. He may decide something, but life is full of
surprises for him, and he always ends up as the one who is acted upon,
not the one who acts. The outbreak of the First World War is no exception. By saying, 'The war has reached me', he becomes literally (syntacti-
cally) the object, not the subject, of the story; his amazement at the turn
of events is underscored by the strongly marked attributes 'surprised'
and 'astonished', his reluctance to accept what is happening is signalled
by the repetition of the temporal syntagm 'sooner or later', while his
bourgeois condition and his self-irony are conveyed by his reckoning
that the war has deprived him 'in one go' of all his family, significantly
including his administrator. He is witnessing the beginning of hostilities while taking a walk in the hills around Trieste, and all his previous
preoccupations with smoking his last cigarette, with his guilt over the
death of his father, with being faithful to his wife, with loving his sister-
in-law, all of a sudden become irrelevant games. His long search for his
individual self abruptly ends in the encounter with and recognition of
the other (society, history). The apocalyptic ending of the novel expands
and universalizes the image of the building going up in flames: it signals
that Zeno's individual 'disease' is truly a collective one, and exposes the
infamous proclamation by Filippo Tommaso Marinetti (1875–1944) that
'war is the only hygiene of the world' as the horrible folly it is. It should
be noted that Futurism's avant-garde innovations had a very limited

influence on Italian narrative prose in general, though they were relevant to poetry (the 'parole in libertà' or words set free of syntax) and political discourse (the rhetorics of the 'manifesto'), not to mention painting and sculpture. In stark contrast, Futurist innovations were influential in French and even British literature – suffice it to recall Ezra Pound, the 'Vortex', and even James Joyce. In any case, the First World War caused a lot of soul- searching among European intellectuals. In Italy, *Esame di coscienza di un letterato* ('A Literary Man's Examination of Conscience', 1915) by Renato Serra (1884–1915) and Carlo Emilio Gadda's *Giornale di guerra e di prigionia* ('Journal of War and Imprisonment', 1955) are exemplary texts in this respect, but few works have the poignancy, lightness and visionary power of the final pages of *La coscienza di Zeno*.

Under the pen name of Italo Svevo, the Triestine Ettore Schmitz had started to write and publish novels, short stories and critical pieces during the last two decades of the nineteenth century, bringing psychological analysis to depths never reached before in Italian literature. Using the same techniques as the later Verga to subvert the expressive codes and modes of Naturalism, he offered unforgettable portraits of anti-heroes in *Una vita* ('A Life'‡, 1893) and *Senilità* ('Senility'‡, 1898), both written in the third person. Only *La coscienza di Zeno*, however, achieved the kind of lucid subjectivity, self-awareness and self-reflexivity that was appropriate to one of the milestones in the modern representation of the (male, bourgeois) self.

Of course, as the earlier reference to Federigo Tozzi implied, Svevo was not alone in this endeavour. From the marginal perspective of his native Sicily, and also using much the same narrative techniques as the later Verga, Luigi Pirandello had started his own analysis of the human psyche and behaviour in such seemingly Naturalistic novels as *L'esclusa* ('The Outcast'‡, 1901) and *Il turno* ('The Turn', 1902). His representative of the modern self burst forth in 1904 in *Il fu Mattia Pascal* ('The Late Mattia Pascal'‡), a revolutionary novel in which the improbable plot (the narrator 'dies' twice) is used to explode the principle of causality, and the very essence of the protagonist is put into radical question. The oxymoronic name Mattia Pascal is not enough to indicate a personality that is split in more than two ways: it is a personality that by the end of the book is shown not to exist at all – the *late* Mattia Pascal. Similar claims can be made for Pirandello's later novels, including the first one to deal with the new art form of cinema, *Si gira* ('Shooting', 1915, later retitled *Quaderni di Serafino Gubbio operatore*, 'Notebooks of Serafino Gubbio Cameraman'‡,

1925) and *Uno, nessuno e centomila* ('One, None and A Hundred Thousand'‡, 1926) – not to mention his theatre.

Unquestionably, Svevo and Pirandello are major protagonists in modern Italian literature. They have contributed greatly to a better understanding of the modern individual, and their knowledge and use of psychoanalytical ideas have considerably expanded the field of the novel. Alberto Moravia (1907–90) in the 1930s and Giuseppe Berto (1914–78) in the 1960s wrote significant works in this same vein, while Guido Piovene (1907–75) and Mario Soldati (1906–) continued in the more traditional, Manzonian vein of a tormented Catholicism.

But what about the feminine self? In this area, too, there are innovative and illuminating texts. Sibilla Aleramo (1876–1970) published her autobiography, *Una donna* ('A Woman'‡), in 1906: her book is the starting-point of and the point of reference for much contemporary *prise de conscience* by women writers searching for a definition of the self that is necessarily different from that of their male conterparts. *Una donna* (just 'a woman', not '*the* woman' of the male tradition, with its idealized and symbolic overtones) is a strong-willed, sensitive and painful account of Aleramo's own liberation from the strictures of cultural and social roles she was unable to accept. Paramount in her autobiography are the conflicts between family and independence, motherhood and writing.

Similar accounts abound, with varying degrees of success both in literary achievement and in the process of self-liberation. I shall mention at least Deledda's *Cosima* (1937), Alba De Cespedes's (1911–) *Dalla parte di lei* ('On Her Side'‡, 1949) and *Quaderno proibito* ('Forbidden Notebook'‡, 1952,), *Le voci della sera* ('Voices of the Evening'‡, 1961) by Natalia Ginzburg (1916–91), Dacia Maraini's *Donna in guerra* ('Woman at War'‡, 1975), *Casalinghitudine* ('Housewifeness', 1987) by Clara Sereni (1946–), and Susanna Tamaro's *Per voce sola* ('For Voice Only', 1991), which is a much more powerful book than her bestseller *Va' dove ti porta il cuore* ('Go Where the Heart Takes You', 1994). Women's voices have contributed a substantial and remarkable level of discourse, both personal and social, in contemporary narrative – from Gianna Manzini (1896–1974) to Lalla Romano (1906–), from Francesca Sanvitale (1928–) to Rosetta Loy (1931–), from Gina Lagorio (1922–) to Isabella Bossi Fedrigotti.

Nassera Chohra's recent *Volevo diventare bianca* ('I Wanted to Become White', 1993) deserves particular mention. Chohra is an Algerian woman from a Saharawi tribe, whose parents emigrated to France. She later settled in Italy, where she wrote her book in Italian with the collaboration of Alessandra Atti Di Sarro. Her autobiographical testimony shows how feminine identity is constructed in the wake of decolonization and in the face of racism, economic hardship and profound cultural diversity. With her witty, energetic and practical attitude, Chohra develops a stimulating discourse not only on the feminine self, but also on the present conditions of Italian and European society, characterized by an emerging and growing multiculturalism.

5 May 1936. After conquering Ethiopia, Benito Mussolini announces the founding of the Italian Empire from the balcony of Palazzo Venezia in Rome.

> Then the reiterated exultation of the whole body, as if a spring were throwing it upward – of the whole abundant person: in order to seem an even greater emir on top of four hoofs; then the sudden protuberance of that phallic proboscis of his, snoutlike in the dimension of a swine [...] 'ecco ecco ecco eja eja eja', the glorious and virile excitement of the no-longer-seen masturbation: and the consequent virile pollution in the face of the many, of the clapping.[5]

> Er Maccheronaro, in via del Gesù [...] had tiled it [the sandwich], inside, with such three slices of fillet [...] all three supported by that sort of small beam of a double loaf, that was a slipper, Madonna!, that nowadays we can't even remember, now that the empire has come in between.[6]

After the First World War, Mussolini was able to take power by capitalizing on popular discontent and the weakness of the Liberal parliament. A fictional but accurate rendition of these events is the Symbolist novel *Rubè* (1921) by Giuseppe Antonio Borgese (1882–1952), while Ignazio Silone (1900–78) was compelled to write and publish his anti-Fascist novels *Fontamara* (1933) and *Pane e vino* ('Bread and Wine'‡, 1937) in German translation while in exile in Switzerland. In both Silone's novels, the anti-Fascist stand is combined with an impassioned denunciation of the incredibly poor conditions of the Southern hired hands and peasants – and this denunciation marked an important date in the persisting 'Southern Question' which inspired the works of writers like Corrado Alvaro (1895–1956), Rocco Scotellaro (1923–53) and Francesco Jovine (1902–50). Alberto Moravia was able to publish *Gli indifferenti* ('Indifferent People'‡, 1929), a scathing portrayal of the Roman bourgeoisie in the 1920s only because it did not contain any direct allusion to the Fascist power structure. Obviously, those intellectuals who openly opposed Fascism could publish their works only after its fall. The most memorable among these was *Cristo si è fermato a Eboli* ('Christ Stopped at Eboli'‡, 1945) by the Turinese physician and painter Carlo Levi (1902–75), a fascinating account of his time in internal exile among the peasants of Lucania during the 1930s

In general, Italian writers abstained from explicit criticism of the Fascist régime so as to avoid censure and persecution. Only after Mussolini's fall did they express their feelings and their judgments, and the favourite form for these reactions was satire. Notable among these writers was Vitaliano Brancati (1907–54), whose main target from the beginning of his career had been the virility so valued by Fascists and Sicilians alike, which he exposed in terms of customs rather than politics in his *Don Giovanni in Sicilia* ('Don Juan in Sicily', 1941), and then explicitly in *Il bell'Antonio* ('Handsome Antonio'‡, 1949) and in *Paolo il caldo* ('Paolo the Hot', 1955).

Not by chance, then, Gadda chose two powerful and ferocious expressionistic means – the sexual metaphor of a public masturbation and the equation (synecdoche–hyperbole) between the Fascist leader and a gigantic phallus, in order to give full relief to his outrage at Mussolini's manipulation of the Italian crowds in his speeches from the balcony of Palazzo Venezia. In so doing, he eloquently condemned the Fascist degradation of Eros, a positive principle of love and life, into Priapus, a violent and destructive possession, a true rape of culture and civilization. Another means by which Gadda attacks Fascism is to undermine it with passing references to its effects on the daily life of the people, such as the difficulty of having a succulent sandwich of the kind 'Er Maccheronaro' used to prepare – 'nowadays we can't even remember, now that the empire has come in between' – the narrative prolepsis jerks the reader from the time of the story (1927) to that of writing (1945–6), when the disastrous effects of Fascism's policies were still widely felt.

But in both passages given above, what is really important is Gadda's style. He writes with a composite, multilayered, colourful language made up of standard Italian, various dialects, technical terms and neologisms – much as Joyce does. His 'spastic use of language' is a most effective tool to express his vision of a world that for him is fragmented into a myriad of conflicting aspects that only such a style can hope to capture on the page. Whether he deals with the Milanese bourgeoisie and his love-hatred for it in *L'Adalgisa. Disegni milanesi* ('Adalgisa. Milanese Drawings', 1944) and *La cognizione del dolore* ('Acquainted With Grief'‡,

1963) (under the veil of a fictional Latin American country), or whether he treats the lower bourgeoisie and the common people of Rome in *Quer pasticciaccio brutto de via Merulana* ('That Awful Mess on Via Merulana', 1957), Gadda wants to portray the richness of the world, although he ends up by leaving many of his works incomplete, unfinished.

The chaotic enumeration, the list and the catalogue cannot exhaust all the possibilities of the real; no single cause can account for any number of effects. Gadda's fictional worlds retain the fluidity and the multifaceted marvel of a life in progress, and his language refracts the abundance that the world can offer, on the sexual as well as on the gastronomical level, in Milan as well as in Rome. That Gadda was also neurotic in his psychological make-up and frustrated about the impossibility of possessing everything only adds to his modernity.

8 September 1943. Italy signs a separate truce with the Allied forces. The Germans set up a puppet government in the North under Mussolini. Beginning of the armed Resistance against the Nazis and the Fascists.

> 'So I had to keep a bit of an eye on what was going on around the girl. You understand me. With you I had nothing to worry about, nothing at all. You always talked, for hours. Or rather, you talked and Fulvia would listen. Isn't it true?'
>
> 'It's true. It was true.'
>
> 'With Giorgio Clerici instead . . .'
>
> 'Yes,' he said with his tongue dry.
>
> Recently, last summer I mean, the summer of '43, you were in the army, I think [. . .] Recently [Giorgio] came too often, and almost always at night. [. . .]'
>
> 'And this went on until when?'
>
> 'Oh, till early last September. Then there was the chaos of the armistice and the Germans. Then Fulvia went away from here with her father. And I, fond as I was of her, was glad. I was too anxious. I am not saying they misbehaved . . .'[7]

The protagonists of this dialogue in *Una questione privata* ('A Private Question'‡, 1963) by Beppe Fenoglio (1922–63) are an old woman who is the custodian of a villa on the Piedmontese hills near Alba, and Milton, the young partisan who has stopped while on patrol to look at the place where he loved Fulvia, talking with her about English literature and listening to American records, especially *Over the Rainbow*. In the course of the dialogue, he learns that Fulvia has in all likelihood betrayed him with his best friend, Giorgio Clerici. This dialogue is both an event and a symbol. As an event, it propels the plot of *Una questione privata* forward, because Milton absolutely must find out the truth from Giorgio, who is fighting in another partisan brigade in the nearby hills; but finding him proves much more difficult than anticipated, since he has been taken prisoner by the Fascists. The novel is the story of Milton's ever more frantic efforts to save Giorgio and learn the truth. As a symbol, Fulvia's possible betrayal is superimposed, through the coincidence of the dates, upon Italy's unquestionable (albeit necessary) betrayal of Germany effected with the separate truce. The private question of the title seems to upstage the historical question of Italy's switching sides and having to find its truth in the struggle for liberation from the Nazis and its own Fascist legacy.

The pathos of *Una questione privata* derives from the ethical rigour with which Fenoglio describes both the urgency of Milton's private plight and the loyalty and idealism with which he nonetheless continues to fight. The Resistance, in this book, is as true as it could ever be described. But Fenoglio's other texts on the subject, the epic *I ventitré giorni della città di Alba* ('The Twenty-Three Days of the City of Alba', 1952) and *Il partigiano Johnny* ('Johnny the Partisan'‡, 1968), should not be forgotten, nor should the others on the harsh life of the peasants in the Langhe hills, *La malora* ('Ruin‡', 1954) and *Un giorno di fuoco* ('A Day of Fire', 1963).

Fenoglio is perhaps the most representative of the Italian authors who have dealt with the traumatic events of the Resistance. Before and behind him are the so-called 'Decade of Translations' and Neorealism. During the 1930s many Italian authors – Elio Vittorini (1908–66), Cesare Pavese (1908–50), Eugenio Montale (1896–1981) among others – engaged in translating American novels (by Melville, Faulkner, Steinbeck, Anderson and Caldwell) as a means to bypass the cultural parochialism of Fascism, and to see their destinies projected on to 'the gigantic screen' of American literature, as Pavese wrote. Vittorini's anthology *Americana* (1941) was perhaps the culmination of what has been rightly called 'the myth of America' for Italian intellectuals.

The lesson they learned was not simply one of political freedom, but also one of stylistic renewal against the centuries-old stuffiness of Italian tradition – with the consequent revaluation of writers like Verga and Aldo Palazzeschi (1885–1974), who had employed spoken dialogue of the type prevalent among American authors. Elio Vittorini's *Conversazione in*

Sicilia ('Conversation in Sicily'‡, 1941) and *Uomini e no* ('Men and Non-Men'‡, 1945) are certainly marked by such freedom and renewal, as is the whole of his career as an influential intellectual. And Cesare Pavese's *La casa in collina* ('The House on the Hill'‡, 1949) and *La luna e i falò* ('The Moon and the Bonfires'‡, 1950), while testifying to a lucid and tormented consciousness of the moral and ideal choices the Resistance required, are splendid literary achievements in their fusion of symbolism and personal myths with social and linguistic realism, while *Dialoghi con Leucò* ('Dialogues with Leucò'‡, 1947) is a poignant testimony to his effort to be part of a community, and to communicate this effort, even though the community takes the form of the Jungian collective unconscious of classical mythology (Leucò is the spoken-style abbreviation of Leucothea, the nymph of consolation).

The Neorealism that exploded on to Italian screens with the post-war films of De Sica, Rossellini, Lizzani and other directors, depicting the harsh realities of Rome as an 'open city', of *sciuscià* (shoe-shine boys) and poor bicycle thieves, spilled over into the literary field and marked a whole generation of writers. Among them were Italo Calvino (1923–85) – who however always kept Neorealism in check with his 'fabulous' vein, in the early stories as well as in *Il sentiero dei nidi di ragno* ('The Path of the Spider's Nests'‡, 1947) – Renata Viganò (1900–76), Carlo Cassola (1917–87), Vasco Pratolini (1913–91) and Primo Levi (1919–87), who distinguished himself for the subdued tone of his testimony of the Holocaust, *Se questo è un uomo* ('If This Is a Man'‡, 1947), and for the inflexible moral defence of the dignity of the human person in all his works, all the way to *I sommersi e i salvati* ('The Drowned and the Saved'‡, 1986).

Although Fenoglio translated English (not American) classic texts, his style clearly reflects the changes brought into Italian literature by the decade of translations and by cinematographic Neorealism; the stoicism of his gaze, the immediacy of his language, the English- and Latin-patterned neologisms of his vocabulary, his dialogues, the speed and inexorability of his narrative pace – all these make him the greatest storyteller of the destinies of the individuals who fought in the anti-Fascist Resistance in the years 1943–45, and of the collective saga that resulted from it.

1953: Federico Fellini directs 'I vitelloni'; 1959: 'La dolce vita'; 1973: 'Amarcord'.

> Both the province of *I vitelloni* and the movie-making world of Rome are circles of hell, but they are equally enjoyable lands of Cockaigne.

This is why Fellini succeeds in troubling to the core: because he makes us admit that what we would most like to keep far away is intrinsically close to us. [. . .] Fellini transforms the cinema into the symptomatology of Italian hysteria [. . .] which he from that geographical middle ground of his Romagna redefines in *Amarcord* as the true unifying element of Italian behaviour. The cinema of distance which had nourished our youth is definitively overturned into the cinema of absolute proximity. For the brief span of our lifetimes, everything remains there, painfully present; first the images of eros and the premonitions of death reach us in every dream; [. . .] the film we deluded ourselves we were only watching is the story of our lives.[8]

The juxtaposition of the Resistance and Fellini's films is not as arbitrary as it might seem. It reflects the dramatic and fast-paced changes undergone by Italian society in the past fifty years, and most notably from the 1950s to the 1970s. After the Liberation and the reconstruction, Italy quickly became an industrialized country with all the characteristic phenomena of a modern, affluent society: urbanization, mass media, rapid transport, consumerism, alienation, pollution, and then women and youth movements, and organized crime, terrorism, corruption. All these phenomena powerfully contributed to a radical reshaping of traditional family and societal structures and values, and all were represented in the films of the great cinematic masters – Fellini, Visconti, Antonioni – as well as in the narrative works of the period.

One can clearly follow these phenomena simply by reading Italian novels and short stories. Calvino's *La speculazione edilizia* ('Speculation in the Building Trade'‡, 1957), *La nuvola di smog* ('The Cloud of Smog'‡, 1958) and *Marcovaldo, ovvero le stagioni in città* ('Marcovaldo, or the Seasons in the City'‡, 1963); Pier Paolo Pasolini's *Ragazzi di vita* ('The Lads'‡, 1955), *Teorema* ('Theorem'‡, 1968) and *Una vita violenta* ('A Violent Life'‡, 1959) – 1959 is also the year of Fellini's *La dolce vita* – a memorable contrast – as well as Ottiero Ottieri's (1924–) *Donnarumma all'assalto*, ('Donnarumma on the Attack'); *Memoriale* ('Memorandum'‡, 1962) by Paolo Volponi (1924–94); *Il padrone* ('The Boss'‡, 1965) by Goffredo Parise (1929–86); Leonardo Sciascia's *Il giorno della civetta* ('The Day of the Owl'‡, 1961), *A ciascuno il suo* ('To Each His Own'‡, 1966) and *Todo modo* ('One Way or Another'‡, 1974); *Vogliamo tutto* ('We Want Everything', 1971) by Nanni Balestrini (1935–); *Ferito a morte* ('Wounded to Death'‡, 1961) by Raffaele La Capria (1922–) with its Neapolitan *vitelloni*; or by contrast the autobiographical account *Padre padrone* ('Father Boss'‡, 1975) by Gavino Ledda (1938–); and even *Porci con le ali* ('Pigs With Wings'‡, 1976) by Marco Lombardo-Radice and Lidia Ravera (1951–) are but a few of the narrative texts that, while showing the remarkable diversity of their respective literary qualities, could be used by sociologists to understand modern Italy. In the case of Pier Paolo Pasolini (1922–75), not only his novels, but also his poetry, films, essays, journalistic contributions and personal lifestyle should be considered in their totality as an intellectual and cultural project that had a considerable impact on the Italian scene and was emblematic of the period.

But Italo Calvino is by far the most representative writer of his generation. I have chosen a quote from his 'Autobiografia di uno spettatore' ('Autobiography of a Cinemagoer', 1974) for several reasons. It underscores the importance of the cinema in reflecting and shaping the collective imagination; it points to the centrality of the visual element in Calvino's own writing and cognitive process ('visibility' is one of the values or qualities of literature he wants to preserve 'for the next millennium'); and it shows the peculiar terseness and sharpness of Calvino's way of narrativizing conceptual views ('distance', 'proximity' and 'meaning' are interrelated).

Certainly, a passage from the fantastic trilogy *I nostri antenati* ('Our Ancestors'‡, 1960), or from one of the combinatorial texts like *Le cosmicomiche* ('Cosmicomics'‡, 1965) and *Le città invisibili* ('Invisible Cities'‡, 1972), or from the later, metanarrative ones like *Se una notte d'inverno un viaggiatore* ('If on a Winter's Night a Traveller'‡, 1979) and *Palomar* (1983‡), or even from an anthropologically oriented one like *Sotto il sole giaguaro* ('Under the Jaguar Sun'‡, 1986) would illustrate Calvino's power as a writer just as well or, conceivably, even better than the one I have chosen. However, by pointing out the reasons of my choice and the list of other possible works, I am metacritically following Calvino's own lead and underscoring his constant use of metanarrative awareness throughout his *oeuvre*. Like Sciascia, Calvino admired the Enlightenment and was profoundly influenced by it; like Gadda, he loved the cornucopia of the world and wanted to possess it by naming it in numerous lists and catalogues. His *oeuvre* is an elegant and profound expression of high modernity: an ironic, light, multiple encyclopaedia in which Italy is a tiny but all-important place in the world.

1981. First edition of 'India, a Travel Survival Kit'. Vittorio Sereni publishes his collection of poems 'Stella variabile' ('Variable Star').

> The taxi driver had a pointed beard, a hairnet and a ponytail tied with a white ribbon. I thought he was a Sikh, because my guidebook described them exactly like this. My guidebook was called *India, a Travel Survival Kit*, I'd bought it in London, more out of curiosity than anything else.
>
> I stretched out on the bottom of the boat and began to look at the sky. The night was truly magnificent. I followed the constellations and thought about the stars and about the time when we used to study them and about the afternoons spent at the planetarium [. . .] And then I thought about variable stars and the book of a person dear to me. And then about dead stars, whose light still reaches us, and about neutron stars.[9]

The attitude displayed by Tabucchi's narrator in *Notturno indiano* ('Indian Nocturne'‡, 1984) while riding in a Bombay taxi and while resting in a boat in Nova Goa is perhaps typical of a contemporary tourist – the product of the affluent society and post-modern culture in which bricolage and irony mix with memory or even elegy. Light years separate him, say, from Pavese's Anguilla contemplating the stars and dreaming of distant lands and future travels in *La luna e i falò*.

The protagonist of *Notturno indiano* is a special tourist. He travels to India in order to find a lost friend, but ends up losing himself instead. His search is punctuated by all sorts of intertextual and intercultural encounters and interchanges (like the allusion to Sereni's *Stella variabile*), and is related in quick strokes, with effective notations about the landscape and the characters, in a highly communicative language which uses copious ironic references to popular culture and the collective imagination. Most of Tabucchi's narrative production, from the short stories of *Piccoli equivoci senza importanza* ('Little Misunderstandings of No Importance', 1985) to the recent novels, *Requiem: un'allucinazione* ('Requiem: A Hallucination'‡, 1992) and *Sostiene Pereira* ('Pereira Maintains'‡, 1994), both set in Lisbon (Tabucchi is an expert in Portuguese literature), displays the qualities and the characteristics of *Notturno indiano* and emphasizes the difficulty of finding, or clinging to, a sure individual Self that is always challenged by the desired, or feared, or sudden encounter with the other. This other might be Fernando Pessoa, the avant-garde Portuguese writer Tabucchi translated into Italian, famous for his heteronyms (in *Requiem*); or Monteiro Rossi, a young activist against the Salazar régime, who provokes a quiet but dramatic change in the life of an old and lazy journalist (in *Sostiene Pereira*).

But the tone of Tabucchi's writing cannot be fully grasped without at least mentioning his taste for adventure and the exotic, running from *Donna di Porto Pim* ('The Woman of Porto Pim'‡, 1983) to *Il gioco del rovescio* ('The Game of the Other Side'‡, 1981) and exemplified in a truly delightful manner in his recent story 'Il mistero del messaggio cifrato' ('The Mystery of the Message in Cypher', 1994). In this story the protagonist is Corto Maltese, the sailor from Hugo Pratt's immensely popular comic strip (and Pratt also appears as an innkeeper specializing in hot-pepper chicken), who tries to help freedom fighters from East Timor in today's Lisbon.

Contemporary Italian literature is not only Italian but also international as far as its geographical referents are concerned, as befits an increasingly homogenized but still multicultural world, and a growing instability of the very notion of the Self. Eco's best-selling novels are perhaps the clearest example of this trend, as are the beautifully written texts by Daniele Del Giudice (1949–): *Lo stadio di Wimbledon* ('Wimbledon's Stadium', 1983), whose narrative quest is concluded in London; *Atlante occidentale* ('Western Atlas'‡, 1985), set in Geneva; *Nel museo di Reims* ('In the Museum at Reims', 1988); and *Staccando l'ombra da terra* ('Detaching the Shadow from the Ground'‡, 1994), whose landscape is the whole sky over the Mediterranean Sea, above national boundaries. But it is worth remembering too Maria Pace Ottieri's Burkina Faso in *Amore nero* ('Black Love', 1984), the California of Andrea De Carlo (1952–) in *Treno di panna* ('Cream Train'‡, 1981), the Austria of Francesca Duranti (1935–) in *La casa sul lago della luna* ('The House on Moon Lake'‡, 1984), the Paris of Rossana Campo (1963–) in *Mai sentita così bene* ('Never Felt so Good', 1995), or *Rimini* (1986) by Vittorio Tondelli (1955–91), titled after the resort town on the Adriatic Sea.

As for the philosophical referents, suffice it to mention *Quattro novelle sulle apparenze* ('Four Short Stories on Appearances'‡, 1987) and *Verso la foce* ('Towards the River Mouth', 1989) by Gianni Celati (1937–), in both of which a Palomar-like perplexity is at play, and it seems that the Self can be rescued only by the Other.

Berkeley, autumn 1995–spring 1996

As I approach the conclusion of this essay, I am increasingly aware of its limitations – my biases and some inevitable omissions. I can only hope that what precedes may stimulate you, the readers, to approach the Italian narratives of self and society, which I have presented here, keeping your minds open and ready to make further intertextual and intercultural connections. Above all, I hope that you and I shall feel that, paraphrasing Calvino, the books that we thought we were merely reading are indeed the story of our lives.

NOTES

1. Giuseppe Tomasi di Lampedusa, *Il Gattopardo* (Milan: Feltrinelli, 1969), p. 36. All translations are the author's own.
2. Giovanni Verga, *I Malavoglia* (Milan: Mondadori, 1968), p. 154.
3. Gabriele D'Annunzio, *Il fuoco* (Milan: Treves, 1904), pp. 556–8.
4. Italo Svevo, *La coscienza di Zeno* (Milan: dall'Oglio, 1966), p. 465.
5. Carlo Emilio Gadda, *Eros e Priapo (Da furore a cenere)* (Milan: Garzanti, 1967), p. 38.
6. Carlo Emilio Gadda, *Quer pasticciaccio brutto de via Merulana* (Milan: Garzanti, 1975), p. 166.
7. Beppe Fenoglio, *Una questione privata* (Milan: Garzanti, 1970), pp. 22–4.
8. Italo Calvino, 'Autobiografia di uno spettatore', in *La strada di San Giovanni* (Milan: Mondadori, 1990), pp. 41–71 (p. 71).
9. Antonio Tabucchi, *Notturno indiano* (Palermo: Sellerio, 1994), pp. 13, 89.

FURTHER READING

Aricò, Santo (ed.), *Contemporary Women Writers in Italy*. Amherst: University of Massachussetts Press, 1990.

Barański, Zygmunt, and Lino, Pertile (eds.), *The New Italian Novel*. Edinburgh University Press, 1994.

Biasin, Gian-Paolo, *Italian Literary Icons*. Princeton University Press, 1985.

Cannon, JoAnn, *Postmodern Italian Fiction*. London and Toronto: Associated University Presses, 1989.

Debenedetti, Giacomo, *Il romanzo del Novecento*. Milan: Garzanti, 1976.

Dombroski, Robert, *L'esistenza ubbidiente*. Naples: Guida, 1984.

Hume, Kathryn, *Calvino's Fictions*. Oxford: Clarendon Press, 1992.

Lazzaro-Weis, Carol, *From Margins to Mainstream: Feminism and Fictional Modes in Italian Women's Writing, 1968–90*. Philadelphia: University of Pennsylvania Press, 1993.

Lucente, Gregory, *Beautiful Fables. Self-consciousness in Italian Narrative from Manzoni to Calvino*. Baltimore: The Johns Hopkins University Press, 1986.

Sartini Blum, Cinzia, *The Other Modernism: F. T. Marinetti's Futurist Fiction of Power*. Berkeley: University of California Press, 1996.

Valesio, Paolo, *Gabriele D'Annunzio*. New Haven: Yale University Press, 1992.

Wilkinson, James, *The Intellectual Resistance in Europe*. Cambridge, Mass.: Harvard University Press, 1981.

9

Searching for new languages: modern Italian poetry*

Tradition: stimulus or millstone?

In newly unified Italy, the Italian literary tradition was particularly venerated. The period's leading poet, Giosue Carducci (1835–1907), in the vigorously anti-Romantic preface to his *Rime* ('Poems') of 1857, had identified only three poetic currents as worthy of cultivation in an 'Italian Italy': Classical Latin; the medieval and Renaissance tradition from Dante to Tasso; and the neo-Classical current from Alfieri to Leopardi. Carducci wrote academic studies on Dante, Petrarch and Leopardi, and echoed Dante's civic poetry in his invectives against those of his own contemporaries who seemed unworthy of their country's past. Both as a passionate Republican and democrat before 1871, and subsequently as a Monarchist, Carducci saw poetry as an elevated civic calling: the 'Congedo' ('Envoy') to the *Rime nuove* ('New Poems', 1887) famously pictures the poet as a blacksmith who, in his fiery soul, fashions glorious national memories into swords to fight for freedom, shields for protection, and garlands to celebrate victory. Thus, to inspire his contemporaries, Carducci's public poetry draws on episodes from Italy's history, often linking them into an ideal narrative culminating in unification. He celebrates Italy's Roman heritage, the triumphs of its free medieval communes, its famous poets and, especially, the heroes of unification. Even his metrics illustrate his belief that the past could nourish the present: his *Odi barbare* ('Barbarian Odes') aim at the effect of classical Latin verse forms, as read during the 'barbarian' period when distinctions between vowel lengths were lost and rhythms were based instead on tonic stress.

In complete contrast, in 1909, only twenty years after the final version of the *Odi barbare*, the inaugural manifesto of the Futurist movement boldly called on poets to sever all ties with tradition. Its founder, Filippo Tommaso Marinetti (1876–1944), proclaimed that their subject-matter and sensibility should, instead, reflect the violent industrial world. Subsequent manifestos demanded a total rejection not only of poetic forms but also of conventional syntax, as the movement vied with the most advanced French avant-garde groups to be the most revolutionary in Europe.

The extreme radicalism of Marinetti's 1909 proposals owed much to his awareness that Italy – whose image abroad depended on the glories of Rome and the Renaissance – was culturally backward with respect to France. Reacting against Positivism, the late nineteenth-century French Decadent and Symbolist poets had taken further the irrationalism, mysticism and cult of originality of the Romantics, producing Mallarmé's complex theories of 'pure poetry' and extensive exploration of the distinctiveness and evocative force of poetic language, the power of analogy, the effects of sound qualities and the musicality of the newly developed *vers libres*. Marinetti composed his earliest poetry – in French – according to such aesthetics, but during the first decade of the new century his notion of 'modernity' came to embrace subsequent, contrasting, French poetic trends, such as the celebration of action and urban society.

Gradual innovation in the late nineteenth century

However, one should not assume that desires for 'modern' poetry (in various senses) had not been expressed earlier in Italy. In fact, the intervening years of intense economic, social and ideological change had seen the emergence of various new concepts of the poet's role and of poetic form, though none as far-reaching as Marinetti's. Indeed, even immediately after unification, Carducci's mainstream classicism did not represent the whole picture. Although there had been no thoroughgoing Romantic revolution in early nineteenth-century Italy, the Milanese *scapigliati* ('Bohemians') had expressed their desolate rejection of bourgeois morality through grotesque imagery and echoes of Baudelaire's *Les Fleurs du Mal*, especially in *Penombre* ('Half-lights', 1864) by Emilio Praga (1839–75). Giovanni Camerana (1845–1905) was influenced by Verlaine's 'Art poétique' in seeking indefiniteness in his verse forms; and, though coming from different starting-points, Carlo Dossi (1849–1910) and

Vittorio Betteloni (1840–1910) portrayed everyday life in a less elevated language than that of the poetic tradition. Symbolist elements were used by various minor poets in the 1890s, especially Gian Pietro Lucini (1867–1914).

The most important transitional figures were Gabriele D'Annunzio (1863-1938) and Giovanni Pascoli (1855-1912), whose wide-ranging *œuvres* would powerfully influence twentieth-century Italian poetic language and technique, even when their views of the poet's role were rejected. A vast gulf lay between D'Annunzio's highly publicized sexual and political adventuring and Pascoli's withdrawn, academic existence, and, indeed, between their themes; but both, while being deeply imbued with Greek, Latin and earlier Italian literature, incorporated certain Decadent elements into the Italian lyric tradition, thereby contributing substantially to its breakdown.

Aestheticism, in various forms, was the first of many foreign-inspired manners adopted by D'Annunzio. Following Gautier's *Emaux et Camées* ('Enamels and Cameos', 1852), he regarded art as decorative, depicting the poet as a craftsman and, specifically, in 'Il sonetto d'oro' ('The Golden Sonnet', 1883), as a goldsmith. Like the English Pre-Raphaelites, he adopted an archaizing manner, imitating Trecento and Quattrocento verse forms in *Isaotta Guttadauro ed altre poesie* ('Isaotta Guttadauro and Other Poems', 1886). His revealing line 'Il verso è tutto' ('Verse is all') became the motto of the paradigmatic Decadent aesthete Andrea Sperelli, the protagonist of his first novel *Il piacere* ('Pleasure', 1889). Subsequently, in the *Poema paradisiaco* ('The Poem of Paradise', 1893), as a corollary to the Decadent sensuality, even sadism, of some of his work, he explored sensual weariness and loss of innocence in the muted tones and simple language of Verlaine and the Belgian Symbolists Maeterlinck and Rodenbach.

The poetics of D'Annunzio's *Laudi del cielo del mare della terra e degli eroi* ('Praises of the Sky, Sea, Earth and Heroes') combine further Decadent and Symbolist literary influences with the political ideology of Nationalism and Activism. Adapting Nietzsche's concept of the Superman, D'Annunzio sees the poet as a man of superior will, capable of taking political action to defend the privileges of the élite and of dominating reality through his imaginative creations. The programmatic prelude 'Laus vitae' ('The Praise of Life'), which constitutes most of the first volume, *Maia* (1903), depicts the poet's epic journey of initiation through Greece and Rome to the fearsome industrial cities of the present. Inspired by Nietzsche's theories that ancient Greek art derived from a Dionysian intoxication with life and change, D'Annunzio represents the poet as revitalized by rediscovering a pre-Christian sense of harmony with nature; and prophesies that the appearance of a new muse called *Energèia* ('Energy') will – through the Superman – usher in a new age of Italian imperialism. The poem's climax celebrates the poet's expressive power, representing it, like Wagner's symphonic writing, as a manifestation of this new age.

The third volume, the celebrated *Alcyone* (1904), depicts the Superman's temporary 'respite' from his heroic mission – including the Nationalistic writing in the second volume, *Elettra* (1903) – but is not a rejection of it. *Alcyone* is constructed as the diary of a summer when the poet recovers the primitive sense of identification with nature and creates 'new myths'. Its far-reaching influence depends not, however, on its ideology but on its Symbolist techniques designed to give poetry the evocative power of music. Delicate analogies skilfully transmute reality into a fragile, evanescent 'dream', as in 'Novilunio di settembre' ('New Moon of September'):

> il viso della creatura
> celeste che ha nome
> Luna, trasparente come
> la medusa marina,
> come la brina nell'alba,
> labile come
> la neve su l'acqua,
> la schiuma su la sabbia[1]

> (the face of the creature
> of heaven whose name
> is Moon, transparent like
> the jellyfish of the sea,
> like hoar-frost at dawn,
> fleeting like
> snow on water,
> foam on sand).

Words are selected for their sound effects; and complex patterns of suggestion are created through alliteration, assonance, internal rhyme, near-rhyme and rhythm.

The lyrics of *Alcyone*, where D'Annunzio experiments *within* the Italian metrical tradition, constitute a crucial staging-post in the development of Italian free verse. While some rework classical and early Italian metrical forms, the most musical use D'Annunzio's own *strofe lunga* ('long strophe'), a free combination of traditional lines of varying lengths, where traditional licences are exploited to create new rhythms. 'L'onda' ('The Wave'), with its underlying ternary rhythm, perfectly encapsulates this interdependence of sound and sense:

> L'onda si spezza,
> precipita nel cavo
> del solco sonora;
> spumeggia, biancheggia,
> s'infiora, odora   (*Alcyone*, pp. 438–9)

> (The wave breaks,
> falls into the hollow
> of the furrow resonantly;
> it foams, it turns white,
> it bursts into flower, it gives off fragrance).

The poem is both an onomatapoeic representation of the movement of the waves and a self-referential 'praise / of my Long Strophe', a celebration of the verse form whose rhythms can evoke the rhythms of the universe (*Alcyone*, p. 100).

Pascoli, who composed poetry in both Italian and Latin, was also, in Contini's words, a 'revolutionary within the tradition'.[2] He wrote narrative and civic poetry, as well as lyrics, but disagreed with Carducci's view of the poet's role. Instead, like the Symbolists, he believed in the autonomy of poetry, though not in formalistic aestheticism. According to the fundamental expression of his poetics, the essay 'Il fanciullino' ('The Little Boy', 1897), poetry could, paradoxically, increase its readers' love for their country, their family and humanity, not by being didactic but by being itself. The poet should gaze at the world like an innocent child, with wonderment and without preconceptions. Thus poetry should have no privileged subjects, but – in an echo of Virgil's *lacrimae rerum* – should find 'in things themselves [...] their smile and their tears'.[3] In his most influential lyric collection, *Myricae* ('Tamarisks'; first edition 1891, definitive edition 1903), humble scenes are captured in detail, without being made to illustrate any political or moral stance: 'The long and shaky gate creaks / and blocks the road; standing at the fence / the gossips chatter in a huddle' ('In capannello', 'In a Huddle', *Poesie*, vol. I, p. 58). However, in a way which will be taken up by later poets, these scenes can become images of emotional states. Thus, anguished isolation and terror at the mysteries of the universe are evoked by the vivid, hallucinatory sensory impressions encapsulated in the noun phrases of 'Temporale' ('Storm'):

> Un bubbolìo lontano...
>
> Rosseggia l'orizzonte,
> come affocato, a mare;
> nero di pece, a monte,
> stracci di nubi chiare:
> tra il nero un casolare:
> un'ala di gabbiano   (*Poesie*, vol. I, p. 95)
>
> (A distant rumbling...
>
> The horizon glows red,
> as though on fire, towards the sea;
> pitch black, towards the hills,
> tatters of bright clouds:
> amidst the blackness a farmhouse:
> a seagull's wing)

and by the haunting vision of a world illuminated by a flash of lightning in 'Il lampo' ('The Flash of Lightning'):

> E cielo e terra si mostrò qual era:
>
> la terra ansante, livida, in sussulto;
> il cielo ingombro, tragico, disfatto:
> bianca bianca nel tacito tumulto
> una casa apparì sparì d'un tratto;
> come un occhio, che, largo, esterrefatto,
> s'aprì si chiuse, nella notte nera   (*Poesie*, vol. I, p. 119).
>
> (And heaven and earth revealed themselves as they were:
>
> the earth heaving, bruised, shuddering;
> the heavens laden, tragic, torn apart:
> white white in the silent tumult
> a house appeared disappeared in an instant;
> like an eye, which, wide open, astounded,
> opened closed, in the black night).

While D'Annunzio enriched his poetic lexicon with rare literary words, even describing modern machines with elaborate Latinate vocabulary,

Pascoli extended his by including everyday language, precise botanical and ornithological terms, onomatapoeic representations of birdsong, and sectorial language, such as that of the Italians who have lived in America:

> '*Ioe*, bona cianza! . . .' 'Ghita, state bene! . . .'
> '*Good bye.*' 'L'avete presa la ticchetta?'
> '*Oh yes.*' 'Che barco?' '*Il Prinzessin Irene.*'
>
>   ('Italy', *Poesie*, vol. I, p. 329).

> ('Joe, good luck! . . .' 'Ghita, all the best! . . .'
> 'Good bye.' 'Have you got your ticket?'
> 'Oh yes.' 'Which boat?' 'The *Princess Irene*.'

The combination of such unconventional language with the rhyme scheme of the *Divine Comedy* typifies Pascoli's particular blend of old and new. Furthermore, he creates new rhythms within traditional metrical forms, not only, like D'Annunzio, by exploiting poetic licences, but also, paradoxically, by imitating Latin forms, though in a way different from Carducci's: he reproduces the pattern of Latin long and short vowels as a pattern of stressed and unstressed syllables, thereby producing a new, regular rhythm.

The new movements of the early twentieth century

Armonia in grigio e silenzio ('Harmony in Greyness and Silence', 1903) by Corrado Govoni (1885–1965) is generally considered the first manifestation of the diffused tendency defined as *crepuscolarismo* ('the poetry of twilight') by the critic G. A. Borgese in his 1910 review of *Poesie scritte col lapis* ('Poems Written with a Pencil') by Marino Moretti (1885–1979). In humble language, like Pascoli's, Govoni and other *crepuscolari* painted melancholy pictures of quiet provincial life, emphasizing motifs such as deserted gardens, hospitals, churches and convents, drawn from the *Poema paradisiaco* and from D'Annunzio's own French and Belgian sources. The *crepuscolari*, however, rejected D'Annunzio's cult of art and his self-aggrandizing view of the poet. While they also rejected Pascoli's belief in poetry's ultimate moral value, the scenes they depicted, like Pascoli's, could become emblems of emotion, and their marginalized characters could represent the disillusioned poet who, lacking any sense of civic purpose, is alienated from modern society. The most celebrated examples occur in the work of Sergio Corazzini (1886–1907), the leading member of the Roman *crepuscolari*: in 'Per organo di Barberia' ('For a Barrel Organ'), from *Il piccolo libro inutile* ('The Useless Little Book', 1906), the monotonous, neglected lament of the barrel organ represents his own writing, and in 'Desolazione del povero poeta sentimentale' ('The Sorrow of the Poor Sentimental Poet'), in the same volume, he paradoxically gives his own poetry validity by denying that it fits into traditional categories, portraying himself not as a poet but as a suffering child longing for death.

Montale was to look back with special admiration to Guido Gozzano (1883–1916), the leader of the *crepuscolari* in Turin, for 'going beyond' the omnipresent D'Annunzio and thus acting as a bridge to Montale's own poetry.[4] Gozzano's distinctive tools of irony and parody set the sublime tones of traditional poetic language alongside the prosaic. Famously, the background to the lovers' conversations in 'La signorina Felicita', in his 1911 collection *I colloqui* ('The Conversations'), is not the melancholy, abandoned aristocratic park beloved of D'Annunzio but a vegetable garden. However, such realism did not constitute a rejection of art. The banal motifs – such as the homely character of Felicita herself – also have literary sources (in such poets as Pascoli, or Gozzano's French contemporary Francis Jammes). Contrasting manners are juxtaposed in a complex exploration of the appeal of literature, despite its artificiality. In *I colloqui* experience is stylized, literary allusions abound, and the structure recalls that of a Petrarchan *canzoniere*, where poems reflecting the poet's development are framed by others expressing the contemplative voice of his later self. Here, memory's multiple perspective produces an ironic tone, as the poet contemplates his earlier self in various Romantic poses, or in the guise of literary characters. The great Romantic themes of Love and Death prove illusions, and, with his dreams destroyed, the poet is denied even the consolation of emotion.

Parody, but in more comic vein, was also the way forward for Aldo Palazzeschi (1885–1974). 'Chi sono?' ('Who am I?', 1909), the riddle-like summation of his pre-Futurist poetics, presents him as another alienated figure, unconcerned with civic duty, formal beauty, or musicality. His themes, like Corazzini's, are melancholy and nostalgia, but with an eccentric, clown-like twist: he memorably described himself as 'Il saltimbanco dell'anima mia' ('the acrobat of my soul').[5] Futurism's radical rejection of Romantic subjectivity intensified Palazzeschi's often grotesque whimsy. In his Futurist collection *L'incendiario* ('The Fireraiser'), the poet's conversation with sexually aberrant flowers in 'I fiori' ('The Flowers') parodies the myth of nature's consoling purity; and in 'La fiera dei morti' ('All Souls' Fair'), the clichéd subject of All Souls' Day, traditionally an occasion for a melancholy description of autumn and a lament for the dead, is transformed into a scene of transgressive popular festivity and an opportunity for witty, disrespectful fantasizing about conventional epitaphs.

However, Palazzeschi's Futurist poetry is not simply negative. 'E lasciatemi divertire!' ('And Let Me Enjoy Myself!') envisages the creation of new poetry from the destruction of the old: pure sounds, the basic building-blocks of language, can be used in a poetry whose justification is solely ludic. Similarly, 'La passeggiata' ('The Walk'), while further debunking D'Annunzio and Romantic tradition, also creates new poetry, in the manner of Cubist collages of *objets trouvés*, out of the visual language of the city.

Futurist ideology in its narrower sense – not shared by Palazzeschi or those on the margins of the movement who sympathized mainly with its cultural iconoclasm – involved an irrationalist cult of action, violence, speed, aggressive nationalism, the glorification of war and the aesthetics of the machine. Futurist poetry celebrated electricity, cars and aeroplanes; and Marinetti nurtured the ideal of a machine-like Futurist hero, no longer debilitated by human morality, affection or Romantic love. He even dreamt of replacing traditional themes with a poetry of the material world.

While early Futurist poetry, influenced by French Symbolism and Lucini's theories, used free verse, Marinetti's 1912 invention of *parole in libertà* ('words in freedom'), which he claimed would better represent modern sensibility in a world of fast communications and global awareness, constituted a revolution in technique. Punctuation and conventional syntax were abolished, along with adjectives and adverbs; infinitives were used to eliminate the personal; and meaning depended on nouns linked together not by logic but by analogies (that crucial device of the Symbolists), in a process of 'wire-less imagination'. The first example of the technique, Marinetti's 'Battaglia Peso + Odore' ('Battle Weight + Smell', 1912), evokes his experience of the Libyan War as confused simultaneous sensations:

> Mezzogiorno ¾ flauti gemiti solleone **tumbtumb** allarme
> Gargaresch schiantarsi crepitazione marcia Tintinnìo zaini fucili
> zoccoli chiodi cannoni criniere ruote cassoni (De Maria and Dondi,
> *Marinetti*, p. 89)

(12.45 flutes groans heat **tumbtumb** alarm Gargaresch crashing
cracking march Jingling knapsacks rifles hooves nails cannons manes
wheels ammunition-chests).

He expresses no emotion or judgement, but evokes associated sensations
through a dynamic sequence of suggestions: 'Sea = lace–emeralds–
freshness–elasticity–abandon–softness' (ibid., p. 91).

Through further typographical experimentation and cross-fertil-
ization with the techniques of the increasingly innovative Futurist
artists, *parole in libertà* swiftly developed into *tavole parolibere* ('free-word
paintings') – strikingly new visual poetry which, despite the widespread restoration of tradition immediately after the First World War,
would influence the concrete poetry of the 1960s and 1970s. Many
varied examples filled the pages of the Florentine periodical *Lacerba* in
1913–14, during the highly fruitful alliance between its editors,
Ardengo Soffici (1879–1964) and Giovanni Papini (1881–1956), and
Marinetti's movement. Soffici, attracted like others to the technique's
potential while not fully sharing Marinetti's aesthetics, produced free-
word poems and *tavole* which stand out for their subjectivity and ironic
wit.

New and old on the eve of the First World War

New approaches were clearly in the air on the eve of the First World War,
even in the work of emerging poets who were formally at the opposite
end of the spectrum to the Futurists. Umberto Saba (1883–1957) and
Camillo Sbarbaro (1888–1967) used traditional metres, especially the
endecasillabi (eleven-syllable lines) and *settenari* (seven-syllable lines)
most closely associated with the Italian lyric, and focused exclusively on
intimate autobiographical subjects. However, they were forward-
looking in their combination of traditional form with unheroic
content, and in their use of prosaic language – not polemically, but as a
natural means of expression. Saba celebrated his everyday experiences
in the poems of *Coi miei occhi* ('With My Own Eyes', 1912); while in
Pianissimo ('Very Softly', 1914) Sbarbaro used subdued, unmelodic tones
and bare language to explore the psychological barrenness of what he
saw as his narrow life. *Endecasillabi* and *settenari* appear, too, in the
Frammenti lirici ('Lyric Fragments', 1913) of Clemente Rebora
(1003 1937), but are interwoven with the contrasting rhythms of eight,

ten, and twelve-syllable lines to express contemporary psychological and moral tensions.

Autobiography, accompanied by moderate formal experimentalism, especially the blurring of the boundaries between poetry and prose, characterized the work of many writers associated with the Florentine periodical *La Voce* ('The Voice'). Piero Jahier (1884–1966), a close ally of Giuseppe Prezzolini (1882–1982), who had founded the journal in 1908 with a programme of wide-ranging cultural reform, alternated prose passages with impressionistic lyrics in *Ragazzo* ('A Boy'), where the deep emotional experiences of his youth, especially those occasioned by his father's suicide, are conveyed in movingly direct language. His poems themselves often approach rhythmic prose in their use of lines which are considerably longer than the *endecasillabo*, a metrical technique which possibly influenced Pavese's poetry in the 1930s.

The prose poetry of Arturo Onofri (1885–1928), especially *Orchestrine* ('Small Orchestras', 1917), was based on different aesthetics. His influential theories, published in 1915 in *La Voce*, now under the more literary editorship of Giuseppe De Robertis (1888–1963), focused on the *frammento*, a brief, dense fragment of lyricism, regarded not as an expression of emotion or ideas but as pure poetry, based on the Symbolism of Mallarmé and Rimbaud.

Rimbaud's *Illuminations* strongly influenced the poetry and the prose poetry of the extraordinary Dino Campana (1885–1932), whose mental instability forced him into the life of an outsider. *Canti orfici* ('Orphic Songs', 1914) includes both forms, united, however, in their powerfully visual and richly colourful language. Futurist technique influenced some descriptions of the external world, such as the opening of 'Passeggiata in tram in America e ritorno' ('Tram Journey in America and Back'): 'Harsh prelude of a muffled symphony, trembling violin with an electrified string, tram which runs in a line in the iron sky of curved wires while the white bulk of the city towers like a dream';[6] but industrial society is not Campana's subject. Rather, his descriptions draw on memories, dreams or hallucinations, and take on a mysteriously symbolic quality, as in 'La notte' ('The Night'):

> I remember an old city, turreted and with red walls, burning in the boundless plain in scorching August [. . .] Unconsciously I lifted my eyes to the barbarian tower which dominated the very long avenue of the plane trees. Over the silence which had become intense it relived its distant and savage myth. (*Canti orfici*, pp. 15–17)

Experimentalism and tradition in Ungaretti's poetry

Perhaps the most lasting synthesis of modern experimentation with the essential elements of tradition appears in Giuseppe Ungaretti's First World War poems. Like Marinetti, Ungaretti (1888–1970) was born in Egypt and had a French literary education. He was familiar with the latest French and Italian avant-garde developments, being close to the groups around *Lacerba* and De Robertis's *La Voce*. The distinctly modern consciousness voiced in his first volume, *Il porto sepolto* ('The Buried Harbour', 1916: part of *'L'allegria'*, 'Joy', in Ungaretti's collected works) involves not a celebration of the industrial world, but rather the awareness that identity, defined through family and religious heritage, can be lost in urban society ('In memoria', 'In Memory') and that the loss of traditional certainties causes suffering ('Peso', 'Burden'). Individual feeling thus remains the stuff of his poetry, but it is not expressed through wordy eloquence. Scenes from reality are divested of their occasional characteristics – but not of their concreteness – so that they can become powerful symbols of something more abstract or universal: in 'Un'altra notte' ('Another Night'), for example, the intensely concentrated description of the poet's fumbling attempt to refamiliarize himself with his features after some shocking experience becomes an analogy of his painful attempt to make sense of his existence:

> In quest'oscuro
> con le mani
> gelate
> distinguo
> il mio viso
>
> Mi vedo
> abbandonato nell'infinito[7]

> (In this darkness
> with my hands
> frozen
> I make out
> my face
>
> I see myself
> abandoned in infinity).

The separation of concrete and abstract, or the two elements of the analogy, into separate stanzas shows how Ungaretti's free form closely reflects meaning. His short lines of *versi liberi* require a measured reading which emphasizes the single word, thereby deepening the layers of meaning despite the apparently simple vocabulary: but traditional metres have not been totally jettisoned, and *endecasillabi* may sometimes lie, half-unnoticed, in combinations of lines. With such techniques Ungaretti succeeds in exploring his complex experience of war: both the destruction, suffering, isolation and loss, and the intoxicating moments of harmony with nature and the revitalizing sense of comradeship, which creates a sense of national identity and symbolizes the power of human brotherhood as a shield against the human condition. At the same time he celebrates the power of art to give permanence to fleeting human experience.#

Ungaretti's intentions in *Il porto sepolto* were to examine the pieces of a watch's mechanism to find out how it worked. The watch was poetry, its pieces words. A second edition included a preface, 'Towards a new classical art', reflecting his return to tradition like other poets, such as Saba and Sbarbaro, in the aftermath of the First World War. If Ungaretti's intentions had originally been to examine the watch's pieces, his intention from *Sentimento del tempo* ('Feeling of Time', 1933) onwards was to reassemble them. Time's manifold manifestations were examined with a sense of transiency tinged with deep melancholy: 'Già verso un'alta, lucida / Sepoltura, si salpa' ('Already towards a high, lucid / Sepulchre, we weigh anchor': 'Le stagioni', 'The Seasons'). The individual words of *Il porto sepolto* here come together in magnificent alliterative verse, exemplified in the opening of 'O notte' ('Oh Night'): 'Dall'ampia ansia dell'alba' ('From the ample anxiety of dawn'). The return to traditional metre was motivated by a desire to move away from the particularity of *L'allegria* towards universality; and that was to be achieved through abstraction, what, in 'Memoria d'Ofelia D'Alba' ('Memory of Ophelia D'Alba'), Ungaretti called 'Cose consumate: / Emblemi eterni, nomi, / Evocazioni pure . . .' ('Things consumed: / Eternal emblems, names, / Pure evocations . . .'). Yet the poetry was far from abstract, rescued from such a risk through its strong sensuality, as seen in 'Nascita d'aurora' ('Birth of Dawn').

Given Ungaretti's French education, Baudelaire, Mallarmé and Valéry can be sensed here; but the seminal influences are Italian – Petrarch and Leopardi, particularly Leopardi's 'Alla Primavera' ('To Springtime') and 'Inno ai Patriarchi' ('Hymn to the Patriarchs'). Plato too is present in the contemplation of the ideal, recognizable in

'Danni con fantasia' ('You Damn with Imagination'); but the Platonic ideal is overshadowed by a sense of the innate corruption of human nature, which derives ultimately from Saint Augustine. Memory, as a consequence of this Augustinian sense of corruption, loses its clarity and innocence to become decidedly darker, as in 'Alla noia' ('To Ennui'): '[. . .] fluido simulacro, / Malinconico scherno, / Buio del sangue . . .' ([. . .] fluid simulacrum, / Melancholy mockery, / Darkness of blood . . .).

The haunting beauty of 'Sirene' ('Sirens') anticipates the later poetry of *La Terra Promessa* ('The Promised Land', 1950) whose earliest fragments date from 1935; but personal grief, along with an awareness of civilization's fragility, resultant on the Second World War interrupted with *Il dolore* ('Grief', 1947) the sensuous abstraction towards which his poetry was moving. The Baroque horror of the void, already present in *Sentimento del tempo*, here finds its objective correlative in the Brazilian landscape of 'Tu ti spezzasti' ('You Shattered') where fabulous turtles emerging from the sea's depths mesmerize the poet's young son, represented in that hostile foreign landscape as a gold-crest, the smallest of Italian birds. On a grander scale, in 'Folli i miei passi' ('Mad My Steps'), Michelangelo and, in 'Defunti su montagne' ('Dead on the Mountains'), Masolino da Panicale's fresco in San Clemente in Rome, both serve as examples of hope that the creative spirit may yet prevail.

La Terra Promessa appeared in 1950, to be followed in 1960 by *Ultimi cori per la Terra Promessa* ('Last Choruses for the Promised Land'), which constituted the greater part of *Il taccuino del vecchio* ('The Notebook of an Old Man'). The Promised Land may have been suggested by Ungaretti's Egyptian birth, but the literary model was provided by Virgil's *Aeneid*, whose protagonist replicated the autobiographical 'superstite / lupo di mare' ('surviving old / sea dog') of 'Allegria di naufragi' ('Joy of Shipwrecks'); and it was that autobiographical strand which guaranteed against abstraction and provided the texts with their poetic and psychological modernity. The opening 'Canzone' described the poet's state of mind, and the nineteen 'Choruses' dedicated to Dido were entitled 'Choruses Descriptive of the States of Mind of Dido'. Yet these subtly nuanced texts found elaboration within poetic vehicles whose complex accomplishment belonged originally and notably to the lyric masters of the fourteenth century, Dante and Petrarch.

Dante and Montale

Ungaretti is perhaps *the* exemplar of the wedding of tradition and individual talent of which Eliot spoke. Eugenio Montale (1896–1981; Nobel prize for literature, 1975) rejected from the beginning the tradition of those modern laureate poets, like D'Annunzio, who moved 'only among plants with little-used names: box-wood privet or acanthus' in favour of his native Ligurian landscape with its 'grassy ditches where in half dried-up puddles boys caught the odd skinny eel' ('I limoni', 'The lemons', from *Ossi di seppia*, 'Cuttlefish Bones', 1925, definitive edition 1931). That realistic note so evident throughout his early poetry was to be a constant in Montale, nowhere better illustrated than in 'L'anguilla' ('The Eel') from his third and finest volume, *La bufera e altro* ('The Storm and Other Things', 1956), where the eel turns up again in a thirty-line poem whose mixture of eleven and seven-syllable lines constitutes one single, uninterrupted syntactical movement.

But if the realism is the same, its purpose has changed, for the eel here undergoes a transformation, becoming in turn 'green soul', 'spark' and 'iris', an iris moreover which is 'twin to the one your lashes frame / and you set shining virginal among / the sons of men, sunk in your mire–'. What these lines reveal is that the poem's true subject is not the eel but a female figure whose vitality it mirrors. The lower-case 'iris' echoes an earlier upper-case 'Iris', the title of the opening poem of 'Silvae' ('Woods'), *La bufera*'s most important section; but there the name is simply one of a number of *senhals* (or fictitious names for the beloved, as in old Provençal poetry) for the dedicatee, I. B., of Montale's second volume, *Le occasioni* ('The Occasions', 1939). The initials are those of an American Dante scholar, Irma Brandeis, whom Montale had met in Florence in 1933. The love poetry inspired by her was to take the form of a homage to her medieval interests through its broadly Petrarchan structure (a structure whereby the physical absence of the beloved becomes a poetic presence thanks to the power of memory), allied to a strong moral impulse reflecting their interest in Dante. The longer poems of *Le occasioni* and *La bufera* have a richness and complexity which make them unique in contemporary Italian poetry; but the shorter poems, the 'ossi brevi' ('short [cuttle-fish] bones') of Montale's first volume, the 'mottetti' (motets) of his second, and the ' "Flashes" e dediche' ('Flashes and Dedications') of his third, may have been more influential on later poets. *Poesie a Casarsa* ('Poems to Casarsa', 1942), by Pier Paolo Pasolini (1922–75), for example, clearly reveal a rare understanding of how their model, Montale's 'mottetti', worked.

And yet, if one considers one of Montale's most memorable poems, 'La casa dei doganieri' ('The Customs House'), it is difficult not to think of him as an instinctive follower of Petrarch; for, as in many of Petrarch's poems, the pre-text here is constituted by the effective absence of the beloved, which becomes in the text an intense presence through memory. Nevertheless in its images and references it is entirely modern.

Montale's second and third volumes, given their inspiration, represented a poetry of 'high' culture (of the 'highest' culture, providing as it did a synthesis of the major strands of the poetic tradition, the cathartic memorial strand so important in Petrarch and the polyphonic richness of Dante's *Commedia*) not at all immediately accessible to the generality of readers: a poetry which echoed the closed nature of medieval Provençal verse, and one which provided a model readily taken up by the poets of the next generation, the Hermetics.

Montale's subsequent poetry, while much more accessible, represented a change in tone rather than subject-matter. The poems in memory of his wife, for example (which have drawn comparison with Hardy's late poems for his first wife), shot through as they are with lines memorable in their simplicity – '[. . .] But it is possible, you know, to love a shadow, being shadows ourselves' ('Xenia' I, 13, from *Satura*, 1971) – are for all that no less Petrarchan (or Dantesque: Brodsky reminds us here of the meeting of Statius and Virgil in *Purgatorio* XXI.130–6)[8] than the earlier poetry, filling as they do the void created by her absence with memories of her alive so vivid in detail as to create the illusion of a presence. There is, however, another strand running through this later poetry, much of it characterized by an epigrammatic quality, and that is self-irony, parodic in nature and targeting his earlier verse, now seen, in his own words, as 'works in regress'.

Petrarch and Quasimodo

The poetry of Salvatore Quasimodo (1908–68; Nobel prize for literature, 1959) seemed to undergo a radical change in mid-stream. The immediate cause was the German occupation of Italy after the armistice of 8 September 1943. The opening of 'Alle fronde dei salici' ('On the Willow Branches', from *Giorno dopo giorno* 'Day after Day', 1947) says it all: 'And how could we have sung / with the foreign foot upon our heart, / among the dead abandoned in the squares?' In his 'Discourse on Poetry', philosophers, Quasimodo stated, had claimed that poetry was not subject to change either during or after war, but that was an 'illusion, because war alters the moral life of a people'. But the deepest causes governing the rhythm of the history of the arts are not, as Kundera suggested, sociological or political, but aesthetic.[9] Confirmation of this was to be found in Quasimodo's 1945 essay on 'Petrarch and the Sense of Solitude'. Mario Luzi (1914–), the most precocious of the younger poets (his first volume, *La barca*, 'The Boat', had appeared in 1935, only five years after Quasimodo's first volume, *Acque e terre*, 'Waters and Lands'), also wrote an essay on Petrarch in 1945, entitled 'Hell and Limbo'. What Quasimodo's essay suggested, in spite of the realism of *Giorno dopo giorno*, was not a break but a continuity, a continuity argued by Carlo Bo, the 'theoretician' of the Hermetic poets, in his 1947 introduction to the volume.[10] But a continuity with what?

Line 5 of the volume's title poem reads: 'And no longer can I return to my Elysium.' Elysium was his native Sicily: not simply the modern island, but the much older one of Magna Graecia. Quasimodo, who had studied Latin and Greek in his twenties, was to excel as a translator of Greek lyrical poetry and tragedy. That classical vein, allied to his innate Petrarchism, is finely illustrated in 'Vento a Tindari' ('Wind at Tindari'), where the harshness of mainland exile and the bitterness of bread which he must break contrast with Sicily's positive aspects in the poem's opening: 'Tindari, I know you mild / among broad hills, above the waters / of the god's soft islands.' It was this contrast, Quasimodo's version of Yeats's quarrel with himself out of which poetry is born, which would continue throughout his poetic career.

Hermeticism's implosive silence: Luzi and Parronchi

The silence imposed by the war on the Hermetics became a critical commonplace which long endured in Italy and beyond. Vittoria Bradshaw's 1971 anthology *From Pure Silence to Impure Dialogue. A Survey of Post-War Italian Poetry 1945–1965* illustrates it well. By 1945, however, the Hermetics were barely out of their twenties, and if we look at Luzi's essay on Petrarch, the endless source in song of which he talks is recognized for what it is: a false paradise, self-centred and inward-looking, cut off from the real world, existing purely in a timeless vacuum. Certainly the imagery of 'Avorio' ('Ivory'), from *Avvento notturno* ('Nocturnal Advent',

1940): 'The equinoctial cypress speaks, obscure / and mountainous exults the buck deer' would suggest just such an introspective aestheticism – as indeed did much pre-war Quasimodo.

But already, in 1936, in 'Cimitero delle fanciulle' ('Cemetery of Young Maidens'), to the Limbo-like world of Petrarch Luzi had juxtaposed his 'solemn craggy existence'. Its first fruits were to be found, appropriately enough, in *Primizie del deserto* ('First Fruits of the Desert', 1952). Thus, the opening of 'Notizie a Giuseppina dopo tanti anni' ('News for Josephine after So Many Years'), 'What do you hope for, what do you promise yourself, my friend / [. . .]?', modelled on one of Petrarch's best-known sonnets, 'Che fai? Che pensi? Che pur dietro guardi' ('What are you doing? What are you thinking? You who still look behind you'), recognized, despite that nostalgic backward glance, its destiny in the present, not the past, and in the other, not in self: 'Everything else which must be still exists, / the river flows, the countryside changes, / there is hail, it stops raining, the odd dog barks.'

Pasolini claimed, in a review of *Onore del vero* ('Truth to Tell', 1957), that the depiction of the real world was merely a projection of Luzi's internal world, redeemed in poems like 'E il lupo' ('And the Wolf') as a result of its moral creed ('Everything, / even the gloomy animal eternity / that moans in us, can become holy'), but that ultimately it was vitiated, even in his finest poems, by 'an insensitivity when faced with the phenomena of human life and history'. Likewise, he was to observe that a contemporary of Luzi, Alessandro Parronchi (1914–), had taken a step forward in *Coraggio di vivere* ('Courage of Living', 1956): 'But he will still have to realize, some day, that to believe in our own existence we have to believe in the existence of history.'[11]

Lyricism versus Realism: Pavese, Bertolucci, Sereni

The question of the nature of Realism, discussed by Pasolini and Luzi in *La Chimera* ('The Chimera') in 1954, seemed encapsulated in the former's remarks on Parronchi. But given the lyrical nature of Italian poetry, a Realist tradition was improbable. Italian literature's mind-boggling lack of concreteness from the fifteenth century until the end of the nineteenth, as noted by Lampedusa,[12] was, in poetry at least, to be neither easily nor quickly remedied in spite of the Neorealist climate of the period. Arguably the only genuine experimenter with narrative verse was Cesare Pavese (1908–50) in his 1936 *Lavorare stanca* ('Work is Tiring'), possibly influenced – as mentioned earlier – by Jahier, although a narrative strand inspired by Gozzano could be said to exist in the early Montale, who, as already noted, much admired Gozzano, as well as in Vittorio Sereni (1913–83), who had written his thesis on him in 1936, and in Pasolini. Sereni's *Un posto di vacanza* ('A Holiday Place', in *Stella Variabile*, 'Variable Star', 1981) might be cited as an example, but it is *La camera da letto* ('The Bedroom', 1984, definitive edition 1989) by Attilio Bertolucci (1911–2000) which perhaps best represents this narrative strand. Writers like Giorgio Bassani (1916–2000) and Leonardo Sciascia (1921–89), who began as poets, had to turn to prose to articulate that belief in history advocated by Pasolini in his Parronchi review. Most poets, however, refused to have poetry serve as social commentary. Louis MacNeice's plea for *impure* poetry, for poetry conditioned by the poet's life and the world around him, would have carried little weight in Italy. Sereni's 'Una visita in fabbrica' ('A Visit to a Factory'), for example, grew from two lines – 'happy with others' bread / which only with an alert mind tastes bitter', lines which echo Dante (*Paradiso* XVII.59) – to ninety-five, its final part inscribing Leopardi's 'A Silvia': *E di me si spendea la miglior parte* ('*and the best part of myself was spent*'). Poetry, even in its purest lyrical moments, even in its closest contact with (industrial) reality such as here, reflects not life but literature. The title poem of Pasolini's *Le ceneri di Gramsci*, too, is written in tercets which approximate those of Dante's *Divine Comedy*, and he also has recourse, like Sereni, to literary inscription, in this instance the English poet William Wordsworth's 'Ode on the Intimations of Immortality' which is literally cited within Pasolini's text ('And O ye Fountains...').

With few exceptions – Camillo Sbarbaro, a botanist; Leonardo Sinisgalli (1908–81), an engineer – most modern Italian poets come from a humanities background and become academics or schoolteachers. Andrea Zanzotto (1921–), for example, taught in his native Pieve di Soligo (Treviso) for most of his life. Sereni too was originally a teacher, but in 1952 he moved to Pirelli and, in 1958, to Mondadori.

War and Resistance: Sereni, Pasolini, Zanzotto

What indelibly marked Sereni's post-war poetry was his absence from the Resistance through having been a prisoner of war in North Africa: '*Late, too late for the feast* / – the foul throat taunted – / *too late!*' ('Il male d'Africa', 'The African Sickness', from *Diario d'Algeria*, 'Algerian Diary',

1947). Pasolini's poetry too was marked by the Resistance, his younger brother Guido being killed by Yugoslav partisans in 1945. The Montello wood in Zanzotto's *Il Galateo in Bosco* ('The Woodland Book of Manners', 1978) was the scene of fierce fighting during the Great War. While the volume's title alludes ironically and distantly to Della Casa's 1558 treatise on manners, *Il Galateo, ovvero de' Costumi* ('Galateo, or on Manners'), much more seriously and closer in time it refers to the destruction of a society which, as Vivienne Hand notes, 'has been irreversibly shattered by the events of historical reality, such as the battles between Austria and Hungary fought in the Montello region in 1918'.[13] The awareness of the fragile veneer of civil society in our century, rent as it has been by war and strife, has been one of the unifying strands of Italian poetry from Ungaretti to Zanzotto.

Explosive silence: Luzi

But to return to the paradigm provided by the dynamic broadening of Luzi's poetic horizons. Those hints of a shift away from an earlier stasis, present in the 1950s texts, come to full bloom in *Nel magma* ('In the Magma', 1963). 'Presso il Bisenzio' ('Near the Bisenzio river') is exemplary, with its radically hypermetric line stretching well beyond the traditional hendecasyllable because such metrical expansion is required by the poem's subject. Here it is no longer pre-existent form that constrains it within predetermined structures; rather, it is that same subject that modulates it in a totally free fashion. To that metrical freedom we should add the self-evidently dramatic nature of a text whose dialogue perhaps anticipates a theatrical calling which Luzi will pursue in tandem with his lyrical verse, from the long dramatic poem *Ipazia* ('Hypatia', 1972), to the more recent *Felicità turbate* ('Disturbed Happinesses') on the early Mannerist painter Pontormo and *Ceneri e ardori* ('Ashes and Ardour') on the French writer Benjamin Constant, on whom Luzi had written many years earlier. But to return to 'Presso il Bisenzio', the burning issue of the Resistance – ' "You were not burnt as we were by the fire of struggle / when it blazed and good and evil were alight on the pyre" ' – and its almost literal partisanship, presented in terms strongly reminiscent of Dante's Farinata canto (*Inferno* x), demonstrated that Luzi was no less conscious of the weakening effect of war and civil strife on the social fabric.

The high point of his poetry, however, is perhaps to be found in the three long poems of *Su fondamenti invisibili* ('On Invisible Foundations', 1971). Their exhilarating verse structure, ranging even more freely beyond the limits of traditional metre than *Nel magma* (where that freedom was already substantial), with its incredible richness and density of imagery allied to its strong dramatic quality, itself a manifestation of the conflictual nature of the moral and intellectual problems which he confronts, are of a quality akin only to Montale's 'Silvae' in *La bufera*.

Paradoxical paradigms of language and dialect: Pasolini, Zanzotto and Bigongiari

Pasolini's *Poesie a Casarsa*, in its remarkable and highly original synthesis of the European poetic tradition from Symbolism onwards, has claims – paradoxically, since it was his first volume and, moreover, in dialect – to being his best work. The Italian poems of *Le ceneri di Gramsci* ('Gramsci's Ashes', 1957), with their unorthodox Marxism reflecting a contrast between history and prehistory, nature and culture lying at the root of all Pasolini's work, have a no less compelling unity and originality. Although he continued to publish poetry up until his murder in 1975, much of it was occasional, subordinate to the cinematographic activity which dominated his last fifteen years.

Pasolini, too, may nevertheless serve as a paradigm. The alternative languages of his verse, dialect or Italian, with their profoundly antithetical autobiographical roots (mother versus father, country versus city), with the increasing dominance of the paternal at the expense of the maternal – that is to say the increasingly homogenized bourgeois Italian at the expense of the country's various dialects – reflected the changing social and cultural reality of the times. In 1952 it had been possible for him to publish (along with Mario Dell'Arco, 1905–97) *Poesia dialettale del Novecento* ('Dialect Poetry of the Twentieth Century') and, in 1955, *Canzoniere italiano. Antologia della poesia popolare* ('Italian Canzoniere. An Anthology of Popular Poetry'). Thirty years later, Biagio Marin (1891–1985), a dialect poet from Grado (Gorizia) singled out by Montale as worthy of greater fame in a review of Pasolini and Dell'Arco's anthology, lamented publishers' reluctance to print even a selection of his poetry. The 1996 *Cambridge History of Italian Literature* discreetly and posthumously recognized the rightness of Montale's judgment.

Dialect poetry's survival may depend on philologists, even foreign ones. Hermann W. Haller's *The Hidden Italy* (1986) was warmly reviewed in Italy itself. Closer to home, Pier Vincenzo Mengaldo's *Poeti italiani del Novecento* (1978) had already incorporated not only dialect poets but also translators as poets *tout court*: Giacomo Noventa (1898–1960), *dialettale*, with Sergio Solmi (1899–1982) and Luzi, *in lingua*; Tonino Guerra (1920–), *dialettale*, with Franco Fortini (1917–1994) and Nelo Risi (1920–), *in lingua*; Giaime Pintor (1919–43), translator of Rainer Maria Rilke, with Sereni and Pasolini.

It is the direction of Zanzotto's poetic development, however, which is most telling. *Dietro il paesaggio* ('Behind the Landscape', 1951) had been awarded the 1950 San Babila prize prior to publication by a jury including Ungaretti, Montale, Quasimodo, Sinisgalli and Sereni. Ungaretti concluded his presentation of the volume by pointing out that Zanzotto was 'now part of an illustrious history'.[14] The adjective underscored that early poetry's literariness; but a shift in the direction of experimentalism from *La beltà* ('Beauty', 1968) onwards, wonderfully exemplified in 'L'elegia in petèl' ('Elegy in Petèl'; 'petèl' is the nonsense talk used by mothers to their children), cast doubt on that early literariness, focusing as it did on metalinguistic concerns which, informed by the insights of linguistics and semiotics, suggested that Zanzotto might be *the* postmodernist poet in Italy. He is, after Montale, the poet who has attracted most attention in the English-speaking world. Within Italy that position would seem to belong to Luzi.

To return to the language–dialect nexus , however, Zanzotto, starting with the poems of *Filò* ('Peasants Wake', 1976), written for Fellini's *Casanova*, has increasingly 'regressed' from literary Italian: witness the poems of *Mistieròi* (a dialect term meaning small, poor trades, 1979), now reprinted in *Idioma* ('Idiom', 1986). But these 'works in regress' are no more 'regressive' than Montale's later work, conscious as Zanzotto is that no dialect has ever existed which was not 'something explosively different, at least potentially'.[15] A similar awareness of the potentiality of language is to be found in Piero Bigongiari (1914–1997), particularly from *Antimateria* ('Antimatter', 1972) onwards. It is not by chance that Stefano Agosti, one of Zanzotto's most attentive readers, has also written on Bigongiari. More telling perhaps than critical interest is the interest of younger poets: Silvio Ramat (1939–), arguably the historian of twentieth-century Italian poetry, Roberto Carifi (1948–), Milo De Angelis (1951–) and Roberto Mussapi (1952–), among others.

The schematic presentation of all too few poets in the second half of this essay has meant, regrettably, that more has been omitted than included; nor has space allowed me, again regrettably, to speak of neo-avant-garde movements such as the 1961 *Novissimi* and the *Gruppo 63* with its forty-three adherents; nor women poets such as Margherita Guidacci (1921–92), Alda Merini (1931–), Maria Luisa Spaziani (1924–) and Amelia Rosselli (1930–96). Critics and theoreticians too (Luciano Anceschi, 1911–95, in particular) have no less regrettably been sacrificed, as have literary journals. *Il verri*, linked to Anceschi, still survives, but *Officina* ('Workshop'), linked to Pasolini, has long since gone as has *Rendiconti* ('Reports'), inspired by Roberto Roversi (1923–), a friend from Pasolini's student days in Bologna who, together with the poet and Francesco Leonetti (1924–), had constituted *Officina*'s editorial board. While it may be true that journals have less influence nowadays, the regular monthly appearance on the news-stands of *Poesia* bespeaks an ongoing interest in the art.

NOTES

* The symbol #, which appears approximately half-way through this chapter, marks the point at which the part of the essay composed by Shirley Vinall comes to an end and that written by Tom O'Neill starts.

1. Gabriele D'Annunzio, *Alcyone*, ed. F. Roncoroni (Milan: Mondadori, 1982), p. 715.

2. Gianfranco Contini, 'Il linguaggio di Pascoli', in Giovanni Pascoli, *Poesie*, 4 vols. (Milan: Mondadori, 1969), vol. I, pp. lxii–xcviii (p. lxxiii).

3. Giovanni Pascoli, *Prose*, 3 vols. (Milan: Mondadori, 1952), vol. I, p. 22.

4. Eugenio Montale, introduction to Guido Gozzano, *Le poesie* (Milan: Garzanti, 1960), p. 14.

5. See Luciano De Maria and Laura Dondi (eds.), *Marinetti e i futuristi* (Milan: Garzanti, 1994), p. 375.

6. Dino Campana, *Canti orfici*, ed. F. Ceragioli (Florence: Vallecchi, 1985), p. 267.

7. Giuseppe Ungaretti, *Vita d'un uomo: Tutte le poesie*, ed. L. Piccioni (Milan: Mondadori, 1979), p. 72.

8. Joseph Brodsky, 'In the Shadow of Dante', in *Less than One* (Harmondsworth: Penguin Books, 1996), pp. 95–112 (p. 103).

9. Milan Kundera, *Betrayed Testaments* (London and Boston: Faber and Faber, 1995), p. 59.

10. Salvatore Quasimodo, *Tutte le poesie* (Milan: Mondadori, 1960), pp. 199–200.

11. Pier Paolo Pasolini, *Passione e ideologia* (Milan: Garzanti, 1960), pp. 457, 460.

12. Giuseppe Tomasi di Lampedusa, *Opere* (Milan: Mondadori, 1995), p. 1787.

13. Vivienne Hand, *Zanzotto* (Edinburgh University Press, 1994), p. xii.

14. Giuseppe Ungaretti, *Vita d'un uomo. Saggi e interventi* (Milan: Mondadori, 1974), p. 993.

15. Andrea Zanzotto, *Filò* (Milan: Mondadori, 1988), p. 75.

FURTHER READING

Cary, Joseph, *Three Italian Poets: Saba, Ungaretti, Montale*. 2nd edn. Chicago and London: The University of Chicago Press, 1993.

Gentili, Alessandro, and Catherine O'Brien (eds.), *The Green Flame: Contemporary Italian Poetry*. Dublin: Irish Academic Press, 1987.

Hainsworth, Peter, and Emmanuela Tandello (eds.), *Italian Poetry since 1956*, Supplement 1 to *The Italianist*, 15, 1995.

Jones, Frederic J., *Giuseppe Ungaretti*. Edinburgh University Press, 1977.

  The Modern Italian Lyric. Cardiff: University of Wales Press, 1986.

Klopp, Charles, *Gabriele D'Annunzio*. Boston: Twayne, 1988.

Montale, Eugenio, *Collected Poems 1920–1954*. Translated by Jonathan Galassi. New York: Farrar, Straus and Giroux, 1998.

O'Neill, Tom, 'Pier Paolo Pasolini's Dialect Poetry', *Forum Italicum*, 9, iv (1975), pp. 343–67.

  'Montale's Fishy Petrarchism', *Modern Language Notes* 106 (1991), pp. 78–116.

Picchione, John, and Lawrence R. Smith (eds.), *Twentieth-Century Italian Poetry: An Anthology*. Toronto, Buffalo and London: University of Toronto Press, 1993.

Sanguineti, Edoardo, (ed.), *Poesia italiana del Novecento*. 2nd edn. Turin: Einaudi, 1972.

Wedel De Stasio, Giovanna, *et al.* (eds.), *Twentieth-Century Italian Poets*, *Dictionary of Literary Biography*. CXIV and CXXVIII. Detroit, Washington, DC, and London: Bruccoli Clark Layman, 1992 and 1993.

10

Drama: realism, identity and reality on stage

Introduction

In the Italy of the second half of the eighteenth century comedy had pre-vailed over tragedy, with authors such as Carlo Goldoni, Pietro Chiari and Carlo Gozzi. This was superseded by the tragic drama of Vittorio Alfieri, Vincenzo Monti, Ippolito Pindemonte, Ugo Foscolo, Silvio Pellico and Alessandro Manzoni.[1] By the mid-nineteenth century the dearth of original texts for the theatre (the emphasis having shifted to opera)[2] was compensated by the skill of 'great actors' such as Gustavo Modena, Adelaide Ristori, Tommaso Salvini and Ernesto Rossi. This has been referred to as *drammaturgia dell'attore*, the actor's drama, and it is notable that later, when in the rest of Europe the producer had taken over, in Italy the actor still predominated until at least the 1930s.[3] Indeed, the term *regista*, 'director', was only coined by the linguist Bruno Migliorini in 1932.[4] Alongside the early nineteenth-century tragedies, in response to the expectations of the emerging bourgeoisie, there was a post-Goldonian vein (as in Augusto Bon, Alberto Nota and others) which took the eighteenth-century dramatist's realism and regionalism into the following century. Overlapping with this trend, and spreading into the period of *verismo*, is the first group of playwrights I shall discuss: they belong to the unification period and are representative of *teatro a tesi*, a theatre primarily concerned with ideas.

Theatre of ideas

The Ligurian Paolo Giacometti (1816–87), who composed historical plays which reveal the influence of French Romantic drama, in 1861 wrote his best-known play, *La morte civile* ('Civil Death') which was first performed with a cast including Rossi and Salvini. The protagonist, an escaped life-prisoner, commits suicide in order to let his wife remarry. The message that emerges from this play is the plea against the indissolubility of marriage, summed up in the famous finale after the suicide: 'Legislators, behold!' The *modenese* Paolo Ferrari (1822–89), after a first manner in the 1850s with popular comedies in dialect, took as his subject-matter recent Italian writers, as in his successful *Goldoni e le sue sedici commedie nuove* ('Goldoni and His Sixteen New Comedies', 1852); in his third manner, like Giacometti, he concentrated on themes of contemporary concern. His *Cause ed effetti* ('Causes and Effects', 1871) comes alive in its female protagonist, who, in the face of all opposition, persists in her idealistic search for something other than frivolous entertainment. Social preoccupations typical of the time are also expressed in the works of the Neapolitan Achille Torelli (1841–1922).

Realism and dialect

During the period of the 'great actors', playwrights were very much at their mercy. But during the latter part of the nineteenth century, with the advent of *verismo*, two transformations took place. First, as writers of the calibre of Giovanni Verga (1840–1922), Luigi Capuana (1839–1915), Federico De Roberto (1826–1927) and Gabriele D'Annunzio (1863–1938) took to writing for the theatre, they were in a position to command greater respect from the actors, from whom a less self-centred and declamatory style also was expected. Secondly, dialect was increasingly used for dramatic texts. Dialect was perceived as being closer to the linguistic reality of both characters and audience, and was also more acceptable to certain companies.

The creative writings of the *veristi* (for whom drama was often secondary to narrative) were accompanied by their theories, which showed the influence of French Naturalists like Zola and Maupassant. One of the advantages of drama, according to De Roberto, was that dialogue was the perfect vehicle for complete impersonality on the part of the author, who made his characters reveal their psychology entirely through their own words. The Sicilian *veristi*, Capuana and Verga, turned various of their narratives into dramas: most notably, Verga rewrote his short story *Cavalleria rusticana* ('Rustic Chivalry').

The Piedmontese Vittorio Bersezio (1828–1900) at first refrained from writing in dialect, fearing it went against the aspirations of a unified Italy; however, he gradually changed his mind, claiming that 'you write better in the language you have learnt from birth'.[5] In his most famous play *Le miserie 'd Monssù Travet* ('The Mishaps of Monssù Travet', 1863), the protagonist, goaded by an attack on his honour, is transformed from a weak-willed clerk into an assertive, independent worker. Another writer who passed from a negative to a positive attitude towards dialect was the Venetian Giacinto Gallina (1852–97), who expressed an ethos of family solidarity and common sense within carefully structured plots. In *La famegia del santolo* ('The Godfather's Family', 1892), a story based, like Ibsen's *The Wild Duck*, on uncertain paternity, there is the decision, however hard, made after an initial condemnation with a single powerful word – 'Vergognosa', 'Shame on you!' – , to ignore the adultery committed by a wife twenty-five years earlier.

The Neapolitan Salvatore Di Giacomo (1860–1934) sometimes based his theatre on his poetry and short stories. The seven sonnets (1895) of *A San Francisco* ('In San Francisco Prison') became a libretto (1896) and then a play (1897) about the inmates of the prison. *'O mese mariano* ('Marian Month', 1900; also a libretto, 1910), based on the Italian short story *Senza vederlo* ('Without Seeing Him', 1886), presents another social drama: a mother is forced to put her eldest child into the poorhouse. These two plays are representative of Di Giacomo's most powerful themes: *A San Francisco* of passion and jealousy, *'O mese mariano* of the tragedy of poverty. Another Neapolitan, Roberto Bracco (1861–1943), whose work encompasses many different phases (some of which will be mentioned later), in his early dramatic career wrote romantic melodramas in which poverty is contrasted with upper-class wealth (*Sperduti nel buio*, 'Lost in the Dark', 1901), and where the shame of family prostitution leads to despair and suicide (*Notte di neve*, 'A Night of Snow', 1906). Perhaps his finest work is *Il piccolo santo* ('The Little Saint', 1909), where the tragedy that strikes the village priest, considered a saint, remains a mystery to characters and audience alike.

Alongside tragic drama in Naples, there was a tradition of comedy dating back to the *commedia dell'arte*'s Pulcinella (the forerunner of the English Punch). Antonio Petito not only played the part of Pulcinella (for which he eventually substituted the role of Pascariello) but also created for the young actor–playwright Eduardo Scarpetta (1853–1925) the character of the empty-headed snob Felice Sciosciammocca. Scarpetta's own plays spanned a wide range, from works like *Nu bastone 'e fuoco* ('A Fire

Stick', 1887), which still contained the character of Pulcinella, to his well known *Miseria e nobiltà* ('Poverty and Nobility', 1888), a drama written in both dialect and literary Italian.

Giuseppe Giacosa (1847–1906), who wrote a positive assessment of Verga's *Cavalleria rusticana*, was influenced in the 1880s by the Sicilian writer. After abandoning the medieval fashion of his 1871 *Partita a scacchi* ('A Game of Chess'), he embraced a bourgeois form of *verismo* in *Tristi amori* ('Sad Loves', 1887) and in *Come le foglie* ('Like the Leaves', 1900). In between these plays came *La moglie ideale* ('The Ideal Wife', 1890) by Marco Praga (1862–1929). There is a continuity between Giacosa's *Tristi amori*, Praga's *Moglie ideale* and Giacosa's *Come le foglie*, with the passage from a dwindling nobility to a middle class which is asserting itself, and from the optimistic successes of this new class to its corruption, adultery and compromises.

D'Annunzio and Svevo

In contrast to the tradition of bourgeois realism, we have the *teatro di poesia* of Gabriele D'Annunzio which bears traces of two figures he greatly admired, Nietzsche and Wagner. Eleonora Duse was D'Annunzio's muse and the protagonist of many of his plays. Even when he took historical themes and presented them in accurate settings, or drew his material from popular culture, D'Annunzio was primarily interested in timeless myths and archetypal characters. His two most successful plays were the verse dramas *La figlia di Iorio* ('Iorio's Daughter', 1903) and *La fiaccola sotto il moggio* ('The Light under the Bushel', 1905). One direction of Italian drama was in fact that of myth in its widest historical sense, ranging from pagan and archaic to Christian and medieval or Renaissance. The mythic drama of Ercole Luigi Morselli (1882–1921) is sometimes ironic, as in *Orione* ('Orion', 1910), sometimes elegiac, as in *Glauco* ('Glaucus', which Pirandello recast into Sicilian, 1919), while the historical trend was followed by Sem Benelli (1877–1949) with his vigorous verse play *La cena delle beffe* ('The Dinner of Tricks', 1909). On the other hand, Benelli's 1908 *Tignola* ('Bookworm'), a bourgeois drama about the disasters that befall a timid and idealistic bookseller's assistant – the bookworm of the title – belongs to the intimist tradition of Giacosa.

The fame of Italo Svevo (1861–1928), like Verga's and D'Annunzio's, rests on genres other than the theatre. Notable are the idiosyncratic plots of his dramatic works which were written throughout his career but published posthumously, except for *Il terzetto spezzato* ('The Broken Trio', 1927) which was performed during his lifetime. The psychology of this play is reminiscent of Strindberg, and it also echoes Bracco's 1893 *Maschere* ('Masks'). In the more complex *Un marito* ('A Husband', 1931), with its Ibsenian return to the past, a lawyer, absolved after killing his unfaithful first spouse, is faced with the possible infidelity of his second wife; however, the roles of the couple are gradually reversed as the position of the wife, Bice, is asserted. Svevo's preoccupation with marriage and infidelity reappears in his most successful play, *Rigenerazione* ('Regeneration', *c.* 1927–8), with the figure of Giovanni Chierici, an elderly businessman who undergoes a rejuvenating operation, behind whose obsession with illness and old age there is a zest and humour reminiscent of *La coscienza di Zeno* ('The Conscience of Zeno').

Futurism and the theatre of the grotesque

The existence of drama alongside other forms of artistic expression is even more marked in the case of the Futurists. The theatre stands in opposition to the visual arts, for which the Futurists are mostly remembered (one only has to think of Balla and Boccioni), while their written texts were more ephemeral. In the tradition of Alfred Jarry's *Ubu roi* (1896), with its puppet-like parodic figures, are the early plays of Filippo Tommaso Marinetti (1896–1944), written in French. Audience participation was one of the principles of the Futurist *teatro di varietà*, which from its early improvisation later developed into carefully constructed works like *Piedigrotta* and *Funerale del filosofo passatista*, both of 1914, directed by Marinetti. The *Funerale* was a polemic against the 'outmoded' philosopher Benedetto Croce, and consisted of chanting Futurist pall-bearers led by Marinetti and accompanied by mouldering books and vegetables.

Following the *varietà* came the *sintesi* of 1915 and 1916. These 'syntheses' consisted of lightning action based on positive and negative structures (often 'Futurist' versus 'antiquated'), or they were the enactment of set phrases, like Cangiullo's *Non c'è un cane* ('Not Even a Dog') in which a dog quickly disappears behind the scenes; objects were the protagonists of Marinetti's *sintesi* as in *Vengono* ('They Are Coming') with its eight chairs and a table. Alongside the theatre of *varietà* and *sintesi* existed a third Futurist dramatic expression, *il teatro della sorpresa*, the theatre of surprise, with its 1921 manifesto signed by Marinetti and Cangiullo. The last theatrical manifesto was the 1924 'anti-psychological' one, in which the physical and the metaphysical prevailed over the psychological.

The term *grottesco* is used to define plays which have in common a certain schematic simplification of the characters, who tend to assume the qualities of puppets or masks; the plot is often paradoxical and fixes the characters, rather than being created by them. This is one of the reasons why many object to even Pirandello's early dramas being given the appellation *grottesco*. Another difference between Pirandello and the theatre of the grotesque concerns the mask, which hides a real face beneath it for the *grotteschi*, but another mask for Pirandello. In *Marionette, che passione!* ('Puppets, What a Passion!', 1918) by Pier Maria Rosso di San Secondo (1887–1956), the unnamed characters ('the Gentleman in grey, the Lady in the blue fox fur, the Gentleman in mourning') first meet in a post office and then, like puppets, are brought together again in unexpected circumstances and combinations. Of the same date as *Marionette* is *L'uomo che incontrò se stesso* ('The Man Who Met Himself') by Luigi Antonelli (1882–1942), in which the protagonist meets himself as a young man and tries to prevent his double from suffering the same fate as himself at the hands of his unfaithful wife. *Nostra Dea* ('Our Dea', 1925) by Massimo Bontempelli (1878–1960) opens with the protagonist Dea being dressed by her maid. While she is in her petticoat she behaves and speaks with the automatism of a puppet, and it is only as she dons one sumptuous dress after another that she acquires a personality, or rather personalities, since what seems an unpredictable and contradictory character to her friends is in fact only a series of external mutations caused by changes of attire.

Pirandello

Luigi Pirandello is hailed by Ferdinando Taviani[6] as one of the three glories for which Italian theatre is known, the other two being *commedia dell'arte* (including Goldoni) and opera. The progression of Pirandello's creative writing is usually given as poetry followed by narrative, over which eventually his theatre would dominate. In fact he wrote very many early plays, of which often only the title has survived. His critical ideas, which informed his creative production, covered many fields and came from varied sources. G. I. Ascoli's *Proemio* ('Preface', 1873) had an impact on his linguistic thought, encouraging him to accept an anti-Manzonian and anti-normative approach. Other thinkers whose theories influenced the development of his thought were Max Nordau, Gabriel Séailles, Alfred Binet, Luigi Capuana and Benedetto Croce (in spite of his disputes with that philosopher). Their ideas contributed to his belief in the relativity of truth and the multifaceted nature of personality, and to his particular view of objectivity and subjectivity and of the nature of humour, with its latent tragedy, its sense of the opposite – 'il sentimento del contrario' – notions which he elaborated in his important essay *L'umorismo* ('On Humour', 1908). Pirandello's *Maschere nude* ('Naked Masks') are the creation of a writer whose personal world was fraught with problems: economic ruin, a wife who gradually lost her reason, and a daughter who tried to commit suicide.

Role-playing is one of Pirandello's most constant themes. In the play whose very title expresses this idea, *Il giuoco delle parti* ('The Rules of the Game', 1918), the traditional triangular relationship between wife (Silia), husband (Leone) and lover (Guido) acquires an unexpected but logical twist when Leone, who is required to fight a duel to defend Silia's honour, sends to fight and to die in his stead Guido, who has in all but name usurped his role. This play also emphasizes a theme, connected with the triangle, which again in Pirandello receives varied treatment, that of vindictiveness and revenge. In *Come prima, meglio di prima* ('As Before, Better than Before', 1920) the different roles of the protagonist are symbolized by her different names: she is Fulvia to her husband, Flora to her lover, and Francesca when she returns to her husband as his second wife. In *Tutto per bene* ('All for the Best', 1920), a play that has affinities with Ibsen's *The Wild Duck*, Lori is thought by everyone to have known about his wife's infidelity and that Palma is really the daughter of his friend Manfroni. When Lori discovers he has been playing a role (or living a lie) for sixteen years, he is unable to accept the new situation, and with Palma's help reconstructs their relationship into one of father and daughter. The play closes with the type of unresolved ending in which Pirandello excels. The theme of illusion which becomes reality is repeated in one of Pirandello's best-known plays, *Enrico IV* ('Henry IV', 1922), in which Enrico, after twelve years of real madness, decides to continue behaving as if he were mad, rather than return to a world where he has no role.

The question 'Which is the real person?' asked of characters with several roles has no answer and is an example of the relativity of truth which Pirandello especially develops in *Così è (se vi pare)* ('It's Like This (If You Think So)', 1917) and *Come tu mi vuoi* ('As You Desire Me', 1930). The first (containing the most striking of Pirandello's *raisonneurs*, Lamberto Laudisi) examines the problem from the perspective of the townspeople who are faced with three mysterious newcomers – mother, daughter and the latter's husband – and the impossibility of pinning down the identity of the wife, Signora Ponza; the second focuses on the individual at the centre of the riddle, on l'Ignota's feelings at being appropriated by a German as his music-hall lover Elma, and by an Italian as his long-lost wife Cia. In both cases the audience is left with the mystery unresolved. The settings of these two plays are well defined. We have the hierarchical petty-bourgeois world of *Così è*, and the debauchery of the Berlin of the Twenties contrasted with the superficial calm of the Udine upper middle class in *Come tu mi vuoi*.

Another well-characterized setting is that of the theatre. The most important plays dealing with this setting are the play-within-a-play trilogy, *Sei personaggi in cerca d'autore* ('Six Characters in Search of an Author', 1921), *Ciascuno a suo modo* ('Each in His Own Way', 1924) and *Questa sera si recita a soggetto* ('This Evening We Improvise', 1930). In them Pirandello explores the relationships between the various aspects of the theatre: in *Sei personaggi* between *capocomico* (director), actors and characters who have their own existence; in *Ciascuno* between drama on stage and drama in 'real' life; in *Questa sera* between director, actors and critics, and between the actors and the characters they are portraying. Abstract notions lurk behind these plays. In the 1925 preface to *Sei personaggi* Pirandello addresses the critic Adriano Tilgher's distinction, applied to his earlier plays, between *Vita* and *Forma*, the flowing life of the human being as opposed to the constricting form of art. But Pirandello never remains abstract – not for nothing did he reject the accusation that his work was above all philosophical – and he turns these notions of *Vita* and *Forma* into creative paradoxes.

In each play of the trilogy Pirandello uses the device of the play-within-a-play differently. In *Sei personaggi* the two plays merge as the company, interrupted in their rehearsal of *Il giuoco delle parti*, devote themselves to trying to perform the characters' drama, which culminates in the scene in Madama Pace's brothel in which the mother surprises the father with the stepdaughter. We have alternating scenes: the characters (re)living their experiences – 'living' is more accurate, for 'it is happening now, it is always happening!', as the mother declares – and the actors giving a professional interpretation to what they have seen. In *Ciascuno* there is a different kind of parallelism, with Moreno and Nuti rejecting the drama *à clef* on stage, yet finding themselves irresistibly drawn to imitate it. Pirandello often took his short stories as the starting-point for his plays. In *Questa sera*, perhaps the most ambitious and interesting of the three, the director Hinkfuss is adapting for the stage the short story *Leonora, addio!*, a tale of Sicilian jealousy and destruction. This provides the subject for the improvisation of the actors, who slip in and out of their roles, so that there is uncertainty as to whether it is the actor or the character who is speaking.

The Sicilian element, which is very strong in the above short story, frequently emerges in Pirandello. Several plays – for instance *Pensaci, Giacomino!* ('Think About It, Giacomino!', 1917), *Il berretto a sonagli* ('Cap and Bells', 1918), *Liolà* (1917) and *La giara* ('The Jar', 1925) – were originally written in dialect. Sometimes a play was started in Italian and then turned into Sicilian, as was the case of *Tutto per bene*. *Liolà* was written in Pirandello's own dialect of Agrigento (the phonetics of which he had analysed in his doctoral thesis at Bonn), whereas the others, with their middle-class settings, were written in the Sicilian of the bourgeoisie.

Mythic elements, which had been present in earlier plays, find an organized development in the myth trilogy of the late 1920s, *La nuova colonia* ('The New Colony', 1928), *Lazzaro* ('Lazarus', 1929) and the unfinished *I giganti della montagna* ('The Mountain Giants', published posthumously in 1938). In simple terms, the trilogy covers the myth of society, the myth of religion and the myth of art, to which one turns as a last resort, but all of which fail to provide solutions. In this negative approach to myth, Pirandello could be said to differ from writers like D'Annunzio who tried to find in myth a thread linking different ages.

Fascism and the avant-garde

The Fascist régime, conscious of the political potential of the theatre, encouraged patriotic history plays like those by Giovacchino Forzano (1884–1970), with his propagandist trilogy *Campo di Maggio* ('Champ de Mai', 1930), *Villafranca* (1931), *Giulio Cesare* ('Julius Caesar', 1939), in which he used drafts prepared for him by Mussolini. Rino Alessi (1885–1970) wrote a mystical history play, *Savonarola* (1935), performed to a mass audience in the Piazza della Signoria in Florence. Another large-scale play, directed by the young Alessandro Blasetti, was *18BL* (1934), in which the protagonist was a lorry that had been in use from the First World War to the establishment of the régime. Fascist interest in the theatre was also expressed by the setting up of travelling companies (*Carri Tespi*, 'Thespis's Carts') and in the creation of the *Sabato Teatrale* (Theatrical Saturdays) as part of the *Dopolavoro* ('After Work') activities, as well as by the broadcasting of more radio plays.

The avant-garde was active throughout the Fascist period. Apart from the Futurists, there were writers like Achille Campanile (1900–77), who, as well as narrative works, produced brief humorous dramatic pieces and was particularly known for his two-liner plays, for example, the 1924 *Alla stazione* ('At the Station'), in which the characters are two puffing engines. One of the avant-garde dramatists who is now rightly receiving more attention is Beniamino Joppolo (1906–63), who took an actively anti-Fascist position, for which he was twice imprisoned and then sent into internal exile. His early plays were *L'ultima stazione* ('The Last Station', 1941), *In cammino* ('En Route', 1942), *Sulla collina* ('On the Hill') and *Domani partiremo* ('Tomorrow We Leave', both 1943). In 1949 he wrote *I carabinieri* (adapted by Godard in his 1963 film *Les Carabiniers*), perhaps his best-known play, along with the two-act *Le acque* ('The Waters', published in 1961) in which water, the element linking the two acts, only causes floods and does not quench thirst.

Alberto Savinio (the pseudonym of Andrea De Chirico, 1891–1952), who started his career in the avant-garde in Paris with his brother Giorgio De Chirico, in 1925 staged for Pirandello's Teatro d'Arte his *La morte di Niobe* ('The Death of Niobe', 1925), a striking one-act mime in which the tragedy of a modern-day Niobe is enacted before an impassive stage audience; while in *Capitano Ulisse* ('Captain Ulysses', 1934) he offered an ironic treatment of the contemporary interest in myth. Also characterized by a mythical theme is *Lunga notte di Medea* ('The Long Night of Medea', 1949) by Corrado Alvaro (1895–1956), which presents the tragedy from the point of view of the 'unfaithful Jason'. Vitaliano Brancati (1907–54) was the author of bitter farces. His 1942 *Le trombe d'Eustachio* ('Eustachian Tubes') is a parody of Fascist detective drama and has amongst its characters an ear and an eye; while his 1952 *La governante* ('The Governess') was banned for having lesbianism as its theme. The satirist and theatre critic Ennio Flaiano (1910–72) wrote for Vittorio Gassman *Un marziano a Roma* ('A Martian in Rome', 1960), in which an alien is welcomed by the Romans, who think that contact with him will make their life genuine and simple. Instead, their visitor takes to Roman life with gusto, acquiring a lover, two bodyguards, three secretaries and the title *Dottore*.

Drama of commitment

Some plays were written by anti-Fascists in exile. Leo Ferrero (1903–33) who left Italy for Paris in 1928, wrote in French his satirical drama *Angélica* (1928), which he later translated into Italian. In the form of a fable, this tells of the contemporary political struggle, as viewed by a writer who chooses the mode of ironic detachment. Ignazio Silone (1900–78) wrote *Ed egli si nascose* ('And He Hid', 1944) in exile, exploring the necessity and hardships of that condition. In August 1943 a manifesto was issued by a group of dramatists, including Diego Fabbri (1911–80), Vito Pandolfi (1917–74) and Tullio Pinelli (1908–), affirming the need to face up to the traumas of a nation suffering war and internal conflicts. Their commitment to contemporary problems was combined with a Catholic viewpoint. The theatre of Ugo Betti (1892–1953) can be linked to this tradition. Betti, by profession a magistrate, had started writing in the 1920s: *La padrona* ('The Mistress', 1926), *La casa sull'acqua* ('The House on the Water', 1928), followed by his well-known *Frana allo scalo nord* ('Landslide at the Scalo Nord', 1933 – taken off the stage by the Fascists), which, like his post-war plays *Corruzione al Palazzo di giustizia* ('Corruption in the Palace of Justice', 1948) and *L'aiuola bruciata* ('The Burnt Flower Bed', 1953), treat the themes of evil and responsibility at a universal level.

The Neapolitan drama of Viviani and De Filippo

Returning to the first half of the twentieth century, there is also another thread to be followed, less literary and more performance-oriented. Raffaele Viviani (1888–1950) was born in Naples where the theatre was dominated by Eduardo Scarpetta, against whose drama, often influenced by French comedies and farces, Salvatore Di Giacomo had reacted, wanting a more genuine Neapolitan product firmly rooted in the reality of the city. Viviani started his career as a child actor, and before the First World War he achieved fame in the *Teatro di varietà*, in sketches in which he impersonated traditional Neapolitan types, both comic and tragic, in particular the victims and the defeated. Viviani's best plays are *Pescatori* ('Fishermen', 1924), *Zingari* ('Gypsies', 1926) and the one-act *La musica dei ciechi* ('Music of the Blind', 1927). *Pescatori* is a bleak family tragedy which takes place behind a foreground of the vividly depicted activities of a fishing community. *Zingari* is less realistic: the protagonist achieves a fantasy killing of his rival in the delirium of high fever. In *La musica dei ciechi* a blind musician is in danger of losing his position through jealousy, until the bitter-sweet twist of his wife's confession that she is so ugly nobody would court her.

An actor–writer whose early activities had links with Pirandello was Eduardo De Filippo (1900–84). Their collaboration started in 1935 when the De Filippo company staged a Neapolitan version of *Liolà*. Much has been said about the Pirandellian nature of De Filippo's theatre. Clearly there are some common elements, like the *umorismo* whereby an outwardly comic situation hides seriousness and even tragedy. However, De Filippo's theatre is more rooted in Neapolitan reality, sometimes including socio-political concerns which may find their resolutions in hope and improvement. It is a far cry from the psychological conflict which consumes Pirandello's characters. Eduardo De Filippo was the son of Eduardo Scarpetta. His long professional life coincided with the spread of the mass media, so that he came to be known not only through his stage performances, but also through radio, and above all television. De Filippo often used political and social problems as a backdrop. A case in point is the immediate post-war corruption and black market of *Napoli milionaria* ('Millionnaire Naples', 1945). The plot of *Filumena Marturano* (1946) hinges on the justified trick played by an ex-prostitute and servant to get her long-standing lover Domenico to marry her. She pretends to be dying and tells him that one of her three sons is his, refusing to say which so that he will accept all three. The unconventional *Grande magia* ('Grand Magic') and *Le voci di dentro* ('The Voices from Within') are both of 1948. The first is based on the illusion which a professional magician creates for Calogero di Spelta, whose wife has run away from him, namely that his wife is safely stored away in a little Japanese box. This incredible explanation is more acceptable to Calogero than the reality of abandonment. In the second, which has the form of a detective story, Alberto, an unemployed organizer of parties, has prophetic dreams of the deaths that will strike his relatives. One of De Filippo's most memorable creations appears in this play: zì Nicola, who has given up communicating verbally with an uncaring world and only makes contact by letting off fireworks.

Neapolitan theatre has continued to flourish, but with a darker, crueller streak, the result of the disintegration of social structures and the stranglehold of the camorra, so that more recent plays seem to have as much in common with Genet and Pinter as with Viviani and De

Filippo. There is Mario Santanelli (1930–) with his Pinter-like *Uscita d'emergenza* ('Emergency Exit', 1981) and *Bellavita Carolina* (1987) on the wartime black market; there is Annibale Ruccello (1956–86) with *Ferdinando* (1985), a drama centred on the bisexual seduction of a beautiful youth against the setting of a decaying Neapolitan villa; there is Enzo Moscato (1948–), with *Compleanno* ('Birthday', 1992), in which rebellion, despair and silence characterize the microcosm of family life.

Dario Fo

In 1984, when De Filippo, who was a life Senator, died and his body lay in state in the Italian Senate, the person invited to give the official commemoration was Dario Fo who, although very different in his approach to the theatre, was seen as De Filippo's successor. Fo was born in 1926 and studied as an architect and scenographer. His skills led him to practical theatre, and he trained with the mime Jacques Lecoq, who had worked with the director Giorgio Strehler at the Piccolo in Milan. In 1952, at the Piccolo, Fo, Franco Parenti and Giustino Durano put on a review, *Il dito nell'occhio* ('Finger in the Eye'), followed the next year by *Sani da legare* ('Sane as Hatters'), even more politicizing and violently anti-conformist. It was at this time that Fo began to run into trouble with censorship and to clash with the authorities. His marriage and professional partnership with Franca Rame, who came from a family of travelling puppet-masters and comedians, gave him experience of a different type of theatre. For their company, set up in 1957, Fo wrote some very successful surreal farces into which he injected topical allusions, for instance *Gli arcangeli non giocano a flipper* ('Archangels Don't Play Pinball', 1959) and *Settimo, ruba un po' meno* ('Seventh, Steal a Bit Less', 1964). After 1967, Fo and Rame abandoned bourgeois theatre, where paradoxically the butt of their satire – the middle classes – by laughing at themselves took the sting out of the criticism, and instead performed in left-wing cultural clubs and fringe theatres, encouraging audience participation in their *Teatro del campo* ('Community Theatre').

Fo's approach was gradually to build up his plays as he rehearsed them so that the written text only emerged at the end. One of his best-known plays is the 1970 *Morte accidentale d'un anarchico* ('Accidental Death of an Anarchist'), which had the serious motive of looking into the death of the Anarchist Giuseppe Pinelli while in police custody, and in which Fo uses genuine passages taken from police statements. The play however makes its point as a farce, with a madman finding his way into the police station and being mistaken for the judge investigating Pinelli's death. Another type of production, *Mistero buffo* ('Comic Mystery'), was developed by Fo as a one-man show from 1969 into the 1990s. This has its origin in medieval and biblical figures, which are endowed with features applicable to the present, and owes its fascination to Fo's brilliance as an actor and to his original creation of languages with which the different scenes are interspersed. In 1997 Fo was awarded the Nobel prize, a recognition which was received with mixed reactions in Italy where he is often considered more important as a performer than as a writer.

Drama from the 1960s to the present

To return to works of a more literary nature, we find contemporary problems also represented by the art critic, poet, novelist and playwright Giovanni Testori (1923–93). In his *Arialda* (produced in 1960 by Visconti, but swiftly banned by the censors), he depicts the life of the poor in Milan, the breakdown of family life, the drug scene, and the problems of Southern immigration. But behind these realist themes there is a highly stylized drama of suffering humanity driven by desire, expressed in a language heightened by popular idiom. The language becomes more personal and formulaic in the trilogy *L'Ambleto* (1972), *Macbetto* (1974) and *Edipus* (1977), distortions of the Shakespearean and classical tragedies, with the extremes of evil and violence turning into infernal sequences.

A personal interpretation of the classics, this time emphasizing not alienation but approachability, was provided by one of the experimental *Gruppo 63*, Edoardo Sanguineti (1930–). In 1968 Luca Ronconi staged Sanguineti's highly successful dramatic representation of Ariosto's *Orlando furioso*, in which different episodes were enacted simultaneously, with the audience moving from scene to scene, and in 1989 Federico Tiezzi produced his *Inferno* in which an expressionistic rendering of Dante's language created a taut, dramatic version. An embodiment of the neo-avant-garde is Carmelo Bene (1937–), a brilliantly versatile man of the theatre, actor and producer sometimes of his own 'texts'. The best known is the 1966 *Nostra Signora dei Turchi* ('Our Lady of the Turks'), an irreverent sequence based on his own southern Italian–Saracen background, rejecting nation and religion, and unconventional in its treatment of the audience.

In 1968 Pier Paolo Pasolini (1922–75) wrote his *Manifesto per un nuovo teatro* ('Manifesto for a New Theatre'), in which he rejected both academic and avant-garde theatre: the theatre of *chiacchiera* ('chatter/ gossip'), and the theatre of *gesto* or *urlo* ('gesture' or 'scream'). Instead he wanted a more abstract, classical, fragmented drama, with a cultural understanding between stage and audience of the scenic *mistero/enigma* as he called it. After translations of the *Oresteia* and the *Miles gloriosus* rendered into a popular idiom based on Roman dialect, in 1966 came Pasolini's own verse plays, *Calderón*, *Affabulazione* ('Affabulation'), *Pilade* ('Pylades'), *Porcile* ('Pigsty'), *Orgia* ('Orgy') and *Bestia da stile* ('Beast of Style'). Not very successful at first, they later achieved fame through Ronconi's productions. Pasolini's is a *teatro di parola* ('theatre of words'), a conceptual drama with debate and conflict in a struggle to achieve Reason, which for him was a form of mythicized historical materialism.

Like Testori and Pasolini, Natalia Ginzburg (1916–91) was not primarily a playwright, and like them she caught in her own characteristic way the dilemma of her age. She wrote eleven plays, and her deceptively simple dialogue creates a sense of loneliness, disillusion, incompatibility and fragile, uneasy relationships which are established and destroyed. Dacia Maraini (1936–), primarily a novelist, has taken up an explicitly social and political position. She set up various theatre companies, including the Teatro della Maddalena in Rome (1973–90), a venture which was run by women to encourage Feminist culture in Italy. Her plays include *Centocelle: gli anni del fascismo* ('Centocelle, the Years of Fascism', 1971), *Viva l'Italia* ('Long Live Italy', 1973) and *La donna perfetta* ('The Perfect Woman', 1974) which depicts the tragedy of a young girl who dies after an abortion. A Feminist stance is also taken in the shows of Franca Rame (1929–), co-authored with Dario Fo: *Tutta casa, letto e chiesa* ('All Home, Bed and Church') and *Parliamo di donne* ('Talking of Women', both 1977), and *Coppia aperta* ('Open Couple', 1981).

In other contemporary dramatists there are frequent expressions of family torments: In *La fastidiosa* ('Awkward', 1963) by Franco Brusati (1922–), a play with echoes of Edward Albee, the conflict is epitomized by the wife's desire to become a nun; his *Pietà di novembre* ('November Pity', 1966) presents the life of Luca (modelled on Lee Harvey Oswald), who cannot accept mediocrity. Ugo Chiti (1943–) has written a trilogy: *Paesaggio con figure* ('Landscape with Figures', 1992), *Allegretto (per bene ma non troppo)* ('Allegretto (All Proper But Not Too Much)', 1987) and *La provincia di Jimmy* ('Jimmy's Province', 1989) which take us respectively to the

Italy of the turn of the century, of Fascism, and of the youth rebellion of the 1950s. Especially in *La provincia*, there is the influence of American cinema and a move towards popular speech. *Fratelli d'estate* ('Summer Siblings', 1995) by Cesare Lievi (1952–) is a family tragedy reminiscent of Eugene O'Neill, with generational recriminations, while *La camera bianca sopra il mercato dei fiori* ('The White Room Above the Flower Market', 1995) by Rocco D'Onghia (1956–) takes place in a De Chirico-style square, recounting the vicissitudes of five individuals who go back in time in each act, from old age to young adulthood, a record of the destruction of illusions and relationships. Lievi and D'Onghia reject the 'middle' language often found on the Italian stage and use shifting registers which pass from Baroque to popular, preferring the tradition of narrative writers like Gadda. Giuseppe Manfridi (1956–) offers us Recanati, the home town of Leopardi in *Giacomo il prepotente* ('Giacomo the Bully', 1987); the violence of *Teppisti* ('Thugs', 1986) where verse is used to alienate us from the situation; and the multimedia environment of *Stringimi a te, stringiti a me* ('Press Me to You, Press Yourself to Me', 1990). The theatre historian Paolo Puppa (1945–) has passed from adaptations of classical and modern drama to his own plays: *Parole al buio* ('Words in the Dark', 1992), twelve dialogues and a monologue, in which a Goldoni rehearsal is interrupted by a character trying to persuade the director to read the poetry of her dead friend; *La collina di Euridice* ('Eurydices' Hill', 1996), another powerful dialogue, in which elderly parents who have lost their only child conceal beneath empty chatter, the trauma of their loss; and the haunting *Tre albe* ('Three Dawns', 1999). Noteworthy too is the dynamic young company of the Teatro Settimo of Turin, who write their own shows, sometimes basing themselves on existing narratives, as in their 1989 *Libera nos*, adapted from Luigi Meneghello's prose-work *Libera nos a malo* (1963). Meneghello's narrative has also been the subject of another dramatization, *L'orto* ('The Orchard', 1998), by Marco Paolini (already well known for his television work *Il racconto del Vajont*, 'The Story of Vajont', 1994).

The final play I wish to mention also draws its inspiration from recent writers, in this case Pessoa and Pirandello. This is *Il Signor Pirandello è desiderato al telefono* ('Signor Pirandello is Wanted on the Phone,' 1988) by the novelist and short-story writer Antonio Tabucchi (1943–). It takes place in a psychiatric hospital, with an actor entertaining the patients. The actor plays the part of Pessoa and imagines he is ringing Pirandello to discuss theatrical problems with him:

I would like to ring Pirandello
perhaps he could help me
get out of this situation
he knows how to deal with characters
who find themselves trapped, slaves
of a role and of a mask.

In view of the centrality of Pirandello in Italian post-unification theatre, Tabucchi's lines seem a fitting conclusion to this survey.[7]

NOTES

1. Giorgio Pullini, *Il teatro in Italia*. III. *Settecento e Ottocento* (Rome: Edizioni Studium, 1995), pp. 183–213.

2. Roberto Alonge, *Teatro e spettacolo nel secondo Ottocento* (Rome and Bari: Laterza, 1988), pp. 3ff.

3. Franca Angelini, *Teatro e spettacolo nel primo Novecento* (Rome and Bari: Laterza, 1991), pp. 139–74.

4. Gianfranco Pedullà, *Il teatro italiano nel tempo del fascismo* (Bologna: il Mulino, 1994), p. 112.

5. Alda Croce (ed.), *Teatro italiano della seconda metà dell'Ottocento* (Rome and Bari: Laterza, 1940), vol. II, p. 156.

6. Ferdinando Taviani, *Uomini di scena, uomini di libro* (Bologna: Il Mulino, 1995).

7. A longer version of this chapter is forthcoming in *The Italianist* 21 (2001).

FURTHER READING

Barberi Squarotti, Giorgio (ed.), *La letteratura in scena. Il teatro del Novecento.* Turin: Editrice Tirrenia Stampatori, 1985.

Bloom, Harold (ed.), *Luigi Pirandello*. New York: Chelsea House, 1989.

Günsberg, Maggie, *Patriarchal Representations. Gender and Discourse in Pirandello's Theatre.* Oxford and Providence: Berg, 1994.

Livio, Gigi, *Il teatro in rivolta. Futurismo, grottesco, Pirandello e pirandellismo*. Milan: Mursia, 1976.

Lorch, Jennifer, 'Setting the Scene: Theater in Italy Before Pirandello', in J. DiGaetani (ed.), *A Companion to Pirandello Studies.* Westport, Conn.: Greenwood Press, 1991, pp. 125–43.

Meldolesi, Claudio and Taviani, Ferdinando, *Teatro e spettacolo nel primo Ottocento*. Rome and Bari: Laterza, 1991.

Puppa, Paolo, 'Itinerari nella drammaturgia del Novecento', in Cecchi, Emilio and Natalino Sapegno (eds.), *Il Novecento*, vol. II. Milan: Garzanti, 1987, pp. 713–864.
Teatro e spettacolo nel secondo Novecento. Rome and Bari: Laterza, 1993.

Squarzina, Luigi, *Da Dioniso a Brecht*. Bologna: Il Mulino, 1988.

Tessari, Roberto, *Teatro italiano del Novecento*. Florence: Le Letere, 1996.

Tinterri, Alessandro (ed.), *Il teatro italiano dal naturalismo a Pirandello*. Bologna: Il Mulino, 1990.

Wood, Sharon, *Italian Women's Writing. 1860–1994*. London: Athlone, 1995.

11

Italian cinema

Italian silent cinema

On 11 November 1895, Filoteo Albertini applied for a patent on the Albertini Kinetograph, and between 1909 and 1916, the Italian silent cinema represented a major force in world cinema before the hegemony of Hollywood was firmly established. Albertini produced the first feature film with a complex plot – *La presa di Roma* ('The Taking of Rome', 1905) – a treatment of a patriotic theme, the annexation of the Eternal City to the new Italian state in 1870. The next year, a major production company, CINES, was founded, which enabled Italian films to capture the world market for a brief period. While Italian silent films reflected a variety of genres – Roman costume dramas, adventure films, comedies, filmed drama, even experimental, avant-garde works – the industry's most popular product was the costumed film set in classical antiquity. The period's greatest director was Giovanni Pastrone (1883–1959), whose majestic silent classic *Cabiria* (1914) established the popularity of the feature film with its depiction of the Second Punic War and influenced D. W. Griffith's *Intolerance* (1916).

The coming of sound and the Fascist era

After the end of the First World War, foreign competition almost destroyed the Italian film industry, forcing production to drop from 200 films in 1920 to fewer than a dozen works in 1927. A few years later, sound was introduced to Italian audiences with *La canzone dell'amore* ('The Song of Love', 1930), directed by Gennaro Righelli (1886–1949) from a short story by Luigi Pirandello. Mussolini himself received a private showing

1. Giovanni Pastrone's *Cabiria* (1914): Maciste (Bartolomeo Pagano) rescues Cabiria from sacrifice to the Carthaginian god Moloch.

of this first venture into the talkies in Italy, a reflection of how important cinema was to his regime. During most of the 1920s, Italian cinemas (numbering some 3,000 at one point) could only import works from abroad. When the Italian government moved to block the American monopoly within the peninsula, Hollywood studios withdrew from the Italian market. No longer forced to face overwhelming American economic pressure, local production boomed. During the Fascist period, over 700 films were produced in

Italy, most not really 'Fascist' films at all but primarily entertainment and documentary.

Outside Italy, little was known of Italian cinema during the Fascist period, and this ignorance created the erroneous idea abroad that post-war Italian film rose miraculously from the ashes of the war and anti-Fascist culture. Many important contributions laying the groundwork for the post-war creative explosion (including the technical and aesthetic preparation for the birth of Italian Neorealism) must be credited to the pre-war period. The Fascist regime played a major role in this development. The government built one of the world's great film complexes, Cinecittà ('Cinema City'), which Mussolini himself inaugurated in 1937. The regime also founded an important film school, the Centro Sperimentale di Cinematografia ('Experimental Centre of Cinematography', 1935). Both institutions are still in operation today and constitute the backbone of the present industry. Several important film journals – *Bianco e nero* ('Black and White', the official organ of the Centro) and *Cinema* (edited at one time by Mussolini's son Vittorio) – helped to spread information about foreign theories and techniques through translations and reviews. Most of the great directors, actors, technicians and scriptwriters of the Neorealist period received their training during the Fascist period, and some post-war figures, such as Roberto Rossellini (1906–77), made their first films in the service of the Fascist government.

Two directors stand out during this period: Mario Camerini (1885–1991) and Alessandro Blasetti (1900–87). Camerini's stylish comedies stressed role-playing in society, and first brought together Vittorio De Sica (1902–74) as an actor and Cesare Zavattini (1902–89) as a scriptwriter in a classic comedy, *Darò un milione* ('I'll Give a Million', 1935). Long before De Sica became identified as the director of post-war Neorealist classics scripted by Zavattini, he was the most popular actor and singer in Fascist Italy. Camerini's comedies – the best of which were those with De Sica, such as *Il Signor Max* ('Mr Max', 1937) – established a level of craftsmanship and witty sophistication that rivals the best products of contemporary Hollywood studios. Blasetti was the first Italian director in the sound period to make use of non-professional actors and on-location shooting in the pursuit of film realism (all supposedly original inventions of post-war Neorealism). These stylistic features are evident in his masterpiece *1860* (1934), a patriotic film about Garibaldi, the original version of which linked Garibaldi's soldiers to Mussolini's Blackshirts much as anti-Fascist partisans would later link Garibaldi's Redshirts to their own guerilla forces wearing red neckerchiefs.

2. On the outskirts of Rome, Mussolini begins construction of the largest film studio in Europe, Cinecittà ('Cinema City'). Underneath his image as a film director is the propaganda slogan 'Cinematography is the most powerful weapon', a remark made by Lenin, whom Mussolini admired.

Blasetti's *Vecchia guardia* ('The Old Guard', 1935) does provide heroic depiction of Mussolini's rise to power with a documentary style glorifying the March on Rome. Yet Blasetti also made one of the most beautiful and fanciful of all pre-1945 films, *La corona di ferro* ('The Iron Crown', 1941), in which ornately stylized studio sets testify to the technical prowess reached by Cinecittà and whose dominant theme was a hymn to peace. His *Quattro passi fra le nuvole* ('A Stroll in the Clouds', 1942) prefigures the poetic style of De Sica's Neorealism.

Italian cinema during the Fascist period was nationalistic and patriotic, much like every other national cinema, including Hollywood. Only about a dozen of all the feature works produced during the régime's lifetime can really be said to embody Fascist ideology or to have been produced with political ends in mind. The Fascist régime preferred a cinema of entertainment, and exerted its ideological control predominantly through newsreels and documentaries rather than through fiction film. The search for a realistic documentary style in Italian cinema began not with the post-war Neorealists but with directors enjoying Mussolini's favour. For example, in *L'assedio dell'Alcazar* ('The Siege of the Alcazar', 1940) by Augusto Gennina (1892–1957), the story of the heroic defence of the Toledo fortress by Franco's Fascist troops during the Spanish Civil War, there is a fascinating combination of fact and fiction, documentary style and fantasy, that would be continued in the major documentaries shot for the Italian armed forces by Francesco De Robertis (1902–59) and by a young Rossellini. Rossellini shot three important pre-war films that may be called his 'Fascist' trilogy: *La nave bianca* ('The White Ship', 1941), *Un pilota ritorna* ('A Pilot Returns', 1942) and *L'uomo dalla croce* ('The Man With a Cross', 1943). They employ the hybrid style later made famous by post-war Neorealism: on-location shooting, documentary photography, many non-professional actors and fictionalized historical plots.

Post-war Italian Neorealism

With the fall of Mussolini and the end of the war, international audiences were introduced to Italian films through a few great masterpieces by Rossellini, De Sica and Luchino Visconti (1906–76). Italian Neorealism underlined social themes (the war, poverty, the Resistance, unemployment); it seemed to reject traditional dramatic and cinematic conventions associated with Hollywood; it stressed on-location shooting rather than studio work, as well as the documentary photographic style favoured by many directors under the former régime; and it often employed non-professional actors in original ways. Film historians have unfortunately tended to speak of Neorealism as if it were an authentic movement with universally agreed stylistic or thematic principles. The basis for the fundamental change in cinematic history marked by Italian Neorealism was less an agreement on a single, unified cinematic style than a common aspiration to view Italy without preconceptions and to employ a more honest and ethical, but no less poetic, cinematic language in the process.

The masterpieces of Neorealism are Rossellini's *Roma città aperta* ('Rome Open City', 1945) and *Paisà* ('Paisan', 1946); De Sica's *Ladri di biciclette* ('Bicycle Thieves', 1948); and Visconti's *La terra trema* ('The Earth Trembles', 1948). *Roma città aperta* so completely reflected the moral and psychological atmosphere of the immediate post-war period that its international critical success alerted the world to the rebirth of Italian cinema. With a daring combination of styles and moods, due in great measure to brilliant scriptwriting by Sergio Amidei (1904–91) and a young Federico Fellini (1920–93), Rossellini captured the tension and

3. Luchino Visconti's *Ossessione* (1942), an unauthorized Italian version of James Cain's novel *The Postman Always Rings Twice*, is one of the films made during the Fascist period that would lead to Italian Neorealist style. Here the debilitating effects of an illicit love affair can be seen on the faces of Gino (Massimo Girotti) and Giovanna (Clara Calamai).

4. Roberto Rossellini's *Roma città aperta* (1945): partisan leader Manfredi (Marcello Pagliero), photographed as a crucified Christ, is tortured by the Gestapo.

5. Roberto Rossellini's *Paisà* (1946): a black GI named Joe (Dots M. Johnson) meets a Neapolitan street urchin named Pasquale (Alfonsino Pasca).

tragedy of Italian life under German occupation and the partisan strug-gle out of which the new democratic republic was subsequently born. *Paisà* reflects to a far greater extent the conventions of the newsreel doc-umentary, tracing in six separate episodes the Allied invasion of Italy and its slow process up through the boot of the peninsula. Yet the grainy film, the awkward acting of the non-professional actors, the authoritative voice-over narration and the immediacy of subject-matter we associate with newsreels do not completely explain the aesthetic qualities of the work. Rossellini depicts the historic encounter of two alien cultures, resulting in initial incomprehension but eventual kinship and brotherhood.

De Sica's *Ladri di biciclette* is the finest example of non-professional acting in Neorealist cinema. While De Sica employs non-professionals,

6. Vittorio De Sica's *Ladri di biciclette* (1948): Bruno (Enzo Staiola) delivers one of the greatest of all non-professional performances as a child who helps his father locate a stolen bicycle.

on-location shooting and social themes (unemployment, the effects of the war on the post-war economy) typical of many Neorealist films, the appeal of *Ladri di biciclette* cannot be explained completely by its superficially realistic style. The mythic structure of the plot – a quest for a bicycle, ironically a Fides (Faith) brand, that has been stolen – suggests to the viewer that De Sica is not merely offering a political film denouncing a particular socio-economic system. Social reform may change a world in which the loss of a mere bicycle spells economic disaster, but no amount of social engineering or even revolution will alter the basic facts of life in De Sica's universe – solitude, loneliness and alienation.

Visconti's *La terra trema* is a far more ambitious ideological and aesthetic undertaking. An adaptation of the 'veristic' novel by Giovanni Verga, *I Malavoglia* ('The Malavoglias', 1881), it is coloured by the Marxist theories of Antonio Gramsci. In many ways, the film fits the traditional stereotypical definition of Italian Neorealism better than any other film from the same period. No studio sets or sound stages were used, and the cast was selected from the Sicilian fishing village of Aci Trezza, the novel's setting. Visconti even refused to dub the film into standard

7. Luchino Visconti's *La terra trema* (1948): deep-focus photography adds to the spatial realism of a Neorealist masterpiece.

Italian, preferring the more realistic effects of Sicilian dialect and synchronized sound. The film's visuals underline the cyclical, timeless quality of life in Aci Trezza. Visconti's typically slow panning shots with a stationary camera, or his long, static shots of motionless objects and actors, produce a formalism that bestows dignity and beauty on humble, ordinary people.

These four masterpieces by Rossellini, De Sica and Visconti, all original contributions to film language, were (with the exception of *Roma città aperta*) unpopular within Italy and achieved critical success primarily among audiences, critics, filmmakers and intellectuals abroad. One of the paradoxes of Italian Neorealism is that the ordinary people such films set out to portray were relatively uninterested in their own screen image: Italians preferred to see Hollywood products. Of the approximately 800 films produced between 1945 and 1953 in Italy, only a relatively small number (about 10%) can be classified as Neorealist, and most of these films were box-office failures. Italian audiences were reluctant to abandon popular Hollywood codes, and a number of less original but more successful Neorealist films were able to achieve greater results at the box-office by incorporating traditional Hollywood genres within their narratives about Italian subjects. Such films as *Vivere in pace* ('To Live in Peace', 1946) by Luigi Zampa (1905–91), *Senza pietà* ('Without Pity', 1948) by Alberto Lattuada (1914–), *Riso amaro* ('Bitter Rice', 1948) by Giuseppe De Santis (1917–97) and *Il cammino della speranza* ('The Path of Hope', 1950) by Pietro Germi (1914–74) expanded the boundaries of Italian Neorealism by shifting away from semi-documentary treatments of social problems toward conventional Hollywood themes and film genres, such as the Western or *film noir*. As a result of their combination of Neorealist style with Hollywood subject-matter, such works managed a respectable performance at the box-office.

The 'crisis' of Neorealism

It soon became obvious that while Italian leftist intellectuals and social critics preferred the implicitly political and sometimes even revolutionary messages of Neorealist cinema, the public was more interested in Hollywood films or Italian films with a Hollywood spirit. Even the greatest Neorealist directors (Rossellini, Antonioni, Visconti) soon became uncomfortable with the restrictive boundaries imposed upon their subject-matter or style by well-meaning but ideologically motivated critics. In Italian film history, the transition beyond Neorealism is often called the 'crisis' of Neorealism. In retrospect, the period from 1950–53 to 1968 can be more accurately described as a natural evolution of Italian film language toward a cinema concerned with psychological problems and a new aesthetic style no longer dominated by non-professional actors, on-location shooting, documentary style and social problems. Crucial to this historic transition are a number of early works by Michelangelo Antonioni (1912–), several works starring Ingrid Bergman by Rossellini and the first films directed by Federico Fellini. In *Cronaca di un amore* ('Story of a Love Affair', 1950), Antonioni's first feature film, the director employs a plot indebted to James Cain's novel *The Postman Always Rings Twice* and to American *film noir*. But his distinctive photographic signature is already evident: characteristically long shots, tracks and pans following the actors; modernist editing techniques

8. Roberto Rossellini's *Viaggio in Italia* (1953): the marriage of Katherine (Ingrid Bergman) and Alexander (George Sanders) falls apart amidst the ruins of ancient Pompeii.

reflecting the slow rhythms of daily life; and philosophical concerns with obvious links to European Existentialism. In *Viaggio in Italia* ('Voyage to Italy', 1953), Rossellini abandons his documentary style to embrace an abstract psychological realism that also reflected the emphasis upon alienation typical of contemporary post-war European philosophy.

It was with Fellini's early films that the Italian cinema moved resolutely beyond a preoccupation with social problems, although his works certainly reflect a deep understanding of Italian culture that no other Italian director can match. In *I vitelloni* (1953), for example, Fellini provides a classic portrait of six provincial characters which a Neorealist director would have presented as an indictment of provincial backwardness. But Fellini is more interested in exploring the private fantasy worlds of his creations than he is in making polemical statements about Italian society. Fellini's concern with private fantasy worlds and his belief in transcendental experiences beyond mere humdrum reality find their greatest expression in two masterpieces, both of which were to receive an Oscar for Best Foreign Film: *La strada* ('The Road', 1954) and *Le notti di Cabiria* ('The Nights of Cabiria', 1956). In each film, Fellini moves beyond a strictly realistic portrayal of provincial life to reveal a new poetic dimension, one motivated by a personal vision and a particular Fellinian mythology concerned with spiritual poverty and the necessity for grace or salvation (defined in strictly secular terms but owing an obvious debt to Catholicism).

New directions after Neorealism

In the decade between 1958 (a time when the so-called 'crisis' of Neorealism had clearly passed) and 1968 (a year of violent social and political upheavals all over Europe which shook Italy to its foundations), Italian cinema reached a level of artistic quality, international popularity and economic strength it had never before achieved. Film production continued at well above 200 films per year in Italy, while a prolonged crisis in Hollywood reduced American competition within the Italian market and abroad. Not only did Italy boast a number of distinguished *auteurs* (Antonioni, Fellini, Rossellini, Visconti) whose names had become household words everywhere and whose greatest films were being produced at this time, but the Italian cinema also witnessed the arrival of a second generation of brilliant young directors who had been apprentices to their masters: Pier Paolo Pasolini (1922–75), Bernardo Bertolucci (1940–), Marco Bellocchio (1939–), Gillo Pontecorvo (1919–), Ermanno Olmi (1931–), Francesco Rosi (1922–), Elio Petri (1929–82), Paolo (1931–) and Vittorio Taviani (1929–) and Sergio Leone (1921–89). Italian films regularly won major prizes at the world's most important festivals (Cannes, Venice, Berlin, New York); Italian films, their directors and their actors were the toast of international critics and film historians who privileged the so-called 'art film'; and perhaps most importantly, the industry made huge profits in the international market by exporting not only the traditional film comedies that had always been the staple product of the Italian industry, but also other genre films, such as the 'spaghetti' Western (a genre usually associated with Hollywood but which Italians revolutionized, making a star out of Clint Eastwood in the process) or the *peplum* film – costume films set in the classical period that recalled Italy's initial success with this genre during the silent period.

Film comedy

Film comedies (the so-called *commedia all'italiana*) and 'spaghetti' Westerns dominated the Italian market during this decade. The Italian

9. Pietro Germi's *Divorzio all'italiana* (1961): in the absence of a divorce law, Fefé (Marcello Mastroianni) must trick his wife Rosalia (Daniela Rocca) into committing adultery with Carmelo (Leopoldo Trieste) so that he can kill her and escape punishment.

cinema was blessed with a number of excellent comic directors, such as Mario Monicelli (1915–), Luigi Comencini (1916–) and Dino Risi (1917–). Even more important, Italian cinema boasted a wealth of great actors: Alberto Sordi (1919–), Vittorio Gassman (1922–2000), Marcello Mastroianni (1923–96), Nino Manfredi (1921–), Ugo Tognazzi (1922–90), Monica Vitti (1931–), Claudia Cardinale (1939–), Sophia Loren (1934–) and Stefania Sandrelli (1946–) – which no national cinema outside of Hollywood could match. Many critics of the left during the period denigrated *commedia all'italiana* as merely 'commercial' cinema without artistic value, just as they ignored the Italian contribution to the Western genre. Their ideological bias ignored the fact that Italian comic films often contained more trenchant social criticism than the more acceptable, ideologically oriented 'art films' of the period. The great comic films of the decade from 1958 to 1968 provide an amusing but often accurate mirror of changing Italian customs and values. They helped to force the average Italian into a greater awareness of conflicting moral standards; they attacked age-old prejudices; and they questioned the rule of inept governing élites and institutions. The film which best reflects the combination of humour and social criticism typical of the *commedia all'italiana* is Pietro Germi's *Divorzio all'italiana* ('Divorce, Italian Style', 1961). Made before Italian law permitted legal divorce, Germi's satire of Sicilian sexual mores chronicles the comic attempts of a Sicilian nobleman to force his hated wife into adultery, so that he can murder her, receive a light sentence for a crime of honour (hence the film's title), and marry his mistress. Utilizing a complex narrative juxtaposing the director's critical view of this affair with the Sicilian's biased justifications of his misdeeds, Germi recreates the oppressive atmosphere of Sicilian provincial life that forces men and women to commit violent crimes in order to obtain sexual fulfilment.

The 'spaghetti' Western and the *peplum* film

The other remarkably successful commercial genre during this period was the Western, dominated by a single man: Sergio Leone. The Italian 'spaghetti' Western owes a debt to another popular genre, the so-called neo-mythological or *peplum* film, which accounted for 10 per cent of Italian production between 1957 and 1964. Set in vaguely classical times and populated by mindless musclemen and buxom damsels in distress, these works appealed to a predominantly male audience that thrived on violent action and strong, anti-intellectual heroes such as Steve Reeves (only one of a number of American actors employed by the Italian industry during this period). The *peplum* film's characteristic emphasis upon action was continued by the 'spaghetti' Western. Between 1963 and 1973, over 400 such Westerns were produced in Italy, but none of them had the impact of Leone's first work, *Un pugno di dollari* ('A Fistful of Dollars', 1964). This film revolutionized what was at the time an almost exhausted Hollywood genre by a conscious departure from what had come to be known as the 'classic' Western formula. Leone plunges us into a violent and cynical world far removed from the traditional West of John Ford or Howard Hawks. The hero is motivated by the same greed as the evil bandits, and graphic violence is accompanied by grotesque comic gags and mannered close-ups indebted to Eisenstein. A crucial artistic element is the skilful music of Ennio Morricone (1928–), who first received international recognition from his collaboration with Leone, and whose unusual sound track composed of gunfire, ricochetting bullets, cries, trumpet solos, Sicilian folk instruments and whistles became an international best-selling record. The classic Western show-

10. Sergio Leone's *The Good, the Bad, and the Ugly* (1966): the site of the climactic gunfight that concludes all of Leone's 'spaghetti' Westerns.

down becomes in Leone's hands a ritualistic act concluding a narrative cycle and employs a crescendo of music not unlike the conclusion of an aria in grand opera. Though few in number, Leone's influential Western films that followed *Un pugno di dollari* were not merely hugely profitable: they also revived the most famous of all American film genres.

Auteurs and the 'art film': Visconti, Antonioni, Fellini

If film comedy, Roman pot-boilers and Western epics produced the industry's most lucrative returns, the so-called 'art films' directed by *auteurs* proved to be almost equally good investments during the decade. In fact, one of the remarkable features of this period in Italian film history was its ability to produce great art that also turned a handsome profit. Works such as Fellini's *La dolce vita* ('The Sweet Life', 1959), Visconti's *Il Gattopardo* ('The Leopard', 1962) or Antonioni's *Blow-Up* (1966) were not only major artistic creations, but also gained a large share of the international film market. Fellini's best work during the period emphasized his introspective fantasy world and brilliant, Baroque imagery, as in his masterpiece *Otto e mezzo* ('8½', 1963), and in *Giulietta degli spiriti*

11. Michelangelo Antonioni's *Il deserto rosso* (1964): the director's careful compositions within the frame underlie his abstract use of colour and form.

('Juliet of the Spirits', 1965) and *Satyricon* (1969). Visconti's best films – *Rocco e i suoi fratelli* ('Rocco and his Brothers', 1960), *La caduta degli dei* ('The Fall of the Gods', 1969) and *Morte a Venezia* ('Death in Venice', 1971) – analyse European decadence and owe a great debt both to grand opera and to the European novel. Antonioni's brilliant modernist photography finds its best expression in the black-and-white trilogy of *L'Avventura* ('The Adventure', 1960), *La Notte* ('The Night', 1961) and *L'eclisse* ('The Eclipse', 1962), and in his innovative treatment of colour in *Il deserto rosso* ('The Red Desert', 1964).

Otto e mezzo, *Il deserto rosso* and *La caduta degli dei* reflect the highly complex stylistic shifts which had occurred in the work of these three *auteurs*, each of whom had his origins in the Italian Neorealist era. Visconti usually aimed at establishing a link between his films and a broader historical context. *La caduta degli dei* provides a powerful visual metaphor for the infernal nature of moral degradation, a pathological case history of Nazi Germany underlined by the violent and hellish colours that dominate the film's visuals. In Antonioni's *Il deserto rosso*, colour photography pre-empts the central function of traditional plot and character by concentrating on the relationship between characters and their environment, represented by the machinery and contempo-

12. Federico Fellini's *Otto e mezzo* (1963): the exhausted director on the set of an alternate ending for the film that was eventually rejected.

rary technology of a modern oil refinery in Ravenna. Antonioni's colour photography is thoroughly modernist (only a single scene, a dream of a desert island, is shot in what we have come to consider as 'natural' film colour). Its hues come from the world of industrial plastics, chemicals and artificial fabrics. In some cases, the director even changes the colours of natural objects (grass, fruit) to reflect the psychological states of his disturbed characters. And he frames each shot as if he were a contemporary abstract painter, asking us to consider objects from the world of technology primarily as art forms and only later as objects with a utilitarian function. Fellini's *Otto e mezzo* embodies its creator's belief that the cinema exists primarily for the purpose of individual self-expression, not historical investigation or abstract photography: fantasy, rather than reality, is its proper domain, because only fantasy falls under the director's complete artistic control. The harried protagonist of the film, the director Guido, possesses many of Fellini's personal traits. Fellini's narrative moves rapidly and seamlessly between Guido's 'reality', his fantasies, and flashbacks to the past of his dreams – a discontinuous story line with little logical or chronological unity. The influence of psychoanalysis is obvious in the view Fellini presents of sexuality in the film, as personal problems prevent Guido from achieving artistic fulfilment. In no other film by Fellini was there to be such a perfect synthesis of his personality, his introspective style and cinematic bravura.

A new generation of *auteurs*: beyond Neorealism

While Visconti, Antonioni and Fellini dominated Italian cinema during the period, their international prestige coincided with the rise of an extremely talented group of younger men whose first works were indebted to Neorealism but who reflected what might be called a critical realism with ideological implications. The best examples of such precociously brilliant works are Pasolini's *Il vangelo secondo Matteo* ('The Gospel According to Matthew', 1964), Pontecorvo's *La battaglia di Algeri* ('The Battle of Algiers', 1966), Bernardo Bertolucci's *Prima della rivoluzione* ('Before the Revolution', 1964), Marco Bellocchio's *La Cina è vicina* ('China Is Near', 1967), Francesco Rosi's *Salvatore Giuliano* (1962) and Ermanno Olmi's *Il posto* ('The Job', 1961).

In *Il posto*, Olmi's use of non-professional actors and his emphasis upon expressive deep-focus shots in office interiors reflect an obvious debt to De Sica's poetic Neorealism. Rosi, following Visconti's example in his belief that film must make an ideological statement, moves beyond Neorealist presentation of 'facts' to what he terms a 'documented' method of making films in *Salvatore Giuliano*. This treatment of a Sicilian bandit's career and death is less a work of fiction than an investigation (*film inchiesta*) into the ambiguous historical circumstances of the figure. The film uncovers corrupt connections between the Christian Democratic Party and the Mafia, establishing itself as the first of many Italian 'political' films that would flourish in the period. Pontecorvo employs a documentary style in *La battaglia di Algeri*, with a narrative structure that uses flashbacks and flashforwards to provide critical commentary on the 'facts' the film presents. His careful recreation of a case history of Third World revolution owes an important debt to the early war films and techniques of Rossellini. Pontecorvo's highly mobile, hand-held cameras employ fast film stock; the telephoto lenses common in television news reporting simulate a documentary style; duplicating the negative of his film in the laboratory recreates the grainy, documentary texture of Rossellini's *Paisà*.

Bertolucci, Bellocchio and Pasolini – all influenced by the aesthetics of Brecht and the cinematic practice of Godard – exhibit a far more ambiguous relationship with the heritage of Italian Neorealism.

13. Francesco Rosi's *Salvatore Giuliano* (1962): an overhead shot of the dead Sicilian bandit opens Rosi's semi-documentary account of his life.

Pasolini accepted many of the superficial characteristics of Neorealist style – non-professional actors, on-location shooting, contemporary themes, natural lighting – but he rejected any attempt to employ cinema to present a naturalistic view of life. For Pasolini, Realism included mythology and dream. The cinematic signature he developed in *Il vangelo secondo Matteo*, a biblical film made by a Marxist atheist, can be described as pastiche, mixing the most disparate cultural and thematic materials. Bertolucci and Bellocchio present a fresh view of Italian politics in their youthful works. With *Prima della rivoluzione*, Bertolucci adapts Stendhal's *The Charterhouse of Parma* (1839) in a poetic and highly lyrical study of a young bourgeois intellectual from Parma (Bertolucci's home) who toys with Marxism but eventually prefers a safe, middle-class marriage to revolution or an incestuous love affair with his aunt. Bellocchio's artistic perspective is angry and provocative rather than lyrical and elegiac. While Bertolucci's Fabrizio retreats into the protective womb of the Italian nuclear family, Bellocchio's protagonists in *La Cina è vicina* attack the very notion of a provincial, middle-class family in a satire on Italian political corruption. The result is a political allegory attacking the compromise between the right and the left in Italy, viewed from the microcosm of a small, provincial family.

Post-1968 cinema: politics and ideology in the dramatic film

Between the upheavals in Italian society that took place around 1968 and immediately afterwards, and the mid 1980s, when a period of 'normalcy' was re-established in Italian society, a number of major critical trends can be traced in the evolution of Italian cinema. Politics and ideology continued to play a major role, moving even normally apolitical directors (such as Fellini) to treat political themes. Nevertheless, it is also fair to say that the emphasis on ideology in the cinema was also responsible for some of the most boring and pretentious cinematic works of the period that are best left unmentioned. Films that combined political themes with intriguing and original cinematic styles (hardly an exhaustive list) include: *Medea* (1969) and *Il Decameron* ('The Decameron', 1971) by Pasolini, Bertolucci's *Il conformista* ('The Conformist', 1970), Fellini's *Amarcord* (1976), Elio Petri's *Indagine su un cittadino al di sopra di ogni sospetto* ('Investigation of a Citizen Above Suspicion', 1970), *Padre Padrone* ('Father Boss', 1977) and *La notte di San Lorenzo* ('The Night of the Shooting Stars', 1982) by the Taviani brothers and Olmi's *L'albero degli zoccoli* ('The Tree of the Wooden Clogs', 1978).

With *Medea*, Pasolini employs the classic tragedy by Euripides as a metaphor to explore the confrontation of Western, industrialized society with the preindustrial cultures of the Third World. In *Il Decameron*, Pasolini transforms Boccaccio's panoramic portrait of the rise of middle-class, mercantile culture in an age dominated by the city of Florence into an amusing portrayal of the subproletariat of Naples and its sexual adventures. The film not only underlines the class-oriented nature of the original literary source, but also proposes liberated sexuality as a characteristic of non-industrialized cultures and uses this innocent sense of sexuality to criticize modern, Western values.

Bertolucci's *Il conformista* and Fellini's *Amarcord* provide two very different interpretations of Italy's Fascist heritage. Bertolucci employs a complicated plot with frequent flashbacks, portraying the creation of a Fascist assassin. Bertolucci's mature grasp of his craft is evident in the famous tango scene between two women, with its quickly shifting camera angles, positions, graceful motions and skilful editing, a virtuoso performance due, in large measure, to the brilliant cinematography of a young Vittorio Storaro (1940–). Fellini's *Amarcord* is much less

14. Federico Fellini's *Amarcord* (1974): sexual immaturity, for Fellini, represents one of the many ways provincial life under Fascism was shrouded in ignorance.

stridently ideological but is no less a condemnation of Fascist restrictions of individual freedom. In an unforgettable evocation of life in a sleepy provincial town, Fellini combines a nostalgic view of his childhood with a searing indictment of Italian conformity during the Fascist period.

Two directors became identified almost exclusively with trenchant critiques of Italian political life in this period: Elio Petri and Francesco Rosi. Petri's works, blending his ideological message with suspense and slick, commercial presentation, have always been popular abroad. *Indagine di un cittadino al di sopra di ogni sospetto*, winner of an Oscar for Best Foreign Film, presents contemporary Italian politics in an abstract, almost philosophical manner akin to Kafka's parables, and Petri's message applies not only to power in Italy but to power in general. Rosi's many interesting political films are less comprehensible abroad, since they contain a more specific connection to actual events in Italian daily life. The richly documented denunciations of the system which he began with *Salvatore Giuliano* are continued in a series of interesting works: *Lucky Luciano* (1973), a probing look into the link between American politicians and the Sicilian mafia; *Cadaveri eccellenti* ('Illustrious Corpses', 1975), a chilling parable of the connection between political power and corruption in Italy, adapted from a novel by Leonardo Sciascia in which

15. *La notte di San Lorenzo* by Paolo and Vittorio Taviani (1982): in recounting a story about the meeting of American soldiers and young Italians in war-torn Tuscany, these post-war directors pay homage to Rossellini's *Paisà* and their own Neorealist origins.

the image of the mafia is transformed into a universal metaphor for corrupt power all over the world; and *Tre fratelli* ('Three Brothers', 1981), a view of contemporary Italian life seen through the lives of three brothers who return to southern Italy for the funeral of their mother.

L'albero degli zoccoli by Olmi is one of the many good Italian films financed by the state-controlled television network (the RAI), an increasingly important source of funding for Italian works or co-productions with other European national cinemas. In it, Olmi offers a patient re-creation of peasant life on a farm near Bergamo at the turn of the nineteenth century and adopts a style recalling the conventions of Neorealism, employing non-professional peasants from the area who speak their local dialect. The three-hour length of the film allows Olmi to duplicate the slow rhythms of life in a preindustrial peasant culture.

The Taviani brothers are perhaps the most interesting of the so-called 'political' directors. Their *Padre Padrone* is an autobiographical account of how an illiterate Sardinian shepherd struggled to become a professor of linguistics. The acquisition of standard Italian thus becomes a metaphor for the acquisition of full citizenship in modern Italian society. *La notte di San Lorenzo* is a post-modern reinterpretation of Italian Neorealism and its central theme, the partisan Resistance and the liberation of Tuscany in August 1944.

Bittersweet laughter: social criticism in the *commedia all'italiana*

While films with predominantly political or ideological content tended to dominate the production of 'art films' between 1968 and the mid 1980s, traditional film comedies continued to provide the backbone for the Italian industry, and were consistently the most popular works in the peninsula while frequently dealing with important social issues. Taken as a group, comedies during this era embody a black, even grotesque vision of contemporary Italian society, and the laughter in these works rings bittersweet. An excellent example of the creative combination of humour and social criticism in this modified *commedia all'italiana* is *Pane e cioccolata* ('Bread and Chocolate', 1973) by Franco Brusati (1922–93), a devastating indictment of the conditions experienced by Italian 'guest workers' in what is depicted as a racist Switzerland.

The dominant director of this bittersweet kind of film comedy is Ettore Scola (1931–), who began working in cinema as a scriptwriter on dozens of comic films produced in the 1950s and the early 1960s. In a number of memorable works – *C'eravamo tanto amati* ('We All Loved Each Other Very Much', 1974), *Brutti, sporchi e cattivi* ('Dirty, Mean and Nasty', 1976), *Una giornata particolare* ('A Special Day', 1977) and *La terrazza* ('The Terrace', 1980) – Scola employed a metacinematic narrative to treat the history of Italian cinema itself, examining not only the heritage of Neorealism (especially his model, Vittorio De Sica) but also the assumptions of the *commedia all'italiana*. *C'eravamo tanto amati* is the most complex of these films, combining a consideration of the many social and political changes which Italy has undergone since the fall of the Fascist régime with an equally comprehensive survey of major developments in the history of post-war Italian cinema.

In a series of excellent films – *Mimì metallurgico ferito nell'onore* ('Mimì the Metallurgist Wounded in his Honour', 1971), *Film d'amore e d'anarchia* ('A Film About Love and Anarchy', 1972), *Travolti da un insolito destino nell'azzurro mare d'agosto* ('Overcome by an Unusual Destiny in the Blue Sea of August', 1974) and her masterpiece, *Pasqualino Settebellezze* ('Pasqualino Seven Beauties', 1975) – Lina Wertmüller (1928–) combines an exuberant imagery indebted to Fellini with a concern for topical political issues, all set within the conventions of traditional Italian film comedy, with its vulgarity, stock characters and frontal attack upon society's values. Wertmüller's films aroused the ire of many Feminists, as

16. Lina Wertmüller's *Pasqualino Settebellezze* (1975): in order to survive in the concentration camp, Pasqualino must seduce its hefty female commandant (Shirley Stroler).

her works did not conform to what many Anglo-American academics considered to be proper for a woman's film. In addition, *Pasqualino Settebellezze*'s treatment of the Holocaust was set within a comic framework and was attacked by some critics as irreverent. Nevertheless, its portrait of the hellish life inside a concentration camp found important critical defenders, while the virtuoso performance of its protagonist, Giancarlo Giannini (1942–), made him an international star.

Another controversial portrait of the Holocaust was *Il portiere di notte* ('The Night Porter', 1974), a work by another woman director, Liliana Cavani (1936–). In sharp contrast to Feminist hostility to Wertmüller's films, Cavani's morbid portrait of a love affair between a woman in a death camp and a sadistic German officer, a relationship which is renewed in the post-war period after a chance encounter between the two in Vienna, was praised by a number of Feminist critics though

17. Bernardo Bertolucci's *L'ultimo imperatore* (1987): Pu Yi (John Lone) is driven out of the Forbidden City in an epic portrait of China's last emperor that earned Oscars in nine categories.

damned by others for its revisionist view of evil in the camps. The treatment of the Holocaust during this period in the Italian cinema that elicited almost unanimous praise (except from Giorgio Bassani, the novelist whose book was its source) was Vittorio De Sica's *Il giardino dei Finzi-Contini* ('The Garden of the Finzi-Continis', 1971), a lyrical, elegiac portrait of the Jewish population of pre-war Ferrara which was awarded the Oscar for Best Foreign Film in 1972.

Italian blockbuster epics

At the height of the Italian cinema's international success, two directors – Bertolucci and Leone – produced three films that seemed more typical of Hollywood blockbusters than of Italian cinematic production. Bertolucci's *1900* (1977) describes the history of the class struggle in Italy from the death of Verdi to our own times through the intertwined accounts of two boys from different classes. It may well be described as a Marxist *Gone With the Wind*. A much more successful epic film was Bertolucci's *L'ultimo imperatore* ('The Last Emperor', 1987), the story of Pu Yi, China's last emperor who ended his days as a humble gardener. With a brilliant flashback/flashforward structure, this work swept the board of Oscar awards for the year, winning in nine categories (including Best Picture, Direction, Cinematography, Costumes, Editing and Music), an unprecedented honour for an Italian director and for a film indebted primarily to Italian technicians. Perhaps the most fascinating epic film to come from Italy was Sergio Leone's last work, *C'era una volta in America* ('Once Upon a Time in America', 1984) – an ambitious attempt to change the generic conventions of the Hollywood gangster film as Leone had already done with the Hollywood Western, with Jewish, not Italian, gangsters.

The passing of the old guard and new faces at the dawn of the millennium

By the time Fellini received a fifth Oscar for his career, shortly before his death in 1993, Italian cinema seemed to be immersed in an economic and artistic crisis. On the other hand, its rich tradition of great directors, actors and films was universally recognized by a number of international awards. In the late 1980s and 1990s, a new generation of young directors rose to prominence within Italy and some even garnered important recognition abroad, holding out the promise of yet a third 'renaissance' of Italian cinema that would follow those of Neorealism and of the generation of Bertolucci and Pasolini. These include such figures as Maurizio Nichetti (1948–), Nanni Moretti (1953–), Gabriele Salvatores (1950–), Giuseppe Tornatore (1956–), Gianni Amelio (1945–), Roberto Benigni (1952–), Francesca Archibugi (1960–) and Carlo Carlei (1961–).

Amelio's *Le porte aperte* ('Open Doors', 1990), nominated for an Oscar, is an adaptation of a novel by Sciascia about justice in Fascist Italy. His *Il ladro di bambini* ('The Thief of Children', 1992), winner of a Grand Jury Prize at Cannes, is a moving treatment of children reminiscent of De Sica's classic Neorealist works. In *Lamerica* ('America', 1994), Amelio focuses upon Albanian emancipation from Communism and looks at a poor country (Albania) from the novel perspective of a nation (Italy) that was once poor and chronicled its poverty in Neorealist film, but is now rich and intent on exploiting the poor in Albania.

Unlike Amelio, many of the younger faces in the Italian cinema prefer the comic genre, and the variety of styles they employ is impressive. Nichetti's *Ladri di saponette* ('Soap Thieves', 1989), a brilliant spoof of De

Sica's Neorealist classic *Ladri di biciclette*, employs techniques the director learned from working in television and advertising, while his *Volere volare* ('To Desire to Fly', 1991) mixes actors and cartoon characters in a technique exploited most notably in Robert Zemeckis's *Who Framed Roger Rabbit?* (1987). Tornatore's tremendously popular *Cinema Paradiso* ('The Paradise Cinema', 1988) owed much of its success to its bittersweet look at contemporary Italy through the prism of its cinematic past. It was awarded a special Jury Prize at Cannes in 1988 and the Oscar for Best Foreign Film in 1989. Salvatores's *Mediterraneo* ('Mediterranean', 1991), another Oscar winner for Best Foreign Film, employs the old formula of the *commedia all'italiana* to portray the Second World War from the perspective of Italian soldiers marooned on a Greek island. While its director (Michael Radford) is certainly not Italian, everything about *Il postino* ('The Postman', 1994) has links to the Italian film industry and the perennially popular *commedia all'italiana*. The film brought actor Massimo Troisi to the attention of international audiences, but Troisi died shortly after shooting was completed for the film. *Il postino* was a smash critical and commercial success, receiving five Oscar nominations and one award, in the category of Original Musical Score. While practically unknown outside Italy, Leonardo Pieraccioni's recent comic films have made spectacular gains at the box office within the lucrative Italian market: *Il ciclone* ('The Cyclone', 1995) and *Fuochi di artificio* ('Fireworks', 1996).

Two actors who script and direct their own films, Nanni Moretti and Roberto Benigni, have enjoyed international success. With *Caro diario* ('Dear Diary', 1994), Moretti – the favourite director of Italians aged under forty – won the Grand Prize at the Cannes Film Festival for an autobiographical portrait that led some critics to label him as 'the Italian Woody Allen' for his cerebral brand of comedy. Roberto Benigni first achieved international attention as the strange Italian learning English in Jim Jarmusch's *Down by Law* (1986) and as the heir to Peter Sellers' role as Inspector Clouseau in Blake Edwards's *Son of the Pink Panther* (1993). His *Johnny Stecchino* (1991), a spoof on the gangster genre, broke all records for Italian or American grosses inside Italy. *La vita è bella* ('Life Is Beautiful', 1997), a tragicomedy about the Holocaust indebted to Charlie Chaplin's *The Great Dictator* (1940), earned Benigni special recognition at the Cannes Film Festival, three Oscars and nine David di Donatello awards (the Italian equivalent of the Oscar). It also broke every American record for box-office returns for a foreign film in the post-war period.

Like the phoenix, post-war Italian cinema seems to arise from the ashes of the past in each generation. With a younger generation boasting the talents of such directors as Benigni, Moretti and Tornatore, its artistic future during the next millennium looks promising.

FURTHER READING

Armes, Roy, *Patterns of Realism: A Study of Italian Neo-Realism*. Cranbury, NJ: A.S. Barnes, 1971.

Bazin, André, *What Is Cinema?* II. Berkeley: University of California Press, 1971.

Bondanella, Peter, *The Cinema of Federico Fellini*. Princeton University Press, 1992.

   The Films of Roberto Rossellini. Cambridge University Press, 1993.

   Italian Cinema: From Neorealism to the Present. 3rd rev. edn. New York: Continuum, 2001.

   'Recent Work on Italian Cinema', *Journal of Modern Italian Studies* 1/1 (1995), pp. 101–23.

Brunetta, Gian Piero, *Storia del cinema italiano*. 4 vols. Rome: Editori Riuniti, 1993.

Gieri, Manuela, *Contemporary Italian Filmmaking*. Toronto: University of Toronto Press, 1995.

Landy, Marcia, *Fascism in Film*. Princeton University Press, 1986.

   Italian Film. Cambridge University Press, 2000

Marcus, Millicent, *Filmmaking by the Book: Italian Cinema and Literary Adaptation*. Baltimore: The Johns Hopkins University Press, 1993.

Sitney, P. Adams, *Vital Crises in Italian Cinema*. Austin: University of Texas Press, 1995.

Sorlin, Pierre. *Italian National Cinema 1986–1996*. London: Routledge, 1996.

12

Art in modern Italy: from the Macchiaioli to the Transavanguardia

The Macchiaioli and the unification of Italy

Until the middle of the nineteenth century, the term 'Italy' was an abstract concept that intellectuals and artists since Dante had used to describe their imagined homeland rather than a political reality. The first group of artists who presented themselves as linked to the nation were the Tuscan Macchiaioli, whose emergence was made possible by the Prima Esposizione Italiana ('First Italian Exhibition') that was held in Florence in 1861, a matter of months after unification. (The name 'Macchiaioli' was taken from *macchia* which means 'sketch' or 'sketch technique'.) It was at this exhibition that, for the first time, artists who were living and working in different parts of the Italian peninsula were grouped together. As is well known, the centuries-long fragmentation of the Italian states and the numerous foreign dominations had significantly contributed to the absence of a 'national' art or culture. Moreover, the divided state of the peninsula did not facilitate exchanges between different regions. Not surprisingly, many nineteenth-century artists who, with unification, wished to expand their boundaries and horizons considered Italian life and art to be marked by cultural provincialism.

To counter this impression, after the declaration of the Kingdom of Italy which designated Florence as its first capital, the Prima Esposizione overtly presented itself as Italy's first *national* art exhibition. The exhibition made possible interaction between regional artistic schools and traditions, and created the opportunity for retracing and redefining a 'national' cultural identity. Although the Macchiaioli were a regionally based movement, redolent of Tuscan backgrounds and scenes, their work struck a national chord, and their influence and fame spread well

18. Giovanni Fattori, *Garibaldi a Palermo* ('Garibaldi in Palermo'), 1860–2.

beyond their local confines to make them the artistic movement most closely associated with the Risorgimento.

The Macchiaioli were a very active group of artists who established their school in Florence in the mid-nineteenth century and who had all frequented the Florentine Caffè Michelangelo, the centre of cultural and artistic life in the years (1824–59) of the reign of Grand Duke Leopold II (1797–1870). Many of the members of the group such as Odoardo Borrani (1834–1905), Telemaco Signorini (1853–1901) and Giovanni Fattori (1825–1908), who painted *Garibaldi a Palermo* ('Garibaldi in Palermo', 1860–2; fig. 18), were patriots and had volunteered to join the forces of Giuseppe Garibaldi (1807–82) in Tuscany. Painters were deemed to have a key function in spreading a sense of patriotism, as well as in adding rhetorical emphasis to historical facts. Another important characteristic of the 1861 exhibition, therefore, was the way it marked the arrival of a new artistic genre, centred on contemporary history, and which included paintings that took as their subject-matter episodes drawn from the wars of unification and other patriotic motifs.

In addition to their political art, the Macchiaioli had ties with the Realism of the day. They painted familiar Tuscan landscapes, the *vedute*, and depicted the simple life of ordinary people. In order to strengthen their sense of the Italian artistic and cultural tradition, the Macchiaioli sought inspiration in the fifteenth-century Florentine school of paint-

19. Odoardo Borrani, *Le cucitrici delle camicie rosse* ('The Seamstresses of the Red Shirts'), 1863.

ing. For instance, a painting such as Borrani's *Le cucitrici delle camicie rosse* ('The Seamstresses of the Red Shirts', 1863; fig. 19) had the effect of turning a simple scene into a deeply political and specifically Tuscan moment. The figures of the women are grouped together in forms that evoke the silence and mystery of frescoed paintings typical of the fifteenth century. Borrani's painting came into being during a time of popular enthusiasm for Garibaldi's campaign to conquer Rome. The historical event which inspired this painting was the failed patriotic war of 1862 during which, without the support of Cavour, Garibaldi (whose portrait we see in the background hanging on the wall) marched on Rome, which owing to papal hostility was not yet part of the Kingdom of Italy. The women depicted in Borrani's painting sewing the red shirts are relatives of Garibaldi's irregulars. The theme of an intimate and domestic environment pervaded an earlier painting by Borrani, his

20. Odoardo Borrani, *Il 26 Aprile 1859* ('26 April 1859'), 1861.

26 Aprile 1859 (1861; fig. 20), which was presented at the national exhibition. Here again, we see a woman sewing pieces of fabric in the colours of the Italian flag. The historical events informing this painting are those of 1859 which forced Grand Duke Leopold II to flee from Tuscany.

Borrani's paintings, and especially the ones considered here, offer vivid examples of two of the main characteristics of the Macchiaioli's art. First, as already stated, the recovery of the Renaissance artistic tradition, seen in the calm majesty of the figures. Secondly, the fascination, common to all the Macchiaioli, with the new medium of photography. In Borrani's 'The Seamstresses of the Red Shirts', there is a diffuse and warm light effect very similar to that which can be obtained by photography. Painters started to draw on photographs for inspiration or to develop their work in innovative ways. It goes without saying that photography, which was present at the first national exhibition, but under the category of 'Chemistry', was very popular and went on to revolutionize perspective.

After the Church's resistance to unification had been overcome, Rome became the capital of the new state in 1870. The various political factions agreed to make Rome the place where Italy's national culture and art would be defined. The planning and execution of monuments celebrating the great figures of the Risorgimento took many years, since deep ideological disagreements characterized the relationships among the different political groups. The conflicts and political disputes involving the nature of the image of Rome as the capital of the newly formed nation testify to the difficulties involved in creating the new Italy and its artistic culture.

Divisionism

The end of the nineteenth century was marked by the co-existence of a variety of artistic currents and forms of experiment. The notion of art itself was problematized, as was its function in society, its potential to enrich the spiritual life of human beings, and its contribution to the understanding of nature and history. The situation of the visual arts in Italy was exceedingly complex: on the one hand, art was expected to help construct the new Italian national identity; on the other, it was supposed also to satisfy a desire for internationalism by crossing local and national boundaries, thus overcoming what was perceived to be its provincialism. This explains the interest in and contributions of Italian artists to European artistic movements and debates such as Impressionism and Symbolism. Giovanni Segantini (1858–99), among Italy's most famous painters of the period both at home and in Europe, was one of the leading protagonists of the artistic current known as Divisionism. Despite his premature death at the age of forty, Segantini's work was exhibited in Vienna in 1898, and later, in 1902, a retrospective was organized, again in Vienna, at the Palace of Secession. It is important to note that many artists at this time were critical of official institutions and took up anti-academic positions, forming alternative groups from which the term 'secession' derived its origin.

Divisionism in Italy gave expression to several concerns that animated European cultural and artistic debates. The movement's novel views on how to represent reality, which included the need for cultural

21. Giuseppe Pellizza da Volpedo, *Il quarto Stato* ('The Fourth Estate'), 1901.

and artistic renewal, combined with a faith in science and intelligence, prevailed over the patriotic sentiments of earlier years. Moreover, Divisionism incorporated some of the ideas of the Lombard group of writers known as the *scapigliati* ('Bohemians'), especially their rejection of empty formalism and refusal to conform to established artistic techniques. Among the exponents of Divisionism, besides Segantini, was the Piedmontese painter Giuseppe Pellizza da Volpedo (1868–1907), famous for his *Il quarto Stato* ('The Fourth Estate'; fig. 21). The painter adhered to Divisionism mainly because of his interest in the movement's rationalist approach. He also had ideas in common with the Socialist intellectuals in Turin, ideas which reinforced his belief in a committed art.

Pellizza's first inspiration for *Il quarto Stato* came from the big industrial strikes of the 1890s. He subsequently changed the subject to a peasant march in the village of Volpedo where he had been born and from which he took his surname. The crowd was, for the painter, the symbol of humanity marching towards progress and redemption. The characters are symmetrically organized into groups of three as they narrate their stories to each other. The scene, especially in its emphasis on the characters' bare hands, recalls Raphael's *The School of Athens* (1508–11), a fresco that Pellizza studied while composing *Il quarto Stato*. He worked on the painting for several years before exhibiting it for the first time at the Turin Quadriennale in 1902.

The opening decades of the twentieth century were marked in Italy by a widespread sense of disenchantment with the state of the nation, which had been unified for less than fifty years. For many, the Italy that had emerged from the unification process was but a pale shadow of the nation in which they had invested their hopes. Disenchantment was felt across the ideological spectrum, while in all areas of Italian intellectual life, including art, significant moves were made to regenerate what was seen as the debased, petit-bourgeois dominated state of Italian culture and politics.

The Futurist movement

Foremost among the new artistic movements were the Futurists, whose project was to effect a deep rupture with everything that the past, and especially the recent past, represented. Inspired by the experiences of the European avant-garde, which was oriented not towards figurative depiction but towards the idea of art for art's sake, the Futurists aimed to reform radically all aspects of art, society and culture. Filippo Marinetti (1876–1947) published the first *Manifesto futurista* ('Futurist Manifesto') in the Parisian newspaper *Le Figaro* on 20 February 1909. Following on from Marinetti's literary manifesto, Futurist painters prepared a manifesto of their own, which was signed by Umberto Boccioni (1882–1916), who became the leader of the movement, Carlo Carrà (1881–1966), Luigi Russolo (1885–1947) and Gino Severini (1883–1966), who at the time was living in Paris. The *Manifesto dei pittori futuristi* ('Manifesto of Futurist Painters'), published on 11 February 1910, was presented in a theatre in Turin where the artists, together with Marinetti, launched the programme with which they aimed to renew the contemporary artistic scene. The artists attacked what they deemed to be the quasi-religious relationship with tradition embodied especially in places like museums. Futurist art was to find inspiration in the present and 'in the tangible miracles of contemporary life'.[1]

The urban environment, its speed and nocturnal atmosphere, constitute some of the favourite subjects of Futurist painting. Interestingly, the descriptions of subjects and atmospheres found in Marinetti's literary manifesto were to provide a much richer source of inspiration for artists than for poets, on account of the manifesto's language and its immediate figurative translatability. For the Futurists, the notions of dynamism and movement were fundamental in conceiving

22. Giacomo Balla, *Dinamismo di un cane al guinzaglio* ('Dynamism of a Dog on a Leash'), 1912.

the representation of a reality that was never seen as static. Furthermore, psychological feelings were thought to be deeply involved in the reception of a gesture or of a given reality. In other words, things and feelings were continuously moving around the painter and the viewer to the point where the Futurist artist claimed to be able to place the viewer inside the picture, as if s/he were part of the painting itself, the real protagonist of the scene created. The image was not conceived in frozen fixity as if evoking a sort of calm finitude, but rather in its 'materiality', as a vital flux of emotion and feelings. A striking visual representation of these ideas is *Dinamismo di un cane al guinzaglio* ('Dynamism of a Dog on a Leash', 1912; fig.22) by Giacomo Balla (1871–1958). Underpinned by a marked sense of intellectual rigour, Boccioni's work, as he himself presented it in his book *Pittura e scultura futuriste* ('Futurist Painting and Sculpture'), stressed the function of the *Stati d'animo* ('States of Mind') as an important principle for Futurist painting; and it is noteworthy that he painted a series of pictures bearing this general designation, whose particular titles are: *Gli addii* ('Goodbyes', 1911), *Quelli che vanno* ('Those Who Go', 1911) and *Quelli che restano* ('Those Who Stay', 1911).

After Boccioni's death in 1916 at the age of thirty-four, the main exponents of Futurism continued to be active in many different artistic and cultural areas. It is important to note that the significance of Futurism was only recognized after the Second World War. In Italy, during the period of their greatest creativity, the Futurists were not taken seriously. Nevertheless, their influence has been extensive.

Metaphysical painting

The Futurists set great store by what they hoped would be the beneficial regeneration offered by war and the *tabula rasa* effect it would have on human endeavour. However, differently from how the Futurists imagined things would turn out, one of the major consequences of the devastation and confusion caused by the First World War was to drive many artists to search for a return to order. As a result, they turned towards a more figurative art (though 'figurative' in this instance should not be understood as equivalent to realistic or naturalistic modes). It was during these years that painters such as Giotto, Piero della Francesca and Raphael were studied once again, and in a new light, thanks to the influence of the art historian and critic Roberto Longhi (1890–1970), who proposed new evaluations of Italian Renaissance art. In addition, much attention was paid to the aesthetic of the form of a work of art rather than its content, following a tradition established by Italy's foremost and most influential twentieth-century philosopher, Benedetto Croce (1866–1952).

In the years before the advent of Fascism in 1922, much of the above-mentioned debate on art took place in the pages of the journal *Valori plastici: Rassegna di arte contemporanea* ('Plastic Values: Review of Contemporary Art'), edited by Mario Broglio (1891–1948), who was both a painter and an art critic. The journal was published in Rome from the end of 1918 until 1922. The painters Carrà and the De Chirico brothers Giorgio (1888–1978) and Andrea (1891–1952) (the latter using the pseudonym Alberto Savinio) contributed to the journal, as did other Italian and foreign artists. In their writings for *Valori plastici*, De Chirico and Savinio theorized so-called 'Metaphysical' painting which had its major protagonist in De Chirico. In De Chirico's paintings, his links to Symbolism and Surrealism are evident as well as a sense of the 'return to order' within the chaos of the present. It is enough to think of the presence of buildings, arches, columns and walls, as well as the statuesque bodies and busts. His clean lines and apparently well-ordered fragments of landscapes allow the viewer almost to feel for a moment the ambiguity of existence which his paintings represent with their mysteries lurking in a

23. Giorgio De Chirico, *Enigma di un giorno* ('The Enigma of a Day'), 1914.

corner of a street, in an empty piazza or in the shadows of a sunny day, as in his *L'Enigma di un giorno* ('The Enigma of a Day', 1914; fig. 23).

Art under Fascism

On 26 March 1923, on the occasion of the opening of the art exhibition *Artisti del Novecento* ('Artists of the Twentieth Century') at the Galleria Pesaro in Milan, Mussolini stated that in a country such as Italy it would be impossible for any government not to care for art and artists. The artists whose works were presented at the exhibition were a group of seven painters, among them Achille Funi (1890–1972) and Mario Sironi (1885–1961), all of whom were gathered around the art critic and journalist Margherita Sarfatti (1883–1961), Mussolini's brilliant Jewish mistress who greatly influenced him. She was the art editor of the national news-paper *Il Popolo d'Italia* ('The Italian People'), director of the party journal *Gerarchia* ('Hierarchy') and a biographer of the Duce. Sarfatti was among the few women who corresponded with important intellectuals, artists and political figures; she also organized art exhibitions, lending her support to artists and writers. Her relationship with the Duce ended in the early 1930s.

In recent years, it has become possible to look back at Fascism in a rather more objective manner than was possible in the decades immedi-ately after the war, and to study its culture and cultural policies to see how it attempted to build consensus among the population, and hence establish and maintain its hegemony. Art and culture in general were assigned an important role by Fascism as it sought to create general consent for itself among Italians. It was as Fascism consolidated its power in the 1930s that Mussolini began forcefully to pose the question of a 'Fascist art' in the overall context of a general 'fascistization' of Italian life and culture. The Fascist bureaucratic apparatus was well organized and capable of ensuring that artists adhered to its tenets, while at the same time allowing painters some artistic freedom of expression. Instead of building an art 'for the régime', Fascism devel-oped a more pragmatic approach. It encouraged – and directed – artists through a network of commissions and exhibitions: five editions of the Venice Biennale from 1930 to 1940; the Quadriennali I, II and III in Rome in 1931, 1935 and 1939; the second Exhibition of Rational Architecture in Rome in 1931; the exhibition of the Fascist Revolution in Rome in 1932; the two national exhibitions of *plastica murale* ('Mural Plastic') in Genoa in 1934 and Rome in 1935. In addition, Fascism encouraged a vast number of local exhibitions, offered space to artists in the press and appointed them to public posts. In these circumstances, it is possible to appreciate how the visual arts played a key role during Fascism, espe-cially at the end of the 1920s and throughout the 1930s, the period which saw the construction of the Fascist corporate state.

On the occasion of the inauguration in Perugia of the Accademia di Belle Arti (Academy of Fine Arts) in 1926, Mussolini declared that he wanted to create a Fascist art, but also added that he had no intention of encouraging anything that might resemble state-controlled art. This dual emphasis well exemplifies Fascist attitudes towards art. Art, according to Mussolini, belonged to the realm of the individual, and the state's role was to encourage artists and to create appropriate conditions for them to develop. Subsequently, however, following the alliance with Germany and the racial laws of 1938, the régime proved to be less generous to the nation's artists. Telesio Interlandi, co-director with Giovanni Preziosi of the journal *La difesa della razza* ('The Defence of the Race'), tried to define a pure 'modern Italian art', which, in Interlandi's view, was characterized by non-imported aesthetic canons and was to be firmly distinguished from the corrupt *arte ebraizzata* ('Jewish-influenced art'). In this respect, it is important to remember that two art shows were organized in 1937 in Munich: one of 'degenerate art' which included avant-garde artists and Expressionists, and one of 'healthy art' with exhibits which exalted Nazi ideology and the superiority of the Aryan race. Thus, after the passing of the racial laws, the Fascist régime tried to follow the example of Germany and stimulate an art that would stress the values of the 'Italian race'. One of the results of this new attitude was the Cremona Prize, set up in 1939 and sponsored by Roberto Farinacci (1892–1945) of Cremona, the former *ras*, or local Fascist leader, and Secretary General of the Partito Nazionale Fascista ('National Fascist Party'). The aim of the prize was to promote a 'true' Fascist art and iconography through the illustration of a number of pictorial themes such as 'States of Mind Created by Fascism' in 1939 or 'The Battle for Grain' in 1940 – all themes suggested by Mussolini himself. Not surprisingly, no serious artist competed for the Cremona Prize. As a counterweight to the Cremona Prize, which he denounced as vulgar and lacking artistic merit, the open-minded Fascist Minister for Culture, Giuseppe Bottai (1895–1959), organized the Bergamo Prize, which represented a totally different way of conceiving art during the Fascist régime. The Bergamo Prize's first exhibition was also held in 1939 and enjoyed considerable prestige among artists. Indeed many of the most important figures of Italian art, such as Renato Guttuso (1912–87), Mario Mafai (1902–65), Filippo De Pisis (1896–1956), whose real name was Filippo Tibertelli, and Pio Semeghini (1878–1964), were given awards.

Architecture, on account of its monumentality, was the art that best suited Fascist aims, as well as Mussolini's desire to leave a permanent and visible mark of his régime. A self-consciously Fascist style of architecture, a mix of classicism and modernism, much of which is still visible in Italian cities today, especially in Rome, was developed. Mussolini intended Rome to become the Fascist city *par excellence*, as well as the model for cities outside Italy which were part of the 'Fascist empire'. Side by side with the glorification of imperial Rome and its grandiosity,

Fascism also emphasized notions of novelty and *giovinezza* ('youth'). In this way the glorification of the past was integrated into the fabric of present needs. Inevitably, this dual focus could not but bring out a series of contradictory elements within architecture and urban planning which mirror the contradictions within Fascism itself. Ideologically, the régime was attempting to straddle two mutually exclusive positions: on the one hand, it underlined Fascism's continuity with the great moments of Italy's past, such as the Roman Empire and the Risorgimento; on the other, it presented itself as a completely new phenomenon which had no precedents and no debts to the past, much as Futurism had done. These two contradictory concerns are enshrined in the very first lines of the *Manifesto degli intellettuali fascisti* ('Manifesto of Fascist Intellectuals') organized by the philosopher and Fascist theorist Giovanni Gentile (1875–1944), in which Fascism is introduced as both 'a recent and ancient movement of the Italian spirit'.[2]

This fundamental contradiction was especially apparent in Fascist architecture. Officially sanctioned Fascist architects were grouped in the significantly titled Associazione dell'Architettura e della Modernità Fasciste ('Association of Fascist Architecture and Modernity'). Mussolini himself declared that he was for 'modern architecture' – by which he meant a relationship of non-continuity with the architecture of the age of Giolitti, the Liberal politician whose policies were associated with the post-Risorgimento decline of Italy. Hence the notion of being 'new' meant to be in step with the times or, in other words, in tune with the Fascist era. However, differing views existed among architects as to how this notion of 'modernity' should be expressed. The architect Marcello Piacentini (1881–1960), who was also an academic, and later on other young architects belonging to the Gruppo 7 ('Group 7'), who had graduated from the newly established faculties of architecture in the 1920s, argued for innovation. Among these, Adalberto Libera (1903–63), one of the best-known architects of this period, assumed a prominent position at the first National Architecture Exhibition in 1928. At the same time, however, the rhetoric of the past glory of ancient Rome set the trend for other Fascist architects. Through the evocation of Italy's past glories, architecture contributed to create a sense of admiration for the régime, as well as serving as a means of persuasion and propaganda. It is enough to think of the monuments in the Foro Italico ('Italian Forum') in Rome. Here, the inscriptions on the huge marble plaques celebrate the victories of the Fascist régime. After the fall of Fascism, two anti-Fascist inscriptions were added to two of the plaques, which had originally been left blank so as to mark what was going to be Fascism's next great achievement, victory in the Second World War. Tellingly, the anti-Fascist inscriptions commemorate the fall of Fascism in 1943 and the proclamation of the Republic in 1946.[3]

The post-war period

The post-war years were marked, initially at least, by the wish for a new beginning which would exorcise the ghosts of Fascism and the war. In the art world, this hope found expression in an intense proliferation of movements and debates, all of which argued for change, and which found expression in the customary manifestos. Milan and its Via Brera were the centre of artistic life. Art, literature and cinema were all pervaded by a great vitality which seemed to embody both a reaction to the dark years of Fascism and the war, and the urge to return to life. Although a strong desire to create a new art was shared by many artists, their aims, styles and ideological positions differed greatly. It should not come as a surprise that considerable effort was expended in exploring the language of art along with its social, political and aesthetic implications. Between the years 1946 and 1948, two important manifestos were published: the manifesto of Realism and that of *Spazialismo* ('Spacialism'). The latter was influenced by another manifesto, the *Manifesto Blanco* ('White Manifesto'), which was drafted in Buenos Aires (hence its Spanish title) in 1946 by Lucio Fontana (1899–1968) and his pupils. In addition, the Fronte Nuovo delle Arti ('New Front of the Arts') was founded in Milan, along with the movement for 'concrete' art.

The art scene of the post-war years was profoundly affected by the opposition between Marxism and Catholicism which dominated all aspects of Italian life: committed art, literature and film associated with Neorealism opposed escapist cinema, art and literature. Other tensions, such as those between Realist or figurative art and Abstractionism, marked relations between different artistic movements, as well as relations within a group such as the Fronte Nuovo delle Arti, which brought together left-wing artists. The group eventually split into two factions. On the one hand, the 'Neorealists', who shared a poetics with Neorealist writers and film directors, aimed to create a figurative art with recognizable mimetic elements, which were organized in a familiar narrative that at times had a popular as well as a populist intent. On the other hand, the second group was more interested in recovering the legacy of the experimental language of the Italian and European avant-gardes.

The need to explore new forms of Realism was motivated by the political and social circumstances of the immediate aftermath of the war. Realism in art responded more to an ethical need than to a search for new forms and vehicles for art, and so was less concerned with effecting any real break with established conventions. As an aesthetic, Realism disappeared towards the mid 1950s, although Guttuso remained the leading post-war figurative painter. Guttuso participated actively in artistic debates, making decisive contributions in the form of articles about painting and its currents. Already in 1937 he had wanted to draw the attention of other artists to art's figurative qualities and to the need for artists to engage with history. He did this most notably through his painting *Fucilazione in campagna* ('Shooting by Firing Squad in the Countryside', 1944), in memory of the murdered Spanish poet Federico García Lorca. Guttuso's talent had already been recognized under Fascism when the artist was in his twenties. His painting *Crocifissione* ('Crucifixion'), which he completed in Rome in 1941, was exhibited in 1942 and won the Fourth Bergamo Prize. The *Crocifissione*, with its Cubist–Expressionist style and dramatic force, stood out among the plethora of still-life paintings. By treating a religious subject with a passionate tension towards pain and death, Guttuso intended to represent the deep sufferings of the Italian people both under Fascism and during the war.

During 1945 and 1946, the debate regarding the two contrasting aesthetics of Abstractionism and Realism continued to focus on complex questions regarding the relationship with the past in the context of the changes that were taking place in the post-war period, and the implications of these for artistic language. The need was felt for artists to broaden their artistic horizons and explore visual language as a cognitive act. In order to pursue this goal, the Alleanza della Cultura ('Alliance of Culture') was founded which, between September and November 1948, organized the first national exhibition of contemporary art in Bologna. Among the prominent artists who participated in this exhibition were Renato Birolli (1905–59), Antonio Corpora (1909–), Guttuso and others.

Differences among artistic projects, and above all those between the works of abstract artists and Realists, continued to characterize left-wing art for at least a further ten years. However, the landscape of post-war Italian art was not confined to the debate on the nature of committed art. Fontana returned from Argentina, where he had been living since 1939, and in 1947 presented in Milan the *Primo manifesto di spazialismo* ('First Manifesto of Spacialism'). The manifesto illustrated his idea of constructing a 'total art' which combined both reason and the unconscious. The following year in Milan on 18 March, Fontana, along with other artists such as Milena Milani (1922–   ), also signed the *Secondo manifesto dello spazialismo* ('Second Manifesto of Spacialism'). Present in this manifesto is a critical, yet lucid awareness of the significance of avant-gardes such as Futurism which bring about a new notion both of art and of the role of the artist. In addition, the tendency to frame an atmosphere or a visual experience, as occurred in Metaphysical art, is rejected. Equally, the manifesto's opening undermines the notion of the eternal monumentality of the work of art, something that was dear to Fascism. Indeed, in the *Primo manifesto* the concepts of eternity and monumentality are placed in direct opposition. A similar view is expressed in the *Secondo manifesto*.

Artistic experimentation from the 1950s to the present

The 1950s and 1960s were marked by experimentation, the rejection of traditional techniques, and an openness towards foreign influences, especially those of French, German and New-York-based artists. Moreover, the economic boom at the end of the 1950s helped to establish a thriving market for art. Typical of this period was the formation of a group of dissident abstract artists based in Rome. Alberto Burri (1915–95), one of its exponents, was originally a doctor who started to paint in 1944 while he was still a prisoner of war in Texas. He had his first exhibition in 1947 in Rome, where he decided to settle. In 1950, along with Giuseppe Capogrossi (1900–72), Ettore Colla (1899–1968) and others, Burri signed the manifesto of the group called *Origine* ('Origin'), which expressed a very distinctive anti-figurative aesthetic. Refusing any codified language of art, their aim was to explore a sort of primordial materiality synthesized by the use of mixed media, which banished any trace of image-making. Burri, in fact, incorporated a variety of materials like wood and plastic to form his canvas, an example of which is his famous series of *Sacchi* ('Sacks'). In these works, the very concept of the canvas and its spaces are completely re-explored and redefined, as in his *Grande sacco* ('Big Sack'), which he exhibited in 1952 at Rome's National Gallery of Modern Art. Burri and Fontana, each of whom developed a personal aesthetic, were to become the best-known Italian artists of this period. In 1952, Fontana exhibited at the Galleria del Naviglio in Milan his *Concetti spaziali* ('Spatial Concepts'), which he created by piercing the surface of a piece of paper inserted in a canvas.

If the post-war years and the early 1950s were marked by a highly charged ideological debate on the function of the arts in renovating culture, the 1960s represented a moment of widespread and varied experimentation. The economic boom, the advent of television and a general improvement in economic and social conditions contributed greatly to the profound changes that occurred in Italy at all levels of society. The drive to experiment reflected these changes, though it was also encouraged by an artistic market and affluent buyers open to innovation. Equally, much higher attendances were registered at art exhibitions all over Italy. In addition, a fruitful international exchange between artistic movements took place. Particularly influential in Italy was Pop-art, which grouped together various Anglo-American artists and was introduced for the first time at the Venice Biennale of 1964. Consumerism and the language of the mass media, represented in a polemical and critical style, were the main targets of this art. The objects in themselves were not considered important. Rather, it was their reified and fetishized image that was foregrounded. It is enough to think of the Campbell's soup-can by Andy Warhol, or his gigantic and multiplied version of Marilyn Monroe's face. Pop artists began to concern themselves with the 'mythologies' of mass consumerist society – as had the French critic Roland Barthes in his collection of essays entitled *Mythologies* (1957), a text which was widely read at the time.

These were also the years during which artists and art critics were posing questions concerning the very notion of a work of art, as well as the problems involved in its reception. The provocative shows of Piero Manzoni (1933–63), which involved, for example, signing almost naked people as *Living Sculptures* (1961) or producing his *Merda d'artista* ('Artist's Shit', 1960–1) in a box, a gramme of which he sold at the same price as a gramme of gold, can be considered as polemical reactions to the fetishization of the art object. In September 1967, in La Bertesca gallery in Genoa, Germano Celant organized an exhibition called *Arte povera e IM-Spazio* ('Poor Art and IM-Space') that included in its *arte povera* section artists like Alighiero Boetti (1940–94), Luciano Fabro (1936–), Giulio Paolini (1940–), Jannis Kounellis (1936–), Pino Pascali (1935–68) and Emilio Prini (1943–). The epithet 'poor' in the exhibition's title was

24. Michelangelo Pistoletto, *Venere degli stracci* ('Venus of the Rags'), 1967.

borrowed from Grotowski's theatre, and Celant used it to refer to works that were realized with natural elements and industrial material of common use. Many of the artists who belonged to this group expressed their ideas about art in various installations as well as in sculptures. An especially striking instance of this trend is *Venere degli stracci* ('Venus of the Rags', 1967; fig. 24) by Michelangelo Pistoletto (1933–), in which contrasting elements and materials were combined: Venus, the classical icon of beauty, is shown surrounded by a mountain of old rags of different colours. Another artist, Pascali, produced a series called *Armi* ('Arms'), anti-militaristic 'toys' including the work in the form of a fake cannon *Cannone bella ciao* ('Bella Ciao Cannon', 1965), which quotes in its title a famous song of the Italian partisans. The piece, which was made of discarded car parts and pipes, was also meant to offer a symbolic critique of the Vietnam War, which was being fought at the time. It is possible to understand some of the conceptual implications which lay behind the various experimentation in the arts by remembering the heated debates going on at the same time about the nature of literature and language.

In the wake of conceptual art and *arte povera*, as well as of the broader discussion on the nature of signs, came experiments in visual and concrete poetry. These experiments combined word and image, and explored the pictorial charge of the verbal sign, both on the iconic and verbal levels. In this regard, particularly important were the works of the poet Adriano Spatola (1941–89), most notably *Verso la poesia totale* ('Towards Total Poetry', 1969) and *Il segno poetico* ('The Poetic Sign', 1977). Several exhibitions were organized in the 1970s and early 1980s which culminated in the exhibitions *Visual Poetry* (*1969–1979*), which took place in Florence between December 1979 and January 1980, and, again in Florence, *Il Colpo di Glottide. La poesia come fisicità e materia* ('The Stroke of Glottis. Poetry as Physicality and Material') held in April 1980.

The year 1968 marked a radical change in art and society. The Venice Biennale of the same year was strongly contested and many young artists went through a deep crisis as regards the nature of language and communication. In this same period, Italian art also lost many of its most famous names. In 1968, Fontana, Colla, Leoncillo and Pascali all died. In the aftermath of 1968, some artists found inspiration in the student protest movement and in the confused ideological climate to produce works with an explicitly political content. Such a work is *Funerali dell'anarchico Pinelli* ('Funeral of the Anarchist Pinelli', 1972) by Enrico Baj (1924–). Pinelli had been wrongly charged with placing a bomb in a bank in Milan, and died while he was being interrogated by the police.

The protests of the late 1960s turned, in some cases, into terrorism, which by the 1980s led to a marked decrease in political commitment. In the art world, this change of mood was reflected by the increasing interest in matters of form over content. The Transavanguardia, comprising Mimmo Paladino (1948–), Sandro Chia (1946–) and Emilio Cucchi (1950–), who were known outside Italy as the Post-Expressionists, recovered and reworked the artistic language and the style of the historical avant-garde, as well as that of the past in general. The tendency to quote from the artistic movements of the past was, in fact, a characteristic of various artists in the 1980s. The *Anacronisti* ('Anachronists'), for example, reworked the iconography of Baroque and eighteenth-century painting.

The 1980s were also the years in which the concept of the

post-modern became fashionable. In this context, the notion of 'citation-ism' was transformed into a general eclecticism and was accompanied by a corresponding lack of historical perspective. This trend found an important voice in the exhibition *Una generazione postmoderna* ('A Post-modern Generation'), which took place in Genoa from November 1982 to January 1983. In the late 1980s and early 1990s, the artistic scene was fragmented not just in Italy, but throughout Europe and the USA. Artistic research became more personal and individualistic, reflecting the increasing lack of faith in all-powerful ideologies and the general lack of confidence in long-term projects. However, with the fall of the Berlin Wall, it is possible to recognize a general search for new perspectives in studying the trauma of Europe's recent past as represented by the continent's totalitarian régimes and by the wars the European nations have fought amongst themselves. It is interesting to note that fifty or so years after the end of the Second World War, one can perceive all across Europe a renewed interest in exploring the relationship between art, society and history. Several exhibitions organized in the last few years testify to this. Many of these exhibitions look back on the historical past, especially the most traumatic moments of Europe's recent past. These exhibitions respond to the need to recontextualize the past and the artistic experiences that occurred at the beginning of our century and between the two World Wars. Some of the most important are *Degenerate Art* in Berlin in 1992; *Art and Dictatorship* in Vienna in 1994; *Art of Freedoms, of Antifascism, of War and Liberation in Europe* in Genoa in 1995; *Art and Power. Europe under the Dictatorships* in London in 1996; in the same year, at the Centre Pompidou in Paris, *In the Face of History*; and finally, at the Museum of Modern Art in Paris in 1997, *Europe in the 1930s. 1929–1939. The Threatening Times*.

Perhaps this recent pan-European phenomenon in the art world, characterized by a renewed interest in looking back on Europe's recent history, is a sign that art is playing the role Walter Benjamin assigned to the Angel of History in his well-known interpretation of Klee's painting *Angelus Novus* – looking back on history, seeing the single catastrophe that has been the twentieth century, and attempting to make sense of the heap of ruins which confronts its gaze.

NOTES

1. Maria Mimita Lamberti, 'I mutamenti del mercato e le ricerche degli artisti', in P. Fossati (ed.), *Storia dell'arte italiana* (Turin: Einaudi, 1979–83), vol. III, pp. 134–204.

2. Emilio R. Pepe, 'Storia di due manifesti', in *Il Fascismo e la cultura* (Milan: Feltrinelli, 1958), pp. 59–102.

3. For additional information on Fascist architecture, see the following chapter, pp. 271–2.

FURTHER READING

Arte Italiana 1960–82. Catalogue of the Exhibition Held at the Hayward Gallery, London: *October 1982–January 1983*. Milan: Electa, 1982.

Barocchi, Paola (ed.), *Storia moderna dell'arte in Italia*, 2 vols. Turin: Einaudi, 1992.

Bossaglia, Rossana, *Il novecento italiano. Storia, documenti, iconografia*. Milan: Feltrinelli, 1979.

Cannistraro, Philip and Sullivan, Brian R., *Il Duce's Other Woman*. New York: William Morrow and Company, Inc. 1993.

Celant, Germano (ed.), *The Italian Metamorphosis: Italy 1943–1968. Catalogue*. New York: Progetti museali editore-Guggenheim Museum, 1994.

De Seta, Cesare, *Gli anni trenta. L'arte e cultura in Italia*. Catalogue. Milan: Mazzotta, 1982.

Matteucci, Giuliano (ed.), *The Macchiaioli: Tuscan Painters of the Sunlight*. Catalogue. New York: Stair Sainty Matthiesen, 1984.

Olson, Roberta J. M. (ed.), *Ottocento: Romanticism and Revolution in 19th-Century Italian Painting*. New York: The American Federation of Arts, 1992.

Soby Thrall, James, *Giorgio De Chirico*. New York: Museum of Modern Art, 1955.

Stajano, Corrado (ed.), *La cultura italiana del Novecento*. Rome and Bari: Laterza, 1996.

Tonelli, Edith and Hart, Katherine (eds.), *The Macchiaioli Painters of Italian Life 1850–1900*. Los Angeles: University of California Press, 1986.

13

A modern identity for a new nation: design in Italy since 1860

Introduction

In the second half of the nineteenth century the face of Italy was transformed in a number of different ways. The political effects of national unification, combined with the economic, social and cultural ramifications of industrialization, engendered a new country complete with a new programme of action designed to take it into the twentieth century. The idea of 'newness' permeated many aspects of Italian life, underpinning numerous efforts to define the character of the new nation. The concept of 'Italianness' was also given renewed impetus in this period. A key theme in its formation was the appeal to past strengths: for example, to moments of high cultural achievement when Italy had made a unique impact in the international arena. Nowhere was this Janus-faced orientation – a simultaneous relationship both with the past *and* with the future – more apparent than in the design of Italy's objects and environments in the second half of the nineteenth century and in the first half of the twentieth. For five hundred years, through their artistic achievement and their high cultural significance, Italian decorative arts had been preeminent. The ceramics, glass, metalwork, furniture, interiors, textiles and costume of the Italian Renaissance of the fifteenth and sixteenth centuries had established a standard of excellence to which many other countries had aspired. Equally, the level of workmanship and creativity in the objects and environments made by Italian Renaissance artists had served to erode the distinction between the 'high' and the 'lesser' arts and to establish an international reputation for Italian decorative art which was still in place several centuries later.

Aesthetic leadership in this area had been made possible by the special nature of the manufacturing and artistic infrastructure which had sustained Italy's decorative art production. The system of small workshops and highly skilled itinerant artists; of masters and apprentices; and of the transferral of two-dimensional imagery, complete with its systems of symbols, available through prints, on to three-dimensional artefacts, resulted in the unique quality of Italian decorative art objects, from maiolica to metal goods, and from textiles to furnishings. It was a model of practice which remained substantially intact until well into the twentieth century, providing a framework for the many design innovations in goods such as mass-produced furniture items, electrical goods and automobiles that were to transform Italian cultural and artistic life at that later date.

If the achievements of the Renaissance had the effect of applying a stylistic brake to the evolution of Italian material culture in the late nineteenth and early twentieth centuries, a strong innovatory push was provided by the joint effects of national unification and industrialization. In its frantic search for a new identity, Italy moved enthusiastically into the new industrial era. This offered new prodution techniques and new materials, such as steel and, later, plastics, with which to innovate. Thus, while one face of Italy's material culture looked back towards its heroic 'artistic' past, another looked towards the products of its engineers – bicycles, trains, ships and new consumer machines – with the aim of finding new 'design' solutions for these goods, as well as for the more traditional decorative art products, such as ceramics, glass, metalwork and textiles.

The story of modern Italian material culture, which reached its apogee in the decades after 1945 when the concept of 'Italian design' reached the height of its maturity, is based on the marriage between art and industry which aligned the strengths of the past with the challenge of the future. It was a union which located its singular identity in the idea of 'design', a newly constructed concept belonging uniquely to the era of industrialization (and distinct from its roots in the indigenous notion of *disegno* or 'drawing') which, by the second half of the twentieth century, had come to characterize an important face of the international achievement of modern Italian culture. As a process the concept of design is a result of the division of labour within mass production – a result, that is, of the separation between 'conceiving' and 'making' goods unknown within the unified craft process. As a feature of manufactured goods, it is the visual manifestation of the way in which functional, aesthetic and semantic requirements have been combined; and, as a feature of modern society, it is a visible marker of the phenomenon we call 'conspicuous consumption'.

Perhaps more than any other country, it was Italy which sought to renew its past reputation for artistic excellence through the nineteenth and twentieth centuries, and in so doing make a bid for entry into the world of modernity through the appearance and nature of the goods which make up the everyday, mass environment. In this way Italy sought to ensure for itself a unique place within international modern culture. By the mid 1960s, the exclusive, luxurious decorative art objects of the nineteenth century had been joined by much more banal material goods – from ashtrays to sewing machines – representing the democratized face of design. They remained imbued, however, with qualities resulting from a rigorous and self-conscious programme of aesthetic and industrial innovation. As a result, for the second time in its history, Italy earned a unique reputation for its attention to the important role that objects play within culture as a whole.

The evolution of the modern Italian design movement was synonymous with many of the key shifts in the economic, technological, political, social and cultural life of the Italian nation in the years after 1860. It stands, in many ways, as a testimony to those shifts, providing a material exposition of them, visible both to the inhabitants of Italy itself and, perhaps more significantly, to the rest of the industrialized world. The story can be broken down into a sequence of historical moments which focus on the periods 1860–1914, 1914–39, 1939–65, 1965–75 and 1975 to the present day. Each moment marks a stage in the development of a phenomenon which had its formative years in the nineteenth and early twentieth centuries; which began to become clearly visible in the 1930s; which reached its zenith in the subsequent three decades; and which experienced a series of crises and redefinitions in the years after 1970.

New goods for a new nation, 1860–1914

The second half of the nineteenth century saw the new Italian nation in search of a self-identity which would be visible both at home and abroad. Where mass material culture was concerned, however, change was slow. The country was predominantly agricultural in nature and the production and consumption of goods – clothing and furniture among them – were essentially local in nature. The goods themselves, for the most part, perpetuated long-standing traditions. During this period, however, the movement of large numbers of people to cities and the emergence of a few large-scale mechanized industries – steel manufacture featuring as a crucial development in this respect – led to a transformation of the Italian material landscape and the introduction of the concept of modernity into many peoples' lives. Nowhere was this more evident than in the emergence of new objects of transport (trains, ships and eventually cars); in objects for the work environment (among them typewriters and items of office furniture); and in the new forms of mass retailing, predominant among them the urban department store. Such advances were concentrated in the area known as the 'industrial triangle' in the north of the country, namely in the area between Milan, Turin and Genoa, where industrialization was most rapid. At the Milan National Exhibition of 1881, held in specially constructed buildings in the Public Gardens, for example, a small electric railway took visitors from one site to another, while a large Machine Hall contained numerous examples of machines destined, among others, for the expanding textile industry. The coach-building manufacturers of Turin and Milan were also represented at the Exhibition, as were more traditional decorative-arts objects, glass, ceramics and furniture in particular.

Inevitably most of the new consumer goods and services were aimed at the wealthier sectors of society, as indeed were the vast majority of the more traditional goods which continued to emanate from the decorative-arts industries. The new products were fashioned in an un-self-conscious 'engineered' style which reflected their means of manufacture, while the traditional goods – ceramics and glass items, textiles, furniture and other items of household display – remained the key status symbols, manifested in the historicist repertoire of fashionable styles, among which Baroque and Rococo featured strongly. By the turn of the century, however, and as was clearly manifested at the Turin International Exhibition of 1902, the more modern Art Nouveau idiom, or, as it was called in Italy, the Stile Liberty, had emerged.

Italy could boast a few innovators of its own in this modern, turn-of-the-century style: important among them was the furniture designer Carlo Bugatti (1855–1940). Still firmly linked to the nineteenth-century world of historicism and bourgeois display, Bugatti succeeded nonetheless in creating a number of furniture designs which earned Italy a place within the international stylistic avant-garde. Although he was part of a larger group of furniture innovators – other members included Eugenio

Quarti (1867–1931) and Carlo Zen (1851–1918) – their contributions did little to stem the continuous flow of traditional designs which characterized the production of the majority of furniture workshops of the period. Most furniture was still made in small workshops in historical styles, as indeed were the majority of the glass and ceramic objects. A few firms, such as the ceramics manufacturer Richard Ginori, rationalized their production; however, the aesthetic of the goods made was still far from innovative. Only the floral style of the Stile Liberty began to make an impact. By the turn of the century it provided a means by which middle-class, style-conscious consumers could represent their desire to enter into modernity.

The new industries, on the other hand, emanating from electrical engineering and from iron and steel manufacture, produced utility, rather than status, goods, clearly demonstrating this fact in their chosen aesthetic. The Olivetti typewriter company, for example, applied the principle of producing innovatory items of function rather than fashion at the same time as it rationalized its manufacturing systems according to principles which Camillo Olivetti (1868–1943) had observed in the USA. The simple, unadorned form of his M1 typewriter, with its black, enamelled body-shell, marked the presence in Italy of a new, 'functional', industrial aesthetic which was to exert a tremendous influence in subsequent years.

At the turn of the century Italian cars were only enjoyed by the wealthy. The products of the Fiat company (founded in 1899), Lancia (founded in 1905) and Alfa Romeo (founded in 1910) were all luxury items, embellished with an appropriate level of conspicuous comfort. These companies drew heavily on Italy's well-established coachbuilding tradition represented by companies such as Castagna and Alessio, both of which were based in Turin. Only Fiat's 'Zero' model, developed between 1912 and 1915 but never produced in large numbers, aimed, like the USA's 'Model T' Ford, to be perceived as a utility car directed at a wide market.

The years 1860 to 1914 were marked, therefore, by an essentially pragmatic approach to design. They also witnessed the formation of the industrial, social and cultural framework which was to sustain subsequent developments in this area. The move towards industrial rationalization, combined with the expansion of the material needs of a new, middle-class urban population which identified itself with the values of a new nation emerging in the context of a transformed, modern environment, created a new stylistic imperative for Italy's goods which was to reach partial fruition in the inter-war years, but which only achieved full maturity in the years following the Second World War. At the same time, however, the traditional values and production methods of the decorative-arts industries continued to exert an important influence, constraining Italy's rush into the future.

The emergence of Italian modernism, 1914–1939

The ambivalence towards modernity continued in the years following the First World War. At the same time, it was in the years 1914–39 that Italy moved one step nearer towards the formulation of a modern Italian design movement. This occurred in the context of an Italy which, from the early 1920s onwards, was transformed politically with the advent of Fascism. Most significantly, where material culture was concerned, Fascism was a political ideology with a strong economic and cultural programme which was implemented through state control, and which brought with it the need for industrial self-sufficiency and the necessity for a strong visual national identity. Mussolini was more progressive than Hitler in his aesthetic preferences, and was sympathetic to the stark forms of the architectural and design movement known, in Italy, as Rationalism. For a few years in the early 1930s, in fact, Rationalism appeared to offer an appropriately progressive visual face for the régime. At the same time Mussolini's political programme depended on the presence both of a number of large-scale industrial enterprises, which continued to emulate their counterparts across the Atlantic, and of a network of small, regional manufacturing workshops to which he gave his full support. This resulted in a dualism which encouraged the perpetuation of the traditional decorative arts, acting, once again, as a brake upon the more forward-looking thrust of Italian material culture. Thus, as had happened before, while the inter-war years saw a highly progressive approach to material culture, they also continued to hark back to the past, both stylistically and where manufacturing processes were concerned.

The progressive attitude was reflected in the startlingly modern appearance of many of the products of the new, mass-production industries. Fiat's 'model 1500' car of 1933, for instance, was a prime example of American-inspired 'streamlining', its flowing body lines clearly indebted to Chrysler's futuristic 'Air-flow' car. Lancia's 'Aprilia' model of two years later was designed like a section of an airplane wing. The Olivetti company continued to lead the way in graphic and product aesthetics. In the 1920s, Adriano, the son of Camillo, returned from a trip to the USA intent on modernizing not only his factory's production methods but also the visual identity of the company as a whole. To this end he employed a number of progressive graphic designers, among them Alexander Schawinsky (1904–79), who had trained at the famous Bauhaus design school in Germany. With this group of innovative artists and designers he succeeded in modernizing all the graphic material emanating from his company. By the late 1930s, he had extended this programme of modernization to the machines that came off the production lines. Marcello Nizzoli (1887–1969) was brought in to head this project, while two leading architects of the day, Luigi Figini (1903–) and Gino Pollini (1903–), designed the company's new factory in Ivrea which was completed by the end of the decade. Other firms keen to emulate Olivetti's example included the Necchi sewing-machine company and Phonola, a radio manufacturer. The latter's futuristic model of 1939, designed by Luigi Caccia Dominioni (1913–) and Livio (1911–79) and Pier Giacomo Castiglioni (1913–68), emulated the shape of a modern telephone – an object which had already been accepted by a large slice of the population – in an attempt to reassure consumers that it was an advanced piece of technology which at the same time was familiar and safe.

The importance of the Rationalist movement in architecture and design, which began to make its mark in the late 1920s and which, by the mid 1930s, had had a considerable impact, more in terms of its influence on theoretical and pedagogical ideas than in terms of actual constructed buildings, cannot be overestimated. Influenced by the work of architects such as Walter Gropius (1883–1969) in Germany and Le Corbusier (1887–1965) in France, it proposed a modern style for the modern environment based on new materials – concrete and steel among them – and simple, functional forms devoid of unnecessary ornamentation. Rationalism embraced the use of new technologies as evidenced by the 'Electric House' (*La Casa Elettrica*), designed by Piero Bottoni (1903–73), together with Figini and Pollini, for the Monza Biennale of 1930, demonstrating the movement's claim to be the way forward for the material environment of the 'new age'. Rationalism allied itself with the internationalism of the architectural Modern Movement of the inter-war years, although, for a short time at least, it was also aligned with the Fascist régime. This association found expression in, among other projects, the competition proposals of 1933 for the new Florence Station and in the Casa del Fascio (1932-6) in Como, by Giuseppe Terragni (1904–43).

In spite of the ideological marriage between Rationalism and Fascism, the style proved too international in essence to represent adequately the fiercely nationalistic ambitions of Mussolini and his party. Much nearer to the essential 'Italianness' that he sought was the much more overtly nationally oriented modern architectural and design style referred to as Novecento ('Nineteenhundred'). Rooted in classicism, it was a simplified version of this style, and served to remind Italy simultaneously of its great past and of its ambitions for the future.

Buildings constructed by Mussolini in the key industrial centres as well as in the 'new' towns – Littoria and Sabaudia among them – helped this new style to become *the* symbolic expression of Fascism. Novecento also influenced the decorative arts, providing a stylistic bridge between the past and the present, with its combination of the familiarity of classicism and a new simplicity. Gio Ponti's (1891–1979) ceramics for Richard Ginori, for example, displayed the simplified classical motifs that characterized the style. Goods in the Novecento idiom also dominated the displays at the exhibition held in Milan known as the Triennale, so called because it was held at three-yearly intervals from 1933 onwards. The exhibition was crucial for Italy's bid for modernity in the international arena, as it was visited by large numbers of people. The building which housed it, designed by Giovanni Muzio (1893–1982) in 1933, epitomized the Novecento style.

The inter-war years proved to be ones of both consolidation and change for Italian material culture. The essentially modern concept of 'design', imported from the USA along with ideas about rational manufacturing, existed alongside a reworking of the traditional concept of the decorative arts, a reworking which began to align itself with the idea of modernity. Additionally, Italian architects and designers had to address the problem of finding a style to reflect the dominant political and ideological imperatives of the day. This last need instilled into Italian material culture a level of significance which was absent in the American model. In the USA design remained primarily commercial in orientation. In the Italian context, however, commerce, industry, culture and politics interacted with each other to create a richer frame for Italy's foray into modern design. By 1939 that infrastructure was fully in place, although it was not until after the Second World War that it was to find its fullest expression.

From reconstruction to conspicuous consumption, 1939–1965

Although the framework which was formed by 1939 exerted a strong influence on the way in which the concept of 'Italian design' was constructed after the cessation of hostilities in 1945, the key instigator behind this notion was the need to represent the post-Fascist Republic through a new and specifically Italian material culture. Spurred on by the desire to oppose all that had gone before, the architects and designers of post-Mussolini Italy sought to create a new environment which reflected the transformation that was taking place in the country. It is ironic, however, that in many ways the evolution of post-1945 Italian design was heavily influenced by events of the pre-war years, most notably by the programme of industrialization, modernization and rationalization that had been undertaken by the Fascist state.

In the immediate post-war years a new Rationalism, articulated most strongly by the architect Ernesto N. Rogers (1909–69) in the important architectural and design periodical *Domus*, which had existed since the 1920s and of which Rogers became the editor in 1945, was seen as the means by which a new domestic environment could be created for the large numbers of people left homeless by the war. More than this, however, it was a means of combining the new ideological and cultural programme with an aesthetic which could represent it. 'It is a question', wrote Rogers in the first January edition of the magazine published in 1946, 'of forming a taste, a technique, a morality, all terms of the same function. It is a question of building a society.'

These ambitions were realized in the new simple furnishings that poured out of the furniture workshops in Brianza and in the simple metal goods that emerged from the factories, increasing numbers of which were reorganized along mass-production lines. The American design idiom known as 'streamlining' was once more in evidence, especially in the forms of the new office machines, in items of coffee-bar equipment, and in objects of transport that symbolized the new democracy. The 'Italian line', as it came to be called, was visible, for example, in designs for cars by Pinin Farina (see fig. 25), in Piaggio's Vespa motor-scooter of 1947, in Gio Ponti's coffee-machine for La Pavoni of 1948 (see fig. 26), in the Cisitalia car of 1951, and in Marcello Nizzoli's 'Lexicon 80' typewriter for Olivetti of 1948. As symbols of the newly democratized

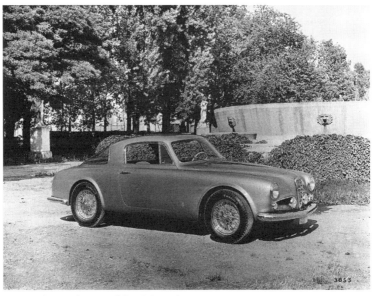

25. Coupé 1900. Photograph by Pinin Farina, 1953.

26. Gio Ponti, Espresso coffee machine for La Pavoni, 1948.

Italy, goods such as these penetrated the mass environment in a hitherto unprecedented manner. Their mass production was part of the renewed industrial effort that took place after 1945, of which these goods became the most visible face.

The rapid evolution and dissemination of a concept of 'Italian design', linked to a sophisticated modern aesthetic in goods making up the everyday environment, occurred in the period of Italian reconstruction and economic boom, namely 1945–60. A product of the twin forces of industrialization and modernization, the new popular concept of design became a key element in the image that Italy presented of itself both domestically and internationally. Its success was dependent on several contingent factors, among them the presence of a number of manufacturing industries – both large and small – which sought to differentiate their goods in foreign marketplaces through their modern, sophisticated aesthetic; the availability of a group of architect-designers, trained within the ethos of Rationalism, ready and able to apply their visualizing skills to a wide range of goods; the rise of an Italian home market wealthy enough to consume many of the new goods; and the emergence of a new Italian image of domesticity that was to have enormous international appeal.

As the Republic moved from its early left-wing phase in the years immediately after the war into a more moderate era dominated by the Christian Democrats, design in Italy became central to the image of the 'good life' that became a key aspiration for many Italians in the 1950s and 1960s. Luxury and comfort became represented, however, less by an appeal to tradition and to the familiar decorative arts and more by the highly expressive image of modernity conveyed through the furniture items, lighting objects and other small goods that made up the ideal Italian domestic landscape. From the sinuous forms of chairs designed by Marco Zanuso (1916–) for Arflex and by Osvaldo Borsani (1911–86) for Tecno, to the sculptural forms of lighting by Gino Sarfatti (1911–) for Arteluce designed in the early 1950s, to the sensuous shells of the new *elettrodomestici* and household goods, among them the 'Spalter' vacuum cleaner designed by the Castiglioni brothers and Sergio Asti's soda water syphon (see fig. 27), Italian 'designs' joined together to create a completely new image of domesticity. In the international arena, this image replaced the craft-based, humanistic environment of the Scandinavian home with a much more aestheticized, dehumanized and aggressively modern living area.

By the end of the 1950s, at the height of Italy's economic boom, all-plastic chairs, in bright synthetic colours, designed by Vico Magistretti (1920–), Marco Zanuso (1916–) and Joe Colombo (1930–71), were presented in glossy magazines, such as *Domus*, *Abitare* ('Living') and *Stile Industria* ('Industrial Style'), appealing through their pages to style-hungry affluent consumers worldwide. Depicted on plinths like sculptures, these chairs represented much more than the mere act of sitting. They conveyed, rather, an image of modernity which Italy had made its

27. Soda water syphon, designed by Sergio Asti, 1956.

own, and through which it was communicating, to the rest of the world, the measure of its economic achievement in the mid-century. In addition, the names of the designers were 'sold' along with their products, thereby reinforcing their status as art objects. The post-war years saw, in fact, the emergence of a group of designer-heroes whose names were as important as their work.

By the mid 1960s a concept of Italian design, linked with a seductive image of a lifestyle for the late twentieth century, had penetrated the international consciousnes. This was partly made possible by Italian design's visibility at the Milan Triennali of these years (1947, 1951, 1954 and 1957) and by the international design press which seized upon it. Its success coincided with a general rise in prosperity in the industrialized world, and with an increased faith in technological progress and in the dream of democracy on the part of a large section of the population of Western countries.

From design to anti-design, 1965–1975

After 1965, however, this sense of optimism was showing signs of fading. In Italy the industrial strikes of the early 1960s had indicated a hiatus in the 'economic miracle' and, combined with the student movement later in the decade, seemed to indicate that the upward curve of growth and optimism about the future was beginning to move downwards. So deeply entrenched was the ideology of the Italian design movement within the enthusiasm for technology and the faith in the 'economic miracle' that reservations about the one inevitably caused doubts about the other. The 1968 Triennale closed early as a result of student agitation, and by the end of the decade it had become apparent that design too could contain its own 'counter-movement'. 'Contro-' or 'Anti-design' grew out of ideas put forward by Italian architects and designers who were responding to the shift in the status quo. More than any other single individual, the Austrian-born designer Ettore Sottsass (1917–), who in 1959 became a consultant to Olivetti working on their early computer, the Elea 9003, and subsequently, through the 1960s, on their innovative range of typewriters, presented a new role for design in Italy. Since the early 1960s, Sottsass had been experimenting with projects in the areas of furniture and ceramics. He was fascinated with the idea of design being its own cultural messenger, rather than the handmaiden of the manufacturing industry. Design, for Sottsass, had to be first and foremost an agent for change, and his 'Valentine' typewriter of 1969 designed for Olivetti – a bright red 'pop' object intended for flexible use in a number of different environments outside the conventional office – demonstrated his commitment to the essential flexibility and mutability of design and its accompanying ideology.

Rooted in the ethic of pop culture, which favoured ephemerality over permanence, Sottsass's statements inspired a larger movement in design thinking which developed into a critique of mainstream practice. Groups of architects and designers, many of them based in Florence and all of them formed in 1966 – among them Archizoom, Superstudio, Gruppo NNNN and Gruppo Strum – rejected the image of the individualized designer-hero which had developed in the post-war years and set about using design as a form of commentary upon Italian culture as a

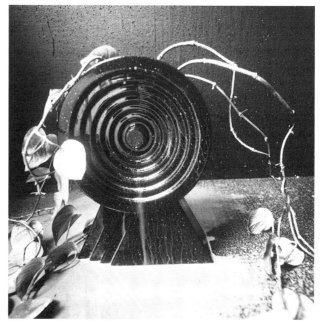

28. Ettore Sottsass, *Yantra Ceramici*, 1970.

whole. In place of the unremitting modernity, seriousness and high cultural intentions which had characterized Italian design a decade earlier, these *agents provocateurs* injected humour, historical references and banality into their radical designs, thereby offering the possibility of design functioning independently of the post-war economic industrial programme. Even manufacturing companies responded to this new radicalized role for design; the Zanotta company, for example, in 1969 produced its famous *Sacco* ('Sack') chair, a formless seat made up of thousands of polyurathene pellets. The *Sacco* was a design anti-statement inasmuch as it had no inherent or fixed form, a strategy which denied it the possibility of standing for luxury or conspicuous consumption. It was a strategy which was repeated in a number of other designs of the period, among them Achille Castiglioni's 'Boalum Lamp'.

For the most part, however, Anti-design found its natural home in the art gallery rather then in the environment of everyday life. In 1973 a major exhibition about Italian design, entitled *Italy: The New Domestic Landscape*, curator Emilio Ambasz (1943–), was held at the Museum of Modern Art in New York. It presented the different faces of Italian design as these had emerged over the previous decade, but focused on

29. Superstudio, 'The Continuous Movement', 1969.

the oppositional nature of many of its contemporary manifestations. The idea of design becoming its own critique dominated the 1970s, providing an alternative route to the more mainstream, chic face of Italian material culture – recognizable through a preference for leather and chrome in furniture and, in products, through an alliance with contemporary sculpture – which continued to represent that country in the international marketplace.

Towards post-modernism, 1975 to the present

By the end of the 1970s, Italian design dominated the international arena but, at the same time, it continued to include its own critique. By the early 1980s, the Anti-design movement, which had been an exclusively Italian phenomenon in the 1960s, began to show signs of reviving. This time it influenced attitudes to design outside Italy as well as within it. Nowhere was this more obvious than in the dramatic and sudden impact of the first show of the Memphis group, held in 1981 in Milan. The group was headed by the veteran agitator, Ettore Sottsass, who since 1979 had been collaborating with a radical group project, known as Studio Alchymia, which had regrouped the older members of Anti-design and recruited new ones. Memphis extended the programme of Studio Alchymia in a more publicly accessible way, and within weeks of the first exhibition it was clear that Italy was leading an international sea-change in design.

The effects of Memphis, characterized by its zany, 'kitsch' pieces of

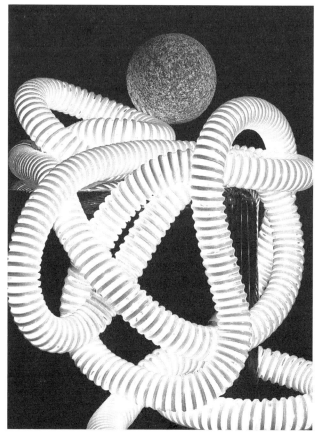

30. Achille Castiglioni, 'Boalum Lamp', 1970.

furniture covered in brightly coloured and highly decorated plastic lam-
inates, and its pieces of glass and ceramic which flaunted craft principles,
were rapidly felt beyond Italy. The work of Sottsass, Michele de Lucchi
(1951–), Matteo Thun (1952–), and others showed a way out of the
impasse of 'good taste' and confirmed that Italian design was still at the
forefront of debate and innovation.

   The 1980s saw a number of Memphis shows and a widening of the
movement to include a host of new names, many of whom came from
outside Italy to work in Milan. While the design avant-garde flourished,
the flexible structure of Italian manufacturing industry made it possible
for their ideas to be realized. The Milan furniture fairs of the decade
were filled with visitors looking for the latest design idea.

In the 1990s, however, Italian design lost its pre-eminence in the face of other countries – France, Spain, Japan and Singapore among them – rising up to challenge its authority in the marketplace. A growing internationalism in design meant that, increasingly, non-Italians came to work in Milan, while Italian influences were felt across the globe. Although the manufacturing giants – Alessi, Cassina and Olivetti among them – continued to impress and push the boundaries forward, the heroes of modern Italian design remained the generation of men then moving into their seventies and eighties. Today, a modern design movement features less strongly in Italy's contemporary identity, viewed both from within and without. The emulation of Italian design by other countries has permitted newly industrialized nations to learn from its achievements. They are now busy harnessing modern design to their own emerging national identities. Design's task of bringing Italy into the modern world seems to have been completed.

FURTHER READING

Ambasz, E. (ed.), *Italy: The New Domestic Landscape.* New York: Museum of Modern Art, 1972.

Branzi, A., *The Hot House: Italian New Wave Design.* London: Thames and Hudson, 1984.

Branzi, A. and De Lucchi, M., *Il design italiano degli anni '50.* Milan: IGIS, 1981.

Dansi, S. and Patteta, L., *Rationalisme et architecture en Italie.* Milan: Electa, 1976.

Fossati, P., *Il design in Italia 1945–1972.* Turin: Einaudi, 1972 .

Fratelli, E., *Il disegno industriale italiano 1928–1981 (Quasi una storia ideologica).* Turin: Celid, 1982.

Grassi, A. and Pansera, A., *Atlante del design italiano 1940–1980.* Milan: Fabbri, 1980.

Gregotti, V., *Il disegno del prodotto industriale: Italia 1860–1980.* Milan: Electa, 1982.

Modern Italian Design. Catalogue. Manchester City Art Gallery, 1956.

Radice, B., *Memphis: The New International Style.* Milan: Electa, 1981.

Sartago, P., *Italian Re-Evolution: Design in Italian Society in the '80s.* California: Museum of Contemporary Art, 1982.

Sparke, P., *Italian Design: 1970 to the Present.* London: Thames and Hudson, 1986.

14

Fashion: narration and nation

There is a scene in *Il Gattopardo* ('The Leopard', 1958), the novel by Giuseppe Tomasi di Lampedusa (1896–1957), in which the character of Don Calogero, who represents the new aspiring bourgeois class, is invited for the first time to dinner at the Prince of Salina's summer residence. The Prince, who is also the narrator of the novel, describes Don Calogero's arrival with a high degree of stylistic virtuosity. Don Calogero – we are told – is the only guest who is not appropriately dressed for the occasion. In fact, he is wearing a formal frock-coat since he wants to show the aristocratic Salina family that he is wealthy enough to afford one. The Prince, however, is wearing an afternoon suit, as he has always done at his rural retreat in order not to embarrass the locals. Don Calogero's outfit is a real 'catastrophe' not so much for its fine fabric as for its cut, which reveals his stinginess and lack of style as he has chosen an incompetent local tailor instead of relying, as the true aristocrats did, on a more expert and expensive tailor based in England. In addition to this fault, the Prince remarks that not only are Don Calogero's shoes wrong but his shirt-collar is shapeless, details which act as clues to his defining trait: his hopeless lack of refined manners and elegance, despite his newly acquired wealth.

This description of Don Calogero's outfit underscores the encounter of the two worlds present in the novel: the aristocracy and the wealthy petty bourgeoisie. The novel is set, in fact, at the moment of the petty bourgeoisie's rise to becoming the new ruling class, and follows its struggle for hegemony during the Italian Risorgimento. In the novel, social dynamism is often depicted in terms of clothes and uniforms. It is possible, in fact, to note a progressive change in the various clothes and military uniforms of the major protagonists as the social and political situation in Italy evolves during the 1860s. The process comes to a head towards the end of the novel in the ball scene, rendered famous by Luchino Visconti's film adaptation, in which the soldiers who formerly wore the Garibaldinian red shirts are now dressed in the more sober and dignified blue of the Piedmontese-Savoyard army, soon to become Italy's first national army.

Clothes do not have symbolic meaning if we isolate them either from their socio-political context or from those elements – the body, grace, elegance, accessories and ultimately the performance of their wearing – which reinforce their narrative function. It is for these reasons that literary texts, paintings, memoirs, letters and so forth help us to reconstruct the nuances of a given historical period through their representation of clothes. Fashion, we might say, is a system of signification as well as an on-going process of communication which narrates history. However, fashion does this at a level different from that on which people live their lives as regards both everyday activity and special rituals.

Let me at once stress that fashion does not exist without the notion of change, and it is for this reason that it has an intimate link with modernity. Fashion in Europe, in fact, emerges as a phenomenon with the early phases of capitalism, the expansion of trade and the growth of cities. Its beginnings can be traced back to the fourteenth century with the breakdown of hierarchical relationships between classes, which led to the rise of an increasingly powerful bourgeoisie. It was during the High Renaissance that bourgeois culture first displayed a self-awareness about the fashioning of the human subject as a controllable process. With the creation of its mythologies, fashion represents a visible narration of a given epoch which illustrates the contradictions and manifestations of class and gender conflicts. Furthermore, through fashion we can identify social and class agendas which go towards the shaping of the political environment at both the individual and the collective levels. Works like *Il libro del cortegiano* ('The Book of the Courtier', 1528) by Baldassare Castiglione (1478–1529), which is the first text of its type in Western culture, addressed the question of the construction of the public image in court society. The book gives practical advice to both men and women which allows us to trace the different contemporary ideological constructions of 'femininity' and 'masculinity'. What we now call 'dress for success' was an aesthetic and political game whose rules the powerful men and women of the Renaissance knew very well, as do some of the characters of *The Leopard*. Fashion, besides being a system of signification and a process of communication, can function as a technique with which to construct gender and identity within a given narrative. With clothes we dress, cover and adorn our bodies. With clothes it is possible for someone to project an identity; or better, we could say that clothes contribute to creating a veil of images in the communicative relationship between people. The concern with and refinement of appearances should not be dismissed merely as a superficial aspect of human activity. Rather it constitutes an important component of what we call identity in the modern age. Human needs and desires cannot be relegated solely to the realm of usefulness. This also helps explain the relationship between fashion and art. Thus, the search for beauty represents another important aspect of the fashion system, an aspect which is initially connected with the self and its psychological implications before going on to constitute a politics of style.

From the sixteenth century onwards, French fashion held sway in Italy and in the rest of Europe. Most men and women belonging to the noble classes bought their clothes and accessories in Paris, and those who could afford it employed a French tailor. A biting portrait of a Milanese *giovin signore* ('young gentleman') is offered by Giuseppe Parini (1722–99) in his poem *Il Giorno* ('The Day', 1763), a text which is dedicated to fashion. As a reaction to this and similar influences, and spurred on by the rise of patriotic movements and the drive towards the peninsula's unification, attempts were made during the nineteenth century to create fashions that could be deemed 'independent' of external influences. For instance, high-society ladies started to dress in red, after Garibaldi's redshirts, calling their colours 'magenta' or 'solferino', referring to the victorious battles of the unification campaign.

However, this patriotic impetus was little more than a fad and did not last long, since French fashion continued to exercise a powerful appeal. Nevertheless, attempts were made in the years preceding Italy's unification to create a distinctive Italian fashion separate from the French. In magazines such as *Il corriere delle dame* ('The Ladies' Newspaper'), several articles stressed that French fashion patterns could not be completely adapted or copied because of the cultural and climatic differences between the two countries. To illustrate the relationship between fashion and the desire to create a national image, we might mention two fashionable items. One is the famous *cappello alla calabrese* ('Calabrian-style hat'), adopted by some Milanese women and derived from a popular, rustic and exclusively masculine world. It thus represented a double transgression of established gender and social norms. It was worn during the Milan insurrections of 1848 and was outlawed later that same year. At the same time, a distinctive *vestire alla lombarda* ('dressing in the Lombard fashion') appeared in the iconography of the period. The political message of this trend was contained in the fabric used to make the clothes: the black velvet which was produced in the region, as opposed to wool, which was imported from Austria or Germany.[1]

These sporadic and timid attempts to build a genuine Italian fashion did not have a real impact. It was not until the first two decades of the twentieth century that a new, more dynamic image of woman, more in tune with the speed of modernity, appeared. With their short hair and shorter skirts, women dressed in a functional manner more appropriate to the less leisured life many working women led after the First World War. This change in the culture of women's clothes, part of the whirl-wind of social change which took place in the opening decades of the century, was noted by the Futurists who published the *Manifesto della moda futurista* ('Manifesto of Futurist Fashion', 1920). Although there existed a strong desire to create an Italian national fashion, the conditions were not yet present for this to happen. French fashion and its industry would continue to dominate foreign markets until the 1960s.

If fashion is the creation of images and simulacra able to mark popular memory through the creation of consciousness and the projection of strong models of social hegemony, we can understand why Mussolini, especially in the autarchic phase of the régime, concerned himself with the rhetoric of fashion and promoted the fashion industry. Fascism was to represent a new way of being, living and appearing. Italians were no longer to shake hands, as this was not considered to be virile enough; instead, they were to greet each other with the Fascist Roman salute of the raised right arm. And, of course, it was the Duce's desire to influence the way people dressed, thereby creating a complex image of the perfect Fascist. At public parades and rallies, each generation was dressed in uniforms created by the Fascist régime, for example the black shirt and the beret with a tassel for men. As a totalitarian régime, Fascism was concerned with the construction and presentation of an image of Italy and Italians which was standardized and controlled by the state. The 'new' image of the Fascist woman was spread through various magazines such as *La Donna* ('Woman'), *Bellezza*, ('Beauty') and *Per voi Signora* ('For You Madam'). She had a strong athletic body, but was not too skinny, in contrast to the dominant image of French women, from whom the Fascist régime was at pains to distance itself. At the same time, the Fascist woman had to project a reassuring and protective image of maternal femininity.

In April 1933, the Queen of Italy, Elena, inaugurated the first Italian exhibition of fashion, which was held in Turin, the city chosen by the régime as the capital of fashion. This was the first concerted official attempt to convince Italian upper-class women that not just French but also Italian fashion was chic. Tailors, dressmakers and women were encouraged to seek inspiration in the regional costumes of Italy. Photographs of the future queen Maria José wearing traditional dress were published in popular female magazines. In 1932, the Ente Nazionale della Moda ('National Fashion Board') was established in Turin with the purpose of 'Italianizing' fashion.[2]

As well as French authority, Fascist Italy had to contend with another foreign influence, this time coming from Hollywood films which were extremely popular. American cinema represented an important source of inspiration for Italian women, who began to copy the dresses worn by the actresses. In 1936, the Ente Nazionale della Moda published a dictionary of fashion by the journalist Cesare Meano with the purpose of purifying Italian fashion jargon of foreign terms. This 500-page dictionary, which was reprinted several times and which contained quotations from Italian authors such as Dante, Boccaccio, Foscolo and Manzoni, set out to create a new Italianized fashion jargon which was to be adopted by people working in the fashion industry. The results of this linguistic 'nationalization' campaign sometimes touched upon the ridiculous, as in the case of words like *cignone* which was supposed to replace the French *chignon*. Unfortunately, in Italian, *cignone* means 'big swan'. In 1938, in the midst of the racial laws, disciplinary sanctions were enacted in order to eliminate foreign influences from Italian life. Even the publication of French patterns in popular magazines, as occurred in the case of *Vita femminile* ('Feminine Life'), was censored. Interestingly, as had already happened in the Renaissance with the sumptuary laws which aimed to control the social body by disciplining how people dressed – especially women, Jews and lower-class people – these kinds of sanctions were unfailingly transgressed.

A more lasting innovation of these years was the introduction of synthetic fibre or so-called 'intelligent fibres' such as rayon. As a consequence, it became possible to produce cheaper mass-produced clothes for an ever-growing market. Department stores such as UPIM and La Rinascente, which still exist today, were opened. We have to remember, however, that a wide gap continued to exist between cities, on the one hand, and the countryside and small towns and villages on the other. For the real 'ready-to-wear' revolution, we have to wait until the 1960s. Nevertheless, the concern with appearances, which is captured in the saying *fare bella figura*, 'to look good', was a concern that extended to all social classes in both rural and urban Italy. The notion of *bella figura*, which also means to create a good impression and to possess a sense of decorum in social and public occasions, is an important component of Italian identity and is part of a tradition which can be traced back to the Renaissance and to texts such as Castiglione's *Il cortegiano*.

The link between fashion and the search for a national identity continued during the post-war years when Italian fashion started to impose itself on the international market, especially in America. The development of an authentic Italian style and a modern fashion system took place within the context of the new international fashion system. The reciprocal attraction between Italy and the USA was the result of the American presence in the peninsula during the last phase of the war. In the 1950s Florence became the capital of Italian fashion and the ideal site for fashion shows. This also occurred thanks to the efforts of the Florentine aristocrat Giovanni Battista Giorgini, who organized the first Italian fashion shows and invited many American buyers to attend them. These society events greatly contributed to making Italian fashion known internationally. The 1950s were the time when Italian fashion designers such as the Sorelle Fontana, Emilio Pucci, Emilio Shubert, Valentino, Germana Marucelli and others started to make a name for themselves both in Italy and in foreign markets, above all in the USA. An important contribution to the creation of the 'Italian look' was made by the very high standards and technological sophistication of the Italian textile industry, which was well known outside Italy and the fashion world. In fact, the textile and clothing industry boomed in the 1950s and played a major role in Italy's economic reconstruction.

As a result of these various circumstances, Italian fashion started to receive wide recognition, and Italian clothes, styles and fabrics began to be identified as specifically Italian.[3] During the same period, a number of American films, most notably William Wyler's *Roman Holiday* (1953), showed an image of Italy which was different from that presented by Neorealist films. Italy was often depicted as the perfect place for romance in which American or foreign tourists were mesmerized by its art and architecture, and not only by the good pasta and olive oil. *Italianità* was romanticized and associated with the beautiful artistic cities steeped in history, which also created an ideal backcloth for fashion photographs and for the idea that Italian clothes and people were romantic and sexy. Indeed, some of Hollywood's most famous actresses wore dresses by Italian fashion designers.

In the mid 1960s, the emergence of ready-to-wear as opposed to high fashion revolutionized the fashion world and started the process of its democratization. It was during this time that Max-Mara, among others, began to play a key role in the ready-to-wear industry, establishing a reputation which, both in Italy and abroad, has continued to this day. Max-Mara contributed to the creation of a 'total look' which, with its co-ordinates (dresses, blouses, coats, sweaters and so forth), established a subtle, understated urbane elegance for professional women.[4] Similarly, in the late 1970s, Fiorucci exercised a strong attraction for the youth market, creating a playful, colourful line of inexpensive clothes: T-shirts, jeans, dresses, etc.

As regards youth culture and styles, post-war Italy differed from the USA and Britain. Teddy-boy, mod, hippie and punk styles were imported via the mass media into Italy, which, in general, has not created its own indigenous youth subcultures. The only such specifically Italian grouping were the *paninari*. These young people, however, did not constitute a transgression of the established order or dress codes, and were completely at ease in consumer society. They appeared in the early 1980s at the same time as a number of sandwich bars (in Italian *paninoteche*, a word derived from *panino*, 'sandwich', from which the designation *paninaro* was also taken) which served as their meeting-places. The *paninari* forged a look based on designer casual clothing, and a jargon of their own which was mainly drawn from the world of English-language popular music. The *paninari* were a typical phenomenon of the 1980s: the decade of conspicuous consumption and of the so-called *riflusso*, or lack of interest in the political activism which had characterized previous decades. The 1980s also saw Milan become one of the foremost international capitals of fashion, on a par with Paris and New York. The 'Italian look' was sold all over the world.

With more women working in high-level positions, a new image and identity were created by the fashion world: that of the woman manager, characterized most effectively by the androgynous look made famous by Giorgio Armani. As well as 'masculinizing' female clothes, Armani also contributed to 'femininizing' the male 'business suit', deconstructing its stiffness and rendering it sexier thanks to the use of soft and luxurious fabrics such as wool and silk, as well as cashemere.[5] To this day, Armani continues to be the foremost Italian designer in terms of sales in the USA. Other high-fashion designers, such as Gianni Versace, took inspiration from punk street-styles, while developing the high-couture version of the motorbike leather jacket. Versace gave an innovative twist to the traditional world of Italian fashion. His image of woman was deliberately provocative, eccentric and exaggerated, the very opposite image of Armani's understated one.

Another designer, Gianfranco Moschino, has played an even more ironically irreverent role in subverting the notion of 'classic elegance'. His clothes have parodied religious garb, and have combined different styles and fabrics in the same outfit. Moschino aims at giving a carnivalesque and derisive character to mainstream fashion – it is enough to think of the dress recalling a ballerina's tutu he made out of what looked like recycled bras – even though he does this from within the system he wishes to undermine. As a matter of fact, several fashion designers have taken this direction in the last two decades, as if to underline the fetishistic and crossdressing elements which are part of fashion. Perhaps this phenomenon hides a constant fear of being taken for granted, and a sort of stylistic restlessness which reveals a lack of new ideas. On the European scene, Vivienne Westwood, Jean Paul Gautier, John Galliano and Alexander McQueen are examples of designers who offer a bricolage made up of 'quotations' from historical costumes, punk styles, paintings and turn-of-the-century coquettes.

By way of conclusion, I should like to go back to literature and recall the well-known text by the nineteenth-century poet Giacomo Leopardi, his 'Dialogo tra la moda e la morte' ('Dialogue between Fashion and Death'). Among many interesting observations, this dialogue, in which fashion and death are sisters, calls our attention to the fact that fashion lives in the utopia of the fleeting moment, the present. This is an important detail on which philosophers and sociologists – among them Georg Simmel and Walter Benjamin – were to ground some of their reflections in their seminal writings on fashion.[6] Fashion, in occupying the dividing line between past and future, feeds on the ungraspable present. From this derive the constant urge towards the new and the need to change.

But if fashion lives in the folds of the present, clothes weave the fabric of memory. Fashion and clothes move at different speeds, and they are not the same thing. The history of a particular item does not necessarily coincide with the history of fashion. Thus, certain clothes, as in some of the cases mentioned in this essay, designate what the historian Philippe Perrot has called 'events' as opposed to 'structure', which Perrot, via Roland Barthes, identifies with fashion.[7] It is through single events, their functions and roles, as well as the associative chains they forge, that we are able to construct and narrate a story, or, if we are patient enough, to discover passages and remnants which might have escaped the distracted gaze of history.

NOTES

1. Grazietta Butazzi, 'La moda a Milano dal regno d'Italia al '48', *Il Risorgimento* 3 (1992), pp. 493–515.
2. Natalia Aspesi, *Il lusso e l'autarchia* (Milan: Rizzoli, 1982).
3. Luigi Settembrini, 'From Haute Couture to Prêt-à-Porter', in G. Celant (ed.), *The Italian Metamorphosis* (Milan: Progetti Museali, 1994), pp. 484–94; Valerie Steele, 'Italian Fashion and America', ibid., pp. 496–505.
4. Nicola White, 'Max Mara and the Origins of Italian Ready to Wear', *Modern Italy* 1/2 (1996), pp. 63–80.
5. Valerie Steele, *Fifty Years of Fashion* (New Haven: Yale University Press, 1996).
6. Georg Simmel, 'Fashion' (1895), in G. Wills and D. Midgley (eds.), *Fashion Marketing* (London: Allen and Unwin, 1973), pp. 171–91; Walter Benjamin, *Parigi: Capitale del XIX Secolo. I Passages di Parigi* (Turin: Einaudi, 1986).
7. Philippe Perrot, 'Suggestions for a Different Approach to the History of Dress', *Diogenes* 114 (1981), pp. 157–76

FURTHER READING

Barthes, Roland, *The Fashion System*. New York: Hill and Wang, 1983.
Butazzi, Grazietta, *1922–1943 Vent'anni di Moda Italiana*. Florence: Centro Di, 1980.
De Giorgio, Michela, *Le italiane dall'Unità ad oggi*. Rome and Bari: Laterza, 1992.
De Grazia, Victoria and Furlough, Ellen (eds.), *The Sex of Things: Gender and Consumption in Historical Perspective*. Berkeley: University of California Press, 1996.
Giordani Aragno, Bonizza, *Moda Italia*. Milan: Domus, 1988.
Levi-Pisetsky, Rosita, *Storia del costume in Italia*. v. *L'Ottocento*. Milan: Rizzoli, 1969.
    'Moda e costume', in *Storia d'Italia*. v. *I Documenti*. Turin: Einaudi, 1973.
    Storia della moda e del costume in Italia. Turin: Einaudi, 1978.
Paulicelli, Eugenia 1994. 'Fashion as a Text. Talking about Femininity and Feminism', in G. Miceli-Jeffries (ed.), *Feminine Feminists*. Minneapolis: University of Minnesota Press, pp. 171–89.
    'Le narrative della moda. Egemonia, genere, identità', *Quaderni d'italianistica* 16 (1998), pp. 315–37.

15

The media

Today, ownership and control of the media in Italy (the press and television broadcasting in particular) are so important as to determine the outcome of elections, and are a burning issue on the Italian political agenda. For this reason, rather than tell the story of the development of the media chronologically through the twentieth century, this chapter will start by outlining the institutional situation in the 1990s, which is illustrated with some facts and figures, and then proceed to discuss the chronological development of radio.

Who and what are the media for?

Firstly, it is generally agreed that the closer a state approaches to the ideal of democracy, the greater the need of the voters for information on which to base their choice of representatives. They need to know what exactly is happening in the country, what measures the elected representatives are enacting, and what policies candidates for election are proposing. Secondly, a nation coheres partly through values and beliefs concerning the history of its society, the meanings that have been given to life and to both personal and communal activity, as well as a common 'language' (verbal, visual, dress-codes, eating habits, etc.) shared or at least discussed by the community. Thirdly, people need to relax and laugh together; solitary people (like the elderly) need contact with others; and creative talent needs to find expression.

In the days when broadcasting was in most countries (Italy was one of them) a state monopoly and a public service, it was asserted that its functions were 'information', 'culture' and 'entertainment', corresponding to the three needs that we have just listed. However, in the United States broadcasting was neither a state monopoly nor a public service, but was rather a commercial enterprise carried on by private companies for profit. In Britain a public service monopoly was 'joined' by a private, commercial sector from the 1950s onwards. This gives us three institutional models for broadcasting: 'public service', 'commercial' and 'mixed'. About public service broadcasting we want to ask how it is controlled, and how much autonomy it has with regard to the state; about commercial broadcasting, whether it is regulated or not, how and by whom; about the mixed system, what the relationship is between the two sectors. The answers are as follows: for public service broadcasting in Britain, it was funded by a licence fee and controlled by an autonomous body whose job was to act as a buffer between the broadcasters and the government; for commercial broadcasting in the USA, it was funded by the revenue from advertising, and strongly regulated by the Federal Communications Commission. When Britain moved to a mixed system, the public service sector remained as it was, while the commercial sector was funded by the revenue from advertising, and was strongly regulated by the Independent Broadcasting Authority which set quality levels to be met, and distributed franchises accordingly.

Italy's state public service broadcasting was controlled by the political party holding a majority in parliament (before the Second World War by the Fascist Party, afterwards by the Christian Democrat Party). But from the start of national (radio) broadcasting in Italy in 1924, it was funded partly by a licence fee, and partly by advertising revenue. No institutional decision was ever made at a policy level to introduce a mixed system in Italy. Instead, in 1976, the Constitutional Court ruled that prosecuting private broadcasting companies for violating a state monopoly was unconstitutional. RAI (Radiotelevisione italiana, the state broadcaster) was ruled to have a monopoly over *national* broadcasting, but not *local* broadcasting; Silvio Berlusconi, the owner of a number of television stations, simply had all his local stations broadcast simultaneously the same programming which was delivered to them in video-cassettes by a trucking company which he owned. In due course, Bettino Craxi, the Prime Minister and an ally of Berlusconi, issued decrees in the 1980s permitting existing networks to broadcast nationally. Finally, the law of 13 August 1992 gave licences to broadcast nationally to the following channels: the three RAI (state) channels, the three Fininvest channels owned by Berlusconi (Canale 5, Italia 1, Retequattro) and three further commercial channels (Telemontecarlo, Rete A and Videomusic).

The functioning of the two alternative systems of control is generally theorized in the following way: public service broadcasting is guided by the criterion of public service: to meet the needs (for information, culture and entertainment) of the various different sectors of the population – men and women, the old and the young, manual workers and intellectuals, practising Christians and non-believers, and so on: in a word, the licence-fee payers, *all* of them at some time, but not necessarily all of them at the *same* time. The word 'pluralism' is used in English to refer to this notion of a single broadcaster satisfying a 'plurality' of different audiences; as we shall see, the same word (*pluralismo*) is used in Italy in a different way. On the other hand, commercial television, in the absence of regulation, functions to meet the needs of its shareholders for profits, and since these come from advertising revenues, the criterion tends to be that of attracting the largest possible audience *at any one time* – what is called 'competitive' programming. Regulation has generally been deemed necessary to ensure that commercial broadcasters do not cater exclusively for the lowest common denominator in their programming, but that they meet the needs of different sectors of the population for the three different types of programming we have described.

In the mid 1970s, Italy could be said to have landed herself with the worst possible institutional arrangement. She had a public service sector whose first duty was to the needs of the ruling political party, and whose second duty was to attract advertising revenue; and she had a totally unregulated commercial sector whose duty was exclusively to its shareholders. Because RAI had to compete for advertising revenue, and therefore audiences, with the commercial sector, it was forced to adopt competitive programming in order to remain solvent.[1]

Viewers who watch commercial programming believing that they are 'buying' the information, culture or entertainment that they choose by purchasing the goods advertised are deluding themselves. They are, it is true, involved in a marketing operation; but it is not the programme that is being sold to the viewer, it is the viewer who is being sold to the advertiser. Viewers and the meeting of their needs are not the end and goal of the whole enterprise; rather, the meeting of the broadcaster's need for revenue is the end and goal of the enterprise, and he meets this need by selling to the advertisers the viewers he attracts with his programming. The viewer is a 'means' to his 'end'.

It is worth following this train of reasoning as far as it takes us. It might be thought that the existence of Berlusconi's three television networks constitutes a contribution to Italian mass culture. But if the programming of those networks is (as it almost exclusively was for many years, and still is, to a large extent) bought-in American material, pre-packaged with national advertising by Berlusconi's advertising conces-sionary (Publitalia), and dumped on the networks according to a plan of audience-targeting, it is hard to see the operation as contributing in a very meaningful way to Italian culture.[2] If the airwaves are public prop-erty, then perhaps we can best describe the situation by using an analogy. Outside a row of apartment blocks and small shops the kerb offers the inhabitants, the businesses and their customers the facility for parking their cars. If a trucking company from around the corner, to save the rental of a lorry park, parks its articulated lorries in front of the apart-ments, it is 'occupying' a public space for private profit, and 'censoring', so to speak, the other small commercial enterprises. Berlusconi's adver-tising concessionary, Publitalia, now has a near-monopoly on television advertising (with the exception of the RAI). Publitalia supplies Berlusconi's own television networks, which have a near-monopoly on commercial broadcasting. An advertiser who places spots with a televi-sion station of which Berlusconi disapproves can be threatened with diminished access to Berlusconi's networks, or seduced over to Publitalia by especially advantageous rates – which is what happened to the adver-tisers who were buying time on an interesting and successful indepen-dent TV station, Videomusic, whose owner had to sell the station at a knockdown price to Cecchi Gori, Berlusconi's one-time partner in film distribution, and the owner of Telemontecarlo.

The point of this line of reasoning is not so much to demonize Berlusconi as to demonstrate that the institutional arrangements for broadcasting have a strong bearing on the cultural contribution of a medium to the life of a nation. There is, however, a further consideration which modifies the conclusions one might draw from the merely institu-tional picture of the Italian media, and this is that the use made of a medium by its consumers is not completely determined by its institu-tional identity. Viewers do not watch television, for example, passively; they integrate it into their social lives. One characteristic of Italian televi-sion which might be considered a shortcoming, its dependence on quiz shows, phone-ins and interviews (all eminently 'cheap' programming, in the sense that production costs are low), could be seen as the integration of the public sphere into the essentially private, domestic life of Italian society. When Italian television first started broadcasting in 1954, for the first few years it was watched communally in bars, clubs and theatres, and people would trek in from miles around in rural areas to watch a show, people who had never contemplated going to the cinema – perhaps partly because of the nature of the 'address' to the audience that television made, its 'phatic' qualities (the way it establishes and maintains direct contact with the audience), rather than its informational content. Part of the experience of communal viewing would be the discussion of what was being viewed.

It might be helpful to introduce here a word or two of theory relating to the press: newspapers carry out similar functions to broadcasting, but ownership and control can have a major bearing on how they carry out those functions. Newspapers can be owned by companies that exist for, and earn their revenue by, publishing (either newspapers alone, or newspapers, periodicals and books). Alternatively, they can be owned by companies which exist for, and earn most of their revenue from, other activities, and for whom the newspaper is merely a tool for promoting those other activities. A third category is one in which a newspaper is owned by a political party as a mouthpiece for its policies. In the latter two cases, readers and their needs are once again a 'means' to an 'end'. Italy at the moment has almost none of the first kind of newspapers (owned by companies which exist solely for publishing – an exception is *Il manifesto*, which is strongly aligned ideologically with Communism); the majority of her newspapers are of the second kind (owned by businesses with other, more important, interests), and a few are of the third kind (run by political parties for their own ends). One last piece of theorizing, this time about journalism in general: journalists can believe that their duty is to seek out and communicate the 'objective truth' concerning the events taking place around them. They can, on the other hand, believe that it is an ideal impossible to reach, and that the nearest to the 'truth' to which a reader or viewer can ever aspire is to read a number of perhaps less than objective accounts of those events, each, however, recounted by someone whose 'bias' and limitations are openly declared. The readers or viewers can then discount the known bias of each report, and construct the 'truth' for themselves out of the multiple perspectives. A number of contemporary philosophical positions challenge the notion of 'objective truth' and 'reality', and the certainties implicit in that notion. One reason why these philosophical positions are so successful is that we perceive ourselves to be living in a world in which public communication (of which 'the media' in their widest sense are the vehicle) has so usurped the place of private conviction and choice in our lives, that competition in the marketplace between rival 'realities', which their purveyors have to communicate in order to pay their mortgages or further their careers, now appears to be the only 'reality' about which we can be sure. Where once farming and heavy industry fed the inhabitants of Britain and Italy, and 'talk' was cheap, now the marketing of hardware and software for the communication of words, images and sounds gives a living to very large sections of the populations of our two countries. The result is that the 'reality' of the money involved in the media, which determines the health of our economies, threatens to render the value of the content of each item of communication almost insignificant. Thus 'reality' is the outcome of competing 'discourses' in a 'market', and at the same time, competition is the only thing that is 'real'. The 'discourse' of this chapter suggests that 'competition' is the least 'real' phenomenon of all.

Italian journalism uses the word *pluralismo* for the second approach to 'truth' in news reporting (multiple 'known' perspectives), and while many criticize this position, the organization of Italy's media institutionalizes it.[3] Whereas, as we have seen, in the UK 'pluralism' refers to one broadcaster satisfying the needs of a plurality of audiences, in Italy *pluralismo* means a plurality of broadcasters satisfying one viewer's need for reliable information. When, in 1975, the RAI was 'reformed' at the instigation of Communist Party parliamentarians, in order to reduce the Christian Democratic Party's control over the information and cultural programming of the RAI channels, what was set up was not a single newsroom that attempted to communicate the news 'objectively', but three entirely separate newsrooms, one for each channel, each controlled by a different political party, each one's bulletin being different from that of the other two (the Christian Democrat one gave much prominence to stories about the Vatican and little to labour disputes, while the Communist one gave more space to strikes and workers' action and less to the Vatican). The name given to this procedure is *lottizzazione*, 'sharing out', and it was applied to radio newsrooms as well. The assertion that journalists and editors in RAI (not only in RAI, and not only in broadcasting) are employed not for their professional ability but for their party affiliation is so widespread and is so little contradicted in Italy that we have no grounds for challenging it.

When, in 1994, Silvio Berlusconi became Prime Minister, he told a reporter 'it is certainly anomalous for a democratic state to have a public service [television] that opposes the majority that elected the government of the country'.[4] He promptly appointed his own people to positions in the RAI. In other words, he controlled all six of the major television networks in Italy. Whatever we might think of the Italian notion of *pluralismo* applied to the news, Berlusconi's actions rendered it impossible. 'Objectivity' was not deemed an achievable end, and *pluralismo* was blocked by monopoly control.

The reader might think 'but there was always the press', and indeed the press staunchly argued the case for freedom during the struggles of 1994. First, however, the circulation of newspapers in Europe is lowest in Greece, and next lowest in Italy. There is no popular daily press in Italy (unless one counts the sports dailies). Giancarlo Bosetti has written: 'People like those who, in other countries like Great Britain, Germany and the US, read a popular newspaper and watch the television, [in Italy] watch television and that's it.'[5] Secondly, newspapers are not written for the ordinary person-in-the-street in Italy. Stories are allusive, rather than giving the 'what, who, when, where, etc.', and the prose style is difficult for the less well educated. Many believe that Enzo Forcella's famous characterization in *Tempo presente* in November 1959 still applies to Italy today:

> A political journalist in our country can count on around 1,500 readers: ministers and under-secretaries (all of them), members of parliament (some of them), party leaders, trade union officials, high prelates, and some industrialists who want to be informed. The rest do not count, even though the paper sells 300,000 copies [. . .] The whole system is based on the rapport between the political journalist and this group of privileged readers. If we lose sight of this factor, we cannot understand the most characteristic aspect of our political journalism, perhaps of Italian politics in general – the feeling of talk within the family, with protagonists who have known each other since childhood.[6]

So far, we have theorized and generalized about ownership and control in the Italian media, and asserted its centrality in Italian politics. The best way to bring home to the reader the full picture is simply to provide hard data, firstly about the sharing out of power between the political parties in state broadcasting (Radiotelevisione italiana – RAI), and secondly about how companies (and therefore the owners of those companies) own the media.

Lottizzazione in the RAI newsrooms in 1991

A news bulletin is called a *telegiornale*, 'Tg' for short. The following were the party affiliations of main editors, newsdesk editors, main journalists on political newsdesks and newsreaders on the three RAI channels:

> Tg1 (out of 22 people counted): Democrazia Cristiana – 16; Partito Democratico Socialista (or known PDS sympathizers) – 3; Partito Liberale Italiano, Partito Repubblicano Italiano, Partito Social Democratico Italiano – 1 each.
> Tg2 (out of 22 people counted): Partito Socialista Italiano – 16; DC – 4; PLI, PDS – 1 each.
> Tg3 (out of 20 people counted): PDS – 14; DC (left faction) – 4; PLI, PSDI – 1 each.[7]

Press and commercial television ownership in Italy in 1989–1991

What follows was the situation around 1989–91. Companies which had once simply manufactured goods or produced publications (like the automobile manufacturers FIAT, or the publishers Rizzoli) had gradually grouped themselves into or been taken over by large 'holding companies' (companies or groups of companies which hold shares in order to control other companies; the companies they control can be in a multitude of different industries for the purpose of 'diversification' and spreading risks, or they can be other holding companies). Such companies are identified by an (H) after their names. It was the implications of the situation we describe below that in 1990 led a number of politicians in Italy, from the left of the DC to the PDS, to decide that the regulation of cross-media ownership and control was long overdue. Silvio Berlusconi (see (vi) below) was acquiring control of Mondadori-L'Espresso (see (ii) below). It would have given him control over the daily *La Repubblica* and the weekly *L'Espresso*, perhaps the two most independent voices in the Italian press, and this at a moment in which pressure was being put on the editor of *Il Corriere della Sera*, traditionally Italy's newspaper of record, by its owners to make it more competitive. However, in April 1991 a judicial decision gave the group of *L'Espresso* and *La Repubblica* autonomy (though under De Benedetti, the owner of Olivetti) from Berlusconi and the rest of Mondadori. Since 1991 various parts of the picture painted below have changed, but this year has been chosen because it is the one in which the nation as a whole first fully realized the enormity of the mess it had got itself into, and because the picture illustrates the complex interweaving of both public and private financial, political and propaganda interests that has characterized the Italian state, and which the *Mani pulite* campaign of the judiciary sought to unravel.

It is necessary to bear in mind that the Italian daily press is much more local and regional than the British press, which means that a paper with a circulation of around 300,000 copies can be the main newspaper for that region, and therefore that there is not really national competition between papers like *La Gazzetta del Mezzogiorno* (Bari), *Il Mattino* (Naples), *Il Messaggero* (Rome), *La Nazione* (Florence), *Il Resto del Carlino* (Bologna), *La Stampa* (Turin) and *Il Corriere della Sera* (Milan) – except perhaps for the last of these, which also operates as a national newspaper in competition with *La Repubblica*.

(i) In the group consisting of Fiat (H)–Gemina(H)–Rizzoli–Corriere della Sera (RCS) (H), Giampiero Pesenti (one of the owners of Poligrafici–Monti–Pesenti–Editoriale (H), see (iv) below) was President of Gemina (H), while the publishing branch, Rizzoli–Corriere della Sera (RCS) (H), was owned 62 per cent by FIAT (H) (which in turn was owned by the Agnelli family, which means that it was controlled by Gianni Agnelli), and 21.6 per cent by Ferruzzi (H) (which owns Montedison (H)) – of which the president was Raul Gardini (see (iii) below).

The group owned the daily newspapers *Corriere della Sera* (Milan, circulation 689,000); *Gazzetta dello Sport* (Milan; circulation 733,000); *La Stampa* (Turin, owned directly by FIAT/Agnelli; circulation 591,400); *Stampa Sera* (Turin, owned directly by FIAT/Agnelli; circulation: 40,600), giving the group a total daily circulation of about two million, or 22.59 per cent of the market. The group also owned the weeklies *Amica*, *Brava*, *Anna*, *Bella*, *Più bella*, *Astra*, *Salve*, *Linus*, *L'Europeo*, *Il Mondo*, *Oggi*, *Domenica del Corriere*, *Novella 2000*, *Domenica Quiz* and *Corriere dei piccoli*, with a total circulation of about three million, giving it 19.47 per cent of the market. It owned the television station Telemontecarlo through Rete Globo, a Brazilian company, though Ferruzzi (H) (see (iii)) was later to take a controlling interest. The station passed eventually to Vittorio Cecchi Gori, Italy's major film producer, who at this time, together with Berlusconi's Fininvest (H), in a distribution company called Penta Film, handled 25 per cent of the films distributed in Italian cinemas. The group owned three advertising agencies, Rizzoli, Publikompass (owned directly by FIAT/Agnelli) and RCS Pubblicità. Its holdings in book publishing were the Gruppo Editoriale Fabbri (H) (which included Fabbri, Bompiani, Sonzogno, Etas, and 48 per cent of Adelphi), Rizzoli (RCS Libri) and RCS Cartiera Marzabotto.

(ii) The Mondadori–L'Espresso (H) group was owned by AMEF (Mondadori) (H)–CIR (H)–Olivetti (H). Carlo De Benedetti owned Olivetti and he and his supporters had 63 per cent of CIR-AMEF. Berlusconi had 8 per cent of AMEF, and when the Formenton family – Mondadori's partners in AMEF – fell out with De Benedetti, they sold to Berlusconi a stake which gave him control of the group (he was made president). Raul Gardini (Ferruzzi) had 18 per cent of *L'Espresso*.

The group owned the national dailies *La Repubblica* (Rome; circulation 839,000), *La Nuova Sardegna* (circulation 101,000), *Alto Adige*, *Il Centro*, *Gazzetta di Mantova*, *Il Lavoro*, *Mattino di Padova*, *Nuova Gazzetta di Modena/Gazzetta di Carpi*, *La Nuova Venezia*, *La Provincia Pavese*, *Il Tirreno* and *La Tribuna di Treviso*, giving it a total circloation of about 1.5 million, or 14.15 per cent of the market. Its weeklies were *L'Espresso* (circulation 410,000), *Panorama* (circulation 508,000), *Nuova Guida TV* (circulation 460,000), *Grazia* (circulation 400,000), *Auto oggi*, *Dolly*, *Epoca* and *Guida cucina*, giving it a total circulation of about 2.6 million, or 17.7 per cent of the market. The group controlled the advertising agency A. Manzoni & Co., and owned the large book publishers Arnoldo Mondadori Editore. (In the mid 1990s, together with the publishers Electa, Mondadori formed Elemond, which has acquired control of the important Turinese publishing company Einaudi.)

(iii) The Ferruzzi (H) group owned Montedison (H), the major chemical company, and was headed by Gardini (who also had 21 per cent of RCS and 18 per cent of *L'Espresso*), publishing the main dailies *Italia Oggi* (circulation only 126,000, but it was an influential business newspaper) and *Il Messaggero* (Rome; circulation 396,000), giving it about 5.7 per cent of the market.

(iv) The Poligrafici–Monti–Pesenti–Editoriale (H) group, owned by Monti 52 per cent, Pesenti 20 per cent, Varasi 10 per cent, Ligresti 10 per cent, owned the dailies *Il Resto del Carlino* (Bologna; circulation 305,400), *La Nazione* (Florence; circulation 268,000), *Il Tempo* (Rome; circulation 158,000), *Il Piccolo* (Trieste), *Il Corriere di Pordenone* and *Il Telegrafo*, giving it about 9.2 per cent of the market.

(v) The Rusconi group owned the daily *La Notte* (Milan; 90,000), and the weeklies *Eva Express* (circulation 314,000), *Gente* (circulation 944,000), *Gioia* (circulation 458,000), *Onda TV* (circulation 304,500), giving it 13.2 per cent of the weeklies market.

(vi) The Fininvest (H) group (now owned by Mediaset (H)) was owned by Berlusconi, who also controlled the Mondadori (H) group, with the exception of *La Repubblica* and *L'Espresso*. Its main daily was *Il Giornale Nuovo*, but it was its weeklies, *TV Sorrisi e canzoni* (one of the largest national weeklies, if not the largest), *Ciak* and *Telepiù*, which gave it about 16 per cent of the market. Its real monopoly power lay in its ownership of the Publitalia advertising concessionary (the biggest turnover nationally), and the four national commercial television networks, Canale 5, Italia Uno, Rete Quattro and Rete Italia (Berlusconi sold off the last of these).

To complete the picture for the period under discussion, the Banco di Napoli (H) controlled the papers of the South, *Il Mattino* (Naples) and *Gazzetta del Mezzogiorno* (Bari), while Italy's most prestigious business-oriented newspaper (the Italian equivalent of the British *Financial Times* or the US *Wall Street Journal*), *Il sole-24 ore* (circulation approximately 300,000), was owned by the Confederation of Italian Industry, Confindustria. Daily newspapers were also owned by political parties: *Il Popolo* by Democrazia Cristiana; *Avanti!* by the Socialist Party; *L'Unità* and *Paese Sera* by the Partito Comunista Italiano; *Il manifesto* called itself Communist, but was independently owned and run by a 'collective'; *Il Secolo d'Italia* by the Movimento Sociale Italiano. The largest and most important Italian news agency, ANSA (Agenzia Nazionale Stampa Associata), was government-controlled, while ASCA was controlled by the DC, ADN-KRONOS by the PSI and Italia by ENI (H) (Ente Nazionale Idrocarburi, Italy's major petroleum group).

It is worth adding a note to illustrate how industrial interests see press and television ownership as instruments to be used for their own purposes. In 1996, Francesco Gaetano Caltagirone, with a controlling interest in, and an option to buy, *Il Mattino*, and ownership of *Il Tempo* (acquired from Monti–Pesenti (iv)), bought *Il Messaggero* from Ferruzzi (iii). Caltagirone also owned the major local television station for Rome, Teleregione. This gave him an overwhelming media dominance in the Rome area. Caltagirone was at the time a developer–constructor, with his eye on government contracts for two major construction projects coming up in Rome: the Jubilee, and the possibility (which existed at the time) that Rome might be chosen for the 2004 Olympics.[8]

The picture that emerges is one of cross-media ownership, a fusing together of public and private financial and industrial interests, and the concentration of control over the media in the hands of a few who had vested interests in controlling it for their own ends. Four men could determine what information Italians were privy to: Agnelli, Berlusconi, De Benedetti and Gardini. Only the state-controlled broadcaster, RAI, stood outside this oligopoly, but that was not to last. The Communist Party (now named the Partito Democratico della Sinistra) promoted a policy for regulating media ownership, limiting the extent to which one organization could own or control more than a certain percentage of the nation's press and broadcasting. Since Berlusconi's business operations depended on monopoly control of advertising and its markets, this policy threatened the profits of Fininvest. When, in 1994, the political alignments in Italy broke down, and it looked likely that the PDS would form part of a government coalition, Berlusconi, in order to protect his interests against their proposed legislation, was forced to form his own political party (Forza Italia), use the massive propaganda resources offered by his television networks to get himself elected as Prime Minister, and thwart the plans of the PDS. As President of the Council of Ministers, Berlusconi was then in a position also to control the information output of the RAI. He controlled all major national television networks except Telemontecarlo, plus a large part of the weekly magazine market, and very nearly owned one of the two major national newspapers, as well as having a near-monopoly on television advertising. Because of the need to compete for audiences, the state channels (with the exception of the third, cultural, channel) had reduced their treatment of current affairs by dropping current-affairs programmes and documentaries, and operating a policy of multiple, short news bulletins throughout the day as opposed to a small number of longer bulletins. Romano Prodi's left-of-centre government, which succeeded Berlusconi's in 1995, reinstalled a governing body for the RAI which reflected the more liberal and pluralist complexion of the government coalition, but the RAI still bears today the chains of the past.

Radio and reliability

A single chapter in a volume of this kind can only cover so much ground, and so it is now proposed to change the subject, and give an account of the development of radio in Italy, in order to introduce a historical perspective into the discussion of the media's role in Italian culture.

The formation in 1924 of URI, the Unione Radiofonica Italiana ('Italian Radio Union'), to become, in 1927, EIAR, Ente Italiano per le Audizioni Radiofoniche ('Italian Corporation for Radio Reception') institutionalized radio broadcasting in Italy as a monopoly funded by a licence fee and advertising. The much-trumpeted broadcast by Mussolini from the Teatro Costanzi on 25 March 1924 that was to herald the uniting of a nation of listeners was marred by interference, and all that could be heard was the confused bubbling sound of his voice with no words distinguishable. This humorously illustrates the extent to which technological development is integral to the development of broadcast media, and has continually conditioned radio in particular.

URI's broadcasts officially began on 6 April 1924, with a mixture of concerts, theatre, news and conversation, its listeners predominantly young people, students, engineers and electronics enthusiasts. The need for radio, its potential as a channel for popular culture and news, brought about its spread: 6,196 hours of transmission in 1927, 15,768 in 1929 and 43,723 in 1934. At first, a radio licence cost as much as a white-collar worker's monthly salary, and radio sets cost 3,000 lire (while the average annual wage was 1,300 lire). In 1927 there were 40,000 licences (while in Britain there were two million), in 1929 61,500, in 1939 one million (whereas by then in Germany and Britain there were eight million each) and in 1943 1.8 million. The listeners were a great deal more numerous than the licence-holders, however, because they listened to radios in public places, just as they were to do with television in the 1950s. Despite the government's attempts to promote the construction and marketing of cheap sets, it was not until 1937 that the Radioballila, costing 430 lire, was made available.

The programming developed its popular character throughout the 1930s, with singing stars, light music, variety, comic sketches and heroic–comic adventure drama. The first audience to be specifically 'targeted' was children. Reports and broadcasts were launched from the war in Ethiopia, and in the late 1930s sports broadcasts began. The sources for the news were the government's press agency, Stefani, and a few approved newspapers, such as *Il Popolo d'Italia*. Radio's potential for propaganda could only be realized to the extent that the 'product' of radio itself, firstly its hardware and then the regular programming, had been sold to the public in the first place. By the outbreak of the Second World War, this potential was being realized, but it was precisely at this moment that another consideration came into play.

In a war that involves civilians, the latter need information. The government used EIAR for propaganda instead, giving a picture of a victorious Italy, minimizing defeats and demonizing the enemy. However, the technology of radio gave the government little control over which stations citizens' radio sets were tuned into. The public found the BBC Italian Service's broadcasts from London (called Radio Londra) more reliable than those of its own broadcasters, and many also tuned into Italian broadcasts from Moscow (Radio Mosca and Radio Milano Libertà), despite the fact that clandestine listening was punishable by law. In a contest over reliability, EIAR was humiliatingly rejected. On 8 September 1943, a strange silence descended: EIAR merely broadcast a repeated message that Mussolini had resigned and that a new government had been formed by Marshal Badoglio. A babble broke out: in the liberated zones ex-EIAR stations restarted under the tutelage of the Psychological Warfare Branch of the Allied Military Government; the German occupying forces broadcast in Italian; the government of Salò officially took over EIAR; clandestine partisan transmitters broadcast in the North. Because the damaged equipment and cabling did not permit the linking of the ex-EIAR studios and transmitters in the liberated zone (Bari, Naples, Palermo and Cagliari), these stations broadcast independently of each other, giving Italians a taste of a radio that was relatively free of centralization, pluralist in the Italian sense, and capable of dealing with regional circumstances. Rather than learn from these experiences, the Italian government, at the end of the war, reinstated a government service, and as the liberation coalition gave way to Christian Democrat hegemony, the newly baptized RAI (Radio Audizioni Italia – later to become Radiotelevisione italiana) adopted a Catholic conservative line. To begin with, two networks were set up, again for technical reasons: Rete Azzurra in the North and Centre and Rete Rossa in the South and Centre, with a gradual centralization of operations in Rome which provoked resistance and protest from the regions. What was set up was not very different from what had been the case during Fascism, except that a different political party was in power.

The 1950s saw firstly the boom, and then the decline of radio in Italy. After 1951 three services were modelled on those of the BBC, the Programma Nazionale, the Secondo Programma and the Terzo Programma (a cultural service). But another technological innovation in the 1960s led to greater programme differentiation: transistors, first developed in 1948. Instead of one radio receiver listened to by an entire household, a number of sets would be used, particularly by a rapidly expanding young audience, who wanted their own programming. As television took over prime-time attention, radio began to function as an 'environmental medium', continually turned on, giving background sound: music for the young, and companionship for housewives and the elderly. Various plans for modernizing the RAI's programming failed to be implemented, and the explosion of commercial broadcasting with the deregulation of the 1970s blew apart the RAI's hold on its audiences.

Whereas the expensive technological and production requirements of television led to the rapid formation of an oligopoly (actually, a duopoly) in television, the lower economic and technical demands of radio permitted far more broadcasters to survive. By the early 1990s, 4,000 radio stations were broadcasting in Italy, 15 at a national level (3 belonging to RAI, and 12 others, of which 9 broadcast music for the young), 150 at a regional level, 1,500 *interprovinciali*, and 2,000 at or below the level of a *provincia* (the level of local government between that of a town or city council like Pisa or Livorno and that of a region like Tuscany). Of the regional and inter-provincial stations, about 250 had an important and stable status; 600 private stations were Catholic.

The ideals with which many a station was launched were *contro-informazione* (an alternative source of news in opposition to that of the state broadcaster and the wealthy newspapers), and *partecipazione* (participation – listener input), or *radio confessionale* (confessional radio – typically Catholic). *Contro-informazione* was only achieved (and still is in some cases) by a few stations in Bologna, Rome, Florence and Milan. Otherwise, most stations gradually subsided into providing music for the young. There were three types of station: commercial ones that made a profit, linked in pools and getting national advertising; promotional ones – sponsored stations operating locally (supported by political, religious, cultural or even commercial interests); and non-professional

ones, staffed by volunteers, often holding to some of the original principles, and including what were called the 'free' radio stations, which
broadcast an independent programming that was an alternative to both
state and commercial broadcasting. A classical music station broadcasts
from Fiesole (near Florence), surviving on subscriptions from listeners,
and borrowing from the example of 'public' radio and television in the
USA, but there are few other non-standard initiatives in Italian broadcasting.

The function of radio became music for the young, information
(news), background wall-to-wall music (*nastroteca*), and breaking the isolation of housewives and pensioners. As radio has accepted these functions, and has accepted also the hegemony of television in the evening,
patterns of listening have taken shape. In the early morning, all categories of listener tend to listen to the RAI's news services. These are followed in the morning by talk and discussion shows, and then music, the
whole sequence being repeated after lunch. After listening to the news
on RAI in the early morning and lunchtime, listeners will often tune to
their favourite commercial channel. RAI's initiative in broadcasting all-
night music on its FM channels, and its (relative) freedom from the
requirement of sticking to the top-fifty records, has led to an increase in
younger listeners during the night. However, radio lost advertising to
television (it had 10.3 per cent of total advertising in 1978, and five years
later only 5 per cent) partly because of the way television developed
nationally, and partly because radio stations, packed closely together on
the FM frequency band, all providing similar programming, were relatively indistinguishable one from another, and difficult to tune into
precisely, so that it was difficult to identify benefits accruing to the
advertiser from advertising on any one particular station. Attempts to
reverse this decline currently aim at targeting specific audiences, and
differentiating programming.

Waste

RAI was in the forefront of developing High Definition Television and
broadcasting by satellite. The media's cultural and technical potential in
Italy has at times been enormous, but it has not always been realized
(though RAI's educational broadcasting has been very successful). Until
recently, technical training in broadcasting was piecemeal, and broadcasters have had a great incentive to look more to their political connec-

tions than to their professional abilities for success in their careers. Too many people and organizations have used the media for their own ends, and too few have used the media's potential for the benefit of the reading, listening and viewing public. Nevertheless, Italians watch television more than anyone else in Europe, and the most prestigious international award for quality broadcasting, instituted in 1949, is the Prix Italia.

NOTES

1. See Mauro Wolf, 'Italy: From Deregulation to a New Equilibrium', in G. Nowell-Smith (ed.), *The European Experience* (London: BFI, 1989), pp. 51–64.
2. See David Forgacs, *Italian Culture in the Industrial Era 1880–1980* (Manchester University Press, 1990), pp. 182–3.
3. See Wolfgang Achtner, *Penne, Antenne e Quarto Potere* (Rome: Baldini & Castoldi, 1996).
4. Donatella Papi, Interview with Silvio Berlusconi, *Il Giornale*, 8 June 1994, quoted in Achtner, *Penne, Antenne*, p. 24.
5. Giancarlo Bosetti, in the monthly *Reset*, October 1994, quoted ibid., p. 77.
6. Enzo Forcella, 'Millecinquecento lettori. Confessioni di un giornalista politico', *Tempo presente* 7 (November 1959); quoted in Robert Lumley, 'Peculiarities of the Italian Newspaper', in D. Forgacs and R. Lumley (eds.), *Italian Cultural Studies* (Oxford University Press, 1996), pp. 199–215 (p. 209), which is the place to start for an understanding of Italian newspapers.
7. Anon., 'RAI Lottizzazione: Giornalisti', *Panorama*, 15 September 1991, p. 52.
8. The sources for all the data in this section are too numerous to list, but a detailed historical account of much of what is described here can be found in Paolo Murialdi, *La stampa italiana dalla Liberazione alla crisi di fine secolo* (Rome and Bari: Laterza, 1998), pp. 236ff.

FURTHER READING

Barański, Zygmunt and Lumley, Robert (eds.), 'Part v. Looking at Television: From Public Monopoly to Competition', in *Culture and Conflict in Postwar Italy*. Basingstoke: Macmillan, 1990, pp. 245–336.
Castronovo, Valerio and Tranfaglio, Nicola (eds.), *Storia della stampa italiana. 7* vols. Rome and Bari: Laterza, 1976–94.
Grasso, Aldo, *Storia della televisione italiana*. Milan: Garzanti, 1992.
Lumley, Robert, *Italian Journalism*. Manchester University Press, 1996.
Monteleone, Franco, *Storia della radio e della televisione in Italia*. Venice: Marsilio, 1992.

16

Since Verdi: Italian serious music 1860–1995

1860–1900

In the years immediately following the unification of Italy, serious musical activity throughout the peninsula was still overwhelmingly dominated by opera, as it had been during the Risorgimento period. In all the major cities, and many smaller ones too, the operatic public was large and various, and was still at least as interested in new operas as in established 'classics'. At this time, one senior living Italian opera composer towered above all others, dwarfing them so drastically that most of them are nowadays hardly remembered even in their own country: Giuseppe Verdi (1813–1901) is now regarded everywhere as the only really lastingly important Italian composer who was active across the third quarter of the nineteenth century, and indeed as one of the greatest opera composers who ever lived. Although Verdi became markedly less prolific in his later years, many (perhaps most) of his finest works date from after 1860, and *Aida* (1871), *Otello* (1887) and *Falstaff* (1893) have long been rated among the highest achievements of Italian genius in any field. However, by the time the two last-mentioned operas were written, the semi-retired Verdi had come to occupy a less unquestionably central place in Italian musical life, and new creative developments were emerging which in various ways showed signs of transforming the character of the new music being written at the time.

Several of these developments had links with innovative Italian literary trends or with the traditions (musical and otherwise) of countries north of the Alps, or both. Arrigo Boito (1842–1918), author of the outstandingly effective Shakespeare-based libretti of *Otello* and *Falstaff*, was a leading writer in the *scapigliatura* ('Bohemian') movement and was also himself a composer. His own single completed opera *Mefistofele* (1868; revised version 1875) is imperfect and eclectic in style; yet it is rightly remembered as an important milestone on the road which led Italian opera away from the powerful but relatively simple-minded world of Verdi's earlier operas (which had more or less covertly reflected the Risorgimento spirit) towards wider cultural horizons and greater awareness of the more complex musical idioms that had recently been emerging outside Italy. Boito was clearly more receptive to Wagner's example (albeit within limits) than Verdi ever was; but a more marked upsurge of Wagnerian tendencies in Italian opera can be seen in the works of two slightly younger composers who were for a time associated with the *scapigliatura*: Alfredo Catalani (1854–93) and the talented but grievously neglected Antonio Smareglia (1854–1929). In responding to Wagnerian and other foreign models neither composer wholly negated his fundamentally Italian character, especially where *cantabile* vocal writing is concerned; yet the last act of Catalani's *La Wally* (1892) is pervaded by an almost Nordic nature-mysticism. Despite a weak libretto, the work has retained a precarious foothold in the repertory in Italy, and demonstrably influenced Giacomo Puccini (1858–1924).

However, it was with the arrival on the scene of Puccini himself that it became increasingly obvious who could be regarded as Verdi's 'heir apparent' in the rising generation of Italian composers: he was quickly recognized as such by the most powerful and influential of Italy's music-publishing houses, G. Ricordi and Co., which owed (and owes) a substantial part of its wealth to the on-going success of Verdi's own operas. Ricordi wasted no time in launching Puccini's works, from *Manon Lescaut* (1893) and *La Bohème* (1896) onwards, on to a wide international market. In so doing, the firm was to some extent driven by rivalry with another Milanese publishing house, Casa Musicale Sonzogno, which in the same period was successfully launching operas by some highly *commerciabile* if lesser composers of the same generation as Puccini: the crude yet fresh and compelling *Cavalleria rusticana* ('Rustic Chivalry', 1890) of Pietro Mascagni (1863–1945) set Sonzogno's run of major successes in motion by winning a lasting worldwide popular acclaim which the composer's numerous later operas never quite recaptured. Close on the heels of *Cavalleria*, Sonzogno's other durable successes included *I pagliacci* ('The Clowns', 1892) by Ruggero Leoncavallo (1857–1919) and *Andrea Chénier* (1896) by Umberto Giordano (1867–1948). So strong, indeed, was the joint influence of Ricordi and Sonzogno on the fortunes of Italian operas in general that in these years a composer who failed to win adequate support from either firm was likely to lose any chance of major operatic success in his own country. Smareglia was a particularly extreme case in this respect: having personally offended Giulio Ricordi for non-musical reasons, he found himself ostracized by most of the major theatres, achieving some degree of lasting recognition only in Trieste.

The responsiveness of new operatic developments to literary trends, both in and out of Italy, continued: *Cavalleria rusticana* was based on Verga's famous short story and play of the same name, with the result that the term *verismo*, which originally referred to the important movement in Italian literature of which Verga was a supreme exponent, came to be applied not only to Mascagni's most successful opera, but also (not always so appropriately) to those of a wide range of other Italian composers active around the turn of the century, including Puccini. Although his musical style has recognizable roots in Verdi and Catalani, Puccini was much influenced by the popular French operatic tradition as epitomized in the successful operas of Jules Massenet (1842–1912). It is therefore appropriate that the plots, too, of several of his operas were of French origin: in *Manon Lescaut* he openly competed with Massenet in his treatment of a subject on which one of the French composer's biggest successes had been based.

Meanwhile the predominance in Italy of opera over all other musical genres, though it continued, was gradually becoming less extreme. During the later nineteenth century, chamber music societies founded in various Italian cities had begun to attract select but increasingly receptive audiences; and in 1872 Italy's first really systematic series of public orchestral concerts (the Concerti Popolari, founded in imitation of Pasdeloup's famous Concerts Populaires in Paris) had been launched in Turin. Further progress in this sphere remained slow, however, with the result that an Italian composer who chose to turn his back on opera, and to devote his energies principally to writing concert works, might be deemed somewhat unrealistic, even foolhardy. Yet such composers had existed inconspicuously throughout the nineteenth century, and became more prestigious (though still relatively little performed) as the turn of the century approached.

Unquestionably the outstanding non-operatic composer in Italy at that time was Giuseppe Martucci (1856–1909), whose Second Piano Concerto (1885), two symphonies (1895 and 1904) and several major chamber compositions raised Italian instrumental music to a level of excellence which had seldom been reached by anyone else working south of the Alps since the end of the eighteenth century. Inevitably Martucci's larger pieces could find few regular outlets in his own country, and some of his most important music significantly had to be published abroad. Though not devoid of Italian characteristics – ranging from the *bel canto* lyricism of *La canzone dei ricordi* ('The Song of Memories', 1887) to the neo-Scarlattian brilliance of some of his best short piano pieces – his style owed a fair amount to the Austro-German tradition, especially to Schumann and Brahms. It is therefore ironic that lack of practical support from his fellow-countrymen prevented Martucci's distinctive and distinguished responses to that tradition from being adequately appreciated by the world at large. Only in the 1990s, thanks to the growing exploratoriness of the record industry outside Italy, has this rewarding aspect of late nineteenth-century Italian music at last become a bit more accessible to an international audience.

1900–1930

In Italy as elsewhere, the first three decades of the twentieth century saw a sustained upsurge of radically innovative movements in music (as in the other arts), all in various ways rebelling against nineteenth-century styles in general and the established Italian opera tradition in particular. Public resistance to these new trends could, however, be strong, and the overall situation in Italy may seem provincial when compared to what was happening in some other countries: it is no accident that several of the more adventurous Italian composers felt the need to travel, and even to live abroad for long periods, in closer contact with new cultural developments such as those in France and the German-speaking world.

The case of Ferruccio Busoni (1866–1924), easily the most 'modern-minded' Italian composer born before 1875, was particularly extreme in this respect: after spending his entire earlier career abroad (mainly in Germany), in 1913 he became director of the Bologna Liceo Musicale, believing this might give him his long-awaited chance to lead a revolution in Italian music. But he found himself surrounded by indifference and obstructive bureaucracy and soon gave up the struggle, thenceforth resigning himself to permanent exile: it is questionable, therefore, whether Busoni's strangely fascinating (if at times perplexingly heterogeneous) music can legitimately be counted as being Italian at all.

However, by the second decade of the twentieth century a new generation of Italian artists was already seeking and proclaiming new creative ideals. The most pugnacious group among them, the Futurists, admittedly achieved far more in the fields of literature and (especially) the visual arts than in music, although the *intonarumori* ('noise-tuners') of Luigi Russolo (1885–1947) – ingenious but somewhat naive contraptions designed to produce a new kind of music based on organized noise – are of interest as primitive forebears of the electronic music and *musique concrète* of the 1950s and beyond. The ferment of new ideas centred on the famous Florentine periodical *La Voce* ('The Voice', 1908–16) proved more fertile where music was concerned: musicians associated with the Vocian circle included Ildebrando Pizzetti (1880–1968) who before the outbreak of the First World War was already establishing himself as a relatively moderate but profoundly serious innovator whose style derived important features from long-neglected Italian music of the remoter past, such as Gregorian chant and the great polyphonic compositions of the Renaissance period. This overtly 'archaic' side of Pizzetti's style is particularly evident in his unaccompanied choral works, of which the *Messa di Requiem* (1922–3) is the supreme example; but he was also a distinguished writer of chamber music and a significant reformer of Italian opera: his operatic methods owe more to the examples of Monteverdi, Mussorgsky and Debussy than to his immediate Italian predecessors.

Of all composers, Pizzetti was the one who collaborated most closely with Gabriele D'Annunzio – notably in his first published opera *Fedra* (1909–12; première 1915), whose libretto was adapted by the poet himself from his play of the same name. D'Annunzio's own obsession with elaborately colourful archaisms, together with his personal responsiveness to music, did much to encourage the revival of interest in previously forgotten early Italian composers, which was soon being reflected increasingly in the works of other composers of Pizzetti's generation – the so-called 'generazione dell'Ottanta' ('generation of the 1880s'). The music of Ottorino Respighi (1879–1936), being more colourful and hedonistic than Pizzetti's, may seem more truly D'Annunzian in spirit, despite Respighi's less close personal connection with the poet. In the long run his picturesque symphonic poems and decorative arrangements of old music have fared better on the international market than the works of his more high-minded Italian contemporaries: pieces such as the famous *Fontane di Roma* ('Fountains of Rome', 1916) and *Pini di Roma*

('Pine Trees of Rome', 1924) have a natural appeal to virtuoso conductors which has kept them in circulation through all the vicissitudes of subsequent changing fashions.

However, the most adventurously innovative composers were undoubtedly Alfredo Casella (1883–1947) and Gian Francesco Malipiero (1882–1973), both of whom defied the Italian musical establishment drastically enough to arouse strong hostility from many of their compatriots. Casella, like Busoni, lived and worked for many years abroad, in his case mainly in France. However, when he returned to Italy in 1915 – he too with the conscious aim of transforming Italian music in the light of his recent experiences north of the Alps – he was better able than Busoni to persist, gradually gaining ground in the teeth of fierce opposition. Casella was a born organizer, and in 1917 he founded the Società Italiana di Musica Moderna, which during its brief existence acted as a rallying point, concert platform and propaganda machine for much that was truly new in Italian music. It is at least symbolic that the Society's subversive and entertaining magazine *Ars Nova* included articles by the leading Metaphysical painters De Chirico and Carrà (who were then at the heights of their powers) as well as by the Vocian writer Papini.

Casella's own music was at its most radically Modernist from 1914 to 1920, when he boldly responded to the examples of Stravinsky, Bartók, Schoenberg and others in his intensely dissonant so-called 'second manner'. After 1920 this gave place to a consciously neo-classical 'third manner', in which he too (following the example of Stravinsky's most recent works) derived significant aspects of his style from pre-nineteenth-century music. All through this period (up to 1928) Casella avoided opera, and instead played a crucial part in the continued resurgence of instrumental music in Italy. In this he was encouraged by the knowledge that Italian composers had made many major contributions in this field in the seventeenth and eighteenth centuries.

The less practically minded but more original Malipiero did not renounce opera altogether, but rebelled against established models far more idiosyncratically than Pizzetti did. Malipiero declared that his *Sette canzoni* (1918–19) – which consists of seven little operatic vignettes, musically linked but dramatically quite independent and each with a song as its musical nucleus – 'was born of the conflict between two sentiments: fascination with the theatre and boredom with opera'.[1] His other theatre works of the period are equally experimental, culminating in the enigmatically dream-like *Torneo notturno* ('Night-time Tourney', 1929).

During and immediately after the First World War theatrical innovation was widespread in Italian spoken drama too: suffice it to mention the famous 'paradoxical' plays of Pirandello, with whom Malipiero collaborated in 1932–3. Malipiero also composed prolifically for the concert hall, and his direct involvement with the revival of old Italian music soon became second to none: in 1926 he himself began to edit what is still the only complete modern edition of the surviving music of Monteverdi, and influences from early music (albeit far from conventionally treated) are prominent, for example, in his *San Francesco d'Assisi* (1921).

All through this time various older Italian composers remained active; but only Puccini had enough powers of self-renewal to go on giving of his best to the end – often stimulated by the examples of composers younger than himself. *Madama Butterfly* (1904) already contains Debussian elements; and in *Turandot* (left unfinished at his death in 1924) he enhanced the opera's more aggressive side by using tough dissonances evidently picked up from Stravinsky and Casella. Right to the end, Puccini remained the living composer most favoured by Ricordi for worldwide promotion; but after Tito Ricordi's retirement in 1919 the firm's former overwhelming preoccupation with popular operatic success gradually gave place to a more open-minded policy: thus the more defiantly non-conformist composers, who previously had often had to turn to foreign publishers, were now increasingly accepted by the Italian publishing establishment. Meanwhile, in 1922, Fascism had come to power; but it had little direct effect on the musical world before the 1930s.

1930–1960

Censorship of the arts under Mussolini never grew to the same monstrous proportions as in Hitler's Germany: there were too many inconsistencies in the Duce's own thinking on the subject for a coherent policy ever to be formulated, let alone carried out, and this was especially true where a non-conceptual art such as music was concerned. Yet the régime exerted pressures of other, more subtle kinds, partly through its propaganda and partly (though not until the 1930s) through its attempts to impose a comprehensive bureaucratic structure on the musical world as on so many other things.

An influential aspect of Fascist propaganda, which affected many composers (including some of those already mentioned), sprang from

Mussolini's megalomaniac desire to revive and surpass the glories of Italy's great past, from ancient Rome to the Renaissance and beyond. This naturally gave a boost to revivalist trends of all kinds, and it must be admitted that some of the most vital as well as some of the most debased Italian artistic tendencies owed at least something to such influences. Italian musicological research was certainly not discouraged; nor was the already existing creative interaction between its findings and the new music of the time.

Closely linked with this cult of Italy's past we find a corresponding denigration of the achievements of other countries: a slogan that was increasingly brandished by conformist Italian critics was the curt condemnation of a composer for being *internazionale*, and therefore, in a sense, a traitor to his country. This was the main accusation levelled against current progressive trends by a group of relatively conservative composers (including Respighi and the now increasingly reactionary Pizzetti) in a notorious anti-Modernist manifesto published in several newspapers on 17 December 1932. However, perhaps the most startling aspect of the fracas which followed the manifesto's appearance is that on this occasion Mussolini came down firmly on the side of the Modernists. After such a persuasive show of solidarity with more 'advanced' trends, and explicitly with Casella and Malipiero, Mussolini's abrupt and characteristically unpredictable banning, less than two years later, of the latter's opera *La favola del figlio cambiato* ('The Fable of the Exchanged Son', 1932–3) inevitably came as a rude shock to all concerned.

This drastic piece of censorship remained isolated, however, and on the whole one is surprised by how much freedom there was in Italian musical life, owing to the non-conformist influence of intelligent and cultured Fascist leaders such as Giuseppe Bottai and the important arts bureaucrat Nicola de Pirro. Thanks especially to the latter, it was possible for Alban Berg's powerfully Expressionist opera *Wozzeck* (1925), which had long been banned in countries under direct Nazi rule, to have its Italian stage première, astonishingly, in Rome in 1942 – even though by then the officially favoured principle of autarchy was on the whole leading to strong preferential treatment for Italian composers over foreigners. By the late 1930s, within the framework of the emerging Corporative System, the state was seeking to control, and also to subsidize, all activities relating to opera, the concert world and the radio; but the system operated mainly at an administrative and economic rather than dictatorially regulatory level, and novelty was in some ways actively encouraged even by the official rules. For instance, opera houses were subsidized only on condition that they presented a certain quota of new or recently composed works – though admittedly these often turned out to be by Italian composers of mediocre gifts and relatively conservative outlook.

Yet it was less surprising than it might have been, all things considered, that the 1930s saw the emergence of some powerful new creative talents in Italian music. The most important of these newcomers were Luigi Dallapiccola (1904–75) and Goffredo Petrassi (1904–), both of whom first made their marks in the context of organizations such as the recently founded Venice Festival of Contemporary Music (launched in 1930, with Casella as one of its directors) and the International Society for Contemporary Music, which had an active if at times controversial Italian section. Although, like almost all Italian composers of the time, Dallapiccola began by naively accepting Fascism at its deceptively persuasive face value, by the end of the 1930s – when Italy's adoption of Hitler's race policies came as a direct threat to the safety of his Jewish wife – the scales fell from his eyes. His fury at the true nature of the rapidly deteriorating situation found expression in his choral *Canti di prigionia* ('Songs of Imprisonment', 1938–41), which remains one of the most powerful of all modern musical protests against tyranny. No less powerful was the opera *Il prigioniero* ('The Prisoner', 1944–8) which Dallapiccola conceived during the very worst part of the war and gave to the world amid the mingled disillusionments and cautious hopes of the immediate post-war period. In creating the tormented, intensely Expressionistic idiom of this opera, Dallapiccola owed much to the Schoenberg school and especially to Berg; yet here again the strong impact of foreign influences did not stifle the composer's evident Italian characteristics – notably in his vocal writing, whose roots can even be traced back as far as Verdi.

Meanwhile Petrassi, whose early music sometimes had a dynamic, celebratory quality owing something (as he later freely admitted) to the pageantry associated with Fascism, abruptly entered a new phase when war broke out. His darkly pessimistic *Coro di morti* ('Chorus of the Dead', a setting of Leopardi, 1940–1) may be less overt in its protest than Dallapiccola's *Canti di prigionia*; yet there is no mistaking the work's deep responsiveness to the grimmer aspects of contemporary reality. By the 1950s Petrassi had moved a very long way from his creative starting-point (despite certain recurrent technical features which define his musical personality through all the changes), and in due course he even proved strikingly receptive to the attitudes of the new generation of avant-garde composers who emerged after the war.

The main pioneering figures in this new generation, among whom Bruno Maderna (1920–73), Luigi Nono (1924–90) and Luciano Berio (1925–) were the first to establish international reputations, were motivated almost from the start by the urge to construct a post-war musical culture utterly different from almost anything that had existed in Italy before 1945. Significantly, all three composers (and other Italians too) made regular visits to that most stimulating and influential breeding ground for radical post-war innovation, the annual Internationale Ferienkurse für Neue Musik at Darmstadt. In Germany the need for a total clean break from the officially approved music of the immediate past was obviously somewhat greater than in Italy. However, for evident political and historical reasons, it was understandable that many Italians, too, should want to make a radically innovative start; and it is no coincidence that several members of this new avant-garde were also strongly attracted to the Gramscian form of Marxism which was to dominate so much of the country's cultural and intellectual life in the third quarter of the twentieth century.

Nono was a particularly clear case in point: several of his most compelling pieces – among which the choral work *Il canto sospeso* ('The Suspended Song', 1955–56) remains one of the most impressive – combine extreme musical modernity with fiercely direct anti-Fascist protest, in which his left-wing political standpoint can clearly be sensed. This sort of polemical attitude to the immediate past, though natural enough in the circumstances, was soon to give rise to unfair distortions of historical perspective which caused even many of the better musical fruits of the Fascist period to become hidden from view, along with the dross that the period undoubtedly produced in quantity.

1960–1995

By 1960 the post-war rebuilding of musical life was already well advanced in practical terms, carried forward on the crest of the 'Italian economic miracle'. New musical creativity was by now being encouraged not only (as previously) by music publishers, festivals of contemporary music, subsidized opera-houses, etc., but also, more than ever before, by the huge, monolithic national broadcasting organization generally known as RAI (Radio Audizioni Italia). RAI's Terzo Programma had originally been created in direct imitation of the BBC Third Programme; but by the early 1960s (*before* the same thing happened in Britain) the programme had been extended throughout the day. Moreover, the broadcast output of serious music was being further expanded with the help of a cable radio network (*filodiffusione*) available in the main cities. Never before had the Italian public had such easy access to so vast a range of music, including an admirably varied offering of serious works of the twentieth century, new and not so new. One may now look back at that situation with nostalgia, so greatly has it deteriorated since RAI gave way to commercial and political pressures after losing its monopoly in 1976.

Meanwhile the post-war Italian avant-garde, though never all-dominating, was gaining in international prestige, often to the detriment of longer-established or more conservative composers. Berio became and has remained especially well known in the English-speaking world, following the widespread acclaim that greeted works such as his *Circles* (1960 – an aptly capricious setting of the poetry of e.e.cummings) and his brilliantly multifaceted *Sinfonia* ('Symphony', 1968–9) with its cunningly deployed quotations from Mahler and others, including himself. Even Nono and Maderna have been thrown into the shade by comparison. In Italy, however, Berio is just one of several composers of his generation who are now rightly regarded as major figures: during the 1960s and 1970s, big reputations were won by (among others) Aldo Clementi (1925–), Franco Donatoni (1927–), Sylvano Bussotti (1931–), Niccolò Castiglioni (1932–96) and the precocious Salvatore Sciarrino (1947–), all of whom attained the status of eminent (if still controversial) senior figures in their country's music.

All these composers initially owed something, directly or indirectly, to the Darmstadt experience, as well as to other important international new musical developments: for example, Italy's first centre for the creation of electronic music, the Studio di Fonologia attached to the Milan branch of RAI, had been founded by Berio and Maderna as early as 1954 in direct response to recent innovations in Cologne. However, it would be wrong to see the Italian avant-garde as a mere reflection of the international radical movements of the time: the main composers all have strong individualities, and great contrasts can be seen, for example, between the colourful, very Italian lyricism of Maderna; the restless, dynamic textures of Donatoni; the kaleidoscopic, rather naive capriciousness of Castiglioni; the provocative, idiosyncratic extravaganzas of Bussotti; the outwardly static yet subtly shifting 'continuum' techniques of Aldo Clementi; and the evanescent, refinedly shimmering sound-world of Sciarrino.

The time is perhaps not yet ripe to draw firm conclusions about the numerous composers younger than Sciarrino who have made their mark in Italy in recent years. But even if none of them has yet made international reputations commensurate with those of, say, Nono or Donatoni (let alone Berio), they nevertheless display a wide variety of stylistic approaches and types of talent. The achievements of, for example, Adriano Guarnieri (1947–), Fabio Vacchi (1949–), Ivan Fedele (1953–) and Luca Francesconi (1956–) are already sufficient to merit more sustained worldwide attention. Although most of the best of these younger composers owe a considerable amount to their immediate Italian predecessors, there seems (in Italy as elsewhere) no longer to be the same almost moral pressure to follow radically innovative paths which was felt so keenly by so many 'new' composers in the immediate post-war years. In the heterogeneous (not to say directionless) post-modern culture of the 1980s and 1990s, the idea of a clearly focused avant-garde movement lost much of its meaning, and in some quarters fashions swung right over in the other direction, towards a frankly populist neo-tonalism whose achievements may be debatable but have undeniably won significant public success: this is particularly true of the eclectic operas of the theatrically skilled Lorenzo Ferrero (1951–).

Although, all in all, there is plentiful creative talent among Italian composers active at the present time, the multiplicity of co-existing trends reflects the uncertainty of a country (and a world) going through a period of unsettling transition. More practical aspects of Italian music, too, are contributing to the disorientation. Since RAI is no longer so committed a cultural and educative force as it was able to be in the 1950s and 1960s (by the mid 1990s all but one of the established radio symphony orchestras had been abolished), it has become considerably harder for visitors to Italy to make systematic contact with the serious contemporary musical scene, unless they are able to travel widely with a view to hearing the music in live performances. There are, it is true, various music festivals – notably the long-established and still remarkable Venice Festival of Contemporary Music – which continue to provide prestigious platforms for modern works. However, in the present unstable, sadly philistine political and economic climate, there are disquieting signs that even these institutions may soon be under threat. Moreover, although the rather limited Italian record industry has become a bit more enterprising in the age of compact discs than it used to be, the current exceptional difficulty of finding sponsorship for anything riskily adventurous is stunting what might have been a promising and long-overdue growth. Significantly, the recent modest expansion in the previously very limited range of twentieth-century Italian serious music available in commercial recordings owes at least as much to foreign as to Italian enterprise.

The real if slow improvement in this last-mentioned sphere does, at any rate, mean that several significant aspects of Italian music of the past century and more, which had previously been in danger of falling into undeserved oblivion, have recently begun to find a new worldwide audience. Market forces have never, of course, allowed such naturally *commerciabile* items as the operas of Verdi and Puccini, or the orchestral tone poems of Respighi, to sink from public view. But only a few years ago the world at large seemed almost to have forgotten about all too many other worthwhile facets of Italy's music of the period with which this book is concerned. Reference has already been made to the recent rediscovery of Martucci, in which the international record industry has played a major part; and the same sort of thing is now starting to happen to those members of the 'generazione dell'Ottanta' (other than Respighi) whose music was so frowned on in Italy in the 1960s, 1970s and 1980s, for reasons which have more to do with political and ideological history than with the qualities of the music as such. With growing historical perspective, it is now becoming easier to perceive that Italy did, after all, make lasting contributions to the serious music repertoire in *all* phases of the twentieth century. The time is therefore ripening for a reassessment of the entire panorama, with its bewilderingly varied mix of contradictions and continuities.

NOTE

1. Gino Scarpa (ed.), *L'opera di Gian Francesco Malipiero* (Treviso: Canova, 1952), p. 192.

FURTHER READING

Bortolotto, Mario, *Fase seconda: studi sulla Nuova Musica*. Turin: Einaudi, 1969.
Budden, Julian, *The Operas of Verdi*, 3 vols. London: Cassell, 1973–81.
Carner, Mosco, *Puccini: A Critical Biography*. London: Duckworth, 1975.
De' Paoli, Domenico, *La crisi musicale italiana (1900–1930)*. Milan: Hoepli, 1939.

Labroca, Mario, *L'usignolo di Boboli (cinquant'anni di vita musicale italiana)*. Venice: Neri Pozza, 1959.

Martinotti, Sergio, *Ottocento Strumentale Italiano*. Bologna: Forni, 1972.

Nicolodi, Fiamma, *Musica e musicisti nel ventennio fascista*. Fiesole: Discanto, 1984.

'Opera Production from Italian Unification to the Present', in L. Bianconi and G. Pestelli (eds.), *Opera Production and its Resources*. Chicago: The University of Chicago Press, 1998, pp. 165–228.

Osmond-Smith, David, *Berio*. Oxford University Press, 1991.

Rosselli, John, *Music and Musicians in Nineteenth-Century Italy*. London: Batsford, 1991.

Waterhouse, John C. G., 'Italy from the First World War to the Second', in R. P. Morgan (ed.), *Man and Music*. Vol. VIII. London: Macmillan, 1993, pp. 111–27.

(with Julian Budden), 'The 20th Century: Italy', in S. Sadie (ed.), *The New Grove Handbooks in Music: History of Opera*. London: Macmillan, 1989, pp. 269–80.

17

Folk music and popular song from the nineteenth century to the 1990s

In 1954, when the ethnomusicologist Alan Lomax (1915–) took a six-month trip to Italy together with Diego Carpitella to record original folk music, the country that he found was scarred by the Second World War and still dominated, in large areas of the southern countryside, by a rural and archaic culture. For the purpose of his research, however, Italy was an untouched paradise, as precious to an ethnomusicologist as Hungary had been to Bartók and Kodály. 'The tradition of Italian folk music is arguably one of the least spoiled, most vigorous, and varied of Western Europe', he wrote. And yet Lomax realized that the situation was changing:

> So far as the Italian amusement industry is concerned, the only worthwhile native song traditions are those of Naples and the Alps. The combined battery of radio, television, and the jukebox pours out a steady barrage of Neapolitan song, American jazz, and opera, day in and day out, as if some unseen musical administrators had resolved to wipe out the enemy, folk music, as quickly as possible.[1]

It is true that, as Italy underwent a major transformation from rural economy to city-based industry, folk music reminded urban people of the oppressive peasant life that they were eager to leave behind. In his massive study of the origins of the tarantella as a medicine ritual, the anthropologist Ernesto De Martino (1908–65) could still experience the richness of southern lore in connection with music.[2] But in the new soundscape provided by radios, the jukebox and public television (which was introduced in 1954), folk music was non-existent. Only some of the Neorealist films caught a glimpse of that fading world: in Visconti's *La terra trema* ('The Earth Trembles', 1948), and in Rossellini's

Viaggio in Italia ('Voyage to Italy', 1953), one can hear voices singing in the background with a purity that is now lost and that even in those days was difficult to hear outside the most remote countryside.

The German scholars who began to study Italian folk songs at the beginning of the nineteenth century were perplexed by the disdain with which Italian men of letters looked at folk material. As Carpitella and Lomax pointed out, 'Since the period of the Renaissance this Italian peasant music [. . .] has lived almost without contact with the great streams of Italian fine-art music. It has followed its own courses, unknown and neglected, like a great underground river.'[3] Luigi Carrer and Giacomo Leopardi were probably the first poets who took an interest in the folk songs of their native regions. Subsequently, the Neo-classical habit of the Italian cultured classes was replaced, albeit slowly, by a more Romantic attitude towards the people, and many researchers paved the road for an Italian ethnomusicology. Printed material became widely available, but only in 1948 did Giorgio Nataletti (1907–72), founder and director of the Centro Nazionale Studi di Musica Popolare ('National Centre for the Study of Folk Music') at the Accademia di Santa Cecilia in Rome, begin to build up an archive of field recordings of peasant music.

Neapolitan, Alpine, Piedmontese and Risorgimento songs (together with the Venetian *villotte* and *canzoni da battello*, 'boat songs') were not peasant music. They stemmed from the 'artisan song' genre – the urban folk music most influenced by Italy's fine-art music. Due to the widespread use of band arrangements and *copielle* (broadsheets), these songs relied upon well-established performing practices. Between the end of the eighteenth century and the first half of the nineteenth century the most popular Neapolitan songs were still attributed to celebrated opera composers: *Te voglio bene assaje* ('I Love You So Much', 1835) was credited to Donizetti, and *Fenesta ca lucive* ('Lighted Window', 1842) to Bellini. At any rate, after the success of *Santa Lucia* (1848), Neapolitan song no longer needed illustrious fathers. *Funiculì funiculà* ('Funicular', 1880) by Luigi Denza, a classically trained composer, sold more than a million *copielle* in a year, and its earthy verve and unusual phrase-structure aroused the attention of several classical composers. The golden age of the nineteenth-century Neapolitan song was exemplified by *'O sole mio* ('My Sun', 1898), and by the poems of Salvatore Di Giacomo (*Marechiare*, 'Clear Sea', 1885, music by Francesco Paolo Tosti). Di Giacomo (1860–1934) indulged on the sentimental side of the Neapolitan soul, but not without a gentle ironic look that was often lost in the work of his populist followers and definitely lost in the *sceneggiata*, a truculent genre of popular theatre based on tear-jerking songs and crime stories.

Francesco Paolo Tosti (1846–1916) was the undisputed king of the *romanza da salotto* (salon song). He was equally famous in Italy and at the court of England (where he was Sir F. P. Tosti), and his friendship with D'Annunzio produced many successful *romanze* ('*A vucchella*, 'Tiny Mouth', 1892). The *romanza da salotto* ultimately gave way to operetta and the different forms of variety show (*cabaret*, *tabarin*, *café chantant*). Armando Gill (Michele Testa, 1879–1945) was perhaps the first singer–songwriter in a modern sense – the first *cantautore*, author and performer of his own songs in the *café chantant* (the word *cantautore* did not come into use before 1960). His songs (for example *Come pioveva*, 'How It Rained', 1918) were sentimental, but the language was plain and updated, not unreminiscent of the *crepuscolari*, the 'Twilight Poets' (Gozzano, Corazzini, Moretti). The world of *café chantant* could not survive the newborn record industry and mass entertainment, and it was replaced by *varietà* or *rivista*. Ettore Petrolini (1886–1936) made a name for himself with *Gastone* (1921), in which he poked fun at the now obsolete *café chantant* characters.

From *rivista* came Rodolfo De Angelis (Rodolfo Tonino, 1893–1965), a gifted lyricist and performer. De Angelis had been in the Futurist movement, and together with Marinetti he wrote the *Manifesto del Teatro della Sorpresa* ('Manifesto for the Theatre of Surprise', 1921). Unlike his mentor, he was not well accepted by the Fascist régime, and from 1922 to 1940 he concentrated on songwriting (*Ma . . . cos'è questa crisi?*, 'So . . . What Is This Crisis Anyway?', 1933).

Far away from the *salotti* of the upper class, other songs were sung: anarchist ballads like *Addio Lugano bella* ('Farewell, My Beautiful Lugano', 1894), Socialist hymns (*Bandiera rossa*, 'Red Flag') and songs of emigration (*Mamma mia dammi cento lire*, 'Mother, Give Me One Hundred Lira'). The First World War produced official patriotic tunes like *La leggenda del Piave* ('The Piave Legend', 1918), as well as strong anti-war statements like *O Gorizia tu sei maledetta* ('O Gorizia, May You Be Damned', 1916).

The Fascist régime made a great use of propaganda songs, from *Giovinezza, giovinezza* ('Youth, Youth', a pre-Fascist song of 1921 which became the official Fascist hymn) to *Faccetta nera* ('Little Black Face', 1935, the unofficial hymn of the Abyssinian war). Far from the public parades, the success of popular song was connected more and more with radio and cinema. *Solo per te Lucia* ('Only for You, Lucia', 1930) and *Parlami d'amore, Mariù* ('Tell me About Love, Mariù', 1932, sung by a very young

Vittorio De Sica) were the centrepieces of two of the first *film musicali* – not musicals, but movies in which the story was based on a song. At the end of the Second World War the *rivista* either disappeared or transformed itself into the *commedia musicale* (musical comedy). Wanda Osiris (Anna Menzio), the post-D'Annunzian *diva* of the most glamorous *riviste*, was replaced by the earthy Anna Magnani, who achieved her first great success with Totò (Antonio De Curtis) in German-occupied Rome. Sandro Giovannini and Pietro Garinei, who wrote scripts for Anna Magnani in 1945, later became the kings of the *commedie musicali* that dominated the Roman scene until the end of the 1960s.

The songs of the 1940s and the 1950s often have a distinctive regional character. In Milan, Giovanni D'Anzi (1906–74) was able to put down an impressive number of hits, ranging from the gentle populism of his Milanese sketches (*Madonina*, 'Little Madonna', 1938) to love ballads of a Cole-Porter-like harmonic complexity (*Viale d'autunno*, 'Avenue in Autumn', 1953). But Neapolitan song was alive and well, and it renewed itself either by mourning the landscape of wartorn Naples (*Munasterio 'e Santa Chiara*, 'St. Chiara's Convent', 1945) or incorporating jazz harmonies (*Anema e core*, 'Soul and Heart', 1950). The influence of American music must not be underestimated. Although banished in the last decade of Fascism, jazz played an important role in the changing musical landscape of the 1940s and 1950s. In defiance of the Fascist police, the young jazz *aficionados* cherished the few dusty records that were smuggled from America. Ironically, one of them was Romano Mussolini, one of the Duce's sons, who after the war forged a career for himself as a jazz pianist. The censors could sometimes be fooled. As the legend goes, *St. Louis Blues*, performed by Bessie Smith and Louis Armstrong, was released under the delightful title *Le tristezze di San Luigi* ('The Sadnesses of Saint Louis') because the censor believed it to be a religious song. In the last days of the Second World War, Resistance songs (at least in Northern Italy) and Glenn Miller's *In the Mood* were the unlikely soundtrack of the Liberation.

After the war, some young entertainers adopted swing with an ironic approach. Renato Carosone (1920–) made a name for himself with *Tammurriata nera* ('Black Drumroll', 1944; Carosone recorded it in 1957), a devastatingly funny account of how Neapolitans coped with the arrival of the American soldiers in 1943 ('A new baby is born, and he is black. Such things are not rare; we've seen countless numbers of them. Sometimes it takes no more than someone looking at the mother, and all of a sudden she is *imprinted* . . .'). After his first hit, Carosone made the charts again with his swingy *Tu vuo' fa' l'americano* ('So You Want To Be an American', 1957) in which he poked fun at the Italian youngsters trying to pose as Americans while 'buying Camel cigarettes with mommy's money'.

Fred Buscaglione's America, on the contrary, was both very foreign and very familiar. Fred (Ferdinando) Buscaglione (1921–60) was born in a working-class district of Turin. He dressed and behaved like a character out of a Damon Runyon or Mickey Spillane novel, and his songs relocated with devastating irony the world of the American gangster movie to the outskirts of an Italian industrial town (*Eri piccola così*, 'You Were as Small as This', 1958).

The most important performer of the 1950s was Domenico Modugno (1928–94). He caused a national commotion by appearing at the 1958 Festival di Sanremo with his new song, *Nel blu dipinto di blu* ('In the Blue Sky, Myself Painted in Blue', 1958). To fly far from the world and into the infinite blue of the sky was a very strange subject for an Italian song, but even more impressive was Modugno's vocal and performing style. His voice was still the voice of a southern *cantastorie* ('story-singer'). Italians were still surrounded by those voices, but they were not used to hearing them on television. With Modugno, vocal Neorealism had reached the media. Renamed *Volare* ('Flying'), the song became a worldwide hit, selling more than twenty-two million copies.

The 1950's still had room for other great voices. Mina (Mina Anna Mazzini, 1940–) is the most versatile pop singer in Italian music. A soprano with an astonishing extension and agility, Mina has been a staple of TV variety shows for many years. Swingy and anti-melodic in her early years (*Tintarella di luna*, 'Moon Tan', 1959), her singing later acquired high dramatic tones. Ornella Vanoni (1934–) went from Giorgio Strehler's Piccolo Teatro to sophisticated schmaltz, while Milva (Maria Ilva Biolcati, 1939–) went from the Sanremo Festival to Strehler, who turned her into an accomplished Brechtian singer. At the beginning of the 1960s, other young female singers were ready to interpret the new female roles: Rita Pavone and Caterina Caselli were both sassy and sentimental, and Patty Pravo (Nicoletta Strambelli) was even sexually aggressive.

Adriano Celentano (1938–) is the closest thing to Jerry Lee Lewis and Little Richard that Italy has produced. When he made a cameo appearance in Fellini's *La dolce vita* (1960), he was a Milanese street boy infatuated with rock and roll. And yet Celentano was very much an Italian original.

Ventiquattromila baci ('Twenty-four-thousand Kisses', 1961) was one of the first post-war songs in which the language of love was drastically updated. Celentano also provided the Italian pop scene with a distinctive urban and working-class posture that was almost unknown. His characters were the young rockers living on the outskirts of the newly industrialized towns. Italy at the time being a gentler place than Liverpool or Detroit, its blue-collar workers and apprentices still clung to the words of the local priest, and their biggest problem was not how to find dope but how to find a date (*Il problema più importante*, 'Our Most Urgent Problem', 1962).

Gianni Morandi (1944–) is the Dorian Gray of Italian song. In his fifties now, he still looks like the teenager who made girls scream when, like Paul Anka, he topped the charts at sixteen, singing thought-provoking lyrics like: 'Have your mother send you to buy milk, I have to tell you something about us. If I see you coming out of school with that other guy, I'll definitely smash his face' (*Fatti mandare dalla mamma*, 'Get Your Mother to Send You', 1963).

Increasing social unrest marked the end of the 1950s. Some young writers and singers, spurred on by the example of French *chansonniers*, Brechtian song and by rumours of a folk-revival movement in America and Britain, began to think that popular songs could be made into a less apolitical medium. A loose association of lyricists, composers and performers called *Cantacronache* ('News Singers') was formed in Turin in 1957. Obscure and amateurish as it was, *Cantacronache* marked the beginning of the modern *canzone d'autore*, or art pop song. With the occasional help of Italo Calvino (who wrote lyrics for them), *Cantacronache* recorded a number of allegorical and overtly political songs. *Per i morti di Reggio Emilia* ('For the Dead of Reggio Emilia', 1960) sounded like a Resistance folk tune with Russian overtones (the chorus quotes a passage from Mussorgsky's *Pictures at an Exhibition*). Due to their widespread use in leftist gatherings, Resistance songs like *Bella ciao* ('Goodbye, My Sweetheart') or *Fischia al vento* ('The Wind is Whistling', based on a Russian tune brought back to Italy by Italian soldiers who had fought in Russia) were the only folk songs that the young city dwellers knew. Resistance songs were therefore instrumental in renewing the interest in folk music. Two young researchers, Diego Carpitella (1924– 90) and Roberto Leydi (1928–) championed the new area of study (Carpitella had been De Martino's and Lomax's field assistant). Tullia Magrini (1950–) followed in their steps and is now editor of *Music & Anthropology*.

Another researcher, Gianni Bosio (1923–71), took a more militant approach. Outside the academic circles, he created the Istituto Ernesto De Martino, named after the anthropologist who had investigated the roots of southern folklore. Bosio and his collaborators were not merely looking for folk art. They aimed at documenting and enriching the counter-culture expressed by the rural and working classes. While, in the same years, Pasolini was longing after the prepolitical condition of the subprol-etarians, Bosio relied upon Gramsci's notes on hegemony and folklore, as well as on the so-called *operaismo* of the 1960s (*operaismo*, 'working class-centered Marxism', was the name of a splinter Marxist theory promoted by the philosopher Raniero Panzieri). While field research was the Istituto's main occupation, its practical arm was the *Canzoniere italiano*, a free-form group of urban singer–songwriters, urban folk singers, grass-root folk singers like Giovanna Daffini (an astonishing *mondina* voice – the *mondine* being the rice-picking women of northern Italy) and a well-trained musician, Giovanna Marini. Marini (1937–) was heading towards a career as a performer of Renaissance music when she decided to devote herself to folk material and the composition of long, intellectually pas-sionate ballads, inspired by American talking-blues, rural music from the Italian South, Brechtian song and Renaissance recitatives (VI PARLO DEL-L'AMERICA,[4] 'I Am Talking about America', 1965). Initially spurred on by a blend of Marxist–Catholic anti-capitalist pauperism which is almost uniquely Italian, she subsequently composed complex modern madrigals for a quartet of female voices, cantatas and oratorios, and a poignant suite based on youthful poems by Pasolini (PER PIER PAOLO, 'For Pier Paolo', 1985).[5] While Luciano Berio (1925–) is the only contemporary classical composer who has shown a constant interest in folk music (*Folksongs*, 1964; *Voci*, 'Voices', 1984), Roberto De Simone (1933–) is, like Giovanna Marini, a folk-oriented composer. Working in association with the Nuova Compagnia di Canto Popolare, he reached international success with the folk operas LA GATTA CENERENTOLA ('Cinderella, the She-Cat', 1976) and LA CANTATA DEI PASTORI ('The Shepherds' Cantata', 1981).

The early 1960s saw the rise of a new Italian cabaret. The early songs of Dario Fo and Enzo Jannacci (*La luna è una lampadina*, 'The Moon Is a Bulb', 1963; *Ho visto un re*, 'I Have Seen a King', 1963) are masterpieces of pop Surrealism, demented urban stories that recount the transition from the simpler, paternalistic Italy of the 1950s to the neo-capitalist country of the 1960s. Jannacci (1935–) has remained more or less true to his roots; Fo (1926–) achieved international success with his satirical plays and, to the surprise of many, won the 1997 Nobel Prize for Literature.

The new breed of singer–songwriters who captured the spirit of the 1960s mostly came from Genoa. In defiance of all the pop schmaltz, Luigi Tenco (1938–67) could freeze the casual radio listener with a line like: 'I fell in love with you because I had nothing to do' (*Mi sono innamorato di te*, 'I Fell in Love with You', 1962). Excluded from the 1967 Sanremo Festival, and perhaps mired in debt, Tenco killed himself (the 1958 Nobel prize-winner, Salvatore Quasimodo, wrote a moving eulogy on him, at a time when intellectuals did not normally bother about singers and their songs). Even more desperate than Tenco was Piero Ciampi (1934–80) from Livorno, who, while drinking himself to death, reached a level of angst unmatched by any other Italian song composer. Gino Paoli (1934–) presented an equally non-conformist image. The handful of songs that he wrote in the early 1960s served as the soundtrack of the first mass vacations and the first sexual freedoms experienced by the young Italian generation entering the neo-capitalist Garden of Eden of the 'Economic Miracle' (*Sapore di sale*, 'A Taste of Salt', 1963).

Among the Genoese singer–songwriters, Fabrizio De Andrè (1940–99) maintained a strong appeal to young audiences. The most literary and intellectual of the group, for many years he provided the musical background for *liceo classico* students (*liceo classico* being a secondary school with a literary orientation). De Andrè reached his artistic maturity with CREUZA DE MÄ ('Alley to the Sea', 1982). The songs were in Genoese dialect and the arrangements were entirely acoustic, with musical references ranging from Southern Italy to the Middle East. His next songs were equally powerful. *Don Raffaè* (in LE NUVOLE, 'The Clouds', 1990), a devastating portrait of a hapless prison guard who falls under the spell of the camorrista that he is supposed to watch, is a stunning reminder of the years of disorientation and corruption that led Italy into the Tangentopoli scandal of 1992.

Between the end of the 1960s and the beginning of the 1970s, many other singer–songwriters emerged, each of whom would deserve a detailed analysis (Franco Battiato, Edoardo Bennato, Lucio Dalla, Francesco De Gregori, Francesco Guccini, Gianna Nannini). Beat, mainstream rock, progressive rock and fusion had their day too, with groups like Area, Banco, PFM and Stormy Six.

Aristocratic, isolated, ironic, Paolo Conte (1937–) stands alone. He wrote songs for Celentano, most notably *Azzurro* ('Blue', 1968), but achieved widespread popularity only in his late forties. Paolo Conte is perhaps the most refined song composer since Giovanni D'Anzi, and the most original lyricist since Rodolfo De Angelis. He is the quintessence of the old 'cool', looking at the world with his older generation's wisdom, unflinched by the vagaries of post-modernity (UN GELATO AL LIMON, 'A Lemon Ice-Cream', 1979).

But, significant as it is, the influence of all these musicians pales before that of Lucio Battisti (1943–98). As the semiotician Paolo Fabbri put it, he did not sing about Italian teenagers; he created them.[6] From 1966 to 1979 he found his lyricist in Mogol (Giulio Rapetti), who became for him what Ira Gershwin was for his brother George (EMOZIONI, 'Feelings', 1970). Battisti was no intellectual. He had a harsh, unpleasant 'soul' voice, a reputation for bad temper, and an unparalleled gift for expressing the sexual frustration of a young male in a country that had seen its reassuring patriarchal values vanish. Increasingly reclusive and aloof, at the peak of his fame he disappeared from the music scene. After his collaboration with Mogol came to a bitter end, Battisti resorted to a young and obscure lyricist (Pasquale Panella) who furnished him with bizarre imitations of experimental poetry (DON GIOVANNI, 1986). Mogol's lyrics, however, deserve attention. Halfway between linguistic inventiveness and kitsch, they combine the failed poetry of a teenager's diary with the shrewd immediacy of a television ad.

At the end of the 1990s, the singer–songwriters are still the most original Italian contribution to contemporary pop culture. Although they never captured British and American audiences, they are well known around much of Europe. Heavy-metal rock bands (Litfiba), rockers (Ligabue) and pop cabaret acts (Elio e le Storie Tese) have their audiences; female singers (Nada Malanima, Fiorella Mannoia and Anna Oxa) still undertake their journey from rebellious youth to adult sophistication; and yet it is the singer–songwriter who is supposed to be the spokesperson of the young. Some of the new artists seem promising (for example, Daniele Silvestri), but many older singer–songwriters are still active, and not easily superseded. The list would not be complete without Nino D'Angelo (1957–), who is probably the last scion of the Neapolitan melodic song. His voice has a populist appeal in which no subtlety is allowed.

The most interesting musical phenomenon of the last decade is the emergence of an Italian form of rap. Italian rap has spread through the alternative network of *centri sociali* (self-managed social centres) and independent record companies. Although some of the groups enjoy cult fame (see the anthology FONDAMENTALE VOL. 1, 1992), none has reached the success of Jovanotti (Lorenzo Cherubini), a former DJ who began his career exploiting rap merely for commercial purpose. In recent years, Jovanotti has somewhat matured, and now produces a blend of rap and *canzone d'autore* not entirely devoid of social concerns (LORENZO 1994, 1994). Rap, in fact, is just one of the ingredients that these new groups have mixed together: others are reggae (Pitura Freska), dub (Almamegretta, most notably with ANIMA MIGRANTE, 'Migrant Soul', 1993), world music (Agricantus, Novalia), and even *tarantamuffin*, a mix of Jamaican ragamuffin (reggae plus rap) and *tarantella*.

Italian rap is committed to protest movements, anti-racist and multi-culturalist. Italian rappers often find dialect to be more expressive and to the point than standard Italian, and they make large use of it. Historical continuity with the tradition of the campaigning song has not been broken, and political consciousness still walks hand in hand with popu-lism. The assimilation of rap proves once again that Gramsci was right when he pointed out that popular music is not necessarily written by the people or for the people.[7] Popular music is the music that is adopted by the people insofar as it conforms to what the people think about the world and life, in opposition to the official views promoted by the estab-lishment (whatever the meaning of 'the people', 'opposition' and 'the establishment' is nowadays, of course).

NOTES

1. Alan Lomax, introduction to *Italian Treasury: Folk Music and Song of Italy*, one sound disc (Rounder Records 11661–1801–2, 1999), p. 1. The first version of this introduction (signed with Diego Carpitella) is in the inside cover of the Columbia World Library series albums (see note 3).

2. See Ernesto De Martino, *La terra del rimorso* (Milan: Il Saggiatore, 1961).

3. Alan Lomax and Diego Carpitella, introduction to *The Columbia World Library of Folk and Primitive Music*. XV: *Northern and Central Italy and the Albanians of Calabria*. XVI: *Southern Italy and the Islands*, four sound discs (Columbia Records, KL 5173 and KL 5174, 1957).

4. To distinguish them from song titles, LP and CD titles are written in small capitals.

5. See Alessandro Carrera, 'Il lamento di Narciso. Le poesie friulane di Pasolini musicate da Giovanna Marini', *Italica* 71/3 (1994), pp. 337–53.

6. Quoted in Tullio Lauro and Leo Turrini, *Emozioni. Lucio Battisti vita mito note* (Milan: Zelig, 1995), p. 109.

7. Antonio Gramsci, *Letteratura e vita nazionale* (Rome: Editori Riuniti, 1971), p. 273.

FURTHER READING

Borgna, Gianni, *Storia della canzone italiana*. Milan: Mondadori, 1992.

Carpitella, Diego, 'Italian Folk Music', in *Grove's Dictionary of Music and Musicians*. V: *Appendix*. London: Macmillan, 1961, pp. 135–64.

Carrera, Alessandro, *Musica e pubblico giovanile*. Milan: Feltrinelli, 1980.

Coveri, Lorenzo (ed.), *Parole in musica. Lingua e poesia nella canzone d'autore italiana*. Novara: Interlinea, 1996.

Falassi, Alessandro, *Italian Folklore: An Annotated Bibliography*. New York: Garland, 1985.

Filippa, Marcella, 'Popular Song and Musical Cultures', in D. Forgacs and R. Lumley (eds.), *Italian Cultural Studies*. Oxford University Press, 1996, pp. 327–43.

Leydi, Roberto, *I canti popolari italiani*. Milan: Mondadori, 1973.

Lomax, Alan, 'Musical Styles in Italy: Text of a Hypothesis', *American Anthropologist* 61 (1959), pp. 927–54.

Portelli, Alessandro. 'Typology of Industrial Folk Song', in *The Death of Luigi Trastulli and Other Stories*. Albany: SUNY Press, 1991, pp. 161–92.

Prato, Paolo. 'Tradition, Exoticism, and Cosmopolitism in Italian Popular Music (1950s-1980s)', *Differentia* 2 (1988), pp. 195–218.

Straniero, Michele, *Manuale di musica popolare*. Milan: Rizzoli, 1991.

Testa, Carlo, 'The Dialectics of Dialect: Enzo Jannacci and Existentialism', *Canadian Journal of Italian Studies* 52 (1996), pp. 19–40.

18

Epilogue: Italian culture or multiculture in the new millennium?

On the threshold of the new millennium, as Italy prepares to play an ever more active part in the European Union, it is not inappropriate that students of Italian culture should ask: 'What is contemporary Italian national identity, and what will the adjective "Italian" mean in the future?' The essays in this volume have primarily looked back over cultural developments in post-unification Italy from the perspective of late twentieth-century contemporaneity. They have also occasionally sought to make conjectures about possible future developments. In this brief epilogue, my focus will be on the present and the future, a prospective stance reflective of some of the collection's general aims, and conditioned of course by current realities. The question of what 'Italian' now signifies, and what the adjective may well encompass in future years implicitly or explicitly informs all that follows.

Italy was belatedly born as a nation under the sign of a constructed political and linguistic unity. Unification has always been more a dream than a reality, however, in spite of the many efforts over the last century to bring about national unity. Historically, Italian society and culture have been fragmented, and today there is an increasing, and new, fragmentation under pressure from both internal and external forces. Among these forces are greatly increased immigration, mainly from so-called developing countries, the revival of regionalism and widespread Americanization. The effects of these social and political phenomena on Italian cultural production have been and continue to be great, and it is no longer the case that a few hegemonic centres (certain cities, universities, dominant political parties, publishing and other media entities, the Catholic Church) direct and control most of what has traditionally been thought of as Italian culture. Added to these forces are the seismic political upheavals of recent years: the scandals associated with Tangentopoli; the emergence of the separatist Northern Leagues; the fall of the First Republic; the rise of Berlusconi's media empire; the concerted efforts to join the European Monetary Union. These upheavals, while occurring specifically in Italy, nonetheless have global repercussions. Thus, Italy is both increasingly fragmented within and intensely involved in extranational, global matters. The result is that its national identity is caught up in transformations of great speed and complexity.

In a newspaper piece published in 1997, Alberto Papuzzi wrote of one of the most significant phenomena affecting Italy today: immigration.[1] In the late 1960s, Italy was still a country of emigration, and there were only around 150,000 immigrants living in the country; twenty years later, Italy had over 500,000 immigrants, while having the lowest birthrate in Europe. By the year 2000 the number of native-born Italians will have dropped by four million, while the number of non-native citizens continues to grow exponentially. From the late 1980s to the late 1990s the (legal) immigrant population doubled, and it now represents around 2 per cent of the overall population of the country. In comparison with other European nations, this percentage is low. More interesting is the fact that Italy hosts the most varied gamut of immigrant nationalities. While German immigration has been dominated by Turks, French by Portuguese, Algerian and Moroccan, and English by people from the Commonwealth (West Indians, Pakistanis, Indians, etc.), in 1997 Italy had over 100,000 Moroccans, 63,000 Albanians, 57,000 Philippinos, 54,000 North Americans, 44,000 Tunisians, as well as contingents numbering from 45,000 to under 20,000 people respectively from such varied places of origin as Serbia, Rumania, Senegal, China, Poland, Peru, Egypt, Somalia, Algeria and Iran. While the immigrants from countries in Africa and from the former Yugoslavia are the most visible, the urban centres of Milan, Turin and Rome are filled with people from all the countries mentioned, and smaller cities and even tiny towns in the provinces have many non-native Italians living and working in them.

With so many immigrants now living in Italy, why, Papuzzi asks, has the presence of 'others' generated so much negative reaction in the form of intolerance, violence and racism? According to him, one answer might lie in the tendency among Italians to amalgamate diverse immigrants into one image of otherness; and that image has a black face. How much simpler it is to see 'them' as completely separate and different from 'us' when skin colour marks difference. This explanation is open to question, however, since many Italians appear, rather, to compartmentalize different national and ethnic groups, much as they pass different collective judgments on Italians coming from diverse regions and cities. In either case, an 'us' versus 'them' mentality would appear to play a significant role in the response to those seen as 'other', as is the case throughout the world. Another source of negativity may be the identification of all immigrants with illegal immigrants, so that they are perceived as criminal and a threat to an ordered society. African immigrants have commonly been called *vu'cumprà* ('will you buy?'), while other immigrants are deemed to be *lavavetri* ('window washers'), according to their humble means of livelihood: street vending and maintenance. Socio-economic difference is thus added to ethnic or racial difference, and a hostile mentality becomes even more entrenched among the Italian population. The situation is made worse by some public figures. Umberto Bossi, the head of the Northern League, plays on the economic fears of middle-class Italians in northern Italy (where a high percentage of the immigrant population lives). Fiercely and vociferously divisive, he delights in ridiculing southern Italians, calling them 'Africans' and 'mafiosi' and commenting on their darker skin and on the ways in which they drain the resources of the more affluent North. The major goals of the Northern League are a less centralist government and more political and economic power for the North; anti-southern and anti-immigrant positions are used to forward this goal. Bossi's view particularly of black 'others' is clear; in a talk at the first national conference of the Lombard League, held in 1989, he opined: 'assimilation is not valid regarding immigrants of colour, for whom integration is not foreseeable, perhaps not even centuries from now. With them the classic mechanisms of integration – marriage and children in common – do not work, and it would be impossible to realize an ethnic bond without generating grave racial tensions inherent in the society.'[2] Interracial marriage, a reality in many societies, is characterized as impossible in Italy; yet no reasons are adduced in support of this claim, with the result that it is made as if it were self-evident. Bossi (and others) seem to forget that Italians are no more 'pure' than other ethnic groups, and that many diverse peoples throughout the centuries settled in what is now the nation of Italy, and became what are now known as 'Italians'.

Whether universally welcomed or not, the Italy of today is inescapably multiethnic. As Papuzzi writes: 'The face of immigration is still obscure, and the condition of the majority of immigrants is still too precarious. But roots have been put down and nothing will be able to extirpate them.' Signs of these roots are the sixty mosques scattered throughout Italy; the many diverse centres for immigrants in Emilia-Romagna; the Islamic butcher's shop opened in Naples in 1992; the Florentine suburb of San Donnino, with a population of 4,500 Italians and 3,000 Chinese; the town of Merlo in the province of Vicenza, half the population of which is made up of Senegalese and Ghanaians. Cuisine, fashion and other aspects of social and cultural life are heavily influenced not only by American trends, but also by the many immigrants who have settled in Italy for the long term, have married Italians and others, have had children, and have begun to contribute to the economic life of the country and to its literature, film, theatre and a host of other cultural expressions.

There is now a flourishing Italophone literature, for example, that has begun to be studied by Italianists. To give but one (salient) example: in the United States, the scholar Graziella Parati has published, over the last few years, more than a dozen articles on Italophone literature and related topics. She has recently edited an anthology of translations of immigrant writings, and sits on the jury of a yearly literary prize presented each summer in Rimini to an immigrant author whose work is subsequently published.[3] Parati is among an increasing number of Italian literary scholars who have begun to acknowledge the presence and significance of 'Italian' literature by non-natives: books written in Italian, but which often reflect an Italian reality quite distinct from that of indigenous writers.

Canonical approaches to literary culture may not yet acknowledge these new texts, but it is virtually impossible simply to ignore them. The same holds true for other arenas of cultural activity, and scholars active in the field of cultural studies, primarily in the United States and Britain, as is discussed in the Introduction to this volume, have begun to work on redefinitions of Italian 'high' and 'mass' culture. For instance, they focus on aspects of today's transformed and continually transforming Italian culture, and on issues such as the role of the media, the fashion industry, immigration and gender.[4] In studies such as these can be found an Italian reality quite different from the view propounded by traditional approaches to 'high' cultural production. Historically, Italy has been studied as the country of 'high' culture *par excellence*, and it is known internationally for its great works of art, its opera and, to a lesser extent, for certain of its writers (Dante, Machiavelli, Calvino, Eco). Few non-specialists are aware of the political and social complexities of today's Italy; at most they may have a superficial knowledge of the terrorism and scandals that rocked and eventually toppled the First Republic. The intricate effects of immigration, the separatist Leagues and other events that have shaped and continue to shape Italy are not part of the general perception of a country still seen to a great extent as the land of sun, song and pasta – with some paintings and monuments thrown in for good measure. Only a small portion of recent Italian cultural production makes its way to the shores of most other countries, including the United States and Britain (although more translated materials are beginning to come on to the English-speaking market), so that stereotypical views continue to hold sway. Scholars of history, culture, film and literature working both inside and outside Italy are, however, gradually beginning to provide information on the 'new' Italy, and visitors to Italy experience for themselves something quite different from what stereotypical perceptions have led them to expect. The face of today's Italy – multiracial, multiethnic and potentially multicultural – is starting to be unveiled to the world.

It is not only scholars of literature and cultural studies who are investigating this new Italy. Political scientists, sociologists and geographers, among others, have also contributed many studies in recent years that focus on the question of multiculturalism in the Italian context. In 1996, for example, a conference on 'Immigration and Multiculturalism in Today's Italy' was held at the University of Macerata, and the Proceedings appeared the following year.[5] The convention drew together scholars from the Geography Department at Macerata, from the Association of Italian Geographers involved in a project called 'Foreign Immigration to Italy' and from the 'Cariplo Foundation for Initiatives and Studies on Multiethnicities'. Divided into several sections under the headings 'Immigration in Italy and in its Regional Aspects', 'Problems Related to Immigration', 'Places of Departure and of Arrival of Immigrants' and 'Didactics and Interculture in Today's Schools', the volume is rich in specific information about the geographical, political, familial, social, cultural and pedagogical aspects of immigration and about growing multiculturalism throughout the regions of Italy. In one of the essays, the geographer Guido Barbina provides a very useful summary of the history of ethnic identity and conflict in the European context, and then focuses his attention on the Italian situation of today, in which he sees genuine multiculturalism as more a goal than a reality.[6] Barbina characterizes the politics of multiculturalism (with reference to the Canadian context) as 'beautiful and attractive, but of difficult applicability'. He continues: 'Italy has never shown proof of any effective multiculturalism. Born in the last century under the sign of nationalism, Italy in reality has never succeeded either in melding itself into a sole culture or a sole language, or in some way respecting its own local cultures.' Given the necessity of dealing effectively with the enormous immigration into today's Italy, and the unlikelihood that the influx of diverse ethnic groups into Italy will stop in the future, Barbina urges a political and cultural awareness of the importance of differences rather than the neutralization of differences in the name of 'a more diffused well-being'.[7] He and other scholars in the volume support the flourishing of multiculturalism in Italy; for the moment, however, multiculturalism remains a future goal rather than a present reality.

In this brief epilogue, it is impossible to enter into detailed analyses of the salient facets of contemporary Italian culture, many of which are analysed in the essays contained in this volume. I have chosen to pay some attention to the pressing reality of immigration and its effects, for today's Italy has been and continues to be changed perhaps most radically by this enormous influx of peoples from other countries and cultures. Americanization and regionalism are also important elements in the shaping of contemporary Italian culture. However, given the complex political, social and cultural nature of these elements, which would require a much more extensive venue than this short epilogue, I wish instead to conclude by giving some necessarily small space to more manifestly academic (as contrasted to socio-political) developments that reflect transformations certain also to have significance for the Italy of the new millennium.

More traditional components of modern Italian culture have long been exported; among them are fashion, cuisine, films, design and, to a lesser extent, literature. What has also begun to be significantly exported in the last decade is *thought*, by which I mean theoretical elaborations in diverse fields of inquiry. Two major areas in which contemporary Italian theory has begun to have more than a local effect among (primarily Western) intellectuals and academics are philosophical postmodernism and Feminism. The export of work in these areas has brought Italy squarely into contemporary global debates centring on new paradigms generated and promulgated internationally.

Furthermore, Italy is now more open than ever before to research methodologies, disciplinary shifts and modes of institutional education from beyond its own borders. Contacts between and among Italian and other European scholars have long been established; now exchanges between Italy and North America are becoming routine, and more Italian critical and creative texts in English translations are available for academic and general readers in the English-speaking world (while, on the other hand, the Italian publishing industry has always routinely provided translations of important scholarly texts from around the world). This wider exchange is due in part to the new electronic media, which transport information and facilitate collaboration in ways unheard of by earlier generations; but it is also the result of widely shared views of what are generically called post-modern and Feminist thought and practice.

Italy did not quickly welcome the term 'post-modern,' as other Western countries did, although similar concepts were discussed under terms such as 'neo-Baroque', 'neo-avant-garde' and 'post-metaphysical', depending on the particular discipline in question. However, critical thought in Italy has, as elsewhere, become enmeshed in post-modern debates generated in great part by the crisis of Marxism and the concurrent crumbling of strong ideologies. With the move away from 'classical rationality' and 'grand narratives', scholars in many disciplines have begun investigating alternative modes of conceptualizing and coming to terms with the inheritance of past forms of knowledge, as well as developing new forms for the present and future. Philosophical thought is quite naturally implicated in this shift in perspective, for metaphysics and the historical forms of investigating basic ontological and epistemological problems are also now open to the effects of a generalized crisis of foundations. Aldo Gargani's 1979 collection of essays entitled *Crisi della ragione* ('Crisis of Reason', Turin: Einaudi) was one of the first important expressions of Italian post-metaphysical thought, while the 1983 collection of essays, edited by Gianni Vattimo and Pier Aldo Rovatti, *Il pensiero debole* ('Weak Thought', Milan: Feltrinelli), created quite a stir with its heterogeneous mix of untraditional pieces by philosophers, literary scholars and writers. 'Weak thought' is one of the Italian versions of post-modern theory in which justification is no longer sought in transcendental categories but rather in the contingent complexity of lived experience. It has certain affinities with Derridean and other French schools, and Vattimo – the leading spokesman of the trend – has travelled throughout Europe and North America promulgating his ideas. The journal *Differentia*, founded by Peter Carravetta in the United States in the late 1980s, has concentrated on the dissemination of current Italian thought in English translations, and has done much to bring this thought into international debates. The major effect of this recent work has been on methodologies and pedagogical styles; the traditional emphases on historical, analytical and philological approaches to knowledge are giving way to a more theoretical orientation that is by now widespread in North America, Britain and France. Although still rooted in its own traditions, Italian research in many disciplines is no longer radically distinct from research carried out in other Western countries; it is no longer overwhelmingly Italian, any more than the country's populace is 'purely' native-born; it is, in short, moving into a kind of academic and theoretical multiculturalism.

Italian Feminist theory is another instance of the growing internationalism of Italy's cultural productions. The essay 'Other Voices' in this volume provides an excellent historical overview of Feminism in Italy, and I shall not repeat what is offered by Wood and Farrell. What is most significant about current Italian Feminist work is that it is beginning to be taken into account in the heretofore dominant contexts of research and theorizing in the field: that is, in France, Germany, Britain and the United States. The feminist thinkers in Italy who have recently emerged as among the most important theorists for the most part have been or currently are tied to the Diotima group at the University of Verona, and are made up of philosophers, linguists and scholars from various other disciplines. The philosopher Luisa Muraro is the acknowledged leader of Diotima, while Adriana Cavarero, formerly an important figure in the group, is no longer a member as a result of intellectual and ideological differences. Teresa de Lauretis, an eminent scholar known internationally for her work in Feminism, cultural theory and film studies, was instrumental in bringing word of recent Italian Feminism to North American shores. Her translation of the ground-breaking *Non credere di avere dei diritti* ('Don't Think You've Got Rights') a collectively authored record of the Milan Bookstore Collective's experiences in consciousness-raising and practical Feminist practices, was among the first books to bring contemporary Italian Feminist thought to the attention of scholars outside Italy.[8] Muraro and Cavarero have both travelled widely to present their work, and their and others' research has started to have real resonance in international Feminist debates. Muraro currently concentrates on past and present sites of autonomous female authority, such as female religious communities – as distinguished from the patriarchal order – while Cavarero is attempting to overcome the clash between fundamentally essentialistic metaphysical approaches to sexual difference (such as mark Muraro's approach) and those post-modern approaches that favour the concept of non-essentialistic, culturally constructed differences (such as mark the work of Judith Butler and Rosi Braidotti, for example). While interested in local issues of pertinence to the daily lives of women living in Italy, these and other Italian scholars of Feminism are keenly aware of directions in research and practice in other countries, and take active account of French, British and North American Feminist theory. Once again, this is an indication of a kind of intellectual 'multiculturalism' now very much a part of Italian intellectual and social life.

In conclusion, it could be said that the terms 'Italy' and 'Italian' now encompass realities and imaginaries that are quite different from those of only a few decades ago. No one can say for sure where the Second Republic is heading, nor how Italian culture will look a few decades into the future. When a volume of essays is put together a century or so from now, one which concentrates on 'post-modern' Italy rather than the 'modern' Italy that this volume encompasses, its contents will tell a tale the storyline of which can only be faintly traced today. Or perhaps the storyline that appears to be emerging now will have been erased and replaced by another that cannot yet be imagined. Perhaps Italy will not even exist any longer as an autonomous nation and a separable culture, as global trends continue to develop. There is no crystal ball, only eyes and minds that need to go on looking and thinking as clearly as the complex present allows.

NOTES

1. Alberto Papuzzi, 'Stranieri, la mappa tricolore', *La Stampa*, 12 April 1997, p. 23.
2. Quoted in Laura Balbo and Luigi Manconi (eds.), *I razzismi reali* (Milan: Feltrinelli, 1992), p. 84.
3. Graziella Parati (ed.), *Mediterranean Crossroads: Migration Literature in Italy* (London: Associated University Presses, 1999).
4. Beverley Allen and Mary Russo (eds.), *Revisioning Italy: National Identity and Global Culture* (Minneapolis and London: University of Minnesota Press, 1997); David Forgacs and Robert Lumley (eds.), *Italian Cultural Studies: An Introduction* (Oxford University Press, 1996).
5. Carlo Brusa (ed.), *Immigrazione e multicultura nell'Italia di oggi: Il territorio, i problemi, la didattica* (Milan: Franco Angeli, 1997).
6. Guido Barbina, 'Conflittualità etnica e multiculturalismo', in Brusa (ed.), *Immigrazione*, pp. 121–32.
7. Ibid., pp. 129, 129–30, 132.

8. *Non credere di avere dei dritti* (Turin: Rosenberg & Sellier, 1987). Translated by Teresa de Lauretis and Patricia Cicogna as *Sexual Difference: A Theory of Social-Symbolic Practice* (Bloomington and Indianapolis: Indiana University Press, 1990).

FURTHER READING

Balbo, Laura and Luigi Manconi (eds.), *Razzismi: un vocabolario*. Milan: Feltrinelli, 1993.

Bettini, Maurizio (ed.), *Lo straniero ovvero l'identità culturale a confronto*. Rome and Bari: Laterza, 1992.

Cavarero, Adriana, *Nonostante Platone: figure femminili nella filosofia antica*. Rome: Editori Riuniti, 1990. Translated by Serena Anderlini-D'Onofrio and Aine O'Healy as *In Spite of Plato: A Feminist Rewriting of Ancient Philosophy*. New York: Routledge, 1995.

Ceserani, Remo, *Raccontare il postmoderno*. Turin: Bollati Boringhieri, 1997.

Ghirelli, Massimo, *Immigrati brava gente: la società italiana tra razzismo e accoglienza*. Milan: Sperling & Kupfer Editori, 1993.

Gnisci, Armando, 'La letteratura dell'immigrazione', *Forum Italicum* 30/ 2 (Fall 1998), pp. 368–74.

Lucente, Gregory, *Crosspaths in Literary Theory and Criticism: Italy and the United States*. Stanford University Press, 1997.

Magni, Roberto, *Gli immigrati in Italia*. Rome: Edizioni Lavoro, 1995.

Muraro, Luisa, *L'ordine simbolico della madre*. Rome: Editori Riuniti, 1991.

Ruberto, Laura E., 'Immigrants Speak: Italian Literature from the Border', *Forum Italicum* 32/1 (Spring 1997), pp. 127–44.

Index

Note: this index is arranged alphabetically word by word, but in titles of works the initial definite/indefinite article is ignored. Page numbers in italics refer to illustrations or tables.

Cambridge Companions to Literature

The Cambridge Companion to Greek Tragedy
edited by P. E. EASTERLING

The Cambridge Companion to Old English Literature
edited by MALCOLM GODDEN *and* MICHAEL LAPIDGE

The Cambridge Companion to Medieval Romance
edited by ROBERTA L. KREUGER

The Cambridge Companion to Medieval English Theatre
edited by RICHARD BEADLE

The Cambridge Companion to English Renaissance Drama
edited by A. R. BRAUNMULLER *and* MICHAEL HATTAWAY

The Cambridge Companion to Renaissance Humanism
edited by JILL KRAYE

The Cambridge Companion to English Poetry, Donne to Marvell
edited by THOMAS N. CORNS

The Cambridge Companion to English Literature, 1500–1600
edited by ARTHUR F. KINNEY

The Cambridge Companion to English Literature, 1650–1740
edited by STEVEN N. ZWICKER

The Cambridge Companion to English Restoration Theatre
edited by DEBORAH C. PAYNE FISK

The Cambridge Companion to British Romanticism
edited by STUART CURRAN

The Cambridge Companion to Eighteenth-Century Poetry
edited by JOHN SITTER

The Cambridge Companion to the Eighteenth-Century Novel
edited by JOHN RICHETTI

The Cambridge Companion to Victorian Poetry
edited by JOSEPH BRISTOW